American Diplomatic History

American Diplomatic History

TWO CENTURIES OF CHANGING INTERPRETATIONS

Jerald A. Combs

UNIVERSITY OF CALIFORNIA PRESS
Berkeley • Los Angeles • London

Library of Congress Cataloging in Publication Data

Combs, Jerald A.
  American diplomatic history.

  Includes index.
  1. United States—Foreign relations—Historiography.
I. Title.
E183.7.C655   327.73   81-24067
ISBN 0-520-04590-4   AACR2

University of California Press
Berkeley and Los Angeles, California
University of California Press, Ltd.
London, England
© 1983 by
The Regents of the University of California
First Paperback Printing 1986
ISBN 0-520-05893-3
Printed in the United States of America
1 2 3 4 5 6 7 8 9

IN MEMORY OF ARTHUR AND
KENNETH COMBS

Contents

Preface

In 1964, during my first year of full-time college teaching, one of my students came up after class and asked me to participate in a "teach-in" against the Vietnam War. Somewhat taken aback, I hemmed and hawed, excusing myself on the grounds that I knew too little about the war to do such a thing, and that what little I did know left me with rather divided feelings. On the one hand, if the Buddhist riots and the coup that had recently overthrown Diem were an accurate indication that the American-sponsored government in South Vietnam was little supported by its own people, then I thought we should get out. On the other hand, I said, if the South Vietnamese did support the government, and the war was a Russian- or Chinese-sponsored invasion by North Vietnam, then it seemed reasonable to aid the South in a limited war to contain the aggression. After all, I proclaimed, Munich had demonstrated the dangers of appeasing dictatorial aggressors. The student expressed some puzzlement at the mention of such a musty historical analogy, but she left open the invitation for me to share my quaint notions with the teach-in, and we parted on amiable terms.

As the error of American intervention in Vietnam became more apparent over the years, my mind often turned back to my encounter with that student and the way I had initially reacted to the war in Vietnam. Naturally it made me receptive to later historians' speculations that the historical lessons derived from Munich had played a part in the decisions of America's leaders to intervene and try to stay the course in Vietnam. As I sought to explain to successive waves of angry and disillusioned students how the historical experience of the previous generation might have led reasonably well-intentioned and intelligent people into such a deadly morass as Vietnam, it occurred to me, as it did to many others, that Munich had been especially influential on diplomatic historians like myself. Not only had it affected the way many of us had reacted to Vietnam; it had also influenced our interpretations of earlier events in American diplomatic history. In studying the diplomacy of the War of 1812, the Mexican War, or World War I, historians could not help but wonder whether those wars had been as inevitable as World War II now seemed to have been and whether earlier histories that criticized those wars might have been as mistaken as the appeasers at Munich.

Obviously not all post-World War II historians agreed in their conclusions. A few of them wrote polemical works applying simplistic lessons drawn from Munich to the rest of American diplomatic history, but most extensively researched histories reflected the inconvenient shades of gray that envelop all historical evidence. Nonetheless, diplomatic historians writing in the wake of World War II almost all seemed to be wrestling with the foreign policy trauma of their own generation as well as the historical evidence directly relevant to the episode they were studying. Some historians reinforced the lessons of Munich. Some contradicted them. Almost all qualified them in one way or another. But the overall effect seemed to me to be at least a mild reinforcement of the predominant public mood, lending the legitimacy of the academy to a modified and restrained version of the Munich analogy, and helping to throw the burden of proof on those whose policies could be seen as appeasement.

As I watched Vietnam shatter the Munich paradigm and replace it with one far less favorable to an activist, interventionist American foreign policy, I was reminded that Munich and Vietnam had not been the only crises that had worked such a sea-change in the public mood and consequently in historical interpretations of past events in American foreign policy. World War I seemed an obvious turning point. So too did the Spanish-American War, although historians debated how far back the roots of the Imperial Age went. These thoughts interested me enough that I decided to go back over the entire literature of American diplomatic history to see specifically how historical interpretations might have responded to such traumatic generational events.

This book is the result of that undertaking. It is a study of the theses and interpretations of the major books in the literature of American diplomatic history, looking to see how they reflected the major foreign policy crises experienced by each generation of diplomatic historians. Naturally, I have also tried to acknowledge and assess other influences on the development of these historical interpretations and, especially, to see how the availability of new evidence might have been a factor in the process. But to do this adequately would require an expertise that would make me capable of writing a multiarchival monographic study of every major diplomatic crisis in American history. Needless to say, my knowledge is not that extensive. Therefore, I have not made a regular practice of announcing which particular interpretation I believe conforms best to the available evidence. Such judgments are far more appropriately rendered by historians writing from the original sources than by one surveying the secondary accounts.

One further caution. A historiography such as this one inevitably will be somewhat misleading by emphasizing the theses of books rather than their factual content. This may drive a neophyte to the conclusion that history is indeed only fiction temporarily agreed upon. Or it may inspire another round of the "graduate school game"—since one can never know the full truth about the past, memorize historical theses rather than historical data.

It would be unfortunate if this book encouraged such aberrations. I believe that the information historians provide is more important than the theses they propound. There is much basic information that all historians agree upon. In addition, most historians have admitted the tentativeness of their interpretations and have sought to moderate the oversimplified assertions of the more popular accounts of politicians and journalists or those of their more polemical colleagues in the historical profession. If overall they have reinforced and legitimized their generation's perceptions of America's diplomacy, they have also urged caution, emphasized complexities, and provided opposing views. Above all, in their extensive factual accounts they have presented material from which readers could draw their own inferences to refute the authors themselves. In the end, that is the historian's greatest contribution.

Because this book is a sort of extended bibliographical essay, there is no separate bibliography. Instead, each book will be found in the index under the author's name. Publication information on each book is contained in the footnote on the page where the book is first mentioned, and that page number is listed in italics in the index.

I have incurred many debts of gratitude in the course of writing this book. The primary one is to Katherine Scott, now a Fellow in the public history program at the University of California, Santa Barbara, whose editorial skills were vital to the composition of the second draft of the manuscript. Dr. Brian George, now of the University of California Press, read the entire manuscript and gave many helpful suggestions as well as encouragement. Bradford Perkins of the University of Michigan commented on a portion of the manuscript. Alexander

DeConde of the University of California at Santa Barbara encouraged me at the outset of this project and sent me a copy of his AHA pamphlet on the historiography of American diplomacy to serve as a starting point. Professor Walter LaFeber of Cornell University read the book in two drafts for the press, and his criticisms and suggestions were invaluable. Professor Richard Leopold of Northwestern University also read the manuscript for the press, and although he disagreed with its overall conception, his close proofreading saved me from many specific errors. My colleagues at San Francisco State, Joseph E. Illick, John Tricamo, and Anthony D'Agostino, each read several chapters at various stages of the manuscript's preparation and lent their special expertise to the project. Lorraine Wittemore and Joan Ovalle devoted many hours to typing and proofreading and maintained an amazing restraint when commenting on my execrable handwriting. My wife Sara provided steady encouragement throughout the ten years of ups and downs in the research and writing of the book despite her own busy career. She even took time to compose the index. Naturally any errors of fact or interpretation that remain are my own responsibility.

PART ONE

The Age of Neutrality and Expansion
1775-1860

In the years prior to the Civil War, historians shared the general American disillusionment with the monarchical governments and foreign policies of the major powers of Europe. They endorsed the popular devotion to the principles expressed in Washington's farewell address. Their historical accounts of such episodes as the Revolution, the Jay Treaty, and the War of 1812 praised those leaders and actions they thought supported American neutrality and condemned all that risked European entanglements. They might differ over which particular actions best promoted neutrality and especially over which party, Federalist or Republican, had done so. But the principle of nonentanglement went almost unchallenged. The burden of proof was squarely on any historian or politician rash enough to propose intervention or alliances in Europe.

As opposed to our own day, this policy of nonintervention in European affairs had little to do with any moral compunctions about interfering in the rights of other nations to self-determination. Americans were supremely confident that any intervention they undertook inherently would promote the self-determination of common peoples against tyranny. So the policy of neutrality was based strictly on the limits of American power and the dangers American intervention in Europe posed for the United States itself.

This was most clearly borne out by American attitudes toward the diplomacy of westward expansion. There was rather little opposition to intervention in the West, where American power was so much more easily brought to bear than in Europe, and where American interests were so directly involved. Americans and their historians might debate the pace and to some extent the tactics of expansion. But they saw little reason for restraint toward the Indians and almost none at all save the exigencies of power for restraint toward the European colonies in the area. Thus, American historians praised the western acquisitions of the Founding Fathers and of later American leaders while condemning all the forces, foreign or domestic, that had stood in the way. The Mexican War, involving the question of slavery as it did, broke the unity of opinion on westward expansion somewhat, but the vast majority of histories still continued to approve of it.

Historical treatments of the diplomacy of neutrality toward Europe will be dealt with in the first chapter, the diplomacy of westward expansion in the second.

ONE

Federalists Versus Republicans: Getting Right with the Farewell Address

Until the publication of the first comprehensive history of American foreign relations by Theodore Lyman in 1826, Americans had to derive whatever knowledge they had of their nation's diplomatic history from scattered snippets offered in congressional speeches, newspaper stories, and partisan pamphlets. Fragmentary as these sources were, two fairly coherent interpretations of American diplomatic history emerged from them that influenced not only contemporary politics but subsequent diplomatic history as well. These interpretations followed the lines laid down by the two rival parties of the time, the Federalists and the Jeffersonian Republicans. Both of these partisan interpretations regarded as gospel the advice George Washington had given his countrymen in his farewell address to avoid "the insidious wiles of foreign influence" and to "steer clear of permanent alliances with any portion of the foreign world." The unhappy experiences of the United States with England and France in the 1790s had made nonentanglement so sacred a principle to Americans after 1800 that no politician could afford to be branded as sympathetic to a foreign power. Thus, it became the goal of each party to demonstrate how its own foreign policies were neutral and impartial while those of its opponents were biased and entangling.

For example, on the eve of the War of 1812, Federalist Josiah

Quincy told the House of Representatives that Republican policy was "the first fruit of French alliance. A token of transatlantic submission." The Republicans had fallen into "a paper fly trap, dipped in French honey."[1] Another Federalist member claimed that Republican policy was guided by Napoleon's "invisible hand."[2] The Republican opposition claimed, on the contrary, that the Federalists were traitorous tools of the British. Republican Robert Wright of Maryland noted that the Federalists in Congress were such able advocates of the British position that they were encouraging Great Britain in its aggressions. The Republicans had been accused of being guided by an invisible hand, he reminded the House; he only wished he could pay the Federalists the same compliment. The hand that guided them was all too visible.[3]

These congressmen did not use any elaborate historical references to prove their charges that the opposition's coziness with a foreign nation was a condition of long standing. But memories of letters, newspaper articles, and previous congressional debates recounting earlier diplomatic crises surely helped lend both passion and credibility to their accusations. Federalists, for instance, no doubt remembered that during the Revolution Benjamin Franklin's compliant attitude toward the French had been supported by future Republicans like James Madison, Thomas Jefferson, and Robert R. Livingston. John Adams never stopped reminding people that when he had tried to counter Franklin's supposedly fawning stance, the members of this pro-French faction in Congress had tried to have him replaced as the peace commissioner to Great Britain. Failing that, they had submerged him in a five-man commission more favorable to France and then issued humiliating instructions that this commission should submit itself entirely to French advice.[4]

Adams and the Federalist party recalled with pride that future Federalist John Jay, supported by Adams, had defied Congress's pro-French instructions and compelled Franklin to go along in negotiating peace with Britain independent of French advice.[5] Adams wrote sev-

1. Josiah Quincy, *Annals of Congress*, February 25, 1811, p. 1024.
2. *Ibid.*, February 9, 1811, p. 956.
3. *Ibid.*, pp. 955–956.
4. For the split in Congress, see William C. Stinchcombe, *The American Revolution and the French Alliance* (Syracuse, 1969). For the split between Franklin and Adams, see Peter Shaw, *The Character of John Adams* (Chapel Hill, 1976), pp. 106–191.
5. John Jay to Robert R. Livingston, November 17, 1782, in Francis Wharton, *Revolutionary Diplomatic Correspondence of the United States*, 6 vols. (Washington, D.C., 1889), VI, 11–49.

eral private letters that became widely known in which he claimed that America would have had to settle for a border well short of the Mississippi River and would have lost its rights to the Newfoundland fisheries if the negotiations had been left to the supine Franklin.[6] Meanwhile members of the pro-French faction of Congress, many of them future Republicans, had been very disturbed by the actions of Jay and Adams. Believing that Jay and Adams had needlessly endangered the valuable French alliance, they had sought to censure the two. Ultimately this caviling was smothered by the nation's exultation at the terms of the treaty, but recollections of the conflict rankled, especially with Adams, Jay, and Madison. There is no doubt that memories of this episode hovered over the later accusations of pro-French or pro-British bias that the parties hurled at one another.[7]

Other highly publicized conflicts between Federalists and Republicans also helped lend passion and continuity to accusations that the opposition had long been subservient to a foreign nation. Republicans considered the Jay Treaty of 1794, negotiated and implemented under Washington's Federalist administration, to be a sell-out to the British. Federalists considered Republican opposition to that treaty to have endangered America's peace and neutrality in hopes of helping the French revolutionaries win their war against Britain. Republicans criticized the undeclared naval war with France in 1798 as an unnecessary conflict manufactured by the Federalists as a means to suppress domestic dissent. Federalists thought that the conduct of the French in the XYZ affair and other episodes had fully justified war, and they divided only on whether Adams had been right to make peace at the last moment. The final bones of contention had been Jefferson's embargo and the War of 1812, with Republicans defending those measures and Federalists denouncing them.

Historians writing about these episodes in the ante-bellum period were naturally affected by the partisan debates over them. Like

6. See Adams to Robert R. Livingston, November 8, 1782, in *ibid.*, V, 865. See also Adams to Jonathan Jackson, November 17, 1782, *Adams Papers* (microfilm), reel 110; Adams to Elbridge Gerry, September 5 and 10, 1783, in *ibid.*, reel 107.

7. Secretary of State Timothy Pickering even used a Federalist version of the episode in an official diplomatic dispatch. See Pickering to Charles Cotesworth Pinckney, January 16, 1797, in *Diplomatic and Consular Instructions of the Department of State, 1791–1801* (microfilm). For the use the Federalists put it to, see Gerard H. Clarfield, *Timothy Pickering and American Diplomacy, 1795–1800* (Columbia, Mo., 1969), pp. 60–68.

the politicians, historians assumed that the dictums of Washington's farewell address were the ultimate test of virtue for American diplomacy, and, also like the politicians, their primary debates were over which party and which actions had best served that policy of neutrality. A few histories were published while the battle between Federalists and Republicans was still raging, before the Federalist party died in the aftermath of the War of 1812. John Marshall offered a biography of George Washington, which naturally praised Washington's neutrality policy and implicitly chided the Republicans for attacking it.[8] Parson Mason Weems published a far less scholarly biography of Washington but echoed Marshall's complaint that some American citizens (supposedly Republicans) could "so far *belittle themselves* as to become willing cat's paws of one nation, to tear another to pieces. . . ."[9] Noah Webster, another good Federalist, published a grammar school textbook called *Elements of Useful Knowledge*. In it he reminded children that the French had aided America during its Revolution primarily to hurt the British rather than to assist the breakaway colonies, and he concluded the book by printing the farewell address.[10]

By the time that Theodore Lyman published the first diplomatic history of the United States in the 1820s, the Federalist party was dead.[11] Still, Lyman could not ignore the partisan issues and accusations that had surrounded the major diplomatic events of America's first years as a nation. Those disputes still lingered in the popular consciousness. Lyman's own father had been allied with his relatives, Timothy Pickering and Harrison Gray Otis, in a faction of the Federalist party dubbed the Essex Junto by its primary enemies, John Adams and John Quincy Adams. The Adamses held the group responsible for attempting to incite New England's secession during the War of 1812, and Lyman had written an account of the Hartford Convention to refute such charges, which were effectively destroying the Federalist party.[12]

8. John Marshall, *The Life of George Washington*, 5 vols. (Philadelphia, 1852), V, 14.

9. Mason Weems, *The Life of Washington*, 9th ed. (Philadelphia, 1809), p. 139; italics in original.

10. Noah Webster, *Elements of Useful Knowledge*, 3rd ed., 2 vols. (Boston, 1808), II, 40.

11. Theodore Lyman, *The Diplomacy of the United States*, 2nd ed., 2 vols. (Boston, 1826–1828).

12. Theodore Lyman, *A Short Account of the Hartford Convention* (Boston, 1823).

Naturally, Lyman's *Diplomacy of the United States* supported the Federalist interpretation of America's early foreign policy. But the bias was milder than might have been expected. Perhaps this was because by the 1820s, Lyman had allied himself uneasily with the Jacksonians against the hated Adamses, and the Jacksonians revered Jefferson. Also, he was writing in the Era of Good Feelings, when Americans sought to forget the petty issues that had divided the Founding Fathers and to regard them all as patriots and contributors in their own way to America's success. Perhaps the chief reason for the mildness of the interpretation was that Lyman's book traced the history of each major treaty negotiated between the Revolution and the 1820s by quoting copiously from official documents and the treaties themselves and contained a minimum of Lyman's own prose.

Still, some interpretations did emerge. Most prominent of the attitudes permeating Lyman's work was a seething distrust of foreign nations. He rarely criticized the U.S. government, be it Republican or Federalist, but he roundly chastised excessive forbearance of foreign insults or any action that might entangle America with Europe. "All seemed to feel and acknowledge the force, wisdom, and soundness" of Washington's advice to have as little political connection with foreign nations as possible, he said, and he trusted that "the government will never be seduced by schemes of ambition, or prospects of immediate temporary advantage, to embark upon this wide, unknown, dark, boisterous sea of alliances. . . ."[13] His view of a proper neutrality, of course, tended to be the Federalist one. He called Franklin's diplomatic posture during the revolutionary war "undignified" and considered the Jay Treaty the salvation of America's neutrality.[14] He even supported the hated John Adams in his decision to defy the sentiments of the most rabid Federalists and to send a second peace delegation to France to end the Quasi-War of 1798. For the peace that resulted permitted the United States to withdraw from the entangling alliance negotiated during the revolutionary war, and "that argument is, we admit, always the most forcible that can be employed on any subject, relating to our diplomacy. . . ."[15]

Lyman also tried to avoid excessive partisanship in his assessment of the diplomacy leading up to the War of 1812. He agreed with the Federalists that Jefferson should have accepted the compromise

13. Lyman, *Diplomacy of the United States*, I, 151–153.
14. *Ibid.*, pp. 91, 104, 106, 120, 127, 188–190, 208.
15. *Ibid.*, p. 366.

with Britain offered by the Monroe-Pinkney Treaty of 1806 despite the admitted shortcomings of the pact.[16] Jefferson's alternative, the embargo, might have been a worthwhile experiment if it had had a chance of working, but it had not. Even outright war against both Britain and France in 1808 would have been better than the course Jefferson had followed.[17] Still Lyman defended the Republicans against Federalist charges that their policies had been motivated by a treasonous attachment to France. Although the Republicans had exercised extreme tolerance toward France and carried their love of peace too far by not declaring war against Napoleon, Jefferson's embargo "belonged to the system of forbearance and neutrality, commenced under the first administration."[18]

Lyman's mildly pro-Federalist paean to neutrality stood unchallenged for some time. Timothy Pitkin offered an extensive report on the work in the *North American Review*, and agreed essentially with all of it. He especially thanked Lyman for vindicating the diplomacy of Jay and Adams during the Revolution and decried the "extraordinary and humiliating" instructions binding America's commissioners to French advice.[19] Lyman's account of the diplomacy of the Revolution received further corroboration in 1833 when William Jay published a biography of his father.[20]

But shortly before William Jay's book was published, Lyman's interpretation of the Revolution came under attack. The critic was Jared Sparks, the first professor of secular history in an American university, who offered one of this period's few interpretations of an episode in American diplomatic history that implied approval of a foreign alliance. Sparks did not disagree with Lyman on partisan grounds. He was himself a New Englander who took a mildly Federalist view of most issues. But his primary sentiment was a reverence for all of the Founding Fathers, and while writing their biographies or publishing their papers, he was not above some judicious manipulation of the evidence to protect their reputations.

This attitude led to no quarrel with Lyman over the Proclamation of Neutrality or the Jay Treaty, both of which were approved by

16. *Ibid.*, II, 11–12.
17. *Ibid.*, I, 413; II, 49.
18. *Ibid.*, I, 414–415, 421; II, 49–50.
19. Timothy Pitkin, *North American Review*, 24 (1827): 103, 108–109.
20. William Jay, *The Life of John Jay*, 2 vols. (New York, 1833).

Washington and therefore good.[21] But Sparks found the strictures of Lyman and others against Franklin and his friends for their excessive trust of America's French allies during the Revolution to be both hurtful and mistaken.

Sparks reminded his readers that it had been Jay and Adams who suspected the French foreign minister, the Comte de Vergennes, of actively plotting against American interests. Jay and Adams had been led to this suspicion by several events. First, Vergennes had advised the Americans to accept the credentials of the British envoy, Richard Oswald, even though these credentials did not officially acknowledge the United States as an independent entity. Jay decided that Vergennes had done this to delay American independence in order to keep the United States in the war until France's other ally, Spain, had conquered Gibraltar. At the same time, Vergennes's secretary, Joseph Rayneval, was supporting Spain's claim to the Mississippi valley over that of the United States. Then the British intercepted and turned over to the American delegation a letter from Barbé de Marbois, the secretary to the French minister in the United States, advising the French government to concert with the British to exclude the Americans from the Newfoundland fisheries. To cap it off, Rayneval left on a journey to London after telling Jay that he was going only to the French countryside. Jay concluded that Rayneval intended to urge the British to resist American claims to the Mississippi and the fisheries.

It was this suspicion of France that had brought the disagreement between Jay, Adams, and Franklin, Sparks wrote. First, against the advice of Franklin and Vergennes, Jay had delayed negotiations until Oswald could receive a new commission recognizing American independence. Then, without Franklin's knowledge, Jay had sent a messenger to the British to tell them not to conspire with Rayneval against American interests. Finally, with the support of Adams, Jay had compelled Franklin to agree to negotiate with the British independent of French advice and to keep the details of those negotiations secret from their French allies.

Jared Sparks concluded that Jay's suspicions of France "had no just foundation in fact." With access to the French archives (arranged by Barbé de Marbois himself), Sparks declared that having perused all the records of Rayneval's conversations with the British, he could find

---

21. Jared Sparks, *The Writings of George Washington*, 12 vols. (Boston, 1834–1837), I, 486–488, 502–504.

"not one word in them relating to the American boundaries and fisheries." There were only two minor exceptions to this, and in each case, Sparks declared quite wrongly, the subject had been raised by the British prime minister, Lord Shelburne, while Rayneval had declined to discuss it in accordance with his instructions "that he had no authority to treat on these topics."[22]

Sparks also discounted the letter of Barbé de Marbois regarding American access to the fisheries and argued that the British intercepters had probably altered the letter, which had been written without authority anyway. The French had been motivated by their own interests, of course, but there was no proof of French perfidy, "and nothing is now hazarded in saying, that no such proof will ever be brought to light. The French court, from first to last, adhered faithfully to the terms of the alliance." Thus, Franklin had been correct all along.[23]

The thoroughness with which Sparks treated this question, his access to the French correspondence, and his presumed impartiality combined to give his interpretation tremendous weight. For years to come, historians of all persuasions accepted it despite its implied approval of a foreign alliance.

The next major contribution to the history of American diplomacy was not written until well over a decade later as the nation was dividing over the issue of slavery and sliding toward civil war. In that atmosphere, Richard Hildreth, an ardently antislavery New Englander, published the most partisan pro-Federalist interpretation of American foreign policy yet offered by a major historian.

Hildreth wrote a six-volume *History of the United States of America*, published between 1849 and 1852, covering the period up to the Missouri Compromise of 1820. He envisioned his history as an antidote to the work of his fellow New Englander, George Bancroft, who had begun publication of his monumental *History of the United States* in 1834. Bancroft had attacked the Bank of the United States in a widely read article published in the *North American Review* in 1831, then had become a Jacksonian Democrat, a member of James K. Polk's cabinet and, as such, an apostate from New England Federalism.[24] So Hildreth had an ideological quarrel with him. More importantly, Bancroft's history was romantic, rotund, and fulsomely patriotic. Hil-

22. Jared Sparks, *The Works of Benjamin Franklin*, 10 vols. (Boston, 1840), I, 493–494.
23. *Ibid.*, pp. 494–498.
24. George Bancroft, *History of the United States*, 10 vols. (New York, 1834–1874).

dreth claimed that his history, in contrast, would be "undistorted by prejudice," and "uncolored by sentiment."[25]

Hildreth's first three volumes, dealing with events up through the Revolution, were indeed quite measured and judicious. But the last three were very strident although Hildreth went out of his way to deny this.[26] In his reasonably objective third volume, Hildreth accepted Sparks's view of the diplomacy of the Revolution. But by the time Hildreth reached Washington's administration, there was no such acceptance of Republican views. He saw Jefferson as a political bigot supported by Democratic-Republican societies that were fanatically devoted to France and determined to undermine American neutrality. Hildreth praised the Jay Treaty for saving that neutrality and condemned the Republicans' alternative policy of commercial retaliation against Great Britain as a foolish one "of which they had afterward ample opportunities to be cured." While upholding John Adams's courage and impartiality in making peace with France in 1799, Hildreth could condemn some Federalists for being as pro-British as the Republicans were pro-French.[27] But he took a very strong Federalist line on the War of 1812.

He insisted that peace should have been made with England by acceptance of the Monroe-Pinkney Treaty. He considered the embargo foolish and rejected Lyman's suggestion that war against both Britain and France in 1808 might have been preferable to war against England alone in 1812. Peace with England had to be maintained at all costs. Better to have fought France. "What was there to prevent the United States from choosing from two nations equally obnoxious that enemy with whom she could contend with the least danger and the greatest advantage, reserving to some more favorable season the settlement of accounts with the other?"[28]

If the Republicans had been truly neutral, this is the course they would have adopted, Hildreth believed. He was not so ready as Lyman to absolve the Republicans of being under the influence of France in 1812. He accepted the old Federalist charge that Madison had been forced into the conflict by a coterie of war hawks in Congress who had

25. Richard Hildreth, *The History of the United States*, rev. ed., 6 vols. (New York, 1854–1856), IV, vii. Since Bancroft limited his history to the colonial era, not reaching the Revolution and its diplomacy until his ninth and tenth voiumes, published in 1866 and 1874, he does not figure significantly in the historiography of American diplomacy of this period.

26. *Ibid.*, pp. vi–viii.

27. *Ibid.*, III, 414, 421–424, 476; V, 3, 287–290, 327.

28. *Ibid.*, VI, 98–99.

threatened to withhold support for his renomination unless Madison requested war. This faction, said Hildreth, had been bent from the beginning on war with Great Britain. Some Federalists may have taken too much of a British view of things, but this was as nothing compared with the villainy of the pro-French faction of the Republican party and the cowardice of Madison.[29]

Opposed as Hildreth was to the war, he did not see it as an aggressive one on America's part or as the crusade for Canada some contemporary critics considered it to be. Instead, the United States had sought "to compel Great Britain, by the invasion and conquest of her Canadian territories, to respect our maritime rights." The war was defensive, the operations offensive. Maritime causes, not land hunger or Indian depredations, had been the main causes of the war.[30]

Well into the 1850s then, the only major syntheses of American diplomatic history approached the subject from the Federalist point of view. These accounts agreed that the Federalist policies had generally been successful and had furthered the proper neutrality policy of the United States. They also agreed that Republican policies had failed although Lyman if not Hildreth could concede that the Republicans had at least attempted to be neutral. Only Sparks's interpretation of the diplomacy of the Revolution ran counter to this trend.

Then, in the mid-1850s, two Southern historians broke the New England and Federalist monopoly of early American diplomatic history and offered mildly Republican interpretations. William Henry Trescot was one of these. He was a South Carolinian known for his personal volatility and the instability of his opinions. His first major historical work was *The Diplomacy of the Revolution*, published in 1852, and his second was *The Diplomatic History of the Administrations of Washington and Adams, 1789–1801*, published in 1857. He wrote these books while a member of the U.S. diplomatic corps, serving first as secretary to the American legation in London and then as assistant secretary of state. The latter post he resigned to join the Confederacy when the Civil War broke out.

Perhaps it was his service abroad in the diplomatic corps that made Trescot less dogmatic in his attachment to the policy of neutrality than the other historians of his day. Lyman's xenophobic book was "accurate, laborious, and useful," he conceded, but it was "not written

29. *Ibid.*, pp. 316, 318–319, 323–324, 333–334.
30. *Ibid.*, pp. 313–314.

from the point of view which I wished to occupy."[31] Trescot insisted that the United States could no longer continue to regard itself as apart from Europe.[32] Neutrality had been a good policy, he admitted, but the Founding Fathers had properly understood that neutrality meant "the perfect independence of the United States; not their isolation from the great affairs of the world. . . ."[33] Unfortunately, many Americans failed to see this.[34]

Another mistaken tendency of Americans was to test "the worth of public measures solely by their agreement with popular passion—a habit which elevates every popular paroxysm into a fit of inspiration. . . ." Unfortunately, popular opinion did not respect a diplomatic corps which operated slowly and whose purpose was to "check the selfish extravagance of one interest by demonstrating the reasonable selfishness of another." Americans should study their diplomatic history, Trescot said, to understand America's connection to the world and its role in the balance of power because the Founding Fathers generally understood these matters.[35]

Whenever America's involvements were undertaken in this realistic spirit, Trescot approved of them, and he credited the Republicans with at least as much of this realism as the Federalists. With his Republican proclivities, he naturally accepted Sparks's view of the diplomacy of the Revolution. He thought most of the Founding Fathers had understood that the French had joined America primarily to reduce England's strength and restore the balance of power rather than from sympathy for republican institutions. America's leaders had found this acceptable because they had sought only independence, not world democracy. Thus they refrained from abusing kings while the French diplomatically avoided criticizing republicanism. This realistic outlook, said Trescot, enabled most of the American leaders to understand France's desire to keep the United States somewhat dependent after the Revolution and to see why France did not feel itself obligated to recognize the United States' huge territorial claims as some sort of inalienable birthright of its Anglo-Saxon posterity. Obviously, con-

31. W. H. Trescot, *The Diplomatic History of the Administrations of Washington and Adams, 1789–1801* (Boston, 1857), p. viii.

32. W. H. Trescot, *A Few Thoughts on the Foreign Policy of the United States* (Charleston, S.C., 1849).

33. Trescot, *Diplomatic History of the Administrations of Washington and Adams,* p. 3.

34. Trescot, *The Diplomacy of the Revolution* (New York, 1852), p. 8.

35. *Ibid.,* pp. 2, 8–14.

flicting interests made the alliance a political experiment demanding caution. Yet the excessive suspicion of Jay and Adams gained them nothing whereas Franklin's trust of the French turned out to be quite justified.[36]

Trescot's interpretation of later American diplomacy was also mildly pro-Republican. He applauded Washington's adoption of a strict neutrality. It was a realistic recognition that the United States and the European system had only two points of practical contact—European colonial possessions on America's borders and commercial interchange with the Continent.[37] But he denounced the Federalists' Jay Treaty as a "confessed failure" and was particularly upset as a Southerner that Jay had failed to get compensation for the slaves carried away by the British army at the end of the revolutionary war. Still Trescot agreed that in the end the United States had little choice but the treaty or war. Jefferson's proposal to refuse the treaty and resort to an embargo was "impracticable."[38] Trescot defended Adams's peace with France in 1798 in the same way. Like the Jay Treaty it was a product of a nation "too weak to hold its own in the face of stronger and unscrupulous powers." The most the nation could do was "to submit without yielding," adjourning "final principles to a day of more equal argument. Neutrality is scarcely ever a brilliant policy. . . .But in the case of the United States, their interests clearly required it. . . ."[39]

Trescot had planned a diplomatic history of Jefferson's and Madison's administrations to accompany his previous two volumes, but he never finished it. In the introduction to his book on Washington and Adams, however, he indicated his approval of Jefferson's expansionist policies in Louisiana and Florida, as well as of the War of 1812, although clearly he had doubts about Jefferson's embargo and other commercial measures that had preceded the war.[40] Overall, then, while he contrived to agree in tone with the Republicans, he backed the substance of most important Federalist policies.

The same might be said of the second Southerner, George Tucker. A member of the Virginia congressional delegation from 1819 to 1825, he was a close friend of Jefferson and Madison and was appointed professor of moral philosophy at the University of Virginia

36. *Ibid.*, pp. 17, 49–56.
37. *Ibid.*, pp. 147, 156.
38. Trescot, *Diplomatic History of the Administrations of Washington and Adams*, pp. 109–111, 122–125.
39. *Ibid.*, p. 223.
40. *Ibid.*, pp. 4–5.

through the influence of Madison. A political economist of the Adam Smith variety, he also found time to write a two-volume biography of Jefferson and a four-volume *History of the United States* which he began at the age of eighty-five.[41] Unfortunately, Tucker was neither widely read nor very influential.[42]

Clearly Tucker was Republican in his sympathies, but like his political mentors he was not a rabid Southerner. He hoped slavery would die out, an event he predicted would occur about 1925. He was willing to acclaim the Federalist Washington as the ultimate hero, the farewell address being "the test of orthodoxy to American patriots." Tucker's bias showed subtly in the care he took to emphasize the role of Madison rather than Hamilton in the writing of the preliminary drafts of the address. He was anxious to demonstrate Jefferson's attachment to neutrality. While praising Washington's Proclamation of Neutrality, he agreed with the claim of Jefferson and Madison that Washington had exceeded his constitutional prerogatives by issuing the proclamation without preliminary consultation with Congress. Tucker admitted that if Jefferson's party had triumphed completely in opposition to the proclamation, America might have calamitously fought England, but he was quick to point out that the Federalists might have involved America in war on the other side.[43]

Strangely, given Sparks's impressive research and Tucker's own inclinations, Tucker sided with Jay and his policy of separate negotiations during the Revolution.[44] However, he roundly berated Jay's later treaty with the British for conceding much and gaining little. He sympathized with the Republican opposition to it, but "now that the passions and prejudices of the time have passed away," he could say that Washington's decision to ratify at least had secured the solid blessings of peace.[45]

Tucker was also willing to criticize the Republicans for their failure to assume a more spirited stance against the French in 1798. Yet he thought their opposition to Adams was understandable because Adams's "language and conduct had the extravagance and inconsistency of a madman." Tucker implied that if Washington had been president, peace might have been made more honorably although he

41. George Tucker, *The History of the United States from Their Colonization to the End of the Twenty-Sixth Congress, in 1841*, 4 vols. (Philadelphia, 1856).

42. Michael Kraus, *The History of American History* (New York, 1937), p. 260.

43. Tucker, *History of the United States*, I, 503, 506, 516, 611; II, 198.

44. *Ibid.*, I, 291–295.

45. *Ibid.*, pp. 570, 573–576.

did not quarrel in the end with Adams's decision to resolve the dispute with France.[46]

Finally, Tucker wholeheartedly supported the Republicans' declaration of war on England in 1812 and rejected the contention of Federalist historians that the Monroe-Pinkney Treaty had offered an acceptable settlement. But he also denounced Jefferson's use of the embargo as an alternative rather than as a prelude to war. Jefferson's known aversion to war had a sinister influence on his foreign policy, Tucker believed, tempting foreign nations to aggression. "Had the United States shown a determination to resist by force the first undoubted violation of right, force had not been necessary."[47] Perhaps the most interesting aspect of his justification for the war against Great Britain was his obvious belief that everyone in his audience agreed with him. Americans of the 1850s did not regret the war but looked back at America's forbearance with "wonder as well as indignation," failing to appreciate the danger of war to the infant nation, he said. The people were right, however, to condemn the Federalists and timid Republicans who defeated "every measure which aimed to maintain the rights and honor of the nation." National honor "seemed imperiously to require" war, and it was fortunate that the friends of the administration, "who felt for their country's rights and honor as every citizen who reads this narrative must now feel," had overcome Madison's hesitance to declare it. Tucker even rejoiced that news of Britain's repeal of its orders-in-council had come too late to forestall the declaration, for the character of the American people would have suffered in the eyes of the world and of the present generation if it had borne "to be robbed and enslaved, without striking a blow in their defense. It was happily ordered otherwise."[48]

Thus, the major historians of American diplomacy writing in the pre-Civil War period endorsed neutrality as the supreme law of American foreign policy. The only exceptions were Trescot's reservations and the case of the diplomacy of the Revolution where Jared Sparks's account legitimized the French alliance. Generally, historians differed only in whether the Federalists or Republicans had been most devoted to the principle of neutrality. Republican-oriented historians like Trescot and Tucker might be somewhat more critical of the Jay Treaty and President John Adams's diplomacy than Federalist-inclined

46. *Ibid.*, pp. 622–623; II, 91–92.
47. *Ibid.*, II, 300, 319, 347.
48. *Ibid.*, pp. 385, 425, 430–432, 465–474; III, 189–190.

historians like Lyman and Hildreth whereas Lyman and Hildreth were more critical of the embargo and the War of 1812 than Trescot and Tucker. But they all approved of George Washington, they accepted the Jay Treaty and Adams's move for peace in 1798 as ultimately necessary, they criticized the embargo, and all but the extremely partisan Hildreth commended the patriotism and good faith if not the wisdom of the opposition.

It is difficult to know the extent to which the information and interpretations of these major historians filtered out to the general public. Hildreth's history sold quite well and seems to have been regarded as representative of ante-bellum historical opinion by post-Civil War historians. Jared Sparks reached many people with his articles and his biographies of Washington and Franklin. But Tucker, Trescot, and Lyman seem to have had a very limited readership.

One vehicle for transmitting these interpretations could have been school textbooks. But few history texts existed prior to the 1860s.[49] One authority found only five published before 1825 and only fifteen before 1865.[50] Such textbooks were so scarce because history did not appear as a separate subject in schools until the 1830s and was not generally required until after the Civil War. Some scraps of diplomatic history might be picked up in readers or geographies, but rather few. And history texts emphasized military events far above any other sort of history, relegating diplomacy to a very minor role. One survey of pre-Civil War history texts found that more than 40 percent of their pages was given over to accounts of battles, generals, and military strategy.[51]

Even when history texts did discuss diplomacy, they rarely reflected the conflicting interpretations of the major historians of the era. One might have expected the texts to be at least mildly pro-Federalist since the only texts of any significance written outside New England were the McGuffey readers.[52] But most textbook authors simply assumed that whatever the American government had done had been right, whether the government had been controlled by Federalists or Republicans. No doubt this was to be expected since most of these books were for young, unlettered children, and complex historical discussions were out of place. In addition, these texts reflected the

49. Ruth Miller Elson, *Guardians of Tradition: American Schoolbooks of the Nineteenth Century* (Lincoln, Nebr., 1964), p. 5.

50. John A. Neitz, *Old Textbooks* (Pittsburgh, 1961), p. 242.

51. *Ibid.*

52. Elson, *Guardians of Tradition*, p. 7.

desire of educators and parents to instill patriotism in the young, so internal bickering between historical heroes went unrecorded as much as possible.[53]

Thus, Peter Parley's *The First Book of History*, published in 1832, said simply that the principal cause of the War of 1812 was that British ships "met our vessels on the sea, and their officers behaved in a very improper manner. They took the liberty to search our vessels," forcibly removing English sailors and Americans they mistook for English. No other cause of the war was mentioned, and no other controversial diplomatic issue handled.[54] Another text published in New Haven in 1840 commended the Jay Treaty for saving the peace, took a measured view of Federalists and Republicans, and actually condemned Federalist opposition to the War of 1812. It spoke of the British and French destroying American trade, the British impressing seamen directly off the American coast, and it briefly mentioned British agents involved in Indian wars on the frontier, although this was not described as a major cause of the war. It attacked the "peace party" for embarrassing the prosecution of the war and spoke of the Hartford Convention as part of the violent party spirit dividing the strength of the nation.[55]

Perhaps the most influential text was Charles Goodrich's *A History of the United States of America*, published originally in Boston in 1833. Goodrich's book set a pattern for later texts, many of which seemed almost carbon copies. Goodrich himself noticed this, commenting in his 1853 edition that some were so identical as to justify the question of legality.[56] Goodrich stressed that all of Washington's cabinet agreed to a policy of neutrality. He praised the Jay Treaty. He credited American resistance to French maneuvers with forcing France to negotiate the Quasi-War and commended Adams for sending the peace mission.[57] The embargo failed to halt British aggressions,

53. "There is a need to infuse patriotism to counter the decline of political virtue," wrote one text author, "and what is so likely to effect this national self-preservation, as to give our children, for their daily reading and study, such a record of the sublime virtues of the worthies of our earliest day . . ." (Emma Willard, *Abridged History of the United States* [Philadelphia, 1843], p. vi).

54. Peter Parley (Samuel Goodrich), *The First Book of History* (New York, 1832), p. 120.

55. J. Olney, *A History of the United States on a New Plan Adapted to the Capacity of Youth* (New Haven, 1840), pp. 190, 202, 207, 233.

56. Charles A. Goodrich, *A History of the United States of America* (Boston, 1853), p. 1.

57. *Ibid.*, pp. 223, 225–226, 229. By treating Adams's decision to send a new peace mission to France as a natural and positive result of Adams's and the

and war was declared over impressment and commercial interference. Goodrich made little mention of the French offenses, and he noted Federalist protests and the Hartford Convention without comment.[58]

The major historians of Federalist-Republican diplomacy in the ante-bellum era thus probably had little effect on the diplomatic thinking of their time. They may have contributed slightly to the already overwhelming consensus on the worthiness of George Washington and his policy of neutrality. Possibly they also helped lay to rest some of the more extreme charges circulated by partisans that their opponents were the conscious agents of a hostile foreign power. But if the impact of these historians on the public-at-large was minimal, their influence on later historians was substantial, particularly that of Sparks, Trescot, and Hildreth.

Federalists' previous strong stand against the French, the controversial aspects of the peace commission could be avoided. The same tack was taken by Willard, *Abridged History of the United States*, p. 267.

58. Goodrich, *History of the United States of America*, pp. 236–237, 241.

TWO

Ante-Bellum Historians and American Expansion

Prior to the Texas revolution of 1836, quarrels among American politicians over expansion were neither so vociferous nor so clearly defined as those over neutrality toward Europe. Probably Federalists in general and New Englanders in particular counseled more restraint in American expansionism than did Republicans. But very few opposed expansion outright. Disputes revolved around the tactics and pace of expansion, not the overall desirability of it.

Historical accounts of American expansion written before 1836 reflected this general consensus. For instance, though most historians extended sympathy to the suffering Indians, they all agreed that American expansion was necessary and good and that the tribulations of the Indians were more the result of Indian shortcomings and the workings of Providence than of U.S. policy. John Marshall described the policy of the American government if not that of the people at large to have been one of peace[1] whereas Theodore Lyman bemoaned the outrages "to which the natives . . . have been necessarily exposed," but said this "seems the order of nature, however difficult to comprehend or much to be deplored, that barbarous nations should always encounter when brought into contact with civilized ones."[2]

1. Marshall, *Life of George Washington*, V, 166, 170.
2. Lyman, *Diplomacy of the United States*, I, 248.

Lewis Cass spelled out this general historical view in an extensive article for the *North American Review* published in 1827. This article was part of the famous "battle of the books," a contest in accusation and recrimination between British and American literary figures over the relative virtues of the two peoples. Cass was responding to an article in the *London Quarterly Review* which charged that:

> However it may be attempted to preserve appearances by fraudulent and compulsory purchases of land, and declarations of benevolent intentions towards their injured possessors, it has always been the boast of American policy that "the Indians shall be made to vanish before civilization, as the snow melts before the sunbeam."[3]

Cass did not deny that the Indians were disappearing, but this was the situation in all European colonies in North America, and was due in part to the "fatuity" of the Indian himself, who refused to "imitate the arts of his civilized neighbors," but instead alternated between "listless indolence" and "vigorous exertion to provide for his animal wants or to gratify his baleful passions." Thus it was "ignorance, or folly, or morbid jealousy" to expect that the United States would permit a few "naked wandering barbarians" to occupy areas Providence had intended to support millions of people.[4]

Still, Cass argued that the United States had been reasonably humane in its expansion. The worst tragedies to befall the Indians had occurred during the colonial period under British rather than American auspices. Later, the British had used the Indians to fight the infant United States, "a hopeless contest, in which [the Indian] had neither rights to assert, nor wrongs to avenge." Since Indians were especially cruel in warfare, being taught from infancy both to inflict and endure torture, they naturally raised the hatred of the frontiersmen and brought further cruelties upon themselves.[5]

The textbooks of the time echoed this view. Both geographies and histories gave considerable space to descriptions of Indian culture, to which history texts devoted 3 to 4 percent of their pages. In these texts, some white injustices would be noted, but these instances were overwhelmed by bloody details of Indian massacres. Indian culture was pictured as savage, bloodthirsty, rude, and lazy. Occasionally some nobility was attributed to it, but white expansion was thor-

3. [Lewis Cass], "The Service of Indians in Civilized Warfare," *North American Review*, 24 (1827): 387.

4. *Ibid.*, pp. 368, 373, 391–392.

5. *Ibid.*, pp. 369, 372, 375, 390–391.

oughly justified and the doom of the Indians seen as a sad but necessary working of Providence. The United States could console itself that Spain had been much worse. The texts portrayed ruthless Spanish exploitation of land and Indians for gold, as against the Anglo-Saxons who tilled the soil and established liberty.[6]

Historians felt even less apologetic about American expansion at the expense of European colonial possessions than they did about the fate of the Indians. They saw American expansion as the development of immense regions "abandoned to a state of nature," a process which peaceably added to "the products and resources of the civilized world." European nations, on the other hand, were "conquering every country within their reach."[7] Thus, Lyman, New England Federalist though he was, praised the Louisiana Purchase. He even accepted the Jeffersonian proposition that the boundaries of Louisiana included West Florida, a contention supported only by the most convoluted logic. He brazenly complained that the Spanish case for West Florida was specious, yet "she refused to deliver the country" when the United States claimed it.[8]

In his discussion of the final acquisition of Florida in the Transcontinental Treaty of 1819, Lyman made only brief mention of Jackson's famous raid into the Spanish colony but discussed at length Spanish violations of American neutral rights and raids across the border by Indians and escaped slaves. In all, he found the American course fully justified. He was also pleased that the Florida treaty brought with it the Spanish claim to Oregon and the opportunity to expand to the Pacific. Some had spoken of situating the temple of the god Terminus at the Rocky Mountains, but Lyman was not ready to do that. Wherever the line was drawn between British and American territories in the West, it was clear that a new dominion based on the Columbia River and dominated by "the Saxon race" would soon arise and perhaps meet "the same race of men, coming from an opposite direction, across the plains of India." English-speaking peoples were encircling and covering the globe, raising empires, not so much by the sword, "as by the influence and authority of a superior order of civilization."[9]

Turning to United States-Latin American relations, Lyman ap-

6. See Ruth Miller Elson, *Guardians of Tradition*, pp. 73–79; and Willard, *Abridged History of the United States*, pp. 153, 320.

7. *North American Review*, 2 (1816): 99, 101.

8. Lyman, *Diplomacy of the United States*, I, 367, 270.

9. *Ibid.*, 106, 120, 129–169.

proved the caution exercised by the United States when recognizing the revolutionary governments in the area. The people of Latin America were, at the outset, almost completely unfit for free government. There were too many dissimilar races in Latin American nations to maintain much internal cohesiveness. He credited the British with preventing European intervention there and did not mention the Monroe Doctrine at all. Neglect of the Monroe Doctrine was not unique to Lyman; the school texts of the time also ignored it. The doctrine simply made little impression on its contemporaries. However, Lyman devoted a good deal of discussion to whether or not the United States should have sent delegates to the Panama Conference. He opposed participation virulently. Entanglements to defend republicanism in South America were no better than entanglements to defend monarchy in Europe.[10]

In 1836, American expansionism became far more controversial when people like John Quincy Adams and Benjamin Lundy denounced the Texas revolt and the subsequent American move to annex the new republic as a plot to extend slavery.[11] Opposition to expansion increased even more a decade later when the Texas issue helped trigger the Mexican War. The war became a bone of contention between the Whig and Democratic parties, and this political debate soon became a historiographical one. The early histories of the Mexican War lacked some of the inside information later historians would discover, and most treatments of the diplomacy leading to the war were very brief, with historians concentrating on military victories rather than on the more controversial diplomatic aspects of the war. Nevertheless, within three years of its conclusion, the outlines of most subsequent historical interpretations of the diplomacy of the Mexican War were already clearly drawn.

There were far more histories defending the American course than there were attacking it. The most complete of these was Roswell Sabine Ripley's *History of the War with Mexico*.[12] He was supported with a bit less vehemence by another significant work, Nathan Covington Brooks's *A Complete History of the Mexican War, 1846–1848*.[13] Brantz Mayer, a former secretary to the American legation in

10. *Ibid.*, pp. 415, 423, 448–450, 455–456, 489–490.

11. Benjamin Lundy, *War in Texas* (Philadelphia, 1836), pp. 3–4, 24–29.

12. Roswell Sabine Ripley, *History of the War with Mexico*, 2 vols. (New York, 1849).

13. Nathan Covington Brooks, *A Complete History of the Mexican War, 1846–1848* (Philadelphia, 1849).

Mexico, contributed *A History of the War Between Mexico and the United States*.[14] Lesser works published in this era and defending America's diplomacy toward Mexico were written by Lucien Chase, John Frost, John Jenkins, Nahum Capen, and Emma Willard.[15]

America had justifiably declared war against Mexico, these historians held, first because Mexico had refused to pay the claims American citizens had been awarded by international arbitration for losses incurred during the Mexican Revolution.[16] Even more important, Mexico had broken relations with the United States and moved an army northward to prevent America's legitimate annexation of Texas. Since Texas had maintained its independence for nine years, Mexico had had no right to oppose the wishes of the Texans to join the United States. These historians denied that either the Texas rebellion or the Mexican War had been part of a slaveholders' plot. The Texas rebellion had been a justifiable measure to prevent Mexico from fastening upon the Texans a despotism worse then absolute monarchy. And although the South had been especially alarmed by Britain's attempts to make Texas an independent antislavery British protectorate, other sections had feared the strategic and commercial threat of Great Britain and supported the war. This broad consensus was demonstrated by the election of James K. Polk on an expansionist platform after the red herring of slavery had caused the Senate to reject the first treaty of annexation negotiated under John Tyler.[17]

Once Polk had completed the annexation of Texas, the Mexican minister had demanded his passports and declared that a state of war

14. Brantz Mayer, *A History of the War Between Mexico and the United States, with a Preliminary View of Its Origins* (New York and London, 1847).

15. Lucien B. Chase, *History of the Polk Administration* (New York, 1850); Chase was a Democratic congressman who backed Polk on the Mexican War but opposed his compromise on Oregon. See also John Frost, *The Mexican War and Its Warriors* (New Haven and Philadelphia, 1848); John S. Jenkins, *History of the War Between the United States and Mexico* (Auburn, N.Y., 1851; copyrighted 1848); Nahum Capen, *The Republic of the United States of America: Its Duties to Itself and Its Responsibilities to Other Countries* . . . (New York and Philadelphia, 1848)—a book as long-winded and pompous as its title, it is a straight Democratic party tract dedicated to James Buchanan; and Emma Willard, *Last Leaves of American History: Comprising Histories of the Mexican War and California* (New York, 1849).

16. Chase, *History of the Polk Administration*, pp. 113–116; and Brooks, *History of the Mexican War*, pp. 7–8. Brantz Mayer argued that Mexico had been culpable in the matter of the claims, but he was not convinced that this justified war (Mayer, *History of the War Between Mexico and the United States*, pp. 25, 29, 34).

17. Ripley, *War with Mexico*, I, 36–37, 53–56, 81; Chase, *History of the Polk Administration*, pp. 80–96, 101; and Mayer, *History of the War Between Mexico and the United States*, pp. 43, 54–58, 63–64, 75, 76–78.

existed between the two nations. According to these historians, Mexico was mistaking American forbearance for cowardice and trusting to "the loud-mouthed opposition of a party in the American Union" and the threat of war to back the United States down.[18] Yet even with this provocation, Polk did not "take up the glove thus rudely cast at his feet," although "all usage, both ancient and modern, of civilized nations, would have justified the American Congress in declaring immediate war, and ordering the armies of the republic into Mexico, without waiting for her to strike the first blow."[19] Instead, after acquiring consent from the Mexican government, Polk sent John Slidell to negotiate. But if the Mexican government wanted to negotiate, the Mexican army and people did not. Threatened by revolution, the Mexican government rejected Slidell on a "frivolous subterfuge" of diplomatic etiquette.[20]

Once Slidell's negotiations had broken down, Polk had ordered Zachary Taylor to move his army from Corpus Christi, just south of the Nueces River that had served as the Texas border under Mexican rule, to the Rio Grande, which the Texans claimed by right of conquest and occupation. It was this order, occasioning the clash between Mexican and American forces at the Rio Grande, that inspired the only major disagreement between the historical defenders of America's diplomacy in the Mexican War. Chase and Ripley accepted the American case in full.[21] Mayer and Jenkins were a bit more hesitant, admitting that the area between the Nueces and the Rio Grande was disputed territory effectively occupied by neither power. But they argued that since the Mexicans had refused to negotiate the border and had given notice that the annexation of Texas was an act of war whatever border was claimed, it was Mexico's intransigence rather than Taylor's march that had caused the war.[22] Nathan Brooks, however, insisted that except for Polk's orders to occupy the Rio Grande, the war would never have occurred. This was not to say that the war was improper. "But

---

18. Ripley, *War with Mexico*, I, 49–50, 81; Chase, *History of the Polk Administration*, p. 116; and Brooks, *History of the Mexican War*, p. 8.

19. Chase, *History of the Polk Administration*, p. 111; and Brooks, *History of the Mexican War*, p. 102.

20. Mayer, *History of the War Between Mexico and the United States*, p. 84; and Ripley, *War with Mexico*, I, 82–83.

21. Chase, *History of the Polk Administration*, pp. 118–119; and Ripley, *War with Mexico*, I, 83.

22. Mayer, *History of the War Between Mexico and the United States*, pp. 112–116, 119–120, 137–138; and Jenkins, *History of the War Between the United States and Mexico, passim*.

while there existed so many causes, all or any of which would have justified a declaration of war on our part, it is a matter of supreme regret, that, after the magnanimous forbearance which we had exhibited towards Mexico . . . war was at length brought on by an act, and in a manner, totally unjustifiable."[23] Polk had ordered Taylor to the Rio Grande without congressional approval, a dangerous constitutional precedent.[24]

Brooks did not speculate on Polk's motive for this. Certainly neither he nor the others accused the American administration of seeking to expand slavery or to use the war as an underhanded means of acquiring California. In fact, Ripley said, the United States could have taken all of Mexico but showed its good faith by attempting to establish a stable government there and taking nothing more than such territory as could be fairly demanded as an indemnity.[25] Brooks thought that this was the best that Mexico could expect. The country was racially unstable and aggressive, its blood mixed with uncivilized "Arab ancestry."[26] In any case, said Lucien Chase, although "proper means" should normally be used to acquire necessary contiguous territory, if our nationality depended upon the forcible possession "of any portion of this earth, it would be as justifiable upon the part of Government to employ the requisite force . . . as it would be for a drowning man to thrust his fellow from a plank, which would not support them both."[27]

William Jay, the son and biographer of John Jay, and a leading abolitionist, led the opposition to this majority view of the Mexican War. Far from being a defensible response to Mexican aggression, Jay claimed the war was the culmination of a plot by the slavery interests of the nation to expand their peculiar institution. Jay's was by far the most complete and influential contemporary history of the Mexican War written from this point of view although numerous short pamphlets and propaganda tracts lent weight to the abolitionists' accusa-

---

23. Brooks, *History of the Mexican War*, p. 102.
24. *Ibid.*, p. 103.
25. Ripley, *War with Mexico*, II, 619.
26. Mayer, *History of the War Between Mexico and the United States*, pp. 6, 10–12. See also Chase, *History of the Polk Administration*, p. 96. This attitude that Mexicans were racially incompetent, lazy, erratic, and cruel permeates the literature of both sides of this issue although Jenkins specifically disowned the idea of racial superiority (Jenkins, *History of the War Between the United States and Mexico*, pp. 16–17).
27. Chase, *History of the Polk Administration*, p. 106.

tions, including James Russell Lowell's influential series, "The Biglow Papers."

William Jay argued that slavery interests had plotted the acquisition of Texas ever since the Missouri Compromise had allotted so much more of the Louisiana Purchase to freedom than to slavery. Conveniently, he ignored the part of such antislavery statesmen as John Quincy Adams in the early attempts to acquire the province. He attributed the Texas rebellion solely to Mexico's antislavery attitude and condemned Jackson's administration for encouraging Americans to aid the rebels by its feeble enforcement of American neutrality laws.[28] Jay opposed annexation of Texas as an act of war so long as Texas remained in a state of war with Mexico. He regarded the issues of the monetary claims against Mexico and the alarmist warnings of British meddling in Texas as mere ruses to gain the support of Northerners for acquisition of this new slave territory.[29] He complained that the slave interests had overcome Northern opposition to annexation by portraying the election of Polk as a mandate for expansion when Polk had actually failed to win a majority of the popular vote.[30]

Once elected, Polk had moved quickly to further the slave oligarchy's career of encroachment and crime to the southward, Jay said. While surrendering to Great Britain much of the United States' claim to Oregon, where slavery could not thrive, Polk plotted to acquire California, which had long stimulated the cupidity of slaveholders. Polk would try first to worry Mexico into surrendering California by puffing up the old Mexican claims and then offering to waive them and throw in a *doceur* of a few millions. When that failed, he would irritate Mexico into striking the first blow in a war that would permit the United States to obtain California by conquest. So Polk sent John Slidell to Mexico to settle all questions between the two nations. He was armed with $8 million of claims to bully Mexico and $25 million to bribe them to dismember their territory.[31]

Mexico "cunningly" offered to receive Slidell as a "commissioner" to settle the "present dispute," thus implying that only the question of Texas was at issue and that since Slidell would be a mere

28. William Jay, *A Review of the Causes and Consequences of the Mexican War*, 2nd ed. (Boston, 1849), pp. 10, 12, 16.

29. *Ibid.*, pp. 47–78.

30. *Ibid.*, pp. 99–100. Jay did not mention that New York, by throwing its votes to a third-party antislavery candidate instead of giving them to Henry Clay, provided the margin for Polk's victory.

31. *Ibid.*, p. 119.

commissioner rather than a regular minister, his reception did not indicate that normal relations had been restored. Yet the United States pretended with equal cunning that this equivocal answer was sufficient. Slidell then refused the Mexican request to delay his arrival and demanded reception as an envoy extraordinary rather than as a commissioner. Obviously, he was seeking a pretext for war if he was not received.[32] Even before Mexico had made a final decision on whether or not to receive him, Slidell wrote Polk that he was not received and Mexico was not desirous of settling. Polk saw that Mexico was on the verge of revolution and therefore probably was incapable of ceding California even if it wished to do so for fear of popular disfavor. So Polk ordered Taylor to march to the Rio Grande.

This was a gratuitous act of war, for the Nueces was clearly the border of Texas, said Jay, and he quoted extensively from Southerners like Andrew Jackson and Thomas Hart Benton to prove it. Taylor provoked war even further by blockading the Rio Grande and attempting to drive Mexicans from the eastern side of the river. In this engagement, which Polk had styled as shedding American blood on American soil, Jay claimed that the Mexicans had not fired a shot until the Americans charged.[33]

Meanwhile the Polk administration arranged to take California as soon as war broke out. Commodore J. D. Sloat and a small fleet were stationed off the West Coast, ready to take Monterey and San Francisco. Sloat actually took Monterey before instructions reached him from Washington, which indicated advance planning. Meanwhile, army Captain John C. Frémont supported a rebellion in California while on a supposedly peaceful mission with sixty-two soldiers. The government blamed Frémont for the entire business. But a Senate investigation showed that a secret agent, navy Lieutenant Archibald Gillespie, had communicated oral orders to Frémont. Gillespie said these orders were simply to watch for foreign influence. Yet they caused Frémont to turn away from Oregon, return to California, and aid in the Bear Flag Revolt. Jay said Gillespie's orders to Frémont must have been to bring on a rebellion without compromising the American government. Thus, the Southwest was to be won for slavery, a plot foiled only by the Gold Rush which attracted free labor to California.[34]

Two other significant critiques of the war reflected both the

32. *Ibid.*, pp. 112–113.
33. *Ibid.*, pp. 125, 127, 140–141, 551.
34. *Ibid.*, pp. 146–157, 181–182, 270.

defenses of men like R. S. Ripley and Brantz Mayer and the attacks of abolitionists like William Jay. These were books by Albert Gallatin, diplomat and long-time secretary of the treasury, and the lesser-known Charles Porter.[35] Gallatin and Porter agreed that the war was "aggressive and reprehensible," but they blamed it on the greed of the entire nation rather than on a slaveholders' plot. The war was "waged for the acquisition of territory" and "was sustained alike by north and south."[36]

Both Gallatin and Porter agreed that the United States had the right to annex Texas, but they argued that this could have been done without war by sending Slidell as a commissioner rather than as an envoy and by negotiating more patiently.[37] Instead, Polk sent Taylor to enforce an unjust claim to the whole territory beyond the Nueces.[38] The Founding Fathers had sustained their just rights, said Gallatin, but also had acted in strict conformity with justice and moderation. "Every acquisition of territory from foreign powers was honestly made, the result of treaties, not imposed, but freely assented to by the other party."[39] Although Gallatin did not charge Polk with plotting a war of conquest, Porter did. He echoed Jay's charges of a long-standing conspiracy to get California and New Mexico and said that Polk's order to march on the Rio Grande was "expected and intended" to bring war.[40] Thus, for both Gallatin and Porter, the war was neither a response to Mexican aggression nor a slave expansion conspiracy but a contemptible result of territorial greed on the part of the people and government of the entire United States.

Senator Thomas Hart Benton of Missouri, a major figure in the events leading up to the Mexican War, offered some new information and perspectives on the war in his memoirs published as *Thirty Years View* in the 1850s.[41] William Jay and the abolitionists had associated

35. Albert Gallatin, *Peace with Mexico* (New York, 1847); and Charles T. Porter, *Review of the Mexican War* (Auburn, N.Y., 1849).

36. Porter, *Review of the Mexican War*, pp. iii–iv. See also Gallatin, *Peace with Mexico*, pp. 5, 12–13.

37. Porter, *Review of the Mexican War*, pp. 37–47; and Gallatin, *Peace with Mexico*, p. 5.

38. Porter thought that Texas's legitimate border was the Nueces. Gallatin pointed out that Texas did actually have two towns across the Nueces, Corpus Christi and San Patricio, and that the line should have been negotiated to divide the territory between the Nueces and the Rio Grande (Porter, *Review of the Mexican War*, p. 79; and Gallatin, *Peace with Mexico*, pp. 8–10).

39. Gallatin, *Peace with Mexico*, p. 12.

40. Porter, *Review of the Mexican War*, pp. 87–88.

41. Thomas Hart Benton, *Thirty Years View*, 2 vols. (New York, 1854–1856).

Benton with John Tyler, James K. Polk, and John C. Calhoun as part of the monolithic slave conspiracy to annex Texas, bring on war with Mexico, and allow conquest of further slave territory. Benton demurred. He, Martin Van Buren, and James K. Polk, all good Jacksonian Democrats, had followed an honorable course to annex Texas while avoiding war with Mexico. Benton claimed that unfortunately they were defeated in these attempts by the dishonorable machinations of John C. Calhoun, his dupe John Tyler, and a group of unscrupulous speculators and adventurers. It was these men who had demanded the "premature" annexation of Texas "for the purpose of increasing the area of slavery, or to make its rejection a cause for the secession of the Southern states. . . ." In any case, annexation would become the dominant issue of the presidential election, and Calhoun hoped to be the beneficiary of it.[42]

The Senate, however, had rejected Tyler's first treaty of annexation in a vote "infinitely honorable" to itself. Believing that "the treaty was a wrong and criminal way of doing a right thing," Benton and others "who had no object but the public good," tried to find a way to annex Texas without forcing a confrontation with Mexico. Benton claimed to have received a promise from Polk that he would annex under a Senate resolution requiring new negotiations with Texas, hopefully delaying the issue until an agreement could be made with Mexico. Instead, Polk had accepted Tyler's decision to annex Texas immediately under a House resolution, and war inevitably followed.[43]

If the war was a product of deception and greed, the taking of California was not, according to Benton. California's fate would have been the same with or without the Mexican War. It was already in a revolutionary state, and the American settlers, along with the leading Californians, rallied around the conciliatory John C. Frémont to save it from the British, whose threat to California was as real as it had been fraudulent in Texas.[44] The fact that Frémont was Benton's son-in-law no doubt had something to do with Benton's interpretation.

In this same memoir, Benton presented the first extensive history of the Oregon question. As Democratic leader of the Senate, he had been instrumental in gaining American acceptance of the compromise border at 49 degrees latitude, and his history was an attempt to defend himself against the charges of Northern expansionists that his actions had constituted part of the slave interests' plot to abandon

42. *Ibid.*, II, 581–589, 600, 640.
43. *Ibid.*, pp. 619, 636–639.
44. *Ibid.*, pp. 586, 692–693.

territory unfavorable to slavery while fighting for land that could support the peculiar institution. He recounted his early advocacy of expansion into the Oregon territory. He even had suggested that land grants be offered to attract "thirty or forty thousand rifles" to defend America's interests beyond the Rockies against the British. But he insisted that America's claim extended properly only to the 49th parallel, the line he said had been drawn between British Canada and French possessions by commissioners under the Treaty of Utrecht. Cries for all of Oregon up to 54°40' were mere partisan posturing. Even Polk, who had campaigned on a platform calling for all of Oregon, had offered to compromise at 49 degrees latitude. British rejection of that offer had embarrassed him terribly because of his earlier promises, so that Polk had insisted he would never consider such a compromise again unless the Senate insisted. Thus, when the British themselves offered the 49th parallel, it was up to the Senate to accept and give the president "a faithful support against himself, against his cabinet, and against his peculiar friends."[45]

One might have thought that these critiques of American expansionism in the Mexican War and Oregon negotiations would have led the historians of the 1850s to reevaluate America's earlier expansionism. But they did not. Richard Hildreth related the events surrounding the Louisiana Purchase and the annexation of Florida in a totally noncommittal way. He specifically disowned the idea that the attack on Canada in the War of 1812 was anything but defensive. He praised the Indian policies of Washington and Jefferson for introducing "the arts and habits of civilized life among the Indian tribes," measures which incidentally made them "the more ready to cede a part of their lands, now no longer needed as hunting grounds."[46]

If Hildreth, the New Englander, was not moved to regret earlier expansionism by the events of the Mexican War, it was not likely that Southerners like Trescot and Tucker would be so moved. Trescot, of course, stopped his history with the Adams administration. But he did indicate that in future volumes he would give full approval not only to the Louisiana Purchase and the acquisition of Florida but also to the acquisition of Oregon and Texas.[47]

Tucker upheld all of American expansionism. He blamed any opposition on party motives and eastern fear of a declining influence until such "local jealousy" was replaced by the slave question. He fully

45. *Ibid.*, I, 13; II, 482, 566, 676.
46. Hildreth, *History of the United States*, V, 556–557.
47. Trescot, *Diplomacy of the Administrations of Washington and Adams*, pp. 4–6.

approved of the Louisiana Purchase, where "the wandering tribes of savages which are now its only inhabitants, and amounting at most to a few hundred thousand, will be substituted by a hundred millions of free, intelligent and civilized men." He saw no impropriety in the way Florida was acquired although he conceded that Jackson was a bit hot-headed.[48]

Tucker, as a congressman, had been an opponent of risky measures in Oregon but believed that modern modes of transportation made his views "if right at first, . . . refuted by the improvements of the age."[49] Thus, Tucker was unworried by the implications of American expansionism. Americans "can never, in the aggregate, feel the same impulses as have operated on the minds of an Alexander, a Julius Caesar, or a Napoleon; and the humanity and liberality shown by the Americans towards the Indian tribes within their limits, give some assurance of their future moderation."[50]

Despite Polk's resurrection of the Monroe Doctrine to justify his expansionist course, most historians continued to ignore it. Tucker did give a brief and bland summary of the doctrine's origins, but even he did not think it important enough to include in his list of the outstanding events of the Monroe administration.[51] His was the only major ante-bellum history that even mentioned it in passing.

However, James Clarke Welling did publish a short article in the *North American Review* in 1856 in which he traced the history of the doctrine to counter the interventionist interpretation of Polk and others. Welling argued that the original enunciation of the doctrine had involved no pledge on the part of the United States to defend or otherwise intervene in Latin America. Even John Quincy Adams, whom the author acknowledged as a principal originator of the doctrine, had said during the debates over the Panama Conference that the United States would not commit itself to defend the Western Hemisphere against further European colonization. It would seek only a pledge that each nation would defend its own territory against the Europeans. "To colonization by purchase, treaty, or lawful conquest, the Monroe Doctrine was not intended to apply, however it may have come to be considered in these latter days," wrote Welling.[52]

48. Tucker, *History of the United States*, II, 206, 389, 391–393, 416–417; III, 249–254, 309.

49. *Ibid.*, III, 357.

50. *Ibid.*, IV, 426.

51. *Ibid.*, III, 364, 407–408.

52. [James Clarke Welling], "The Monroe Doctrine," *North American Review*, 82 (1856): 478–512.

Textbooks generally followed the trends established by the major historians of this era. Not one text mentioned the Monroe Doctrine. They championed the Louisiana Purchase and the Florida settlement while fully approving of Indian removal.[53] Controversy and criticism even in the case of the Mexican War were almost nonexistent, and where they did exist, were very thoroughly veiled.[54]

Overall, the consensus of historical opinion rendered a favorable verdict on American expansionism. The Mexican War was a significant exception to this, but still the vast majority of historical accounts justified that war and the resultant extension of American territory. Whatever opposition was expressed to the expansionism of the war was not extended to the previous course of America's westward march. Just as historians might debate the proper approach to neutrality but not neutrality itself, so did they approve of expansion and only question the methods used at particular times. The Civil War, however, would change some of these attitudes and substantially affect several of the specific historical interpretations that had supported them.

53. Goodrich, *History of the United States*; Willard, *Abridged History of the United States*; and G. P. Quackenbos, *Illustrated History of the United States* (New York, 1864; originally published 1857).

54. See, e.g., Goodrich, *History of the United States*, pp. 289–293; and Quackenbos, *Illustrated History*, pp. 421–423.

PART TWO

The Age of Manly Neutrality and the Bloody Shirt
1860-1898

Prior to the Civil War, foreign policy had played an extremely important role in American history. The Federalist and Republican eras had been dominated by diplomatic questions, and if foreign policy intrusions into American life had been brief after 1824, they had generated great public interest. But after 1860 the Civil War, Reconstruction, and the issues of a burgeoning industrial economy dwarfed the minor tempests that surrounded the purchase of Alaska, abortive schemes to annex Santo Domingo, and the Pan-Americanism of James G. Blaine. Most Americans felt little concern for foreign policy.

This disinterest was reflected in the nature of American historical studies of the time. There were very few specialized studies of American diplomacy like those of Trescot and Lyman. The most important diplomatic history appeared in the multivolume tomes on general American history produced in this era by Hermann Von Holst, James Schouler, John Bach McMaster, and Henry Adams, in the tradition of Bancroft, Hildreth, and Tucker. Also, Justin Winsor edited a large series of critical essays covering much of early American history. All of these significant and lasting contributions to historical scholarship were based on painstaking research in primary documents and written for the most part in a readable, narrative form. They were more carefully annotated than the histories of their predecessors although most of these writers preferred to acknowledge a primary source rather than any obligation to fellow historians. More historical sources were available and history was becoming professional, with the majority of the significant historians of this era holding university posts at one time or another. Still, the age of the specialist and the monograph had yet to arrive.

The Civil War worked a major transformation in the interpretations of American diplomatic history. It had a particularly profound effect on historians' attitudes toward past westward expansion, making their accounts of the diplomacy of annexation far less favorable than those of the ante-bellum period. The issue of slavery was the key ingredient in this transformation. With the South's voice largely silenced by defeat, Northern historians almost unanimously endorsed the charge that the Civil War had been the culmination of an aggressive slavocracy's long-standing attempts to expand the area of slavery. The annexation of Texas, the Mexican War, and the acquisition of California and the Southwest, previously part of civilization's march at the expense of inferior peoples who largely deserved their fate, were now seen as part of a reprehensible plot to extend slavery. Sometimes this distaste for slavery even reverberated into criticism of expansionist episodes in which slavery had been involved only peripherally, such as the Louisiana Purchase and the Florida treaty. Although the slavery issue was the primary cause of the more critical interpretations of American expansionism, the growth of America's population and power also seems to have stimulated some second thoughts about earlier American expansion. Those whom previous generations had regarded as formidable enemies, the Indians and the Spanish, now could be represented as underdogs who had been bullied by the United States and whose displacement was pitiable.

But if the images of slavery and bullying brought a more critical tone to historical accounts of American expansion, this was neither because they had convinced Americans that expansion per se was wrong nor because they had reduced the general level of belligerence in the nation. Historians still reminded their readers that while there might have been some tragic aspects of America's march to the Pacific and while the tactics of the United States sometimes had been distasteful, American entry into the relatively empty areas of the West had been inevitable and good. And where the victims of American expansion had been the major European colonial powers, England and France, historians were critical only if they thought the United States had been excessively deferential or had sought its goals by indirect conniving rather than by straightforward challenges. Here too the Civil War and the rising sense of national power combined to shape historians' viewpoints. Americans resented the favorable attitudes Britain and France had exhibited toward the Confederates during the war, and this resentment showed in historical interpretations of previous confrontations with those nations whether over American territorial expansion or neutral rights on the high seas. *Historians of the previous era who had praised Franklin's cooperation with France, approved the Federalist appeasement of Britain in the Jay Treaty, or condemned the declaration of war on Great Britain in 1812 fell from favor. Historians of the post-Civil War era still held fast to neutrality toward Europe but only when it was a properly defiant neutrality rather than a cringing one.*

The rise of imperialism at the end of the nineteenth century surprisingly did little to alter the tone of historical interpretations that had predominated in the earlier years of this era. Only the Monroe Doctrine became the subject of a significant historiographical debate between imperialists and antiimperialists prior to the Spanish-American War. This was because the Monroe Doctrine had been revived by the attempt of Ferdinand de Lesseps to build a French canal across the Isthmus of Panama in 1881. Despite the rising strength of the imperial view, historians of the time concluded that the historical record supported restraint. Perhaps the major reason why no other episode in the history of American diplomacy became a bone of contention between imperialists and antiimperialists was that imperial publicists cited European rather than American historical precedents to support their point of view. Thus, the Civil War remained the primary influence on the late nineteenth century's outlook on foreign policy, which viewed favorably instances of manly belligerence against Britain and France and frowned upon expansionism that had benefited slavery.

THREE

A Manly Neutrality

A few years after Charles Francis Adams had returned from his post as minister to Great Britain during the Civil War, the New York Historical Society asked him to speak at one of their meetings. Undoubtedly Adams felt very comfortable giving a historical paper. He was the president of the Massachusetts Historical Society and an indefatigable historical editor, besides being the son of one American president and the grandson of another. His own three sons, Charles Francis, Jr., Henry, and Brooks, would also become historians of note. Adams selected as his topic, "The Struggle for Neutrality in America," a struggle to which he believed his father, grandfather, and he himself had made significant contributions.[1] America had won its right to remain neutral during foreign wars by four major actions, almost all of them actions of restraint rather than belligerence. Washington had issued the Neutrality Proclamation and then had accepted the admittedly weak Jay Treaty to preserve peace with England. John Adams had sacrificed his popularity to make peace with France during the Quasi-War and in the process had ended the embarrassing and entangling French alliance. Finally, the War of 1812 had brought Britain to her senses. From then on, Britain had defended the rights of neutrals, even

---

1. Charles Francis Adams, "The Struggle for Neutrality in America," pamphlet (New York, 1871).

justifying its own policies during the Civil War by citing American precedents.[2]

Charles Francis Adams was particularly proud of the role his Civil War diplomacy had played in solidifying America's neutral rights by "adhering to precedents so honorably established in earlier times." He applauded the decision to defy American popular opinion and to release the two Confederate diplomats who had been seized by American Captain Charles Wilkes from the British ship *Trent*, a seizure which had been made in violation of America's own concept of international law. Because of this restraint and admission of wrong, the nation had been saved from a needless war.[3] No question ever would be raised again "of the right of the United States to remain at peace. . . . These be thy victories, O Peace," Adams concluded ecstatically.[4]

Henry Dawson, the combative editor and literary critic of *The Historical Magazine*, wrote contemptuously of Adams's testimonial to a restrained and pacific neutrality. The real struggle for neutrality was not with foreign nations, said Dawson, it was domestic. Some Americans wanted a spirited and manly neutrality; others, presumably including Adams, wanted a weak-kneed and cowardly one. Jefferson and his followers had been on the side of manly neutrality. Unfortunately, Hamilton and his monarchist allies had betrayed France and tried to throw the nation into the arms of Britain. The Jay Treaty and John Adams's policy prior to his surprise peace move were not the salvation of neutrality but unneutral offenses against France.[5]

Dawson's biting tone was probably as much due to the widespread anger in the United States at England's policies during the Civil War as to any special proclivities Dawson may have felt for Jefferson. A spirited and erudite defense of British Civil War policy by Oxford don Montague Bernard, published in England in 1870, made no impression on American historians.[6] Even historians who favored a prudent and restrained neutrality agreed that England's policies had been harsh and unfriendly. George Bemis attacked Britain's "hasty" recognition of Confederate belligerency as deliberately designed to aid the

---

2. *Ibid.*, pp. 1–4, 11–13, 20–25, 36, 40–41, 44–45.

3. *Ibid.*, p. 7.

4. *Ibid.*, pp. 45–47.

5. Henry Dawson, *Historical Magazine*, 2nd ser., 9 (January 1871): 129–150.

6. Montague Bernard, *A Historical Account of the Neutrality of Great Britain During the American Civil War* (London, 1870).

Southern traitors.[7] Charles Francis Adams's son, Henry, gave a very hostile interpretation of Britain's negotiations over the Declaration of Paris, which had involved the rights and duties of neutrals.[8] Thomas Harris's account of the *Trent* affair concluded that

> there seemed to be an eagerness on the part of the British government to seize on the occasion and to grasp the pretext for making war. . . . A kindred people were already engaged in a struggle for their very existence, yet, for a difference which it was easily possible to arrange by diplomatic means, this professed leader of civilization and boasted enemy of human slavery did all in her power to make a conflict inevitable and the triumph of an insurgent slave republic certain.[9]

Even historians who were not particularly antagonistic to Britain, like Lincoln's biographers, John Nicolay and John Hay, believed that England was "by active sympathy favorable to the South."[10] But Nicolay and Hay, unlike most historians of this era, were willing to allow some slight excuse for Britain's abominable behavior. President James Buchanan's abdication of responsibility in the face of secession could have led Englishmen to believe that division of the Union was inevitable, thus making recognition of Confederate belligerency not wholly malicious.[11] James Ford Rhodes agreed. His was a surprisingly moderate account, perhaps because he had access to a large number of British sources and was writing at the end of the century when Anglo-American relations began to take a dramatic turn for the better. He noted that while England's government and ruling classes were hostile to the Union, the lower classes and religious nonconformists had favored the North because a Union victory would mean the end of slavery. But the upper classes dominated British policy, "gloating" over the prospect of a divided republic that would provide a more easily managed source of cotton and the opportunity to play balance-of-power politics in the Western Hemisphere. All Rhodes could say in defense of England was that if some "American Jingo" still wished to retaliate "for the depredations of the Confederate cruisers, the cynical

7. George Bemis, *Hasty Recognition of Rebel Belligerency: And Our Right to Complain of It* (Boston, 1865).

8. Henry Adams, "The Declaration of Paris," in his *Historical Essays* (New York, 1891).

9. Thomas L. Harris, *The Trent Affair* (Indianapolis and Kansas City, 1896).

10. John G. Nicolay and John Hay, *Abraham Lincoln: A History*, 10 vols. (New York, 1886–1890), IV, 266.

11. *Ibid.*, pp. 266–269.

ill will of Palmerston, the speech of Gladstone [advocating recognition of the independence of the Confederacy], the leaders in the *Times* and the *Saturday Review*, he must remember that the England which arouses his indignation has passed away."[12]

Anger at Britain combined with a growing sense of national power to make the United States increasingly assertive of its rights and protective of its dignity and reputation in the post-Civil War era. Few Americans challenged the tried-and-true policy of neutrality, but more and more people urged that this be an assertive rather than a restrained neutrality. Even those who argued for a policy of restraint, like Nicolay and Hay, tried to demonstrate that their policy was a manly one based on a consciousness of strength rather than a cowardly one based on weakness.[13] Examples of this appeared in two monographs dealing with America's neutral policy—Eugene Schuyler's *American Diplomacy and the Furtherance of Commerce*[14] and George Bemis's *American Neutrality: Its Honorable Past; Its Expedient Future.*[15] Schuyler argued that in the past the United States had erred more from extreme prudence than from rashness, and he urged future assertion to protect and extend commercial rights and interests abroad. Bemis, on the other hand, argued for continued restraint in America's neutral policy.

Bemis was writing in opposition to a move in Congress led by Nathaniel Banks, chairman of the House Foreign Affairs Committee, to reduce the obligations imposed on American citizens by U.S. neutrality laws. Banks was arguing that these neutrality laws had stemmed from early America's weakness and that the Founding Fathers, especially the two Adamses, had planned to throw them off once the United States had the strength to defend itself. According to Banks, since the British had refused to impose neutral controls on its citizens, as in the case of the *Alabama*, the United States should not feel

12. James Ford Rhodes, *History of the United States from the Compromise of 1850*, 7 vols. (New York, 1893–1906), III, 420n., 503–543; IV, 349–359, 360. See also Nicolay and Hay, *Abraham Lincoln*, V, 40. For an analysis of contemporary sources proclaiming the heroic resistance to Confederate sympathies in the face of the cotton famine by antislavery English workingmen, see Joseph Park, "English Workingmen and the American Civil War," *Political Science Quarterly*, 39, (1924): 432–457.

13. While praising the prudence of Lincoln, Seward, and Adams, the authors were also careful to praise their "unyielding firmness and fortitude" (Nicolay and Hay, *Abraham Lincoln*, VI, 49).

14. Eugene Schuyler, *American Diplomacy and the Furtherance of Commerce* (New York, 1866).

15. George Bemis, *American Neutrality: Its Honorable Past; Its Expedient Future* (Boston, 1886).

obligated to cater to the British as it had in the *Trent* affair.[16] In response, Bemis proclaimed that America's neutrality laws stemmed from pride and righteousness, not weakness. They were a triumph of right and duty over interest and expediency.[17] America was strong now, he said, but that was no reason to abandon neutrality. Interventions and filibusters in Latin America were in accord with neither our duties nor our interests.[18] Bemis concluded that reliance upon justice and the moral principles of our neutrality laws would better preserve American rights than a strong military force and a quarrelsome attitude.[19]

Like Charles Francis Adams, these authors drew on historical precedents to illustrate their views of a proper neutrality. One source of precedents was the historiographical debate over revolutionary war diplomacy. Should the Founding Fathers have been more restrained or more assertive in their dealings with the European powers and in their desires for neutrality and nonentanglement? Ultimately the weight of the post-Civil War era's historical outlook would swing away from Franklin's more restrained treatment of France toward approval of the more assertive, independent policies of Jay and Adams. However, the era did not start auspiciously for Jay or Adams.

George Bancroft, perhaps the most respected historian of his time, reached the revolutionary war portion of his multivolume history in 1866. His elaborate account of the peace negotiations was based on more thorough research in documents both here and abroad than had been possible for his predecessors. He was able to see the papers of British Prime Minister Lord Shelburne, even before Shelburne's biographer, Alleyne Fitzherbert, published large extracts of them. He worked through the documents in the French Foreign Office with Adolphe de Circourt, who later published these documents in conjunction with a French translation of Bancroft's own history in 1876.[20] This research led Bancroft to agree with Jared Sparks that John Jay had needlessly delayed the negotiations over what was actually an adequate preliminary recognition of American independence in the original letter of commission for the British negotiator. Jay's blind suspicion

16. *Ibid.*, pp. 50–51.
17. *Ibid.*, pp. 26–28.
18. *Ibid.*, pp. 126, 132–133.
19. *Ibid.*, p. 135.
20. Justin Winsor, *Narrative and Critical History of America*, 8 vols. (Boston and New York, 1884–1889), VII, 168, n. 3; and Adolphe de Circourt, *Histoire de l'action commune de la France et de l'Amérique pour l'independence des Etats Unis*, by George Bancroft, trans. le comte de Circourt, 3 vols. (Paris, 1876).

of Vergennes had cost the Americans seriously, for the delay gave British special interests a chance to influence Lord Shelburne. By the time negotiations resumed, Shelburne had stiffened the British position on American debts and on compensation for the Loyalists.[21] Franklin had recognized Shelburne's weak political position and had wanted to make peace quickly.[22]

But Bancroft was not as sanguine about French policy as Sparks had been. The post-Civil War era demanded manly conduct toward Britain and France. Bancroft insisted that Franklin had been far from a dupe of the French, being the first of the American delegates to defy congressional instructions tying the negotiators to French advice. Ignoring the French, he had offered the British negotiator a list of peace terms which included the suggestion that if Britain ceded Canada to the United States, America would no longer need the French alliance to help protect its borders.[23] It had been Jay rather than Franklin who had been the dupe of the Europeans. He had overreacted to France's maneuvers by suggesting that the British should have free navigation of the Mississippi and by urging the British to keep Florida rather than allowing Spain to take it.[24]

Bancroft's interpretation was seconded by Edward Everett Hale and his son in their extensive study *Franklin in France*.[25] It was also endorsed by Francis Wharton, solicitor for the Department of State, who was commissioned to publish a new edition of Sparks's *Diplomatic Correspondence of the Revolution* once it was recognized how many liberties Sparks had taken with the documents.[26] Wharton even went beyond both Sparks and Bancroft to claim that Jay's delays had not simply stiffened British terms but actually had cost the United States possession of Canada. Since the British negotiator, Richard Oswald, had been receptive to Franklin's original list of peace terms containing the request for Canada and since he had reported Shelburne as favorable also, Wharton thought the only explanation for the failure of the Americans to acquire the province had to be that Shelburne's position had been so weakened by Jay's delays that he

21. George Bancroft, *A History of the United States*, 10 vols. (Boston, 1834 and 1874; rev. ed. up to 1789, 6 vols., New York, 1876); all citations are from the 1891 edition, the author's last revision, 8 vols. (Boston), V, 549–551, 567, 570.

22. *Ibid.*, pp. 547, 551.

23. *Ibid.*, pp. 548, 570.

24. *Ibid.*, pp. 571–575.

25. Edward E. Hale and Edward E. Hale, Jr., *Franklin in France*, 2 vols. (Boston, 1887–1888).

26. Wharton, *Revolutionary Diplomatic Correspondence*.

could no longer afford to make the cession. "Had Franklin been left to manage in his own way the negotiation with Shelburne, the probability is that Canada could have passed to the United States as one of the conditions of peace," Wharton concluded.[27]

Just as Franklin's diplomacy seemed fully vindicated, the Jay family struck back. John Jay, grandson of the Founding Father, and George Pellew, nephew to this younger John Jay, each published accounts that reverted to the old Federalist version.[28] Their first target was Jared Sparks. They asserted that Sparks had mistranslated Rayneval's letter recounting his secret mission[29] and had interjected "with misleading positiveness a note that Jay's suspicions of France were unfounded," a suggestion, "itself unfounded," that had "until recently been followed implicitly by historians, even by Mr. Bancroft."[30] New material from the French and British archives proved "the absolute correctness of [John Jay's] convictions, and the consequent necessity of the course of action he adopted," they claimed.[31] "We now know from Vergennes' own correspondence what Congress did not know then—that France had secretly assented to the desire of Spain to abridge the boundaries, the resources, and the power of America."[32]

This could be proven in several ways. The Marbois letter urging that America be denied the fisheries was clearly genuine. Marbois himself had admitted the substantial accuracy of the translation in a conversation recorded in John Jay's manuscripts.[33] Moreover, the letter could be shown to reflect actual French policy. A memoir in the archives of France, which the younger Jay maintained was either prepared under Vergennes's direction or submitted for his approval, stated that it was French policy to prevent the United States from

27. Francis Wharton, *International Law Digest*, 2nd ed., 3 vols. (Washington, D.C., 1887), III, 913.

28. John Jay, *The Peace Negotiations of 1782 and 1783* (New York, 1884); John Jay, "The Peace Negotiations of 1782 and 1783," in Winsor, *Narrative and Critical History of America*, VII, 89–184; and George Pellew, *John Jay* (Boston and New York, 1890 and 1898).

29. Jay, *Peace Negotiations of 1782 and 1783*, pp. 42–43.

30. Pellew, *John Jay*, p. viii.

31. *Ibid.*, p. ix. Actually Bancroft had seen most of these documents and so had Wharton (Winsor, *Narrative and Critical History of America*, 168–169ns.). The new material from the French archives was in Henri Doniol, *Histoire de la participation de la France à l'établissement des Etats-Unis d'Amérique*, 5 vols. (Paris, 1885–1892).

32. Jay in Winsor, *Narrative and Critical History of America*, VII, 94.

33. *Ibid.*, p. 120. See also Pellew, *John Jay*, pp. 169–170.

extending its boundaries, spreading its revolutionary ideas, or gaining access to the fisheries.[34] In addition, British diplomat Alleyne Fitzherbert quoted Rayneval as saying that "nothing could be further from the wishes of his court than that the claim [of the Americans to a share in the Newfoundland fisheries] should be admitted" and that rejection of the claim was in keeping with both British interests and "with the strictest principles of justice."[35] According to Fitzherbert, Vergennes himself always echoed these sentiments.[36] Shelburne's biographer, with access to his papers, wrote that in Rayneval's secret mission to London, he "played into the hands of the English ministers by expressing a strong opinion against the American claims to the Newfoundland fisheries and to the valley of the Mississippi and the Ohio."[37] According to the Jay family, John Jay had won acknowledgment of American independence in a new commission given to Oswald by sending a messenger to counter Rayneval.[38] Neither the younger John Jay nor Pellew commented on charges that the delay cost the Americans Canada or concessions on debts and Loyalists, nor did they mention their ancestor's role in pushing the British toward Florida and the Mississippi.

Despite the prestige of historians like Bancroft and Wharton, this Jay family version received the endorsement of the leading historical arbiter of the time, Justin Winsor. It was also seconded by John Morse, editor of a popular collection of biographies entitled the American Statesman Series. Morse concluded that the Jay family version was "a very full and accurate presentation of this entire affair, drawn from those sources which have only very recently become public, and which go far to remove former questions out of the realm of discussion."[39] As we shall see, it failed to do that. But Jay's and Pellew's accounts did coincide better with the age's belligerent neutrality than

34. Jay in Winsor, *Narrative and Critical History of America*, VII, 121.
35. *Ibid.*, p. 120.
36. *Ibid.*
37. *Ibid.*, p. 124. See also Pellew, *John Jay*, p. 174.
38. Jay in Winsor, *Narrative and Critical History of America*, VII, 125 and n., 140.
39. John T. Morse, Jr., *Benjamin Franklin*, 2nd ed. (Boston and New York, 1898), p. 390n. In the Jay version, however, Morse, like the original John Jay and his historian-descendants, did not render Franklin a dupe or villain, as John Adams had done in his letters. Once Franklin's reluctance to break with France and the congressional instructions had been overcome, he had supported the independent policy of his colleagues with a firmness that "seems hardly appreciated by those writers who have insisted that Dr. Franklin had continued to believe in the devotion of France to the American claims and that when he

did Bancroft's, despite the latter's emphasis on the subtle independence of Franklin's diplomacy.

The same devotion to a bellicose defiance of Europe could be seen in historical treatments of America's early national period. The major accounts of Federalist and Republican diplomacy were contained in the massive multivolume histories of Hermann Von Holst, Henry Adams, James Schouler, John Bach McMaster, and Justin Winsor.[40] Along with Richard Hildreth's earlier work, these volumes formed the basic sources for the popular histories and biographies of the time, such as the American Statesman Series of John Morse and the various publications of John Fiske.

Hermann Eduard Von Holst, a German historian who lived and taught occasionally in America and whose *Constitutional and Political History of the United States* commanded great prestige in the late nineteenth century, was the first to publish an extensive account of Federalist and Republican diplomacy since Richard Hildreth.[41] Unlike the later portions of his history covering the coming of the Civil War, Von Holst's analysis of the Federalist and Republican eras was brief, thinly researched, and highly derivative. It was also quite out of step with the aggressive nationalism which permeated the post-Civil War era. With his European heritage, he scorned the "pharisaical self-righteousness, which is one of the most characteristic traits of the political thought of the masses of the American people" and ridiculed Americans for raising "half-true and vague ideas . . . to the dignity of unimpeachable principles" by which "the ship of state should be steered."[42] He also accepted fully Hildreth's Federalist outlook that favored restraint rather than retaliation against European powers. He praised Washington's policy of neutrality and John Jay's "statesmanlike moderation" in negotiating his treaty of 1794 with England, and he con-

---

consented to join Jay and Adams in concealing their negotiations from the French court, he inwardly regarded himself and his colleagues as guilty of an act of national ingratitude and bad faith" (Jay in Winsor, *Narrative and Critical History of America*, VII, 136). See also Pellew, *John Jay*, pp. 187–188.

40. George Bancroft ended his history with the establishment of the Constitution in 1789 whereas James Rhodes began his history with the Mexican War, so they made no contribution to the historiography of the diplomacy of the years between 1789 and 1815.

41. Eric F. Goldman, "Hermann Eduard Von Holst: Plumed Knight of American Historiography," *Mississippi Valley Historical Review*, 23, no. 4 (March 1937): 511–532.

42. Hermann Von Holst, *The Constitutional and Political History of the United States*, 8 vols. (Chicago, 1876–1892), I, 34, 74.

demned the Republicans for fighting an "unnecessary and not very honorable war" against the British in 1812.[43]

Two young reviewers of the first volume of his history quickly told Von Holst that his counsels of restraint ran counter to the belligerent spirit of post-Civil War America. These critics, Henry Adams and Henry Cabot Lodge, informed Von Holst that the vast majority of Americans never had been deeply hostile to the War of 1812. In fact, it was the page of history Americans would least like to efface because it was the first, albeit clumsy, assertion of America's self-respect. The war and its supporters represented a rising sense of nationality that could find no outlet either in the "timid and undignified policy of Jefferson" or in the "narrow factiousness of the remnant of the Federalists."[44]

This assertion became the theme of Henry Adams's own great historical work, *The History of the United States During the Administrations of Jefferson and Madison*.[45] Disappointed in his hopes of a political career, Adams had turned to history and served for a brief time as a professor at Harvard. He had rehearsed for his great multivolume history by writing biographies of Albert Gallatin and John Randolph.[46] Independently wealthy and a frequent traveler, Adams researched his topics exhaustively both in the United States and abroad. The depth of his research, combined with his brilliant pen, acerbic wit, and ironic tone, made his history a formidable one which dominates the writing on this era even today. Adams's volumes were popularly considered something of a Republican answer to the virulently pro-Federalist writings of Hildreth and Von Holst, but in truth they were Republican only insofar as they caustically criticized the Federalists. Jefferson and Madison received quite ungentle treatment. The true heroes of the volumes were Albert Gallatin and the Adams family, each of whom had promoted resistance to Britain and France yet had avoided the cowardice and factiousness of the Federalists and the puerile reliance on economic retaliation of the Republicans. Adams's ironic tone made for some inconsistencies in his outlook. Nonetheless, what did emerge was a constant concern that the United States assert its rights in a dignified, a consistent, and, if necessary, a violent manner.

43. *Ibid.*, pp. 113–114, 122, 219.
44. Henry Adams and Henry Cabot Lodge, "Review of Von Holst's History of the United States," *North American Review*, 123 (1876): 356–358.
45. Henry Adams, *The History of the United States During the Administrations of Jefferson and Madison*, 9 vols. (New York, 1889–1891).
46. Henry Adams, *Albert Gallatin* (New York, 1879); and Henry Adams, *John Randolph* New York, 1882).

Except for his unqualified praise of his great-grandfather's restrained handling of France during the Quasi-War, Henry Adams almost always took a rather belligerent line.[47] He denounced the Jay Treaty as a violation of America's neutrality toward France and said that since 1812, there had never been a time when the United States would not have preferred war to Jay's terms. Of course, the careful reader might note that this defiant assertion stopped short of recommending rejection of the treaty at any time prior to 1812.[48] A similar ambiguity accompanied the bravado with which Adams wrote about the events leading to the War of 1812. He condemned Jefferson for reducing military expenditures and resting American diplomacy on commercial interests and weapons, which left the country "at the mercy of any power which might choose to rob it." Still, he said, the embargo was a worthwhile experiment that had failed. Unlike the war, the embargo had merely "opened the sluice-gates of social corruption," making many traitors and smugglers, but not a single hero.[49]

Naturally, Adams also rejected the contention of Hildreth and Von Holst that acceptance of the Monroe-Pinkney Treaty of 1806 was preferable to the embargo or to war. Not only had the treaty been signed by the American negotiators in direct contradiction of orders, but Britain reserved the right to break it if France retaliated. If any man but Monroe and Pinkney had signed it, "it would have answered for a lifetime, and his mortification would have ended there."[50] The proper course for the United States, Adams maintained, was to have declared war on Great Britain in 1808, when America was unified, its moral position uncompromised, its government still efficient and prosperous, and impressment more flagrant. By experimenting with the embargo, Jefferson and Madison had sapped America's will to fight so that by 1812, most Americans would have preferred to remain at peace. However the congressional war hawks pushed for the hard line, and Madison followed them willingly into war.

Adams did not criticize Madison for going to war, but he ridiculed the manner of entry. First, Madison had accepted at face value the promises contained in a letter from the French foreign minister, the Duc de Cadore, that France would respect America's neutral rights. Then, in conformance with the congressional act known as Macon's Bill No. 2, he had cut off trade with the British to force them to

47. Adams, *Albert Gallatin*, p. 221.
48. *Ibid.*, p. 158.
49. Adams, *History of the United States*, I, 243; IV, 276–277.
50. *Ibid.*, III, 415.

respect those neutral rights as well. His acceptance of France's blatantly false promises had enabled Madison to single out one opponent
at a time and was a purposeful maneuver rather than the naïve
blunder Madison's enemies and later historians had considered it to
be. Unfortunately, so flimsy a base for retaliation against Britain had
undermined America's moral position and raised much domestic opposition to the ultimate declaration of war. This led Madison to distort
his list of justifications for war with Britain when his attempt at commercial pressure had failed. To regain his moral position, he listed
impressment as the primary grievance even though it had dwindled
considerably. But impressment was the most direct and emotional
violation of American sovereignty, so Madison ranked it above ship
seizures and British support of the Indians on the frontier. Such incompetent diplomacy, not the declaration of war itself, was the target
of the belligerent Adams's scorn and irony.[51]

Henry Adams's pugnacious outlook was shared by his fellow
Harvard graduate and citizen of Massachusetts James Schouler.
Schouler also turned to historical writing after a professional disap-
pointment when deafness interfered with his career in law. Like
Adams, he considered the War of 1812 a necessity and rejected Hil-
dreth's contention that peace was worth securing at the price of the
Monroe-Pinkney Treaty. He denigrated Hildreth's whole pro-Federal-
ist history as one marked "by the horizon line of his generation."[52]
Indeed, Schouler's assertiveness and support for a manly neutrality
took a considerably more pro-Republican cast than did the history of
Henry Adams, which Schouler considered too disparaging. He praised
Washington for maintaining neutrality and criticized the pressure
both Hamilton and Jefferson imposed to distort neutrality toward
Britain or France. Yet he clearly considered Hamilton's distortions
more noxious than Jefferson's. Hamiltonian speeches had a "cowardly
tone, as though appealing to the fear of Americans" whereas Jefferson's primary offense was merely neglect of the proper war preparations in favor of the Republican program of commercial retaliation.[53]
Schouler praised John Adams for making peace with France in 1798,

51. *Ibid.*, IV, 375; V, 296–303, 395–400; VI, 116–118, 222–225.
52. Harvey Wish, *The American Historian: A Social-Intellectual History of the
Writing of the American Past* (New York, 1960), pp. 214–215; and Bert James Lowen-
berg, *American History in American Thought: Christopher Columbus to Henry Adams* (New
York, 1972), p. 502.
53. James Schouler, *History of the United States of America Under the Constitution*, 7 vols. (New York, 1880–1913), I, 242, 263, 293.

but where most previous historians had seen this as an instance of restraint, Schouler emphasized the aggressive aspects of Adams's conduct. Adams had won a "bloodless diplomatic victory," forcing the "bland and self-justifying Talleyrand to hasten cringing, to the gate through which the ruffled envoys had filed out, and, cap in hand, ask their return."[54]

Schouler's interpretation of the events leading to the War of 1812 closely paralleled that of Henry Adams although naturally Schouler was less harsh with the Republican leadership. He thought the embargo would have been proper as a temporary stalling technique to buy time for military preparation. Jefferson was greatly mistaken to believe that it would suffice, in itself, to win concessions from the belligerents.[55] Still, Schouler insisted, the embargo was not a product of Jefferson's secret subservience to Napoleon, as the Federalists of that day had maintained. "Neutrality, the neutrality of Washington, was the cold, twinkling pole-star by which Jefferson and his cabinet shaped their course, however they may have maneuvered for foreign effect." The Federalists, on the other hand, were not neutral. No foreign policy would suffice for them except open espousal of the British cause against Napoleon. However, this cowardly, pro-British policy was not to be blamed on the whole of Schouler's native New England. Like Adams, he considered it the product of the tiny but influential Essex Junto.[56]

Schouler also agreed with Henry Adams that Madison had accepted the Cadore letter in the hope of dividing the belligerents, not because he was deluded by Napoleon's false promises. Schouler was more willing than Adams to credit the war hawks for forcing Madison into war against his will although Schouler left it a "mystery" whether or not Madison was confronted with a threat to his nomination in a specific meeting with them. In any case, Schouler rejected John Randolph's charge that the war was an offensive one for Canada. Canada was only a means of reprisal. The War of 1812 was necessary to defend "maritime and neutral rights."[57]

The third great historian of early America writing in this period was John Bach McMaster. McMaster differed from Adams and Schouler in that he did the bulk of his research in newspapers rather than in official documents to determine popular responses as opposed

54. *Ibid.*, p. 432.
55. *Ibid.*, II, 158–165, 176.
56. *Ibid.*, pp. 151–152, 176–182.
57. *Ibid.*, pp. 348–349, 355, 357.

to the actual courses of negotiations or decision making. Yet it is testimony to the influence of Adams and Schouler that the ardently pro-Federalist McMaster used them rather than Richard Hildreth and Hermann Von Holst as the guides to his narrative of events. McMaster still praised Hamilton and vilified the Republicans, but he did not denounce the decision to fight Great Britain in 1812 as Hildreth and Von Holst had done. He relied instead on the prowar interpretations of Adams and Schouler.[58]

Thus, the post-Civil War era witnessed the triumph of manly neutrality in the pages of its histories. Any defiance of Great Britain during the Civil War was praised, and Charles Francis Adams's defense of instances of American restraint went thoroughly out of fashion until rescued by the Anglo-American rapprochement at the end of the century. Young Turks like Henry Adams, Henry Cabot Lodge, James Schouler, and John Bach McMaster now applauded America's decision to fight in 1812 and rejected the appeasing views of Hildreth and Von Holst. Franklin's restrained approach to the diplomacy of the Revolution lost ground to the histories eulogizing the more independent and assertive policies of Jay and Adams. There remained disagreements and minority views on these issues. George Bancroft and Francis Wharton offered strong support of Franklin. Montague Bernard defended British Civil War diplomacy thoroughly whereas James Ford Rhodes at least mitigated British offenses by pointing to the support of the British working people for the North's antislavery cause. And there was almost no agreement whatever about the relative virtues of Republican and Federalist foreign policy. Yet clearly nationalistic belligerence infused the histories of America's attempts to shape a neutral policy toward the major European powers.

58. McMaster praised Hamilton and Washington for their stands on neutrality and for accepting the Jay Treaty while he denounced Jefferson, Madison, and the Republicans as fanatic Jacobins. He also lauded Adams for ending the Quasi-War and accused Adams's Federalist opponents of seeking war with France while attempting illegitimate forms of control over the president. McMaster agreed with Henry Adams and James Schouler that Jefferson was right to reject the Monroe-Pinkney Treaty and implied that America should have fought in 1808 over the Chesapeake affair instead of resorting to the embargo. Contrary to Henry Adams, McMaster considered the war hawks truly representative of the majority of the American people and rated them highly for vindicating the nation's rights. Although McMaster detailed the story of the war hawks confronting Madison with a threat to his nomination, he agreed with Adams and Schouler that this did not prove Madison had been coerced into the war (John Bach McMaster, *A History of the American People*, 8 vols. [New York, 1883–1912], II, 979; III, 114–115, 213, 430, 448–449).

However, few of these historiographical concerns or permutations found their way into the textbooks of the day. This may have been due to a natural time lag between the latest research and its incorporation in lower-school texts. (There were no college-level texts at the time.) Perhaps it was even more the result of the general absence of diplomacy in these texts, which were much the same as the antebellum ones. Their authors still copied one another shamelessly, devoted most of their pages to military affairs, made few judgments on historical controversies, and generally hailed whatever the American government did. They rarely mentioned the diplomacy of the revolutionary war except to say that France had had quite selfish motives for helping the United States. They praised Washington's neutrality while gently reprimanding or thoroughly condemning the Republicans for excessive attachment to France. They recognized the Jay Treaty's unpopularity but deemed its acceptance wise. Adams's peace with France in 1798 was praiseworthy whereas Jefferson's embargo was a disastrous policy since the behavior of both French and British had thoroughly justified declarations of war against them.

Concerning the actual outbreak of the War of 1812, there was some disagreement. None of these authors argued directly that the war should have been avoided, but Federalist-oriented texts made the war seem somewhat less than heroic and generally accepted the argument that Madison was forced into it against his will. They implied that the Republicans unjustly resented British offenses more than French transgressions. While all agreed that maritime offenses were the major cause of the war, Federalist-oriented texts gave some attention to expansionists' ambitions for Canada. These texts were quite respectful in their treatment of Federalist opposition to the embargo and the war, but even these historians saw the outcome of the War of 1812 as very positive, securely fixing America's independence and its position as a great power.[59]

Textbooks more favorable to the Republicans ignored the accusations that the war hawks forced Madison into war. They emphasized the maritime outrages of Britain more than those of France and often ignored American ambitions for Canada. Finally, they disapproved

59. George F. Holmes, *New School History of the United States* (New York, 1884), pp. 174–179; John Clark Ridpath, *History of the United States* (Cincinnati, Chicago, and Philadelphia, 1880), pp. 235–237, 245–249; and Horace Scudder, *A History of the United States of America* (New York and Chicago, 1884), pp. 271–300.

much more strongly of Federalist opposition to the war.[60] But none of these books presented a real analysis of American diplomacy. They mentioned these events briefly and uncritically, moving quickly on to the more dramatic military aspects of war.

James Angell, president of the University of Vermont, was one of the major critics of textbooks that ignored foreign policy. Angell, who had served briefly as minister to China and Turkey, became president of the American Historical Association in 1893 and entitled his presidential address to the society, "The Inadequate Recognition of Diplomatists by Historians."[61] He noted that history was being broadened from a record of battles, court intrigues, and royal genealogies to developments in letters, science, economics, and religion, but was still neglecting great diplomatic transactions, gifted negotiators, and epoch-making treaties. General histories like those of Hildreth, Bancroft, Lyman, and Henry Adams were setting a better example, but school texts were woefully lacking, and a fully connected narrative of American diplomacy was still required.[62]

Clearly, Angell was more disturbed by the absence of coverage than he was by the absence of critical analysis in school texts. His own work was far more exhortatory than critical. He wrote the chapter titled "The Diplomacy of the United States, 1789–1850" for Winsor's *Narrative and Critical History of the United States*. As Angell saw it, American diplomatic history was just one glorious event after another. Americans had supported the rights of neutrals, shown "generosity towards semicivilized nations," exerted "patient and skilful [*sic*] pressure . . . for justice on strong powers that the United States were not in a position to coerce," and made "timely plans of enlargement of the nation's territory." Because of this, Angell claimed, American statesmen had no occasion to fear comparison with the greatest European

60. Thomas F. Donnelly, *A Primary History of the United States* (New York and Chicago, 1885), pp. 122–123, 130–132, 139; and David B. Scott, *A School History of the United States* (New York, 1883), pp. 236, 244–245, 248. Other textbooks consulted: William Swinton, *A School History of the United States* (New York, 1871); Thomas Wentworth Higginson, *Young Folks' History of the United States* (Boston, 1879); John Bach McMaster, *A School History of the United States* (New York, 1897); Mary Sheldon Barnes and Earl Barnes, *Studies in American History* (Boston, 1893); and [Frederick H. Clark], *History of the United States*, compiled under the direction of the California Board of Education (Sacramento, 1888).

61. James B. Angell, "The Inadequate Recognition of Diplomatists by Historians," American Historical Association, *Annual Report, 1893*, pp. 15–24.

62. *Ibid.*, pp. 15, 21, 23.

diplomats of their time. They had "rendered a worthy service to their country and to all mankind."[63]

Angell did find one dark spot in this glorious record although he confined his criticisms of it to a footnote. This was the Mexican War, which he blamed on those Americans who wanted to expand the area of slavery.[64] Angell's comment indicated that this interpretation of the Mexican War, so controversial in the previous era, was almost unanimously accepted by the historians of Angell's day. This was by far the most significant historiographical development of the post-Civil War period.

63. Angell in Winsor, *Narrative and Critical History of America*, VII, 512–513.
64. *Ibid.*, p. 506, n. 3.

FOUR

The Bloody Shirt
and Manifest Destiny

Although there had been substantial opposition to the Mexican War in
the 1840s, even most of the war's opponents had found the conspiracy
theory of abolitionists like John Quincy Adams, Benjamin Lundy, and
William Jay to be extreme. The balance of favorable to unfavorable
histories of the Mexican War in the ante-bellum period reflected that
situation. But the Kansas-Nebraska Act of 1854 helped convince many
that there was indeed an unholy conspiracy of slaveholders to expand
the peculiar institution until it dominated the whole Union. The Republican party was founded on that premise, basing its existence on an
adamant opposition to the expansion of slavery. The passions of confrontation and ultimately of war itself elevated the suspicions of a
minority to the convictions of a majority. The Civil War became a war
against slaveholders conspiring to force slavery on the whole nation
or, failing that, to secede. Every major historian of the post-Civil War
era who had occasion to write extensively on the Mexican War came to
endorse the view expounded by Lundy and William Jay. The multivolume histories of Von Holst and Schouler were now joined by those
of James Ford Rhodes and Hubert Howe Bancroft to provide a united
historical front on this episode of American diplomatic history.[1]

1. John Bach McMaster's history did not reach the Mexican War until
1910, well after the close of the post-Civil War historiographical period.

Von Holst was the first historian to write a major history of the Mexican War in the post-Civil War era. Von Holst researched this period far more extensively than he had the Federalist and Republican eras. Despite the passion that permeated his book, Von Holst's European origin, Germanic training, and broad research gave him a reputation for objectivity. His conclusions were widely believed whereas those of Jay, Lundy, and John Quincy Adams had been rendered suspect by their contemporary political ambitions and abolitionist sympathies.

Von Holst considered both the Texas revolution and America's subsequent annexation of the region to have been a product of the slavocracy's fear that it "would have to die . . . if it could not devise some means to get more land and to create more states."[2] He was convinced that Mexico never would have gone to war over Texas, despite its bombastic conduct, and that Polk had purposely provoked a clash on the Rio Grande "in order to win by a war California and New Mexico, which he had been unable to buy. . . ."[3] Von Holst recognized that the South had not unanimously supported the war and pointed out that John C. Calhoun himself had had his doubts. But the South had ignored Calhoun's "unuttered warnings" and had gone so far as to agitate for the acquisition of all of Mexico.[4] Von Holst thought it fortunate that the All-Mexico Movement had failed. Considering "the character of the Mexican population and the semi-tropical nature of the country," an attempt to hold all of Mexico in subjection "would have been simply suicidal." The combined influence of slavery and "Mexican anarchy" would have made the South even more degenerate and pitiable than Mexico itself.[5]

But if Von Holst's hostile analysis of the Mexican War signaled a shift of the post-Civil War generation's outlook toward a more critical view of America's past expansionism, it was far from a complete revolution. Von Holst recognized that many people from nonslavery sections of the nation had favored the Mexican War, not to mention other instances of expansion. But he was insistent that reproach should not fall on them, for while Polk and the slavocracy had conducted themselves in a sordid and secretive manner, most other Americans truly had believed that Mexico's sins had been sufficient to justify war. In

2. Von Holst, *Constitutional and Political History of the United States*, II, 580–582, 702–703.

3. *Ibid.*, III, 82, 207–210, 253.

4. *Ibid.*, pp. 287, 342.

5. *Ibid.*, p. 341.

any case, it was a historical necessity that America seek to overshadow the entire continent. In the hands of Mexico, California "was not only as good as lost to civilization, but it also lay exposed, a tempting prey to all the naval and colonial powers in the world." The Mexican War might have been a war of conquest, but "decayed or decaying peoples must give way . . . [to] peoples who are still on the ascending path of their historical mission. . . ." Thus, Von Holst's most severe criticisms of American expansionism, like those of most other historians of this era, were aimed at instances that threatened to enhance slavery or to incorporate large alien populations into the Union.[6] Americans of the post-Civil War period may have been isolationists, but if historians accurately reflected the popular mood, there remained a large fund of belligerent nationalism behind this era's criticisms of America's westward march and behind its attachment to neutrality.

Shortly after the appearance of Von Holst's account of the Mexican War, Hubert Howe Bancroft published his own history of that episode. Bancroft was responsible for an immense number of historical publications on the southwestern area of North America, many of them written by others under his supervision. This method resulted in some unevenness in tone, interpretation, and depth of research. Bancroft did more research on the Mexican side of this war than his predecessors, but he seemed to rely on William Jay for the American side. He called the war "a premeditated and predetermined affair," engineered by a government yielding "to the pressure of slave-holding interests." He took the Mexican side so thoroughly as to conclude that America's annexation of Texas was just and sufficient grounds for Mexico to declare war on the United States. Bancroft did note the widespread clamor for war in Mexico and detailed the unavailing attempts of the Mexican government to mollify the Mexican people's anger and avoid war. Still, Bancroft said, it was American policy to provoke Mexico into striking the first blow, a policy that met with most infamous success.[7]

Hubert Howe Bancroft's history endorsed but did little to advance the slavocracy interpretation of the Mexican War. However, James Schouler's history of the affair made a notable contribution to the theory.[8] Schouler reinforced the claim that Polk had plotted to

6. *Ibid.*, pp. 270–273.
7. Hubert Howe Bancroft, *History of Mexico*, 6 vols. (San Francisco, 1883–1888), V. 152–158, 289–308, 332, 338–344.
8. James Schouler, *History of the United States*, rev. ed., 7 vols. (New York, 1892–1913), IV, iii, 524n. See also James Schouler, *Historical Briefs* (New York, 1896), p. 121.

acquire California by whatever means were necessary. Schouler recounted a conversation George Bancroft reported he had had with
Polk in which Polk had proclaimed four goals for his administration:
"one, a reduction of the tariff; another, the independent treasury; a
third, the settlement of the Oregon boundary question; and, lastly, the
acquisition of California." Adopting "the fraud of the Texas revolutionaries," Polk had laid claim to the Rio Grande, then sent John Slidell to
negotiate. Schouler and the other historians of this time evidently did
not have access to Slidell's instructions, but Schouler did see Polk's
diary before he published the revised edition of his history, and from
this he surmised that Polk had ordered Slidell to offer a good round
sum for California. When this offer was rejected, Polk sent Taylor to the
Rio Grande to provoke Mexico into striking the first blow, all of which
Schouler assumed was aimed at satiating the "glut of our slaveholders."[9]

Schouler seemed to have seen Polk's diary for so brief a time
before writing this account for his revised history that the insights to
be derived from the diary were not fully incorporated in his narrative.
He spelled out the implications of the diary more fully in two later
magazine articles printed in a volume entitled *Historical Briefs*. The
diary and the correspondence of Polk confirmed "the worst that was
ever imputed to this administration in its deadly and depredating
course."[10] The primary revelation of the diary was that Polk had
wanted to use the monetary claims as justification to declare war on
Mexico even before news of the attack on Taylor at the Rio Grande had
arrived. This made "his dissimulation even greater than has been
supposed."[11] It proved conclusively that Polk sought California and
New Mexico, not merely the Rio Grande border. Taylor had already
occupied the Rio Grande border without a fight, so far as Polk knew,
when he announced to the cabinet his intention to declare war.

The diary contributed other insights. It convinced Schouler that
Polk had truthfully denied having promised to annex Texas under
Senator Thomas Hart Benton's plan intended to give Mexico more
time to negotiate. The diary also explained why George Bancroft as
secretary of the navy had issued an order permitting Santa Anna to
pass through America's naval blockade to Mexico from his exile in
Havana. Polk had held a secret interview with a Colonel Alexander
Atocha in which Atocha had said that Santa Anna would concede

9. Schouler, *History of the United States*, IV, 498, 519, 524–527.
10. Schouler, *Historical Briefs*, p. 143.
11. *Ibid.*, pp. 149–151.

much territory if the United States would aid his return to power. Polk then had sent Commander Alexander MacKenzie to confer with Santa Anna and to relay the order to let Santa Anna through the blockade. MacKenzie had received confirmation of Santa Anna's cooperativeness. Thus, a long-held suspicion of complicity between Polk and Santa Anna had been confirmed.[12]

Most surprising of all, the diary revealed that Polk was "a true lover of the Union, like Jackson before him, strongly contrasting with Calhoun and many others of his own slaveholding section." Polk had rejected Calhoun's plan to block statehood for California. Calhoun had reasoned that the people flocking to California for gold had no slaves and would bring the area into the Union as a free state. Polk, nonetheless, insisted that California "decide slavery or no slavery, and no Southern man should object."[13] In fact, Polk had viewed "with alarm and evident surprise" the slavery struggle set off by the war.[14] After the turn of the century, other historians would use this same information to destroy the slavocracy interpretation of the Mexican War. But Schouler remained blind to the implications of his own discoveries. His history further bolstered the standard interpretation of his day, as Schouler insisted that Polk had demanded expansion because he had seen what the American people, "or at least the Southern portion, coveted."[15]

Still Schouler, like Von Holst, did acknowledge the important, if secondary, role that expansionist sentiments in all parts of the country had played in the war. These territorial additions were advantageous and would have been even more so "had the luscious fruit been legally acquired." Instead, with the "satanic spirit of manifest destiny . . . alluring us on, . . . the weakness all about us whetted the appetite to expand our domains."[16] Slaveholders, of course, took the lead in this, and their rapacity ultimately resulted in the "overthrow of that very social system for whose preservation it was chiefly contrived."[17]

James Ford Rhodes, writing on the Mexican War as prelude to his great *History of the United States from the Compromise of 1850*, followed Schouler very closely.[18] He had completed his first volume

---

12. *Ibid.*, pp. 153–154.
13. *Ibid.*, pp. 156–157.
14. *Ibid.*, p. 156.
15. *Ibid.*, p. 143.
16. Schouler, *History of the United States*, IV, 249–250.
17. *Ibid.*
18. James Ford Rhodes, *History of the United States from the Compromise of 1850.*

before Schouler's revised edition and the information from Polk's diary had been published, so Rhodes did not incorporate Schouler's latest conclusions into his account. For instance, Rhodes still claimed that Benton had been promised that Polk would annex Texas under the Senate resolution.[19] Otherwise his interpretation paralleled Schouler's. Like all the major historians of this era, he considered the Mexican War a vicious war for slavery.[20]

Thus, the consensus of the period was acceptance of the slave conspiracy theory of the Mexican War.[21] Little was said in the war's defense. General Cadmus Wilcox, a former Confederate, raised a lonely voice to claim that when seen in perspective, the American government proved to have been judicious, its policy wise and prudent, its aims honest and patriotic. But after two quick pages of this, Wilcox raced on to the safer ground of military maneuvers.[22]

Most school texts of the post-Civil War era accepted the opinion of the great historians of their time that slavery had played a vital role in the Mexican War. But their indictments were generally more restrained than those of Von Holst, Schouler, Rhodes, and Hubert Howe Bancroft. Many saw the slavocracy's war guilt as moderated because the majority of Americans, pro- or antislavery, had demonstrated support for the annexation of Texas through election of Polk (thus discounting some doubts of that held by the major historians). Texts also emphasized the aggressiveness of the Mexicans and that a Mexican detachment had attacked Taylor first. Finally, some textbook authors

19. *Ibid.*, I, 85.
20. Many writers justified the war because it was an immensely valuable domain, said Rhodes. But in fact there was "more reason for humiliation than pride" (*ibid.*, p. 75). The "consideration above all others that prompted the Southern faction was the desire to restore, by an accession of slave territory, the balance of power lost by the gain in population at the North. If four slave states could be carved out of Texas, the South might retain her control of the Senate, although she had lost the House" (*ibid.*, p. 79). Tyler and Polk had claimed Polk's election was a mandate for expansion, but it was more a referendum on slavery. Clay had been defeated by antislavery forces in New York because he had hedged on the Texas question and said the issue of slavery should have nothing to do with it. This had thrown the election to Polk (*ibid.*, pp. 83–84). In this way Polk was given his opportunity to provoke war with Mexico and take California and New Mexico (*ibid.*, pp. 87–88).
21. Even a military history of the war written for the series, "Minor Wars of the United States," accepted these conclusions. It condemned the origins of the war while praising the military successes of the United States (Horatio O. Ladd, *History of the War with Mexico* [New York, 1883]).
22. Cadmus M. Wilcox, *History of the Mexican War* (Washington, D.C., 1892), pp. 1–2.

avoided taking a position by saying only that the Whigs saw the hand of the slavocracy behind the Mexican War while most Democrats supported the war. This tone of moderation probably was adopted to avoid undermining the patriotism of young American students by damning a past action of the American government in unequivocal terms.[23]

The Mexican War was not the only episode in America's past diplomacy that inspired doubts about the virtues of American expansionism. Expansionism's effects on the Indian also came under attack, and the public mood changed to such an extent that a major reform of Indian policy was undertaken in the Dawes Act of 1887. The book which did most to inspire this shift of attitude was Helen Hunt Jackson's *A Century of Dishonor*.[24] Her passionate, impressionistic chronicle of the many outrages suffered by the Indians at the hands of white Americans was fully endorsed by the works of Hubert Howe Bancroft, who stated flatly that the United States had treated the Indians as dishonorably as any people had been treated in the history of the world.[25] Other historians agreed that American policy had been cruel although they did not condemn it as thoroughly. Von Holst admitted that the rationales for dispossessing the Indians had been "preposterously stupid sophistry with which the most reckless justification of the right of the strongest is clothed in the garb of justice and even of humanity."[26] But he blamed most of these injustices on slaveholders rather than on the generality of whites and thought that preservation of Indian independence had been impossible under any conditions.[27]

Like Von Holst, Henry Adams also objected less to the nation's Indian policy than he did to the fatuous posturing which white Americans used to hide the reality of their conduct from themselves.[28] And

---

23. The texts most outspoken against the Mexican War were Higginson, *Young Folks' History of the United States*; Scudder, *History of the United States of America*; Swinton, *School History of the United States*; Barnes and Barnes, *Studies in the American History*; and McMaster *School History of the United States*. More moderate in tone were Donnelly, *Primary History of the United States*; Scott, *School History of the United States*; and Clark, *History of the United States*. Those who blamed the war on Mexico totally were Ridpath, *History of the United States*; and Holmes, *New School History of the United States*.

24. Helen Hunt Jackson, *A Century of Dishonor* (Boston, 1881).

25. Hubert Howe Bancroft, "Treatment of Native Races," in *Essays and Miscellany*, vol. 38 of *The Works of Hubert Howe Bancroft* (San Francisco, 1890), p. 74.

26. Von Holst, *Constitutional and Political History of the United States*, I, 451, n. 4.

27. *Ibid.*, II, 291–294; I, 451–452, n. 4.

28. Adams, *History of the United States*, VI, 69–72.

James Schouler insisted that while whites had been cruel, the Indians had been equally treacherous. Thus, Jackson's removal policy had not been "without justifying reasons."[29] But of all this era's major histories, only Theodore Roosevelt's widely read *Winning of the West* would claim that the Indians had been more at fault than the whites, devastating the frontier "generations before we in any way encroached upon or wronged them."[30]

None of the other significant episodes of American expansionism was handled as critically as the Mexican War or America's treatment of the Indians. But none escaped unscathed either. The Louisiana Purchase was praised by all, with only minor caveats about the unconstitutionality of the proceedings and the ignorance of Americans who did not yet recognize the problem inherent in the expansion of slave territory.[31] The only major objection was entered by Henry Adams because he thought Jefferson's policy had not been strong enough. He believed that Jefferson's threats against French occupation of Louisiana had been only feeble bluffs and that Napoleon had handed the territory over for his own reasons, not because Jefferson had coerced him. Adams believed that the United States should have gone to war rather than permit Napoleon to solidify his hold on New Orleans.[32]

What criticisms there were of American acquisition of Florida from Spain were of the same variety. Expansion into Florida was proper, but American methods had been cunning and cowardly rather than manly and straightforward. Henry Adams scorned the argument of Jefferson and Robert R. Livingston that the Louisiana Purchase had included the right to occupy West Florida. That would have required the United States to maintain that "Spain had retroceded West Florida to France without knowing it, that France had sold it to the United States without suspecting it, that the United States had bought it without paying for it, and that neither France nor Spain, although the original contracting parties, were competent to decide the meaning of their own contract."[33] Such a claim, if backed by military force, would have been just as effective "as though it had every attribute of morality and good faith," Adams said, but unfortu-

29. Schouler, *History of the United States*, IV, 275.

30. Theodore Roosevelt, *The Winning of the West*, 6 vols. (New York and London, 1889–1896), I, 102.

31. Von Holst, *Constitutional and Political History of the United States*, I, 184–185; and Schouler, *History of the United States*, II, 51–52, also 52n.

32. Adams, *History of the United States*, I, 421–422, 424, 442–443, 445; II, 114.

33. *Ibid.*, II, 246–248.

nately Jefferson and Madison meant only to use it to pressure France into forcing Spain to disgorge the territory.[34] Adams's preferred course would have been for Jefferson to march into Texas, to which the Louisiana Purchase gave America a far better right, and then seize Florida when Spain declared war.[35]

Adams's cynical view of Jefferson's claim to West Florida, if not his belligerent alternatives to Jefferson's policy, was supported by most historians of the era. Only Justin Winsor and James Schouler accepted Jefferson's claim, although twelve of the fourteen standard school texts still faithfully agreed with the argument that West Florida had been part of Louisiana.[36]

Andrew Jackson's later raid into Florida occasioned some criticism even from James Schouler who had been willing to accept Jefferson's grab for West Florida. Schouler thought Jackson's impetuosity had threatened unnecessarily to embroil the United States with Britain as well as Spain. Negotiations had already reached a promising stage, and "perfidy can never be wisdom where nations negotiate," he said. Still John Quincy Adams properly refused to apologize when disowning Jackson's actions. This helped induce Spain to sell Florida "to the rising republic which had so well demonstrated both its self-restraint and the ability to take possession at any time."[37] Reactions to Polk's expansive diplomacy concerning the Oregon territory were similarly mixed. Historians disliked the deceptiveness and bluff involved, but they also had a sneaking admiration for Polk's willingness to stand up to Great Britain.[38]

Thus, post-Civil War historians were somewhat more critical of America's past expansionist diplomacy than ante-bellum historians had been. But their criticisms were of a limited sort and usually stopped well short of condemning expansion itself. There was near unanimity against expansion when it substantially increased the area of slavery. The same was generally true of opinions concerning expansion into areas already well populated by potentially hostile alien civilizations. But expansion into relatively "empty" areas of North America was accepted as inevitable and good, and only the methods

34. *Ibid.*, p. 71.
35. *Ibid.*, III, 80.
36. H. E. Chambers, *West Florida* (Baltimore, 1898).
37. Schouler, *History of the United States*, III, 68–80.
38. *Ibid.*, IV, 504–505; Schouler, *Historical Briefs*, pp. 142–143; Von Holst, *Constitutional and Political History of the United States*, III, 176–178, 220; and Rhodes, *History of the United States*, I, 86.

used were considered questionable. Many argued that displacement of the Indians might have been more humane and limited or that the United States might have been more patient in acquiring territory from its weaker neighbor, Mexico. But most assumed that this merely would have delayed America's necessary expansion, not stopped it. As to expansion at the expense of European colonial powers, the only criticisms were of tactics that historians might deem conniving or dishonest, and often the alternative offered was not more restraint but a more manly belligerence.

With such mixed and limited criticisms of past expansionism, it is not surprising that historians divided over the rising imperialist tide that began in the United States in the 1880s and 1890s. Some, like James Schouler, Hermann Von Holst, and Henry Adams's brother, Charles Francis Adams, Jr., became leading antiimperialists who used the historical record to attack further expansion abroad. Their primary argument was that this would involve distant areas that were already populated by non-Anglo-Saxons. Ruling these areas as colonies would subvert America's constitutional dedication to self-government whereas the alternative of incorporation into the Union would under-mine the domestic tranquility of the nation. The record of America's treatment of supposedly inferior races had not been a proud one, and the difficulty of amalgamating Indians, blacks, Asians, and the new immigrants from Southern Europe, was enough without adding new peoples. Finally, not only would this new imperialism require a larger military force that might endanger domestic liberty, but it would violate Washington's admonition against foreign alliances and en-tanglements.[39]

Henry Adams was not so certain that the new imperialism ran counter to the lessons America should have learned from its history. He was horrified that Charles Francis Jr. had aligned himself with "all the other Harvard College 'mokes,' the professors of history, by talking out loud" against Cleveland during the Venezuela crisis. Charles and the Harvard professors had made "apes of themselves," Henry

39. James B. Schouler, "A Review of the Hawaiian Controversy," *Forum*, 16 (February 1894): 671; Hermann E. Von Holst, "Some Lessons We Ought to Learn," University of Chicago *Record*, 3, no. 46 (February 10, 1899): 301; Charles Francis Adams, Jr., *Imperialism and "The Tracks of Our Forefathers"* (Boston, 1899), pp. 9–12, 19, 25–26 (Charles Francis Adams became disillusioned with the antiim-perialist movement only a short time later); and Robert L. Beisner, *Twelve Against Empire: The Anti-Imperialists, 1898–1900* (New York, 1968), pp. 107–132.

thought.[40] Yet he was torn by the same historical dilemmas as they. In 1890, he had written favorably of taking Hawaii. But a few months later, his horror at the effects of colonialism in Tahiti brought him to shift his perspective and look to "empty" areas instead. "On the whole, I am satisfied that America has no future in the Pacific," he wrote Henry Cabot Lodge. "Her best chance is Siberia. Russia will probably go to pieces. . . . If it can be delayed another twenty five years, we could Americanize Siberia, and this is the only possible work that I can see still open on a scale equal to American means."[41]

Still other historians supported the new wave of American expansion unambiguously. Among them was Henry Adams's younger brother, Brooks, and Henry's friends Alfred Thayer Mahan and Theodore Roosevelt. Other historical contributors to the early imperialist cause were John Fiske and Josiah Strong. But while the works these historians published prior to the Spanish-American War made a few references to American history to support their position, none of them attempted an elaborate reinterpretation of past American expansionism to give imperialism more legitimate credentials. Brooks Adams, in *Law of Civilization and Decay*, cited historical events in Europe and the Far East to justify his contention that civilizations must either expand or die.[42] Alfred Thayer Mahan's famous book, *The Influence of Seapower upon History*, drew its historical lessons from the British Empire. Even John Fiske, author of numerous books on American history, cited the example of the Roman Empire to justify imperialism.[43] Theodore Roo-

40. Ernest Samuels, *Henry Adams*, 3 vols. (Cambridge, Mass., 1948–1964), III, 141.

41. Quoted in *ibid.*, p. 28. Henry Adams's ambiguity about imperialism showed up again later in the controversy over the Spanish-American War and the Philippines. An ardent advocate of intervention in the Cuban Revolution to free the island from Spain, he became fearful of the costs of taking the Philippines and expanding into the Orient. He supported John Hay in behind-the-scenes attempts to moderate the peace treaty of 1898 in favor of the Cubans and the Philippine insurgents. When the Philippine insurgency began against the United States and negotiations broke down, Adams was disappointed because he thought the "Philippine excursion to be a false start in the wrong direction." Filipinos were "usually worthless Malay types," he said, and he preferred American movement toward north China and eastern Russia instead (*ibid.*, pp. 196, 239–241, 248).

42. Brooks Adams, *The Law of Civilization and Decay* (London and New York, 1895); his most important later works were *America's Economic Supremacy* (New York, 1900) and *The New Empire* (New York, 1902).

43. Alfred Thayer Mahan, *The Influence of Seapower upon History, 1660–1783* (Boston, 1890); and John Fiske, "Manifest Destiny," *Harper's Magazine*, 120 (March 1895): 578–590.

sevelt was again an exception to this tendency to ignore earlier American expansionist episodes as precedents for the acquisition of overseas colonies. In his book *The Winning of the West*, he supported expansion at the expense of weaker peoples. Yet his *Naval War of 1812*, when it dealt with diplomatic rather than military affairs, followed solidly in the footsteps of Henry Adams.[44] Since imperial-minded historians made only side-long references to American history, and the antiimperialist historians already had completed most of their elaborate narratives prior to the 1890s, the major historiographical impact of the imperialist movement would await the dramatic victory over Spain in 1898.

However, the imperialist surge prior to the Spanish-American War did affect one historiographical issue. This issue was the Monroe Doctrine. During the early years of the post-Civil War era, the doctrine still was ignored. Von Holst barely mentioned it.[45] Even publication of John Quincy Adams's diary in 1874, which revealed much new information about the original formulation of the doctrine, seemed to cause little stir. Adams's diary revealed that James Monroe had been inclined to accept George Canning's offer of a joint Anglo-American note, a note to warn the Continental powers against forcible attempts to help Spain regain its lost colonies in Latin America. Monroe had been advised to join with Britain by Thomas Jefferson, James Madison, and John C. Calhoun. Adams, however, had urged a unilateral policy that would avoid the appearance of America's coming in as a cockboat in the wake of the British man-of-war. The diary also revealed that Adams had opposed Monroe's intention to plead for European recognition of the Greek Revolution. Adams had feared that this intrusion into European affairs might be used to justify reciprocal intervention in the Western Hemisphere.[46] Adams's brave stand for unilateralism, had it been known before, might have given both Adams and the doctrine more prominence in earlier histories when historians seemed to judge the significance of events in American diplomacy by the degree to which they illustrated the wisdom of the farewell address. Unfortunately for Adams, events conspired to make his stand for unilateralism less relevant to the issues of the day. Ferdinand de Lesseps began to build a French canal across Panama in 1881. The doctrine's contributions to the policy of nonentanglement with Eu-

44. Theodore Roosevelt, *The Naval War of 1812*, 2 vols. (New York, 1882).
45. Von Holst, *Constitutional and Political History of the United States*, I, 420.
46. Charles F. Adams, ed., *Memoirs of John Quincy Adams*, 12 vols. (Philadelphia, 1874–1877).

rope then took a back seat to the issue of whether the doctrine justified U.S. intervention to thwart European expansion in Latin America.

De Lesseps inspired a sudden rash of publications that examined the history of the doctrine to see whether it favored assertive interventionism or restraint.[47] The most extensive of these was the first full book on the topic by George F. Tucker (no relation to the earlier George Tucker).[48] His mildly interventionist view was reinforced most vigorously by John Kasson, a prominent Republican politician and diplomat who wrote a two-part history of the doctrine for the *North American Review*.[49] Claiming that the doctrine was now "quoted as the supreme, indisputable, and irreversible judgment of our national union,"[50] the interventionists only mentioned Adams's stand for unilateralism in passing and looked instead for evidence that the doctrine required American assertiveness.[51] Kasson, for instance, pointed out that while Jefferson and Adams might have differed on unilateralism, both had urged bold action. Jefferson had said that while America's first maxim was never to entangle itself in European affairs, the "second [was] never to suffer Europe to intermeddle with Cis-Atlantic affairs." Meanwhile, Adams was warning the Russians that the United States would oppose the transfer of any Latin American territory from one European nation to another.

Unfortunately, the "cautious, even timid" Monroe included in his message only strictures against further colonization and against attempts to impose monarchical institutions on Latin American republics, said Kasson.[52] Thus, Europe could interfere in Latin America by war or by treaty so long as this involved neither colonization nor the imposition of a monarchy. Jefferson and Adams would have made the doctrine broad enough to bar such intervention in specific terms. They had wanted a principle that would serve the needs of the future whereas Monroe's caution brought him to make a declaration only for

47. For a list of newspaper articles and a survey of their contents, see Milton Plesur, *America's Outward Thrust: Approaches to Foreign Affairs, 1865–1890* (De Kalb, Ill., 1971), p. 174.

48. George F. Tucker, *The Monroe Doctrine: A Concise History of Its Origin and Growth* (Boston, 1885).

49. John A. Kasson, "The Monroe Declaration," *North American Review*, 133 (September 1881): 241–245; and his "The Monroe Doctrine in 1881," *North American Review*, 133 (December 1881): 523–533.

50. Kasson, "Monroe Declaration," p. 241.

51. Tucker, *Monroe Doctrine*, pp. 9–15, 22–23.

52. Kasson, "Monroe Declaration," p. 250; and Kasson, "Monroe Doctrine in 1881," p. 533.

his own time.[53] They had seen that a European presence in Latin America meant "a flanking position, a military and naval rendezvous, in time of war, and an exclusive commercial position in time of peace." America should protect its southern flank, even if this required opposition to voluntary treaty cessions of Latin American territory to European powers.[54]

H. C. Bunts, in an article for *Forum*, offered the rebuttal to this interventionist view.[55] Bunts agreed with Kasson that "probably no feature of the fundamental policy of our government is regarded by the average American citizen as more essential to it than what is generally known as the 'Monroe Doctrine.' " But Bunts argued that erroneous ideas about the doctrine abounded and were "attributable to ignorance of the circumstances in reference to which the declaration was made."[56] John Quincy Adams, "in all probability the author of the declaration," had intended only a simple warning against further colonization. Instead, the doctrine had been "perverted and magnified" to prohibit acquisition of any territory by any European power on either American continent by any means, "be it by conquest, voluntary cession, treaty stipulation, purchase, or even by succession through family alliances."[57] Certainly it had not been the intention of the doctrine's authors "to proclaim to the world that the United States had arrogated to themselves exclusive guardianship over the entire western hemisphere. . . ."[58] It was true that the doctrine protested armed intervention to oppress or control Spanish colonies, but attempts to stretch that to prohibit peacefully acquired foreign control of the Panama Canal were out of bounds.[59]

Kasson's interventionist view received a major boost in 1895 when Secretary of State Richard Olney announced to Great Britain that the United States considered the border dispute between Venezuela and the British colony of Guiana to fall under the umbrella of the Monroe Doctrine. Any attempt by Britain to increase its territory at the expense of Venezuela would be regarded as an extension of European colonization and would therefore be opposed by the United States under the doctrine. Besides, Olney declared: "Today the United States

53. Kasson, "Monroe Doctrine in 1881," pp. 523–526.
54. *Ibid.*, pp. 525–529.
55. H. C. Bunts, "The Scope of the Monroe Doctrine," *Forum*, 7 (April 1889): 192–200.
56. *Ibid.*, p. 192.
57. *Ibid.*, p. 193.
58. *Ibid.*, p. 194.
59. *Ibid.*, pp. 192–200.

is practically sovereign on this continent, and its fiat is law upon the subjects to which it confines its interposition."

Olney and the Cleveland administration had been urged into this declaration by an inflammatory pamphlet written by America's former minister to Venezuela, William Scruggs, entitled *The Venezuelan Question: British Aggressions in Venezuela or the Monroe Doctrine on Trial.*[60] Initially, Cleveland received a wave of adulatory support for his strong stand against Great Britain. But a reaction set in rather quickly, and most historians who wrote on the Venezuela crisis condemned such broad use of the doctrine. John Burgess challenged Olney's course as "Recent Pseudo-Monroeism."[61] A pamphlet written by John Bassett Moore, who would later become one of America's greatest international lawyers and diplomatic historians, agreed that Olney had stretched the doctrine beyond its legitimate bounds.[62] This growing consensus of American historians around a restrained interpretation of the doctrine was reinforced by publication of the second major book on the subject, written by an Englishman named William Reddaway. Reddaway said that the originators had intended a limited doctrine. His own country of England was now prepared to live with such a policy, as opposed to the interventionist view asserted by Olney in the Venezuela affair. But Reddaway feared that the Cuban rebellion, which had recently resumed "without apparent justification," was swinging Americans back again to the mistaken activist notion that the doctrine required American intervention in Latin America.[63]

What Reddaway anticipated came to pass. Not only did the United States intervene in Cuba, but in the process Reddaway's restrained version of the Monroe Doctrine was swamped by the exuberant one of Kasson and Tucker, a version better suited to the Age of Imperialism.[64] In addition, expansionist incidents like the Mexican

60. William L. Scruggs, *The Venezuelan Question: British Aggressions in Venezuela or the Monroe Doctrine on Trial* (Atlanta, 1894).

61. John W. Burgess, "Recent Pseudo-Monroeism," *Political Science Quarterly*, 11 (1896): 44–67.

62. John Bassett Moore, *The Monroe Doctrine: Its Origin and Meaning* (New York, 1895).

63. William F. Reddaway, *The Monroe Doctrine*, 2nd ed. (New York, 1905), pp. 85–141.

64. While some historians saw the Monroe Doctrine as a keystone of American foreign policy, few texts followed along. Most did not mention it at all, and only one attributed much importance to it. The text compiled by Frederick H. Clark for the California Board of Education in 1888 said that the principles of the Monroe Doctrine "are in accordance with Washington's advice to keep free from European politics, and with Jefferson's idea of America for

War would be reevaluated in light of the nation's new imperial commitments. Toward the end of the imperial era, even the policy of neutrality and nonentanglement toward Europe would be challenged, bringing about revisions in the interpretations of almost all of America's past diplomacy.

Americans. They are broad principles of American patriotism, plainly stated by a patriotic President. . . . It might be called also the doctrine of Washington, Jefferson, Adams, or any genuine American" (Clark, *History of the United States*, p. 237). Clark's enthusiasm for a U.S. role in South America can be seen further in his comment that the opposition to John Quincy Adams's plan to send representatives to the Panama Conference stemmed solely from the reluctance of slave states to associate with South American republics that had abandoned slavery, with no mention of congressional fears of possible foreign entanglements (*ibid.*, p. 241). But this was the only text of the ten surveyed as representative of this period that gave any serious attention to the question occupying the minds of historians in the post-Civil War era.

PART THREE

The Age of Imperialism
1898-1919

On the eve of the Spanish-American War in 1898, the argument from historical precedent still seemed to favor the antiimperialists. Interpretations of America's earlier westward expansion, especially the Mexican War and the displacement of the Indians, were far more critical than they had been in the Age of the Farewell Address, and the restrained view of the Monroe Doctrine was predominant as well. Historians like Schouler and Von Holst might praise other early expansionist episodes where slavery had been less involved and where there was no danger of incorporating large numbers of aliens in the American Union, but they saw no further opportunities for expansion of that sort. Acquisition of territories like Hawaii or Cuba would seem a clear violation of American historical principles as set forth by Washington and the other Founding Fathers. Such densely settled areas would have to be either forcibly ruled as colonies or their alien peoples accepted into the Union. Historians of the post-Civil War era, having condemned the All-Mexico Movement on the same grounds, were bound to argue that the Founding Fathers never had attempted such imperialism and always had limited their expansionist activities to contiguous rather than overseas territories. Finally, these historians warned that overseas expansion would inevitably entangle the United States in the colonial rivalries of the European powers who were seeking influence in the same areas.

At first the imperialists tended to concede the argument from American precedent to the antiimperialists, citing instead examples from Rome and

Great Britain to support their policies and arguing that the United States had outgrown its earlier principles and restraints. But after the Spanish-American War, imperialist historians were no longer content to leave the Founding Fathers in the antiimperialist camp. Accepting the contentions Theodore Roosevelt had offered in his Winning of the West, *they insisted that imperialism was nothing more than the continuation of the expansionism initiated by the Founding Fathers because the targets of earlier expansion had never truly been empty. The nature and number of inhabitants in a desired area were irrelevant since American rule benefited rather than harmed those who came under its sway.*

This imperial view ultimately prevailed in the historical interpretations of the early twentieth century. Not only did historical accounts generally approve of the Spanish-American War, the acquisition of the Philippines, the Open Door notes, the securing of the Panamanian canal route, the Roosevelt Corollary to the Monroe Doctrine, and American intervention into World War I, but this approval of American assertiveness and expansion was reflected in revised historical interpretations of earlier issues such as the origins of the Monroe Doctrine and the Mexican War.

Still, if historians almost unanimously endorsed the imperial surge, they did so with increasing reluctance as the imperial age advanced. Despite their belief that American expansion abroad was justified by strategic, economic, and moral factors, they remained uneasy about the fact that many of the colonized peoples did not welcome American rule and that the precepts of American democracy and civilization had to be waived to maintain America's position abroad. They were disillusioned over the Philippines, as the revolt there took more lives than had the Spanish-American War itself. They also worried that America's power was being overextended. These reservations contributed to a new attitude toward Great Britain and its empire. Perhaps cooperation with Britain could bolster U.S. protection of its possessions and interests abroad. The tendency toward cooperation with Britain vastly accelerated with the outbreak of World War I. Germany's militarism was perceived as a major threat to the United States and to the democratic system America shared with Britain and France. Americans therefore felt far more confident of the morality of their intervention in Europe than they had of intervention in Cuba or Latin America. They assumed that the beneficence of their intervention and the democratic system it served was appreciated in Europe as it never could be in "less civilized" areas. Thus, historical interpretations of past diplomacy increasingly reflected these pro-British and pro-French attitudes, and even the hallowed policy of neutrality and nonentanglement toward Europe came under question. These trends were es-

pecially notable in the historiography of early American diplomacy from the Revolution through the Civil War.

As the Spanish-American War and the subsequent imperial surge drew Americans' attention to foreign affairs, diplomatic history increased in volume and significance. This period saw the first textbooks devoted solely to the history of American foreign policy. Greater numbers of specialized works in diplomatic history also appeared, reflecting changes in the historical enterprise at large. The multivolume general history of the United States, which previously had contained the most definitive work on American diplomatic history, was now in decline. Some of the great multivolume works begun in earlier decades continued into this age, such as those of McMaster and Rhodes, but only one such work was initiated, Edward Channing's A History of the United States. *The age of professionalization and specialization had begun. The typical historian was now a college professor rather than a gentleman of leisure or a retired statesman. His vehicle was the monograph rather than the multivolume narrative general history. Citation of sources was more careful and complete, making it far easier to understand the bases of historical interpretations. Perhaps the general level of research also improved in the age of the monograph although earlier historians like Schouler and Henry Adams needed to take a back seat to no one in this regard.*

This age also saw the beginning of the debate between "progressive historians," who insisted that historical truth was relative and should be shaped to present concerns, and those who thought present concerns and personal opinions should play no part in historical analysis. Diplomatic historians came to this debate rather late, and it did not strike sparks among them until after World War I. But even the most "scientific" historians failed to keep their own assumptions and attitudes from affecting their historical interpretations of past American diplomacy. Whether blatant or disguised, the influence of the Spanish-American War, the acquisition of the Philippines, and World War I upon the diplomatic historiography of this era was tremendous.

FIVE

The Spanish-American War

Americans were probably more united and enthusiastic toward the Spanish-American War than toward any other war in the nation's history. The postwar annexation of the Philippines created a serious and bitter division, but the effort to expel Spain from Cuba was supported by all segments of the population. Within a year of the war, historical accounts of the glorious episode flooded the American market. Most were ephemeral memoirs and descriptions of battles, but there were also several fairly extensive analyses of the prewar diplomacy. Among these early histories was Henry Cabot Lodge's *The War with Spain*[1] and briefer, less partisan accounts by two professional historians, James Morton Callahan and John Holladay Latané.[2]

These historians agreed that Spanish rule in Cuba had been brutal and was fully deserving of summary expulsion. The Cuban Revolution of 1895 had degenerated into a stalemate, and the frustrated combatants had turned more and more savage. Lodge, Callahan, and Latané especially condemned the Spanish policy of *reconcentrado*, which involved herding thousands of Cubans from the countryside

1. Henry Cabot Lodge, *The War with Spain* (New York, 1899).
2. James Morton Callahan, *Cuba and International Relations* (Baltimore, 1899); and John Holladay Latané, *The Diplomatic Relations of the United States and Spanish America* (Baltimore, 1900).

into pestilential concentration camps to deprive the rebels of civilian support. Under American pressure, Spain had offered some concessions to the rebels, including a degree of autonomy within the Spanish Empire. But these historians agreed with the Cubans that Spain's proposals had always been too little too late. The interception and publication of a cynical letter from the Spanish diplomat, Dupuy de Lôme, brought the sincerity of Spain's offers into question as well. Finally, the explosion of the American battleship *Maine* in Havana harbor had driven the United States to the brink of intervention. When an American investigation concluded that the *Maine* had been sunk by a mine exploding against the exterior of the ship, most Americans were quick to blame the Spanish for it, and a great clamor for war to oust Spain from Cuba arose in Congress and the countryside.

Lodge, Callahan, and Latané were fully in sympathy with this demand for war. Lodge sharply criticized big business for its reluctance to join the consensus and even implied some criticism of McKinley for delaying his war message in the vain hope that Cuba could be freed by peaceful negotiations. Belatedly and grudgingly Spain had bowed to two of the demands McKinley's administration had made in the course of its last-minute negotiations. Spain had ended its reconcentration policy and agreed to offer an armistice to the rebels but had given no hint that it was willing to grant Cuban independence. Since independence for the island was the essential condition for peace, American intervention had been thoroughly justified, "and whether our minister had made the fact plain to the Spanish government or not, no peaceful settlement was possible on any other basis."[3]

As Lodge's statement implied, there was some uneasiness among the defenders of American intervention about whether the necessity for Cuban independence had been communicated clearly to the Spanish. The diplomatic correspondence leading to the war had not been published at the time Lodge wrote his book, but it was already common knowledge that a series of telegrams had been sent by State Department officials to the American minister in Spain, Stewart Woodford, setting forth America's demands, and that although independence had been included in one of these messages, it had been added rather tentatively. In addition, Woodford had known the outcry such a demand would raise among the Spanish public, and so had transmitted the insistence upon Cuban independence privately and

3. Lodge, *War with Spain*, pp. 32–33.

orally to the Spanish prime minister.[4] The ambiguity of America's ultimatum would nag at historians from that time to this, but none in the Age of Imperialism attributed much significance to it. All assumed that Cuban independence had become essential by 1898 and that one way or another the Spanish were aware of the American government's sentiments on it. The question raised by critics of the war at this time was simply whether American military intervention had been necessary to achieve it.

These criticisms began in 1901, in the wake of the publication of the diplomatic correspondence relating to the war. *The Nation* magazine surveyed those documents and, ignoring several earlier telegrams in which Cuban independence was specifically if belatedly demanded, printed only the final one, characterizing it as the embodiment of America's ultimatum. In addition to the demands for the end of reconcentration and an immediate armistice, this final telegram ordered Woodford to add "if possible, Third. If terms of peace not satisfactorily settled by October 1, President of the United States to be final arbiter between Spain and insurgents." *The Nation* chastised McKinley for ignoring the great diplomatic triumph represented by Spain's acceptance of the first two demands, proper emphasis of which could have stopped the movement toward war. "Our two categorical demands were both granted, and the third conditional one would easily follow," the editorial stated, citing the authority of Woodford himself for this opinion.[5] Did this mean that Spain was willing to accept Cuban independence since surely an American arbitration settlement would include that? *The Nation* did not face that issue explicitly.

But two later monographs written from *The Nation*'s viewpoint did. Horace Edgar Flack's *Spanish-American Diplomatic Relations* and Elbert Jay Benton's *International Law and the Diplomacy of the Spanish-American War* both emerged from a Johns Hopkins graduate seminar taught by Professor W. W. Willoughby and bore a close resemblance to each other.[6] Both labeled Spain's rule as harsh and the reconcentration system as brutal but reminded readers that the Cuban rebels had shown no greater respect for the rules of warfare or for ordinary humanity.[7] Benton particularly condemned the sensationalist, one-

4. *Congressional Record*, April 20, 1898, pp. 4096–4098.
5. *The Nation*, 73 (1901): 4.
6. Horace Edgar Flack, *Spanish-American Diplomatic Relations Preceding the War of 1898* (Baltimore, 1906); and Elbert Jay Benton, *International Law and the Diplomacy of the Spanish-American War* (Baltimore, 1908).
7. Benton, *International Law*, pp. 26–29; and Flack, *Spanish-American Diplomatic Relations*, p. 9.

sided reporting by the newspapers for stirring the war fever in the United States and for creating opportunities for unscrupulous politicians to make political capital out of jingoism.[8] Both Benton and Flack regarded the verdict of the American investigating commission that the *Maine* had been destroyed by an outside explosion as inconclusive. There was no proof that the Spanish were responsible even if that report were correct. Flack regarded it as more plausible that the rebels had blown up the ship.[9] Both believed that Spain had made adequate concessions to justify peace, and both argued explicitly that Spain ultimately would have accepted the necessity of Cuban independence if McKinley had resisted the war party in Congress and given more time for negotiations.[10]

In several ways these early critics of the Spanish-American War established the mold for future denunciations of America's intervention in the Cuban rebellion. They equated rebel tactics with those of the Spanish, which reduced sympathy for the insurgents. They blamed the yellow press for stirring unreasonable popular emotions. They attacked congressional partisans for seeking political capital through boisterous jingoism which ultimately pushed the weak McKinley into a war already made unnecessary by increasing Spanish concessions. But historical critics of the war were not yet charging that an American imperialist clique had contrived the war to provide an excuse for conquering new colonies. Critics of the war were still willing to believe the claim Henry Cabot Lodge had made earlier that "no one had dreamed that the war meant the entrance of the United States into the Orient."[11]

However influential the criticisms offered by Flack and Benton may have been in later periods, historians writing in America's imperial age seem to have been little affected by them. Most books published after those of Flack and Benton cited these critical works in their footnotes and bibliographies but ignored their conclusions. However, these critics may well have influenced the most extensive and authoritative historical defense of the war published in this era, that written by French Ensor Chadwick.[12] Chadwick had been an admiral

8. Benton, *International Law*, pp. 32, 76.
9. Flack, *Spanish-American Diplomatic Relations*, pp. 45–47; and Benton, *International Law*, p. 79.
10. Flack, *Spanish-American Diplomatic Relations*, pp. 85–95; and Benton, *International Law*, pp. 82–83.
11. Lodge, *War with Spain*, pp. 18–19.
12. French Ensor Chadwick, *The Relations of the United States and Spain: Diplomacy* (New York, 1968; originally published 1909).

in the American navy who had served on the commission investigating the sinking of the *Maine*. Such credentials might have led people to expect a book as chauvinistic as Henry Cabot Lodge's had been, but instead Chadwick's was almost painfully ambiguous and apologetic.[13]

Chadwick thought the Cuban rebellion was justified by the monstrous conditions in the Spanish colony, but he professed an admiration for the Spanish people and culture and accepted the argument that some of the rebel atrocities had been worse than the Spanish reconcentration policy. He regretted that the Spanish had rejected Cleveland's offer to mediate in favor of Cuban autonomy in 1896, and he considered war to have been almost inevitable from this point on. Spain's procrastination in offering an armistice after the sinking of the *Maine* had made chances for peace even slimmer. Still Chadwick thought McKinley might have avoided war if he had been stronger. "Spain had . . . practically accepted the American demands in full," unless the confusing series of telegrams exchanged between the American State Department and Woodford had meant that America was demanding immediate independence for Cuba. Chadwick agreed with Woodford and with Flack, Benton, and *The Nation* that with a few more months of pressure and negotiations, McKinley could have won Cuban independence without war. Yet, after conceding this, Chadwick concluded that McKinley's decision to "put aside the diplomatic success attained," and to go to war immediately rather than to await the results of the armistice was "the best, judged by our knowledge today, for Spain, for Cuba and for the United States."[14]

Although Chadwick's work was the most complete and best researched of the books on the Spanish-American War written in this era, its apologetic tone, along with the criticisms of Benton and Flack, were simply overwhelmed by the positive views taken by the other major diplomatic historians of the day in numerous shorter, more popular surveys. Reading these, one would hardly have been aware that there was any controversy over the American intervention. One of these surveys was written by the leading diplomatic historian of the Age of Imperialism, Harvard Professor Albert Bushnell Hart. Hart's *The Foundations of American Foreign Policy* was the first general history

---

13. Interestingly, Chadwick would later be an ardent opponent of U.S. intervention into World War I; see Charles Callan Tansill, *America Goes to War* (Boston, 1938), pp. 30–31.

14. Chadwick, *Relations of the United States and Spain*, pp. 12, 403–410, 464–466, 494, 554, 561–572, 575–576.

of American diplomacy written since the Civil War.[15] An ardent supporter of Theodore Roosevelt, for whom he was a delegate to the Republican convention in 1912, Hart admitted that he felt little but "pride in the purposes and results of American diplomacy,"[16] and he had no doubt of the justice of the Spanish-American War. Few nations had shown more good temper, patience, or self-restraint than the United States had in this crisis.[17]

Hart was the editor for a prestigious series of historical works called the American Nation Series. The author selected to write the volume in the series which included the Spanish-American War was John Holladay Latané, who had already published one of the earliest brief accounts justifying the war. Recent information and critiques did not change his mind. He did not believe that Spanish acceptance of the first two American demands constituted a surrender, and he agreed with Hart that war was inevitable because Spain would never grant Cuba independence.[18] He took care to deny as well that the United States might have entered the war to acquire colonies rather than to free Cuba.[19]

Lending further authority to these justifications of the war was the survey by John Bassett Moore, a renowned international lawyer and diplomatic historian who had served as assistant secretary of state during the crisis and as secretary to the American peace delegation.[20] Another influential figure who defended the war was Archibald Cary Coolidge, Harvard professor of European history, whose *United States*

15. Albert Bushnell Hart, *The Foundations of American Foreign Policy* (New York, 1901).

16. *Ibid.*, pp. v–vi.

17. *Ibid.*, pp. 48, 132. See also his *The Monroe Doctrine: An Interpretation* (Boston, 1916), p. 373.

18. John Holladay Latané, *America as a World Power, 1897–1907* (New York, 1907), pp. 24–25.

19. *Ibid.*, pp. 7, 25, 36, 175.

20. John Bassett Moore's major work was *A Digest of International Law*, 8 vols. (Washington, D.C., 1906), a revision of Francis Wharton's previous compilation. He also edited two collections of international arbitrations to which the United States was a party. His interpretive works on American diplomacy were "The Monroe Doctrine: Its Origin and Meaning" (New York, 1895), a short article reprinted from the *New York Post*; "A Hundred Years of American Diplomacy" (New York, 1900), another short piece, and very uncritical; *American Diplomacy: Its Spirit and Achievements* (New York and London, 1905); *The Principles of American Diplomacy* (New York and London, 1918), which incorporated the 1905 book; and *Four Phases of American Development: Federalism—Democracy—Imperialism—Expansion* (Baltimore, 1912). For Moore's justification of the war, see his *Principles of American Diplomacy*, pp. 205–208.

as a World Power went through six reprintings between 1908 and 1919.[21] Coolidge was particularly anxious to show that contrary to European suspicions, America had not been motivated to intervene by greed for Cuba.[22] In addition, acquisition of the Philippines had been entirely accidental, as no plans had been made for taking advantage of Admiral Dewey's hoped-for victory at Manila.[23] Finally, the first history of American foreign policy designed as a college textbook, Carl Russell Fish's *American Diplomacy*, gave a solid if unenthusiastic endorsement of American intervention, arguing that while the war now appeared unnecessary, McKinley had had no reason to trust the assurances of a Spanish government that dared not announce its concessions to its own people.[24]

Thus, despite some powerful critiques, American historical interpretations of the Spanish-American War in the pre-World War I era were overwhelmingly favorable to the United States. Perhaps more surprising, the vehement antiimperialist crusade against keeping the Philippines did not prevent historians from endorsing the imperial adventure following the war as unanimously as they had endorsed the far less controversial decision to intervene in the Cuban rebellion in the first place.

21. Archibald Cary Coolidge, *United States as a World Power* (New York, 1908).

22. *Ibid.*, pp. 128–130.

23. *Ibid.*, pp. 148–149.

24. Carl Russell Fish, *American Diplomacy* (New York, 1915), pp. 408, 412–417.

SIX

Imperialism and the Historical Climate of Opinion

Historians writing in the first two decades of the twentieth century were convinced that the Spanish-American War had been responsible for converting the American people to an imperial policy. Almost all historians considered this change a salutary one. They came to write approvingly of the taking of the Philippines, the pronouncement of the Open Door policy in China, the securing of the Panama Canal, and interventions in Latin America. Not a single major historical work written in this period about contemporary diplomatic affairs took an outright antiimperialist line. Hermann Von Holst and James Schouler wrote brief articles in which they mobilized the precepts of the Founding Fathers to oppose imperialism, but they seemed to make little impression. They were of an older generation of historians whose major work was behind them. They failed to incorporate their views organically in a large-scale historical narrative after 1898, as the younger, more imperial-minded historians were doing. Antiimperialists also became convinced that their policies were passé. They seemed to be running against the opinions of the majority of the American people, worldwide historical currents too strong to be breasted, and some powerful analyses produced by the imperialists.

Charles Conant supplied the economic rationale for imperialism, arguing that the United States was facing a congestion of capital which America's potential domestic demand was incapable of absorbing. America had to expand economically if it wished to avoid business depressions, whether that expansion took the form of colonies, protectorates, or just commercial treaties. He was not "an advocate of 'imperialism' from sentiment," Conant said, but he did not "fear the name" if it meant America was determined to share in the world's markets.[1] Alfred Thayer Mahan spelled out the strategic implications of Conant's theories in detail immediately following the Spanish-American War.[2] Mahan insisted that in order to maintain access to the markets of the world, especially those of China, the United States had to have naval bases in the Caribbean, the Isthmus, Hawaii, and the Philippines to protect its major routes of transportation and communication.[3]

The policies laid out by Conant and Mahan had great currency in the Age of Imperialism, forming something of a blueprint for Theodore Roosevelt and much of the Republican party. Roosevelt clearly appreciated the importance of foreign markets, military preparedness, a balance of power, and the vigorous assertion of America's national interests. He continued to champion the Open Door in China; he "took" Panama and encouraged the building of the canal; he began wholesale interventions in the Caribbean area to forestall potential European intervention (the Roosevelt Corollary); and he intervened personally in the Russo-Japanese War and the Algeciras Conference to help stabilize a balance of power in Asia and Europe.

Gradually, however, even enthusiastic Rooseveltian imperialists became a bit more cautious. This new reluctance appeared in the analysis produced by Roosevelt's friend (later to be his biographer), Lewis Einstein, a State Department officer who in 1909 anonymously published a book entitled *American Foreign Policy, by a Diplomatist*.[4] Einstein warned that America's foreign policy commitments were beginning to outstrip its resources. It would require substantial effort to balance commitments to a defense perimeter so far-flung as to include Cuba, the Caribbean, and the Philippines with America's available power. Einstein's solution was not just an increase in American military forces but also a British alliance. If Britain restrained her

1. Charles Conant, *The United States in the Orient* (Boston and New York, 1900), pp. iii, iv–v, 25–29. Ironically, Conant's work may have been the basis of the famous antiimperialist analyses of J. A. Hobson and Lenin, according to William Langer.

2. Alfred Thayer Mahan, *Lessons of the War with Spain* (Boston, 1899; reprinted in New York, 1970); and his *The Problem of Asia* (Boston, 1900).

3. Mahan, *Problem of Asia*, p. 180.

4. [Lewis Einstein], *American Foreign Policy, by a Diplomatist* (Boston, 1909).

ally, Japan, and helped America maintain the Open Door in China, the United States could dispose of the Philippines without fear that the islands would be acquired by a serious rival. Thus, Einstein reflected Roosevelt's own disillusionment with the Philippine colonial experiment. But this did not mean that either Einstein or the Rooseveltians had lost all their taste for imperialism. Einstein still believed that it was necessary "at all costs" to protect the independence of nations in the Caribbean "even against themselves," and he thought it inevitable that in the future the United States would absorb both Cuba and Santo Domingo.[5]

With the demise of the antiimperialist campaign in 1900, the Democratic party offered only a mild opposition to Rooseveltian imperialism. Democratic analysts were just slightly more cautious and apologetic in their imperialism than the Republicans. They reluctantly accepted acquisition of the Philippines, Hawaii, and the Panama Canal, but they caviled at the methods used and argued particularly that the United States should find a way to extricate itself from the colonial problems of the Philippines. They seemed somewhat less confident that American rule would inevitably benefit those subject to it. Often they denounced the insensitivity of the Roosevelt Corollary and urged an apology to Colombia for the methods used by the United States to acquire the Panama Canal route. As World War I began in Europe, Democrats were generally less assertive than Republicans, counseling greater neutrality toward the Allied powers and resisting the preparedness campaign urged by Roosevelt and his allies. Among the political analyses of American diplomacy which adhered to the cautionary, Wilsonian, Democratic party line were works by Richard Olney, formerly secretary of state under Cleveland, and Paul Reinsch, later to be Wilson's minister to China.

Olney did not oppose expansionism in the Western Hemisphere. But he regretted annexations in the Pacific, saying they would probably require a temporary alliance with the British to protect them. Only this tone of regret and some uncomplimentary comments about Theodore Roosevelt marked Olney's interpretations as different from those of outright imperialists.[6] Paul Reinsch's famous book, *World Politics*, was somewhat more antiimperialistic. He warned against further territorial expansion, believing America should seek only open markets abroad and prosperity at home. In China for instance, he

5. *Ibid.*, pp. v–vii, 4–12, 17, 25–27, 42, 50–51, 79–83, 88–89, 95.
6. Richard Olney, "The Growth of Our Foreign Policy," *Atlantic*, 85 (1900): 287–301.

would approve the use of European troops to maintain the Open Door, uphold law and order, prosecute brigands and rebels, and secure the highways of the China trade. But acquisition of foreign territories was not worth the cost either to the United States or to the "so-called inferior races," whom the capitalists regarded as "guilty of an underdevelopment of their natural resources." He urged a measure of independence for Cuba and the Philippines but only to the degree consonant with the general peace of the world and security of life and property on those islands.[7]

As analysts of American foreign policy endorsed America's new imperial status with varying degrees of reluctance, they often referred briefly to America's past foreign policy to justify or gain perspective on this sudden surge of expansionism. These analysts, along with less profound politicians and propagandists, were divided in their use of America's history. Some, like Alfred Thayer Mahan and Lewis Einstein, agreed that America's diplomatic tradition had been one of isolation and antiimperialism but said that America had outgrown such policies. Many imperialists, however, including Charles Conant, Theodore Roosevelt, and Henry Cabot Lodge, were not so willing to admit that imperialism was a departure from past precepts. Roosevelt pointed out that America's "whole national history has been one of expansion," and Henry Cabot Lodge maintained that "if the arguments which have been offered against our taking the Philippine Islands because we have not the consent of the inhabitants be just, then our whole past record of expansion is a crime."[8]

As historians joined the propagandists and contemporary foreign policy analysts in the debate over imperialism, naturally this historical question was one of their major concerns. In the end, most historians decided that imperialism was indeed in line with America's past expansionist diplomacy. Perhaps James Morton Callahan put it most blatantly, declaring in his history of American expansionism that there was no more magnificent movement in modern history than that of the "motley, heroic, sublime migrating procession which . . . breaking barrier after barrier . . . has swept across the American continent within the last century . . . and finally across the fretful Pacific,

7. Paul Reinsch, *World Politics* (New York, 1900), pp. 10–12, 194–195, 310–312, 326, 356–371.

8. Theodore Roosevelt writing in the *Independent* in 1899, quoted in Richard E. Welch, Jr., *Imperialists vs. Anti-Imperialists: The Debate over Expansion in the 1890s* (Itasca, Ill., 1972), p. 119; and Henry Cabot Lodge, speech in Senate, *Congressional Record*, March 7, 1900.

the theater of great future historical events, to the portals of the Orient. . . ." This movement, "adding territory after territory to the American union, and extending her commerce and beneficent influence to distant lands and peoples, is the great central fact of American history. Expansion, non-parasitic, vigorous and attractive, developing by affinity, contending against both restriction and secession, has been America's greatest feat."[9]

Callahan's bumptious tone was somewhat atypical of most of the extended histories of American imperialism. If historians almost unanimously endorsed American imperialism as a continuation of earlier praiseworthy expansion, they did so with considerably less enthusiasm than had Rooseveltian analysts like Conant, Mahan, and Einstein. The difficulties and atrocities of the war to put down the Philippine revolt brought home both the moral and practical problems of ruling an area against the will of a significant number of its inhabitants. An apologetic and ironic tone soon crept into the accounts of even Rooseveltian historians. The gap between Rooseveltian and Wilsonian outlooks on imperialism narrowed.

The work of Albert Bushnell Hart illustrates this process among the Rooseveltian historians. Hart advocated keeping the Philippines and asserting America's interests in Latin America and Asia. He considered America's march into the Caribbean and the Pacific "as inevitable as it was into Texas and California" because of the proximity of "badly ruled, rich, and strategically important lands."[10] Regretfully, Hart noted that recent American expansion would mean ruling people without their consent. Still, strategic and commercial necessities required this, and Hart remained confident that American rule would benefit the natives despite their misguided resistance to it.[11] For "the general tendency of American expansion is toward freedom," he declared.[12]

Of course, the reluctance of Hart's imperialism was far more noticeable in his discussion of expansion under the Democrats than it was when the subject was Republican expansion. He ridiculed the pugnacious attitude of Grover Cleveland and Secretary of State Richard Olney in the Venezuela crisis.[13] He had nothing but scorn for

9. James Morton Callahan, *An Introduction to American Expansion Policy* ([Morgantown, West Va.], 1908), p. 1.

10. Hart, *Foundations of American Foreign Policy*, p. 51.

11. Albert Bushnell Hart, *National Ideals Historically Traced, 1607–1907* (New York, 1907), p. 30; and his *Foundations of American Foreign Policy*, pp. 169–170.

12. Hart, *Foundations of American Foreign Policy*, p. 52.

13. Hart, *National Ideals Historically Traced*, p. 320.

Woodrow Wilson, who professed sympathy with Latin-American powers while removing their problems by "removing their independence."[14] On the other hand, Theodore Roosevelt had every right to intervene in Latin America and to secure the Panama Canal. Still Hart advocated restraint in the collection of protectorates, and he wanted Americans to recognize that their purpose was American self-interest, especially the protection of the Panama Canal, not the promotion of cloudy ideals of democracy among backward nations.[15] Thus, the qualms Hart felt about American imperialism stemmed more from fears of the harm overextension might do to America than from fears that it might do harm to subject peoples. This seemed the case with most historians of this era.

The historian who wrote the last volume of Hart's American Nation Series covering the period from 1907 to World War I[16] was a like-minded Rooseveltian named Frederick Ogg, who had already written a book on westward expansion.[17] Ogg favored contemporary American expansionism as much as he had the earlier march to the West and especially praised Theodore Roosevelt while condemning Wilson's apology to Colombia for the taking of Panama.[18] He was also critical of Wilson's inconsistent policy in Mexico.[19] Indeed, the pre-World War I imbroglio with Mexico, especially Pancho Villa's raid in New Mexico, inspired a more indignant interventionist tone toward Latin America in the writings of many historians of this time.

John Holladay Latané, who wrote the volume immediately preceding Ogg's in the American Nation Series,[20] was slightly less Rooseveltian and more Wilsonian than Hart and Ogg, urging a bit more restraint and concern for morality in America's expansion policies. After World War I, when some of the Republicans, including Roosevelt's friend, Henry Cabot Lodge, sabotaged Wilson's League of Nations, Latané became known as an ardent Wilsonian and a severe critic of the isolationist policies of the Jazz Age. This was so much the case that when David Wainhouse was asked in 1934 to update Latané's 1927 text on the *History of American Foreign Policy*, it was announced

14. Hart, *Monroe Doctrine*, pp. 234, 238, 302.
15. *Ibid.*, pp. 374–377.
16. Frederick A. Ogg, *National Progress, 1907–1917* (New York, 1918).
17. Frederick A. Ogg, *The Opening of the Mississippi: A Struggle for Supremacy in the American Interior* (New York, 1904).
18. Ogg, *National Progress*, pp. 248, 252–253, 276.
19. *Ibid.*, p. 290.
20. Latané, *America as a World Power*.

that he had been selected because he was in sympathy with Latané's "liberal point of view."[21]

However, prior to 1919, Latané's only major break from the Rooseveltian line was his assertion that America had acted unjustly in taking the Panama Canal route. He believed that the United States could as easily have used the Nicaraguan alternative.[22] As might be expected, in his later writings Latané approved of Woodrow Wilson's apology to Colombia for this episode, an action that was anathema to Roosevelt and his followers.[23]

Latané also may have been a bit more antagonistic to America's course in the Philippines than most Rooseveltians. He thought that McKinley had taken the Philippines because larger business and commercial interests of the country had wanted access to the China market and would allow "no mere abstract theory of government . . . to stand in the way of the opening of new markets in the Orient." The resulting Philippine revolt had led to a vicious guerrilla war and a record of atrocities on the part of Americans that was "humiliating." Latané's hope was that the Filipinos would develop a fair degree of governmental efficiency, whereupon the United States would "be glad of the opportunity of giving up the internal government of the islands, retaining simply a protectorate."[24]

Yet despite Latané's doubts about American policy in the Philippines and Panama, his book, overall, supported an expansive foreign policy close to that of Roosevelt. He thought it absolutely out of the question that Cuba should remain independent if it fell into insurrectionary habits.[25] He praised the Open Door policy and urged America to accept its role as a world power, claiming that Washington's counsels of isolation had been merely a temporary policy until the country had matured.[26]

Archibald Cary Coolidge was another example of the reluctant imperialist historian. His *United States as a World Power* was quite Rooseveltian in its frank acceptance of the supremacy of power and self-interest over morality in American foreign policy, but that did not

21. John Holladay Latané, *A History of American Foreign Policy* (Garden City, N.Y., 1927); all citations are from the 1934 edition, revised and enlarged by David Wainhouse.

22. *Ibid.*, pp. 204, 213–218.

23. John Holladay Latané, *From Isolation to Leadership: A Review of American Foreign Policy* (New York, 1918), pp. 142–144.

24. *Ibid.*, pp. 72–73, 96, 174.

25. Latané, *America as a World Power*, pp. 175, 179–181, 190–191.

26. *Ibid.*, pp. 259–263, 319–320.

keep him from chiding his fellow Americans on the means they had used to achieve empire. He warned especially against the vague moralistic passions that might lead Americans to injudicious interventions and overexpansion.[27] He was particularly concerned that incorporation of hostile and "inferior" races would weaken America. Still, he saw no alternative to intervention in Latin America, he justified the acquisition of the Panama Canal route, and he praised the taking of Puerto Rico while hoping for the eventual independence of the Philippines.[28]

John Bassett Moore expressed similar views in his important historical surveys of this period. He supported taking the Philippines, Puerto Rico, and Guam but worried about the imperialistic passions that accompanied the end of the Spanish-American War. Many people, convinced that this imperialism was a tremendous departure from past American policy, enthusiastically assumed that the United States would now "break with its past and enter upon a new career in which previous guides and limitations would be discarded." Paradoxically, Moore seemed to believe that if he could convince people that imperialism was not a new departure, they would be more willing to accept limitations on their ambitions.[29] So he stressed the continuity of expansion in American history, ridiculing America's pretensions to a pacific temperament and noting its tendency to blame others for all conflicts.[30] Yet he praised the United States for absorbing provinces which had languished for centuries under the leaden sway of stationary regimes.[31] People unfamiliar with America's expansionist history had been startled by acquisition of Puerto Rico and the Philippines, and their excitement had led them to "abnormal vaticinations and proposals" for still more colonies until "realities, with the aid of a certain continuity in thought and in temper on the part of the less vocal element of the population, eventually regained their normal sway."[32] In this mild and convoluted style, Moore suggested that the Roosevelt Corollary and the Panama incident had been a bit excessive but that Wilson's policies were applying proper correctives.[33]

27. Coolidge, United States as a World Power, pp. 81, 88–89.
28. Ibid., pp. 116–117, 146, 151, 157–162, 277.
29. Moore, Principles of American Diplomacy, pp. 438–439.
30. Moore, Four Phases, pp. 147–149, 195–196.
31. Moore, Hundred Years of American Diplomacy, pp. 20–21; see also his Four Phases, pp. 147–148.
32. Moore, Principles of American Diplomacy, pp. 438–439.
33. See, e.g., Moore, Four Phases, pp. 141–147; and his Principles of American Diplomacy, p. 416.

This attitude of reluctant and ironic support for America's inescapable role as a great colonial power and the belief that imperialism was essentially in accord with America's past diplomatic history permeated not only specialized works of historians like Hart, Latané, Coolidge, Ogg, and Moore but also the two significant textbook surveys of American diplomatic history written in this era by Willis Fletcher Johnson and Carl Russell Fish. Johnson's 1916 textbook, *America's Foreign Relations*, provides an excellent example of the taming of the imperialists that occurred in this era.[34] In a book written thirteen years before, *A Century of Expansion*, he had surveyed past American diplomacy to prove that as expansion was in the American tradition, so also was holding and governing dependencies without their consent.[35] Admirably, the English-speaking people had avoided the Spanish and French mistake of intermarriage with the Indians and had "held themselves sternly aloof from the natives with an unconquerable pride of race, driving them ever from the land and taking it all for themselves."[36] He wished the United States had taken all of Oregon. He commended the Spanish-American War for stopping the dangerous anarchy in Cuba. He fully approved of taking the Philippines. He even supported intervention in Europe and claimed that neither the Monroe Doctrine nor Washington's farewell address were meant to prohibit such activities.[37]

By 1916, Johnson's expansionism had been tempered. He no longer insisted that the United States should have had all of Oregon, a turnabout perhaps owing as much to his support of the British in World War I as to a cooling of his expansionist passions. He even appealed to the principles of nonintervention and nonentanglement, which he earlier had condemned as outdated, to denounce America's Samoa policy as "one of the most thoroughly discreditable passages in American history." He admired McKinley's attempts to avoid the Spanish-American War and chastised Congress and the yellow press for their prejudice and passion.[38]

Carl Russell Fish's *American Diplomacy* was a far more informed survey than Johnson's. It was unrivaled as a college-level text until John Holladay Latané's *History of American Foreign Policy* was pub-

34. Willis Fletcher Johnson, *America's Foreign Relations*, 2 vols. (New York, 1916).

35. Willis Fletcher Johnson, *A Century of Expansion* (New York, 1903).

36. *Ibid.*, p. 5.

37. *Ibid.*, pp. 197, 298–302.

38. Johnson, *America's Foreign Relations*, I, 402–429; II, 159, 243–256.

lished in 1927. Fish's book reflected the latest monographic research and interpretations of early American diplomacy to a much greater degree than Johnson's. Fish saw some foolishness and excessive belligerence in both past and present American expansionism, especially in the War of 1812, in Florida, in the Venezuela incident, in the Hawaiian annexation rejected by Cleveland, and in the Spanish-American War. But, overall, he approved of the expansionist movement and reluctantly accepted annexation of the Philippines as necessary under the circumstances.[39]

In searching for monographs upon which to base his text, Fish found many recent studies of incidents involving westward expansion. The Age of Imperialism, involving as it had a rapid extension into Asia and Latin America, had sent historians scurrying for precedents in America's past and inspired tremendous research on events like the Louisiana Purchase, the acquisition of Florida, and the Mexican War. By contrast, historical events which involved America's policy of neutrality and nonintervention in Europe seemed far less dramatic or relevant. Only the turn-of-century political rapprochement with England provided some contemporary incentive for a reassessment of America's past relations with Europe.

Then came the outbreak of World War I in 1914. Suddenly questions of neutrality and isolation toward Europe were catapulted into prominence, Historians began an intensive questioning of America's historical relationship with European diplomacy, and America's 1917 intervention in World War I converted almost the entire historical community to the view that a reversal of America's isolation from Europe was long overdue.

Scott Nearing, one-time University of Pennsylvania historian fired for his militant socialism, was the only historian to publish a major work against America's participation in the war in the period between 1914 and 1919. His book, *The Great Madness*, joined the essays of Randolph Bourne and the speeches of Senators George Norris and Robert La Follette as articulate and influential expressions of antiwar sentiment in this period.[40] But once the United States was in the war, Nearing was overwhelmed by the output of historians supporting American participation.

Many historians contributed propaganda speeches and pam-

39. Fish, *American Diplomacy*, pp. 158, 200, 280–281, 394, 406, 408, 416–417, 497.

40. Scott Nearing, *The Great Madness* (New York, 1917).

phlets under the auspices of the government or private organizations devoted to the war effort. James Shotwell organized the National Board for Historical Service, adopting the idea that historians should cease being mere chroniclers and use their talents for prophecy and guidance. Once America was in the war, the government took a hand in this work. George Creel's Committee for Public Information had a Division of Civic and Educational Cooperation made up almost exclusively of historians. Contributing to the publications of this agency were historians like Edwin Corwin, Bernadotte Schmitt, Charles Beard, Sidney Fay, Carl Becker, Carl Russell Fish, William Dodd, J. Franklin Jameson, and Frederic Paxson.[41]

Other historians such as Albert Bushnell Hart and John Holladay Latané contributed their prowar efforts to a rival private organization, the National Security League. The league was highly Republican in its coloration and supported by ardent preparedness advocates Theodore Roosevelt, General Leonard Wood, Elihu Root, and Henry Stimson. It had been very critical of Wilson's reluctance to enter the war, and its members had often characterized the president as spineless. Hart was a leading member of the league and composed a pamphlet for it entitled *America at War: A Handbook of Patriotic Educational References.*[42] Latané was not quite so enthusiastic a member, distrustful of overly patriotic organizations and attitudes, but he assisted with a speaker training camp for the league in 1917.[43] He also contributed considerably to the bad blood between the league and the Creel Committee historians by attacking one of the Creel pamphlets as full of errors, and he received the public endorsement of Hart for doing so. Many of the Creel Committee historians already bore resentment toward Latané because, in 1913, in their capacities as ranking officials of the American Historical Association, they had been subjected to charges from Latané that they were too conservative and repressive.[44] Thus, there was a note of personal bitterness in the debates among historians over whether the United States should have intervened in World War I earlier than Wilson had permitted.

Still, this was the only issue that seriously divided contemporary

41. George T. Blakey, *Historians on the Homefront: American Propagandists for the Great War* (Lexington, Ky., 1970), pp. 16–22.

42. Albert Bushnell Hart, *America at War: A Handbook of Patriotic Educational References* (National Security League, Committee on Patriotism Through Education, New York, 1918).

43. Blakey, *Historians on the Homefront*, pp. 26–31.

44. *Ibid.*, pp. 53–55.

historians of World War I. All assumed American entry had been necessary. Even Carleton Hayes, who had signed a telegram against the declaration of war in 1917, praised American intervention in his *A Brief History of the Great War*.[45] The most extensive of the histories of American entry, John Bach McMaster's *The United States in the World War* and John Spencer Bassett's *Our War With Germany*, both characterized intervention as necessary to protect America's interests, ideology, and even survival against Germany's ruthless autocracy.[46] They were supported in this by other, lesser histories, including Christian Gauss's highly colored account of *Why We Went to War* and Roland Usher's *The Story of the Great War*.[47] While these historians understood that the British blockade had violated America's neutral rights and channeled most of America's valuable exports to the Allies, they did not believe this had excused Germany's submarine warfare. America had tried to be neutral and had protested British illegalities so that the United States could seek compensation in an international tribunal after the war. More than this could not be expected from the United States, for to dispute British violations beyond this point "would have made us participants in the war, and on the side of Germany," wrote Bassett.[48] After German atrocities in Belgium, this would have been unthinkable.

Further German atrocities in the form of submarine warfare finally had brought the United States into the war. The key was not that the submarines violated American neutral rights but that they confirmed that Germany "was a horrible menace to civilization."[49] If Germany won the war, "a great central empire would be founded with the prospect that it would dominate Europe and imperil the safety of the Americas."[50] Documentation of espionage and sabotage by paid agents under the control of the German Embassy in the United States and the interception of the Zimmermann note offering a German alliance to Mexico in case of American intervention in the war

45. Carleton J. H. Hayes, *A Brief History of the Great War* (New York, 1920). For Hayes's opposition to the war, see Walter Millis, *The Road to War: America 1914–1917* (Boston and New York, 1935), p. 385.

46. John Bach McMaster, *The United States in the World War*, 2 vols. (New York, 1918–1920); and John Spencer Bassett, *Our War with Germany* (New York, 1919).

47. Christian B. Gauss, *Why We Went to War* (New York, 1918); and Roland G. Usher, *The Story of the Great War* (New York, 1919).

48. Bassett, *Our War with Germany*, p. 26.

49. Hayes, *Brief History of the Great War*, p. 206.

50. Bassett, *Our War with Germany*, p. 95. See also McMaster, *United States in the World War*, I, 23–50, 87, 102.

confirmed that Germany was a threat to American security. Almost all American historians at this time assumed then that the war was a realistic one for security and survival, not a narrow idealistic defense of neutral rights against submarine warfare.

However, some historians who, like the National Security League, thought Wilson had been too backward in his war policies, entered an important caveat. They agreed that the war was a war for survival and security, but they were not sure that Wilson had understood this. Frederick Ogg, in his volume for the American Nation Series, denounced Wilson for leading the nation to believe that America was unconcerned with the causes and objects of the Great War "until he and the country were rudely awakened by what had become clear to many much earlier—that this was a contest between democracy and autocracy and that America should have taken a firmer stand long ago, throwing its weight against the Prussian autocratic idea." The United States would have to fight imperialistic Germany alone if "the Teutonic powers" were victorious, he warned.[51] Latané agreed and surmised that Wilson had fought originally only because German submarine warfare had violated American neutral rights. If Germany had obeyed international law, Latané thought Wilson would have permitted a German victory, even though it upset the European balance of power and would have led eventually to a conflict between Germany and an isolated America.[52] Latané rejoiced, however, that Wilson and America had finally seen the threat Germany had posed to the United States and, once in the war, had taken up the fight for human freedom throughout the world. "Having once abandoned neutrality and isolation, we are not likely to remain neutral again in any war which involved the balance of power in the world or the destinies of the major portion of mankind," Latané said.[53]

This question of whether the United States entered World War I as a realistic search for security or an idealistic crusade for neutral rights would agitate post-World War II historians far more than it did contemporaries. Historians like Latané, Hart, and Ogg, who were sensitized to the issue by their National Security League affiliations, might examine it overtly. But most of the other historians assumed that the issues of security and submarine violations of neutral rights went in tandem. Roland Usher implied that the United States would have intervened even if Germany had not declared unlimited submarine

51. Ogg, *National Progress*, pp. 396–399.
52. Latané, *From Isolation to Leadership*, pp. 179–186.
53. *Ibid.*, pp. 186–187.

warfare.[54] But McMaster, Bassett, Gauss, and Hayes failed to deal with the question at all.

However divided historians might have been over this issue, almost all welcomed the abandonment of isolation. Here they were as unanimous as they were toward imperialism, and considerably more enthusiastic. The war thus elevated the issue of European involvement, an issue somewhat neglected earlier in the century when imperialism and expansion had held center stage, to a major historical theme ranking alongside that of territorial expansion. But this came late in the Age of Imperialism. Most histories of early American diplomacy concentrated on incidents involving expansion rather than neutrality, expansion seeming more relevant to contemporary concerns.

54. *Ibid.* See also Bassett, *Our War with Germany*, pp. 332–333; Usher, *Story of the Great War*, pp. 233–235; and Hayes, *Brief History of the Great War*, pp. 201–203.

SEVEN

The Impact of the Age of Imperialism on the Historiography of Early American Diplomacy

The interest in past expansion aroused by the imperialist movement had a profound effect on the historiography of the diplomacy of the American Revolution. Fittingly, it was Frederick Jackson Turner who made the first contribution to the historical debate. He noted that a document, recently found in Vergennes's papers and cited by the Jay family in defense of their ancestor's hard line against France, had even more ominous implications for Franklin's indulgent policy than the Jay family had realized. The document indicated that France not only had supported Spanish pretentions in the West but had sought to regain an empire for itself in Louisiana. Turner did warn that authorship of the document was uncertain because no copy of it had been discovered in the official archives of France. But he was convinced that the document genuinely expressed French policy because Vergennes had followed its dictates and because Manuel de Godoy, the famous Spanish diplomat, had stated late in his life that Vergennes had tried to acquire Louisiana from Spain.[1] Turner's views were endorsed by the most authoritative historian of the imperial era, Edward Channing,

---

1. Frederick Jackson Turner, "The Policy of France Toward the Mississippi Valley," *American Historical Review*, 10 (January 1905): 249–279.

the last to write a multivolume general study of the United States from the original sources.[2]

Turner's contentions inspired P. C. Phillips to undertake research deep into the French, British, and American archives, which culminated in his major study, *The West in the Diplomacy of the American Revolution*.[3] Phillips concluded that Turner's document was a forgery. The style was not that of Vergennes, and the document referred to Florida as Spanish territory at a time when the British possessed it, a mistake Vergennes never would have made. Since the document had not been published in France until 1802, Phillips considered it possible that Napoleon had had it forged to support his own efforts to reacquire Louisiana.[4] Thus, Phillips insisted that Vergennes had been faithful to his allies.[5] Jay's open break with the French had been unnecessary and merely had relieved the British from the need to make the concessions Franklin had been hinting were essential.[6] The later concessions Jay and Adams won by firmness were minor by comparison.[7]

Edwin Corwin had been ready to publish a work based on these same archives when he had been scooped by Phillips. So Corwin delayed publication for three years and focused his study on the whole history of the Franco-American alliance rather than on just the diplomacy of the Revolution. Corwin agreed with most of Phillips's analysis although he was somewhat harsher with France's motivations and less convinced that Jay's delay had cost America any substantial concessions. Rayneval's mission already had informed the British of the Franco-American split before Jay's actions revealed it, and in any case the real motive for Britain's harsher terms had been news of the failure of the siege of Gibraltar. Corwin's incisive analysis was sufficiently well researched, balanced, and convincing that it remained one of the two or three standard works on the diplomacy of the Revolution until very recently.[8] Minor works by John Foster,[9] Willis Fletcher John-

---

2. Edward Channing, *A History of the United States*, 6 vols. (New York, 1906–1925), III, 350–357, 384.

3. P. C. Phillips, *The West in the Diplomacy of the American Revolution* (New York, 1913).

4. *Ibid.*, pp. 30–32n.

5. *Ibid.*, pp. 3, 170.

6. *Ibid.*, pp. 216–221.

7. *Ibid.*, p. 224.

8. E. S. Corwin, *French Policy and the American Alliance of 1778* (Princeton, 1916), pp. 9–13, 56–57, 212, 318, 334–351.

9. John W. Foster, *A Century of American Diplomacy* (Boston and New York, 1900), pp. 3–4, 31, 47, 59–64, 82–86.

son,[10] and James Breck Perkins[11] perpetuated the debate on the relative virtues of Franklin's accommodating policy and the belligerent one of Jay and Adams, but since the outstanding books of Phillips and Corwin endorsed Franklin and defused Turner's charge that France had sought an empire at America's expense, the old French alliance was in better repute within historical circles on the eve of America's entry into World War I than it had been since the publication of the Jay family view in the 1890s. Perhaps this helped slightly to lessen prejudices against European entanglements and smoothed the way for intervention.

The new concern for expansion also had an effect on historical interpretations of the War of 1812. Alfred Thayer Mahan's *Seapower in Its Relations to the War of 1812*, published early in this era, still adhered closely to the older interpretation of Henry Adams, citing maritime causes for the war, blaming the Republicans for their lack of military preparedness, and arguing that the United States should have gone to war in 1807 rather than resorting to a feeble system of commercial restrictions.[12] But in 1911, Howard Lewis and Dice Anderson published short articles carrying an expansionist interpretation of the war.[13] If maritime offenses had caused the war, the sea-going peoples of New England logically would not have furnished the major opposition to it, nor would the frontier sections of the South and West have spearheaded the drive for war. And since the French maritime offenses had been every bit as baneful as the British, there seemed no reason except the lure of Britain's frontier provinces to bring the Americans to fight the British rather than the French. Finally, the Americans had continued the war even after the major maritime grievances against England, the orders-in-council, had been re-

10. Johnson, *Century of Expansion*, p. 48.

11. James Breck Perkins, *France in the American Revolution* (Boston and New York, 1911).

12. Alfred Thayer Mahan, *Seapower in Its Relations to the War of 1812*, 2 vols. (Boston, 1905). Edward Channing, who cited Henry Adams and Mahan as his major sources on the War of 1812, professed to see a major difference between the two. Channing claimed to side with Mahan, who he said took a pessimistic view of Republican diplomacy, against Adams, who Channing thought took an optimistic view of the policies of Jefferson and Madison. Actually, there seems to be little distinction between Mahan and Adams, and Channing's account differs little from either of them (Channing, *History of the United States*, IV, 374).

13. Howard T. Lewis, "A Re-analysis of the Causes of the War of 1812," *Americana*, 6 (1911): 506–516, 577, 585; and Dice R. Anderson, "Insurgents of 1811," *American Historical Association Report*, 1 (1911): 167–176.

pealed.[14] Obviously, Americans had continued to fight in hopes of taking British Canada and eliminating British support of the Indian threat to the frontier.[15] In addition, the "usually imperialistic" South saw a chance to take Florida and justified the conquest by claiming that Britain had bolstered Spain's resistance to surrendering the territory to the United States.[16] Anderson and Lewis assigned different priorities to western desires. Anderson emphasized the Indian threat whereas Lewis spoke more of land hunger on the part of the frontiersmen. But both wrote of the congressional war hawks with a slightly disapproving tone. Lewis stated that men of "keener judgment" opposed them.[17]

Many earlier authors had mentioned the western issues in their accounts of the War of 1812, but none had ranked them as comparable with the maritime issues in importance, and this era saw little change in that evaluation despite the revisionism of Lewis and Anderson. Only Carl Russell Fish seems to have paid their views much heed, and his text, *American Diplomacy*, still accepted the maritime explanation in the final analysis.[18] Full acceptance of the theory of western causation waited upon the work of Julius Pratt in a later period. For now, Lewis and Anderson stood as minor indications of the impact of the imperialist movement on interpretations of previous expansion.

Lewis's and Anderson's disapproval of the war hawks demonstrated that while the imperialist movement sensitized the history of westward expansion, it did not produce universal approbation of all of its aspects. H. B. Fuller roundly condemned America's method of acquiring Florida.[19] Isaac Joslin Cox, the first historian to use the Spanish archives extensively in connection with the issue, was less vehement but still critical.[20] Only Edward Channing, among all the major historians writing in the imperial era, defended America's course in Florida unequivocally.[21]

14. Lewis, "Re-analysis of the Causes of the War of 1812," pp. 507, 583; and Anderson, "Insurgents of 1811," pp. 170, 174–175.

15. Lewis, "Re-analysis of the Causes of the War of 1812," p. 583.

16. *Ibid.*, p. 578; and Anderson, "Insurgents of 1811," p. 171.

17. Lewis, "Re-analysis of the Causes of the War of 1812," p. 578.

18. Fish, *American Diplomacy* (1915 ed.), pp. 171–174.

19. Hubert Bruce Fuller, *The Purchase of Florida: Its History and Diplomacy* (Cleveland, 1906), pp. 241–243, 330.

20. Isaac Joslin Cox, *The West Florida Controversy, 1798–1813: A Study in American Diplomacy* (Baltimore, 1918), pp. 660–665.

21. Channing, *History of the United States*, V, 336. For opposition, see Foster, *Century of American Diplomacy*, pp. 258–260; Johnson, *Century of Expansion*, pp. 113, 142–146; Coolidge, *United States as a World Power*, p. 32; Fish, *American Diplomacy*,

Even the sacrosanct Monroe Doctrine, and the Roosevelt Corollary which had been endorsed unanimously if unenthusiastically by the historians of this period, came under at least one strong attack. Hiram Bingham, a professor of South American geography and history at Yale who would later become a Connecticut governor and senator, published a controversial tract entitled *The Monroe Doctrine: An Obsolete Shibboleth.* Bingham did not quarrel with the early doctrine. He believed it had helped Latin American republics maintain their independence for the first seventy-five years of their existence.[22] But the doctrine was based on conditions which had long since disappeared and was looked upon by contemporary Latin Americans as "neither disinterested nor unselfish, but rather an indisputable evidence of our overweening national conceit." Bingham advocated a declaration that the United States had outgrown the Monroe Doctrine, that it realized the Latin nations could take care of themselves, "and that we shall not interfere in their politics or send arms into their territory, unless cordially invited to do so, and then only in connection with, and by the cooperation of, other members of the family."[23]

Bingham did make some converts, including Edward Channing and Archibald Cary Coolidge. Even opponents conceded that the United States ought to avoid intervention in the major nations of South America like Brazil, Argentina, and Chile. But they feared that intervention in the weak, unruly, and strategically placed nations around the Caribbean might remain necessary, a conclusion reinforced by the imbroglio with Mexico and Woodrow Wilson's inability to avoid interference in the Caribbean despite his earlier condemnation of it. Ultimately, even Bingham recanted and agreed that the United States owed it "to the progress of the world . . . to see to it that the republics of tropical America behave."[24]

While historians in the imperial age supported use of the Monroe Doctrine as justification of intervention in Latin America, most also assumed that the doctrine seconded America's historic isolationist policy toward Europe. Worthington Ford, one of the first histo-

p. 200; and Kendric Charles Babcock, *The Rise of American Nationality, 1811–1819* (New York and London, 1906), p. 22.

22. Hiram Bingham, *The Monroe Doctrine: An Obsolete Shibboleth* (New Haven, 1913), pp. 6–7.

23. *Ibid.*, pp. 111–112.

24. Thomas L. Karnes, "Hiram Bingham and His Obsolete Shibboleth," *Diplomatic History*, 3, no. 1 (Winter 1979): 39–57.

rians to gain access to the Adams family papers, applauded John Quincy Adams's insistence on a unilateral policy that would prevent entanglements when Monroe, Jefferson, Madison, and Calhoun had been willing to accept Britain's seductive offer of a joint declaration. Ford considered this sufficient to name Adams as the author of the doctrine.[25] James Schouler defended Monroe as both the author of the doctrine and a true isolationist, citing a letter Monroe had written to Jefferson shortly after the president's message to Congress. In that letter, Monroe had not mentioned Adams's advice but had said he had made the declaration unilateral because the British foreign minister George Canning had already cooled to the idea of cooperation.[26]

While the growth of the Anglo-American rapprochement in this period raised some questions about the sanctity of isolationism, the outbreak of World War I came close to shattering it and changed the terms of debate about the origins of the Monroe Doctrine. Initially the doctrine was cited to support abstention from the war.[27] But interventionists like Albert Bushnell Hart insisted that the authors of the doctrine had never pledged total abstinence from intervention in Europe, only that "we would intervene in America even though there were no distinct aggression upon us, while in Europe we would intervene only when our interests plainly demanded it."[28] Wise as the doctrine had been for its own time, even this mild restraint on intervention in Europe was outmoded, Hart believed. America was a major power and could no longer stand aloof, especially in the present "battle of Armageddon—once more Europe against the Huns."[29] John

25. Worthington C. Ford, "John Quincy Adams and the Monroe Doctrine," *American Historical Review*, published in two parts: 7 (July 1902): 676–692; and 8 (October 1902): 28–52. See also Worthington C. Ford, "Genesis of the Monroe Doctrine," Massachusetts Historical Society, *Proceedings*, 2nd ser., 15 (1902): 373–436.

26. Monroe had also given as reasons the possible offense the Russians would take from an Anglo-American note while the Russians were trying to woo America from rapprochement with England, and the possibility that the United States might lose some credit if Latin America inferred from a joint declaration that the United States was under British influence (James B. Schouler, "The Authorship of the Monroe Doctrine," *American Historical Association Report*, 1 [1905]: 125–131).

27. Roland Usher, *Pan Americanism: A Forecast of the Inevitable Clash Between the United States and Europe's Victor* (New York, 1915).

28. Hart, *Foundations of American Foreign Policy*, pp. 211–216. Hart considered Adams the real author since no one who knew "the cautious and somewhat sluggish mind of Monroe" could suppose that he had had the genius to originate it.

29. *Ibid.*, pp. 225–229, 233–240.

Holladay Latané even argued that the isolationism of John Quincy Adams and the doctrine had been wrong for their own time and that Monroe, Jefferson, and Madison had been right to favor an alliance with Great Britain and a broad declaration against aggression anywhere in the world.[30]

Most of the historical works on the Monroe Doctrine written in this period were better political statements than models of historical research. But this was not the case in the other historiographical area where the Age of Imperialism had its most profound effect, the Mexican War. A host of outstanding works on this topic appeared, notably George Garrison, *Westward Extension, 1841–1850*,[31] Jesse Reeves, *American Diplomacy under Tyler and Polk*,[32] George Rives, *The United States and Mexico, 1821–1848*,[33] and Justin Smith, *The War with Mexico*.[34] All of these works concluded that the Mexican War had not been a part of a slave-power conspiracy, and so this primary instance of early American expansion regained much of its respectability. It owed some of this improved reputation not just to newly discovered historical information and the light cast upon expansion by the imperialist movement but also to new attitudes toward slavery and the Civil War. For the Age of Imperialism was the culmination of what Paul H. Buck has called "The Road to Reunion."

Reconstruction long since had been abandoned, and Northern intervention to secure black rights in the South was a thing of the past. North and South had come together in agreement on the racial inferiority of black people, and both sections now condemned the "excesses" of radical Reconstruction. The "bloody shirt" had palled as a means to rouse Republican antipathies against the Democrats and Southerners, to be replaced by more urgent contemporary issues, such as trust policies and "free silver." As wartime antipathies faded, they were succeeded by paeans to national unity. Southern novelists conquered the North with the pathos of the Lost Cause, and Robert E. Lee's nobility in defeat made him a hero of both sections. The reunion

---

30. He did say, however, that Adams might have been justified since interest in the joint declaration on the part of the British foreign minister, George Canning, had fallen off (Latané, *From Isolation to Leadership*, pp. 28–32).

31. George P. Garrison, *Westward Extension, 1841–1850* (New York and London, 1906).

32. Jesse S. Reeves, *American Diplomacy Under Tyler and Polk* (Baltimore, 1907).

33. George L. Rives, *The United States and Mexico, 1821–1848*, 2 vols. (New York, 1913).

34. Justin Smith, *The War with Mexico*, 2 vols. (New York, 1919).

of the sections was celebrated and symbolized by the appointment of the old Confederate war-horse "Fighting Joe" Wheeler as a commander of American troops in Cuba during the Spanish-American War, an appointment only slightly marred by Wheeler's occasional forgetful cry, "Go get them damn Yankees."

One of the casualties along the "road to reunion" was the slave conspiracy theory of the Mexican War. The first shot against the thesis was fired by Edward Gaylord Bourne in 1900.[35] Bourne noted that expansion into Texas and California had been "on the one hand strongly opposed by some of the ablest champions of [slavery] and on the other hand ardently advocated by its enemies, while the body of its support was in no inconsiderable degree made up of men on the whole indifferent to the slavery question." He argued that the basic motive for the annexation of Texas and the Mexican War was expansion for its own sake.[36]

In rapid order, Bourne's article was followed by numerous books and articles agreeing with and expanding upon this conclusion, including the outstanding works mentioned above. They pointed out that since John Quincy Adams himself had tried to annex Texas for many years, the charge that the movement to acquire it was part of a slave plot was ludicrous, especially as some ardent proslavery advocates like Duff Green had opposed the annexation. These historians recalled that Calhoun himself had opposed the Mexican War whereas the West furnished its major support and that the West rather than the South had been behind the All-Mexico Movement. They now recognized the significance of Schouler's discovery that while Polk's diary demonstrated he had welcomed the Mexican War as a chance to take California, Polk had believed that California would be a free, not a slave, state. These historians maintained that slavery had retarded expansion rather than accelerated it because fear of raising the slave issue prevented the United States from annexing Texas far earlier than it did, and John Calhoun's public announcement that the primary reason for annexing Texas was to save slavery caused the defeat of the first Texas annexation treaty in the Senate.[37]

35. Edward Gaylord Bourne, "The United States and Mexico," *American Historical Review*, 5 (April 1900): 491–502.

36. *Ibid.*, p. 492.

37. George P. Garrison, "The Movement for the Annexation of Texas," *American Historical Review*, 10 (October 1904): 82; Garrison, *Westward Extension*, pp. 30, 225–226; Bourne, "United States and Mexico," p. 492; Reeves, *American Diplomacy Under Tyler and Polk*, pp. 59–60, 137, 324–327; Rives, *United States and Mexico*, I, v, 626–627, 647; II, 129–130, 657–658; William E. Dodd, "The West and

The conversion of historians to this view was extraordinarily rapid and complete. Hermann Von Holst watched the conversion with great chagrin, bewailing the "tendency in the younger historical students to look upon the expansion of the country as the important consideration, and the slavery question as incidental."[38] One of those younger students was his own protégé, Albert Bushnell Hart. In his 1901 *Foundations of American Foreign Policy*, Hart had rated expansion as an important cause of the war with Mexico but secondary to slavery. By 1907, in his *National Ideals Historically Traced*, he had abandoned the slave conspiracy theory completely, a fact that did not escape the notice of his fellow historians.[39]

With slavery dismissed as a cause of the Mexican War, much of the aura of shame that had permeated earlier accounts of America's diplomacy toward Mexico dissipated. The monetary claims against Mexico, which the previous age had seen as trumped-up excuses for aggression, were now portrayed as somewhat exaggerated but "nevertheless . . . worthy causes for protest and even for war."[40] Historians also agreed that America's annexation of Texas had been perfectly legitimate. The Texans had had every reason to rebel. The Mexican regime was "alien in race, language, customs and every social, political and religious conception." It enforced its will on Texas through an "irresponsible, ignorant, vicious and brutal . . . soldiery, led by one of the most greedy and unscrupulous of chiefs."[41] The U.S. government had been quite restrained and neutral toward the Texas rebellion. It had recognized Texas's independence only after the major European powers had done so and had waited nine full years before annexing the province, despite Mexico's obvious inability to reconquer and de-

the War with Mexico," *Journal of Illinois State Historical Society*, 5 (1912): 159–172; and Smith, *War with Mexico*, I, 185–187.

38. Eric F. Goldman, "Hermann Eduard Von Holst; Plumed Knight of American Historiography," *Mississippi Valley Historical Review*, 23, no. 4 (March 1937): 521.

39. Hart, *Foundations of American Foreign Policy*, pp. 68–73; Hart, *National Ideals Historically Traced*, pp. 26, 113; Charles Hunter Owen, *The Justice of the Mexican War: A Review of the Causes and Results of the War, with a View to Distinguishing Evidence from Opinion and Inference* (New York, 1908), p. 154n.

40. Clayton Charles Kohl, *Claims as a Cause of the Mexican War* (New York, 1914), pp. 78–79; Garrison, *Westward Extension*, p. 194; Reeves, *American Diplomacy Under Tyler and Polk*, pp. 85–86; Rives, *United States and Mexico*, I, 418, 432–433, 718; and Smith, *War with Mexico*, I, 74–81, 134.

41. Justin Smith, *The Annexation of Texas* (New York, 1911), p. 21. For general agreement, although more moderately stated, see Rives, *United States and Mexico*, I, 350–351; and Garrison, *Westward Extension*, p. 26.

spite the importunities of the Texans for earlier acceptance into the American Union.[42] But had the Mexican War that followed been equally necessary and justified? Or had Polk cynically provoked it to acquire California? On these questions there was still some division among historians. George Garrison assumed the war was justified since Mexico had broken relations with the United States and declared its intention to fight over the annexation of Texas.[43] Jesse Reeves disagreed. According to Reeves, Polk knew that Mexico was merely blustering and that it would not have fought over the annexation of Texas. But Polk had wanted California. He had intended at first to acquire it by peaceful negotiations, using the monetary claims and the Rio Grande border for leverage. Then Colonel Atocha had conveyed the offer from Santa Anna to give up the Rio Grande border in exchange for $30 million if the United States would make it appear that this had been forced on Mexico. So Polk had turned to warlike measures.[44]

Reeves's account was the only major history of the Mexican War in this era to condemn it as an unjustified war of aggression. Perhaps one reason other historians did not accept his conclusions was that his narrative had a serious logical flaw. He had included as major war provocations the wording of Slidell's commission and the ordering of General Taylor to the Rio Grande, both of which had occurred before Polk's contacts with Colonel Atocha, when Polk was still supposedly following a policy of peaceful negotiations. The contemporary situation also may have contributed to the general rejection of Reeves's outlook. Shortly after the publication of Reeves's book, Mexico overthrew the Porfirio Díaz government. Relations between Mexico and the United States became steadily more acrimonious and culminated in the occupation of Vera Cruz, Pancho Villa's raid into New Mexico, and General John J. Pershing's expedition across the Mexican border. In this atmosphere it was easy for Americans to approve earlier punishments of their exasperating neighbors to the south.

In any case, the two major works published after that of Reeves rejected his contention that Polk had provoked an unjust and unneces-

42. Rives, *United States and Mexico*, I, 382, 718. See also Garrison *Westward Extension*, pp. 33, 88–89, 149; Smith, *Annexation of Texas*, pp. 21–26; Smith, *War with Mexico*, I, 82–83; and Reeves, *American Diplomacy Under Tyler and Polk*, pp. 58–85.
43. Garrison, *Westward Extension*, pp. 106, 132, 136, 149–150, 200–206, 219–226, 236–237. Garrison said that Frémont's plan to stir rebellion in California had been unauthorized and had come instead from Senator Benton by secret instructions through Lieutenant Gillespie.
44. Reeves, *American Diplomacy Under Tyler and Polk*, pp. 188–189, 287–298.

sary war. George Rives agreed that despite its threats, Mexico posed no real danger of war to the United States. But he thought Polk justified in pressuring Mexico for the Rio Grande border and California because Mexico was "persisting in a hopeless and disastrous effort to retain territories which she was wholly unable either to develop or protect."[45]

Justin Smith, on the other hand, refused to concede that Mexico was merely blustering about war over the Texas annexation. Quoting numerous Mexican newspapers, politicians, and historians, he insisted that the Mexicans had wanted to fight. They had avoided an official declaration of war on the grounds that their earlier warnings had made one unnecessary and that without an official declaration they could move their forces northward and begin fighting at any time, leaving America no excuse to strike at Mexico's seaboard or seize territory. Smith believed that Polk had sincerely tried to pacify the Mexicans by sending Slidell with orders to conciliate Mexico over all other considerations. He had sent Taylor to the Rio Grande truly believing that it was the correct border, as well as the best defensive position for the American army. Proof of Mexico's aggressive intent was demonstrated in a letter the Mexican president had written Arista, the commander of the Mexican army, stating that "it is indispensable that hostilities begin, yourself taking the initiative."[46] Smith admitted that Polk had wanted California but argued that Polk had thought he could buy it or simply let American immigration take its natural course, and so his instructions to Larkin, Gillespie, and Sloat had contemplated intervention only if another nation like Britain threatened the province or war actually broke out with Mexico.[47]

Smith's defense of the American course was far more bombastic than that of the majority of historians of his time. Nevertheless, his was the most authoritative book on the Mexican War, based as it was on the archives of Mexico, Britain, France, Spain, Cuba, Colombia, and Peru, as well as numerous books, pamphlets, and periodicals.[48] If historians took Smith's conclusions with a grain of salt, they did generally accept the view that the Mexican War and American expansion had been far more justified than the previous age had allowed. As in the case of Hart, John Bach McMaster's newer writings handled the Mex-

45. Rives, *United States and Mexico*, II, 58, 64, 71, 78–80, 118–119, 129–141, 657–659.

46. Smith, *War with Mexico*, I, 83–96, 116, 138–139, 154–155.

47. *Ibid.*, pp. 127–129, 322–333.

48. *Ibid.*, p. ix.

ican War much differently than had his older textbook.[49] The texts of Carl Russell Fish and John Bassett Moore also joined the consensus.[50] Only Willis Fletcher Johnson, the erratic amateur, clung to the idea that the war was the result of "needless aggression designed and waged for the extension of the slave power," a theme incorporated into his 1916 text, *America's Foreign Relations*.[51]

As the atmosphere of the Age of Imperialism brought historians to new interpretations of the Mexican War, so also did it drive them to look once again at Great Britain's opposition to America's expanding power. The Anglo-American rapprochement and increasing sympathy for the Allies in World War I certainly encouraged revisions in assessments of British enmity in such episodes as the Mexican War, the Oregon controversy, and the Civil War. Since the advocates of Texas annexation and the war for California had defended many of their actions on the grounds that Great Britain was threatening in both areas, the question of British activities and intentions was an important one. Ephraim Adams of Stanford went to the British archives to see if Polk's fears had been justified. Adams did find evidence of British tampering in Texas and California. Palmerston particularly had been interested in an independent Texas as a balance to the United States. But the Mexicans foolishly refused Britain's offer to oppose any American attempt to take Texas in return for Mexico's acknowledgment of Texan independence. Consequently, Palmerston's successor, Aberdeen, had determined to give up attempts to restrict American expansion rather than risk war.[52]

Ephraim Adams also found evidence of British agents seeking to acquire California. However, these agents had acted without instructions and were either checked or reproved for the slight openings they effected. "The theory of an active British governmental design upon California is then wholly without foundation," Adams concluded.[53]

---

49. McMaster; *School History of the United States*, pp. 320–327; *A Brief History of the United States* (New York, 1907), pp. 317–320; and *A History of the American People*, VII, *passim*.

50. Fish, *American Diplomacy*, pp. 244–279, esp. pp. 280–281; and Moore, *Four Phases of American Development*, pp. 167–175.

51. Yet this account was toned down from what it had been in 1903 in Johnson's *Century of Expansion*. Compare p. 174 of *Century of Expansion* with Johnson, *America's Foreign Relations*, I, 307–402, esp. 398.

52. Ephraim D. Adams, *British Interests and Activities in Texas, 1838–1846* (Baltimore, 1910), pp. 226–233.

53. *Ibid.*, p. 264.

He convinced most historians. Rives, for instance, said flatly that Polk's suspicions of British machinations were based on erroneous information.[54] The controversy lived on, however, because later historians accused Justin Smith of ignoring Ephraim Adams's work and "bearing too heavily on the hypothesis of a British conspiracy."[55] As a consequence, much would be written to counter Smith, whose work was considered the standard one on the Mexican War. In fact, Smith had worked next to Adams in the British archives and generally accepted his conclusions.[56] Thus, historians wasted much ink emphasizing the absence of a British conspiracy in a needless attempt to contradict Justin Smith.

Although historians could agree that there was no significant British plot in California and Texas, they reached no such agreement on the controversial aspects of the Oregon settlement. Compared with the research spent on the Texas and Mexican War issues, Oregon was handled shallowly and shabbily by historians of this era. Willis Fletcher Johnson actually believed that Polk could have had 54°40′ without a fight and argued that while the Mexican War was "criminal aggression," the Oregon settlement was "criminal concession." But this was in 1903.[57] By 1916, in his *America's Foreign Relations*, he no longer spoke of taking all of Oregon, and he bewailed the excessive anti-British feeling rampant at the time in the United States.[58] Garrison and Reeves both praised Britain for its conciliatory stand on Oregon in the face of Polk's bluff and gave England primary credit for the compromise settlement.[59] Some historians could not help a sneaking admiration for Polk's defiance of Great Britain. Rives liked his boldness, and Carl Russell Fish noted that America always had found it necessary to compromise when confronted by the British but that "bluff on our part had often hastened agreement."[60] Yet almost all accounts of the Oregon question were moderate toward the British and avoided the obvious opportunities to twist the lion's tail.

The same spirit entered into histories of Civil War diplomacy.

54. Rives, *United States and Mexico*, II, 168.

55. Nathaniel Stephenson, *Texas and the Mexican War* (New Haven, 1921), p. 260.

56. Smith, *Annexation of Texas*, p. vii; and Smith, *War with Mexico*, I, 524n.

57. Johnson, *Century of Expansion*, p. 197.

58. Johnson, *America's Foreign Relations*, I, 403–429.

59. Garrison, *Westward Extension*, pp. 172–173; and Reeves, *American Diplomacy Under Tyler and Polk*, pp. 261–263.

60. Rives, *United States and Mexico*, II, 126–127; and Fish, *American Diplomacy*, pp. 270–271.

The Anglo-American rapprochement helped swing historians to a more moderate view of Britain's conduct during the Civil War. James Schouler, whose account of Civil War diplomacy appeared in 1899 in the sixth volume of his history, still took a hostile view of the British.[61] James Ford Rhodes's two volumes on the Civil War published in 1895 and 1899 were considerably more moderate. But the most striking turning point came with the publication of Frederick Bancroft's biography of Seward in 1900. Bancroft said that for Seward "and the others who wrote in the excitement of the time, there is some excuse" for exaggerated suspicions of British Civil War diplomacy, "but a subsequent generation should avoid this error. Great Britain was neither especially friendly or especially unfriendly." Where Henry Adams had portrayed the negotiations over the Declaration of Paris as a trap laid by the British for the Americans, Bancroft said they were Seward's trap for the British. Bancroft praised the British government for its moderation over the *Trent* affair and the British common people for their steadfast loyalty to the antislavery cause of the Union.[62] James Morton Callahan's *Diplomatic History of the Southern Confederacy* adopted the same view, noting that Lord John Russell had been regarded as unfriendly by the secessionists and reminding readers that "today an undivided nation looks upon England not with the jealousies and suspicions of former days, but as a friendly power, and even as a possible ally in case of national danger."[63]

As the imperial age continued, moderation toward Britain turned to enthusiasm. In 1907, the American Nation Series reached the Civil War with James Kendall Hosmer's *The Appeal to Arms*. Citing a recent article by Goldwin Smith, the last survivor of the English Liberal opposition that had backed the North in the Civil War, Hosmer said that this "warm friend of the North sees little to blame in the conduct of his nation and much to commend; while as regards the great Liberal leaders, John Bright, Richard Cobden, and W. E. Forster, there has been nothing wiser or more magnanimous in the whole history of English statesmanship than their steadfast friendship for the

61. Regarding Britain's recognition of Confederate belligerence, he wrote, "Contempt for the legitimate sovereignty of a friendly nation could hardly have been shown more positively" (Schouler, *History of the United States*, VI, 114).

62. Frederic Bancroft, *The Life of William H. Seward*, 2 vols. (New York and London, 1899–1900), II, 176–177, 192–193, 302–304, 340–341.

63. James Morton Callahan, *The Diplomatic History of the Southern Confederacy* (Baltimore, 1901), pp. 100, 108, 165, 274–275.

Union." Hosmer acknowledged that "such a view . . . runs counter to preconceptions" but insisted on its accuracy.[64]

The final seal of approval for British diplomacy came from Charles Francis Adams, Jr. His biography of his father, published in 1900, had been quite harsh with Britain. Adams had accepted the contention of his brother Henry that Britain had laid a trap for the United States during the negotiations over the Declaration of Paris. In 1912, Adams shifted to Frederic Bancroft's idea that it had been Seward laying the trap and that Britain had negotiated in good faith.[65]

Thus, the United States approached the end of World War I with a historical climate of opinion favorable to interventionist policies and to cooperation with Great Britain and other friendly European nations. Historians had contributed to this climate with their commentaries on contemporary policy and with historical interpretations of past events that implicitly or explicitly endorsed an expansionist and interventionist foreign policy. Accounts of the Spanish-American War on the whole justified America's intervention into the Cuban Revolution and approved of an increased American role in Latin America and Asia. Further interventions in those areas under the Roosevelt Corollary and the Open Door policy were also legitimate although historians accepted them with somewhat greater reluctance and a more ironic tone. Historical accounts of the Monroe Doctrine reinforced an activist policy in Latin America and quoted the opinions of the doctrine's originators to legitimize these actions. Accounts of the Monroe Doctrine also increasingly criticized those aspects of the doctrine that could be interpreted as isolationist toward Europe. Interpretations of various episodes involving Oregon, Texas, California, the War of 1812, and the Civil War softened the once harsh anti-British tone. How much influence such changing interpretations actually had in forming public opinion is impossible to determine, but the historical consensus was clearly in line with the activist spirit of the age.

64. James Kendall Hosmer, *The Appeal to Arms, 1861–1863* (New York and London, 1907), p. 307.

65. Charles Francis Adams, Jr., *Charles Francis Adams* (Boston, 1900); and his "Seward and the Declaration of Paris," Massachusetts Historical Society, *Proceedings*, 46 (1912): 23–81.

PART FOUR

The Aftermath
of the Great War
1919-1939

World War I dampened the interventionist spirit of the Age of Imperialism. Many historians continued to cling to the Wilsonian faith and some even to Theodore Roosevelt's brand of imperialism. But all historical interpretations favorable to America's past interventions and expansion were subjected to severe challenges, and many were overturned. Policies of neutrality and restraint returned to favor.

This sea-change in historical consciousness had begun with the Treaty of Versailles. Wilson's concessions to the demands of America's European allies brought criticism from both the Left and the Right. Even Wilson's defenders excused rather than praised the peace that emerged from the Versailles Conference. The unsatisfactory peace terms helped discredit Wilson's great achievement at the conference, the creation of the League of Nations. Even avid supporters of international cooperation paused when asked to join a League dedicated to preserving what they thought were unjust peace terms on behalf of allies who had proven to be greedy and untrustworthy. The League continued to have many defenders; Wilsonian internationalists may well have formed the majority of historians in the United States even as criticisms of World War I diplomacy reached their peak in the mid-1930s. But clearly the tide had turned away from assertive interventionism.

The Treaty of Versailles had contained an article in which Germany accepted full responsibility for the outbreak of World War I. Historians in America and abroad, using secret materials brought to light at the end of the war, soon challenged this war guilt thesis. Much of the responsibility for the war was now cast upon the Allies. Partly because of this, American historians began to question the wisdom of America's intervention, formerly a sacro-sanct proposition.

As Europe fell into chaos, and fascism cast its shadow over the future, America's historians, politicians, and people tried to learn from their World War I experience. Some argued that the United States should isolate itself from major foreign powers as effectively as it could by barring foreign al-liances, embargoing arms, and even stopping trade with belligerents when-ever a clear interchange threatened to draw America into a foreign war. This spirit led to the Neutrality Acts of the 1930s. Another smaller group believed that an aggressive defense of America's old neutral rights was best calculated to keep America out of war, at least if neutrality was equitably enforced instead of skewed to favor one side or another as the American government had favored the Allies prior to 1917. Still another group of Wilsonian inter-nationalists argued defensively that cooperation with the League was the best hope of world peace. They feared that if Europe went to war, America would inevitably become involved whether it had formed ties to the League or not.

Disillusionment with World War I and the Treaty of Versailles had a significant impact on the historiography of earlier episodes involving Amer-ica's relations with Europe. New interest was generated in the diplomacy of the revolutionary war, the Federalist era, the Monroe Doctrine, and the Civil War. Generally those historical leaders who had advocated neutral and re-strained policies received the most accolades whereas those who could be accused of favoritism toward a European power or of seeking foreign alliances were reproached.

Revulsion against World War I also brought increased criticism of American imperialism in Asia and Latin America. In this case, Wilsonian internationalists joined liberal and conservative isolationists in condemning the imperial surge that had been so unanimously if reluctantly endorsed by historians in the previous era. Now almost all historians of whatever political persuasion welcomed policies that would rectify some of American imperial-ism's greatest abuses. They favored such actions as releasing the Philippines, abrogating the Platt Amendment, recompensing Colombia for Panama, and replacing the Roosevelt Corollary with the Good Neighbor policy. But behind this agreement there lay rather different assumptions held by historians of varying political persuasions.

Conservative isolationists assumed that American rule was probably beneficial to all who fell under its sway but were afraid that imperialism overextended American power and risked foreign entanglements that might lead to further major wars. Liberal and radical isolationists were inclined to think that American imperialism was harmful to the colonized peoples. These critics were more affected by the rise of cultural relativism in this era, which made them less convinced of the benefits of American civilization for different peoples and more respectful of foreign or even primitive cultures. They wished in any case to be rid of commitments that detracted from domestic reform. Wilsonian internationalists also tended to esteem different cultures and to accept the rights of national self-determination. They too were less chauvinistic about the superiority of "the American way" than most earlier historians. But they still thought an activist policy was necessary in "backward areas" like Asia and Latin America. They sought to overcome their qualms about intervention abroad by supporting cooperative enterprises with the League of Nations or some sort of Pan American organization rather than unilateral American action.

Condemnation of America's past continental expansion was not so unanimous among historians as was opposition to imperialism in the post-World War I era. There were more criticisms of the Mexican War, U.S. policy toward the Indians, and other expansionist episodes than there had been in the Age of Imperialism. Yet there were also some strong defenders of westward expansion. Conservative isolationists still made a clear distinction between expansion on the near-empty continent and imperialism in thickly populated areas abroad. Frederick Jackson Turner's favorable interpretation of frontier movements still had tremendous influence, projecting a democratic, egalitarian, and pragmatic image of the frontiersmen who led the march westward. So the pendulum of historical interpretation did swing back toward policies of neutrality, restraint, and antiinterventionism, but in a complex and somewhat limited way.

The post-World War I era also saw the emergence of diplomatic history as a separate and identifiable discipline within the historical profession. The quality of historical research in the field of diplomacy took a significant step forward with the work of such men as Samuel Flagg Bemis, Julius Pratt, Dexter Perkins, and Arthur Whitaker. The quantity of monographs on diplomatic topics rose appreciably as well, and textbooks on American foreign policy by Bemis, Latané, and others incorporated the new findings into coherent narratives of the whole of America's diplomatic history. In addition, progressive history reached the pinnacle of its influence within the historical profession. Diplomatic historians had always been heavily present-minded and anxious to relate past experience to modern concerns, so the preachings of Charles Beard and James Harvey Robinson brought no revolution in that regard. The liberal ideology of the progressives, on the other hand, would continue to have an important bearing on the historical interpretations of diplomatic historians. There were many varieties of progressive ideology, however, and liberal reactions to World War I took some startlingly diverse directions, leading to a variety of interpretations of past diplomatic events.

EIGHT

The Treaty of Versailles and the League of Nations

Contemporaries generally agreed that Woodrow Wilson was at the height of his prestige on the eve of the Paris Peace Conference. He had led a united America into World War I and invested intervention with a moral purpose that had won many skeptical liberals to his side. Wilson's call for a world organization to prevent future holocausts also commanded well-nigh universal support in the United States, despite the fact that it meant permanent foreign entanglements. The wild greeting Wilson received in Europe seemed proof that his ideas of a just peace and a League of Nations would triumph there as well. Such a peace would provide at least some consolation for all of the blood the western world had shed.

But by 1920, when the Senate rejected the Treaty of Versailles for the second and final time, opinion in the United States had shifted drastically. While Henry Cabot Lodge and the Senate Foreign Relations Committee had stalled the issue for months, calling witness after witness to chip away at the treaty's shortcomings, popular support for Wilson and his peace had eroded. There did remain throughout this period enough Senators to provide a two-thirds majority in favor of the treaty if certain of the Lodge reservations were accepted. But a combination of anti-League Senators and uncompromising pro-League Democrats foiled Senate ratification. By 1920 Americans on all sides regarded the treaty as a poor one, and the spirit of intervention that lay behind it was severely discredited. The beneficiaries of American intervention in Europe were seen as unworthy of the effort, the risk, and the bloodshed it had entailed.

The sense of a wasted war and a failed peace permeated the historical atmosphere of the 1920s and 1930s. Wilson's detractors vilified the president and his peace. Wilsonians admitted the peace's defects but excused Wilson's failures by blaming them on vindictive statesmen abroad and partisan opponents at home. Most histories of the peace negotiations written by Americans in this era actually defended Wilson and his League. But clearly the authors of these histories felt themselves outnumbered among the general population of the United States, and interventionism seemed to be on the defensive in the historiographical battle.

Wilson's opposition on the League issue was a strange composite. Among his opponents were a few isolationist liberals who all along had considered Europe unworthy of American intervention. They had opposed World War I and the League of Nations as a diversion from essential domestic reforms. They were joined by a far more numerous and influential group of disillusioned Wilsonian liberals who had supported the war in hopes that it would be followed by a peace modeled on Wilson's Fourteen Points. This would be a peace generous to America's late enemies and based on the ideals of democracy and self-determination. Thus, future American intervention would necessarily be just, for it would be in support of this peace and in cooperation with the League of Nations. When the Treaty of Versailles fell short of the liberals' expectations, many of them abandoned interventionism, condemning the treaty as a Carthaginian peace and a betrayal of Wilson's principles. One of their major spokesmen was William Bullitt, a former aide to Wilson. Wilson had sent Bullitt to Russia to negotiate with Lenin during the Paris Peace Conference but subsequently had rejected Bullitt's advice that the new Soviet regime be accommodated. Bullitt had then turned against Wilson's treaty, and his testimony before Lodge's Foreign Relations Committee had done much to inspire opposition to the Versailles pact.

Another significant part of this antitreaty coalition was a more conservative group led by Henry Cabot Lodge. Lodge and his friend, Theodore Roosevelt, along with a good portion of the Republican party, had been strongly in favor of World War I. In fact, they had berated Wilson for not going to war sooner and for failing to prepare the country's military forces for the coming fray. They did not object to an interventionist foreign policy so much as to what seemed Wilson's utopian dream that the mere existence of a League would deter war and prevent the need for further military preparedness on the part of the United States. If America were to intervene abroad, it should do so more unilaterally, conscious of the sacrifices required, and in pursuit of substantial American interests, not hazy idealistic internationalism. To gain a solid peace was to crush Germany, not to tie the United States to a League of Nations and expect such a weak reed to keep the peace in the face of a revived Germany. A week after Wilson left for Paris, Lodge told the Senate that Europe should be permitted to dismember Germany and exact heavy reparations from it. When Wilson returned with the finished treaty, Lodge and his allies gleefully borrowed every argument they could from the disillusioned Wilsonians. But they were notably silent on those parts of the treaty that the former Wilsonians considered unduly harsh toward Germany.[1]

Finally, the antitreaty coalition did its best to attract some people on ethnic grounds. Germans, of course, would be expected to oppose the treaty as excessively harsh toward the Old Country. The Irish, who detested the British and their empire, damned the treaty as hypocritical for supposedly supporting self-determination yet creating a League of Nations dedicated to preserving the territorial integrity of its members. Conceivably, this meant that the whole world would aid Britain in suppressing Irish independence.

Antitreaty material was widely distributed through newspapers, magazines, and especially through the Senate Foreign Relations Committee hearings. There quickly followed book-length histories and memoirs giving complete accounts and interpretations of both the peace negotiations in Paris and the battle over the treaty in the United States.

Ironically, the most influential books making the case for the disillusioned Wilsonian liberals were written by Englishmen rather than by Americans. The first was *The Economic Consequences of the Peace* by John Maynard Keynes. Keynes had been the Treasury Department representative on the British peace delegation and had resigned in protest against the treaty terms. He criticized the treaty for being too harsh toward Germany, depriving that nation of territory necessary to its economic survival. Besides this, the treaty failed to place an upper limit on the amount of reparations Germany was expected to pay. By permitting the Allies to include pensions and military separation costs

---

1. For an excellent analysis of this position, see William C. Widenor, *Henry Cabot Lodge and the Search for an American Foreign Policy* (Berkeley, 1980).

under the heading of civilian damages to be reimbursed by Germany, the sum was guaranteed to be more than Germany could afford. Such terms would destroy the German economy, and since the rest of Europe was tied to Germany by hidden psychic and economic bonds, all of Europe would collapse, leaving the way open for the horror of Bolshevik revolution.[2]

Keynes could excuse a suffering France its insistence on a Carthaginian peace. So long as Germany remained intact, its superior population and resources would overshadow France. But Wilson knew that a harsh peace would only inspire German revanchism, and his negotiating collapse was "one of the decisive moral events of history."[3] Although most of Wilson's advisers were "dummies," Colonel House had had "vastly more knowledge of men and of Europe than the president" and might have saved him from his catastrophic concessions had Wilson heeded him more.[4] Unfortunately, the president had not only compromised, but in his Presbyterian sanctimoniousness denied that he had done so, setting the "subtlest sophisters and most hypocritical draftsmen" to work to clothe with insincerity the language and substance of the whole treaty.[5]

Keynes, an economist, had concentrated his criticisms on the economic portions of the treaty. Other disillusioned liberals emphasized the ways in which the treaty had violated the principle of national self-determination. Wilson's failure to overturn the secret treaties signed between the Allies prior to U.S. intervention had meant that Italy had taken over the German-speaking Tyrol and Slavic-speaking areas of the eastern Adriatic. Other Germans had been sliced away from the homeland and placed under the control of Poland, Czechoslovakia, and France. China's Shantung Peninsula had been handed to Japan. And the League of Nations, with its commitment to defend its members against aggression, would be more likely to preserve the unjust portions of the peace rather than correct them. Thus, these liberals saw little to regret when the Senate voted down ratification.

Although disillusioned liberals had great influence on the intellectual world and on later historians, their impact on contemporary popular opinion was not very profound. Conservative critics struck a more responsive chord in the American public. While liberals criti-

2. John Maynard Keynes, *The Economic Consequences of the Peace* (New York, 1920), pp. 5–7, 113–225.
3. *Ibid.*, p. 37.
4. *Ibid.*, pp. 39, 43–45.
5. *Ibid.*, pp. 51–52.

cized the peace terms as draconian and praised the concept of the League of Nations, conservative critics did not see the peace as unduly harsh but objected instead to the European entanglements required by the League. This was the position of most newspapers that opposed the treaty.[6] Certainly it was the position of Henry Cabot Lodge. In his Foreign Relations Committee, Lodge encouraged both liberal and conservative attacks on the treaty. But in his own book, *The Senate and the League of Nations*, he took the conservative position.

According to Lodge, Wilson should have said "that the boundaries to be fixed in Europe were nothing to us, that we wanted a peace which would put it beyond Germany's power for many years to attempt again to destroy the peace of the world and the freedom and civilization of mankind. . . ." Lodge did oppose the Shantung concession and some aspects of the Central European territorial settlement, and he took a sidelong swipe at the violations of self-determination contained in the mandate system and the British Empire.[7] But he concentrated his attack primarily on the League of Nations. Lodge never made clear in his book whether he had honestly favored the League so long as reservations were added or wanted it killed outright. He implied that he supported the League with reservations, and he censured Wilson for allowing the treaty's defeat by refusing to compromise. Yet he spent an entire chapter defending himself against charges of inconsistency by showing that in 1917 he had already publicly repudiated his earlier 1915 advocacy of a League. He also admitted that he did not regret the ultimate defeat of the treaty and the League.[8]

Lodge buttressed his arguments against Wilson's peace with the opinions of Wilson's own secretary of state, Robert Lansing. Lansing's opposition to certain aspects of the Treaty of Versailles became public knowledge during the treaty fight. Lodge's committee had drawn him out somewhat when he had testified personally before them. Then William Bullitt had revealed to the committee some further hostile opinions Lansing had expressed to him in private conversations. Lansing was upset at this because he still wanted the treaty ratified. Ratification would end the state of war and provide a chance to restore

---

6. Thomas A. Bailey, *Woodrow Wilson and the Lost Peace* (New York, 1955), pp. 305–306.

7. Henry Cabot Lodge, *The Senate and the League of Nations* (New York and London, 1925), pp. 98–99, 170–171.

8. *Ibid.*, pp. 133–134, 214–215.

stability in Europe before the Bolshevik movement took advantage of the chaos existing there.[9]

To deal with the controversy caused by all of this, Lansing published a personal history of the treaty negotiations. His opinions emerged from this book as a mixed and confusing lot, but on balance they supported the conservative critics of the peace. On the liberal side, he vigorously opposed handing the Shantung area of China over to Japan.[10] He also gave at least some support to the liberal contention that the treaty was too hard on Germany.[11] Yet Lansing emphasized these liberal criticisms very little in his book. He did not even mention the reparations issue, and his critique of the colonial mandate system had nothing to do with national self-determination.[12]

By far the more important charges Lansing leveled at the Treaty of Versailles were conservative ones. He condemned the attempt to make national borders conform to the principle of popular self-determination because this conflicted with strategic and economic interests and imperiled national safety, "always the paramount consideration in international and national affairs."[13] He opposed the League of Nations because he thought judicial settlements of international quarrels more practical than the use of force, and he objected to any surrender of America's right to a unilateral foreign policy.[14] He also criticized Wilson's decision to attend the Paris Conference personally, his unwillingness to seek the advice of his fellow delegates, and his refusal to accept the Lodge reservations when they became necessary to gain senatorial consent to the treaty.[15] All of these criticisms would become the subjects of later historiographical disputes.

Although the critics of the Treaty of Versailles triumphed in the Senate and the majority of American people came to oppose U.S. participation in the League, Wilson had his defenders among historians. Probably the most important was Ray Stannard Baker, a newspaperman who had handled press relations among other chores for the president. Wilson authorized Baker to use the presidential papers to write an account of the treaty issue. Baker first wrote a short volume

9. Robert Lansing, *The Peace Negotiations, A Personal Narrative* (London, 1921), pp. 240–248.

10. *Ibid.*, pp. 217–239.

11. *Ibid.*, pp. 164, 272–273.

12. *Ibid.*, pp. 133–143.

13. *Ibid.*, pp. 85–87.

14. *Ibid.*, pp. 34–37.

15. *Ibid.*, pp. 8, 247–248.

based on his own memories, entitled *What Wilson Did at Paris.*[16] He followed this with a three-volume gloss on this earlier memoir, entitled *Woodrow Wilson and World Settlement.* It included large excerpts from Wilson's papers as well as a connecting historical narrative.[17]

It is one measure of the thoroughness of the victory of Wilson's opponents that Baker was willing to go as far as he did in admitting the shortcomings of the Treaty of Versailles. Baker's primary purpose in writing his book was to account for Wilson's failure to achieve the new order he so ardently had desired. Baker blamed Wilson's failure first on his domestic opponents like Robert Lansing, who had been fearful of the principle of self-determination and who believed still in an isolated America devoted to its own "selfish development."[18] On the other side of the Atlantic, Wilson faced the formidable opposition of Europeans dedicated to the principles of the "old diplomacy." Like Lansing, they would base territorial settlements on the principles of national security and balance of power rather than on self-determination and the welfare of the inhabitants of disputed areas. Despite the lip service paid to Wilson's Fourteen Points, these European leaders had come to the conference determined to adhere to the terms of the secret treaties they had signed among themselves during the war.[19]

Why had Wilson led his constituents to expect a glorious and just peace when he knew the secret treaties would make such a peace difficult to achieve? Why had he led Germany to believe it could expect peace on the basis of the Fourteen Points when the secret treaties stood in the way of their fulfillment? Wilson had been attacked for ignoring these treaties and had gotten around it ingenuously by professing to a group of Senators that he had been unaware of their terms prior to his arrival in Paris. Baker himself tried to obscure the issue. "In America we knew little and cared less about these European secret treaties," he said. Wilson himself, although knowing generally of some agreements between the Allies, did not recognize their importance, and his indifference was shared by Lansing, Colonel Edward House, and others who knew of their existence. "While the president must have known in general of these secret agreements, for he often excoriated the practices of 'secret diplomacy,' he apparently made no at-

16. Ray Stannard Baker, *What Wilson Did at Paris* (Garden City, N.Y., 1919).
17. Ray Stannard Baker, *Woodrow Wilson and World Settlement*, 3 vols. (Garden City, N.Y., 1922).
18. *Ibid.*, I, 15–17.
19. *Ibid.*, pp. 24–26, 80.

tempt to secure any vital or comprehensive knowledge," Baker claimed. When one of the British commissioners, Arthur J. Balfour, came to Washington and briefed Colonel House on the treaties, House said he was not particularly interested and "apparently let it drop without reference to the president." With this preparation, Baker then quoted Wilson's flat denial to the Senate of any knowledge of the treaties, without noting the contradiction between that and his previous admission that the president must have known at least something. Baker passed it off by criticizing instead "American ignorance and failure to 'pay any attention' to such vital diplomatic matters."[20]

Baker also defended Wilson's decision to attend the conference in person. Wilson was viewed by people all over the world as the embodiment of the high principles and hopes he had enunciated, an influence which still might triumph over the old diplomacy.[21] Wilson had, after all, fought the good fight in Paris. Contrary to the assertions of Lansing, Baker thought Wilson had consulted widely with his advisers, although perhaps not as much as he should have with his fellow American delegates. Wilson was always open to new information, but he was not open to challenges to his basic principles, principles to which he had dedicated his life. Since Lansing had challenged Wilson's principles rather than offering practical information, Wilson shunned him. But this should not be mistaken for arrogance or refusal of counsel.[22]

Perhaps Baker's major contribution to the historiographical melee over the treaty was his extremely critical view of Colonel House. After Wilson had held his own against the Carthaginian proposals of his European counterparts, he had returned briefly to the United States in mid-conference to sign bills passed by Congress in his absence. He left Colonel House in charge of the American delegation. According to Baker, the Europeans used the opportunity to get from Colonel House what they had failed to get from Wilson himself. Their vehicle was a preliminary military peace settlement that Wilson had agreed should be promulgated in his absence to restore order and prevent the rise of bolshevism. The European ministers crammed into this supposedly bare-bones military agreement most of the important substantive questions in which they had an interest. Conspicuously absent from the matters inserted into the military settlement was the

20. *Ibid.*, pp. 32–36.
21. *Ibid.*, pp. 3–4, 99.
22. *Ibid.*, pp. 114–115, 188.

League of Nations Covenant that the conference had adopted just before Wilson's departure. Baker saw this as an intrigue of the Europeans to separate the League from the most important elements of the peace, settle their own demands in this preliminary treaty, and leave the League to the formal separate settlement where it could be defeated without affecting the other major provisions of the peace.

On Wilson's return, the president had managed to thwart this nefarious plan by suddenly publishing to the world a statement to the effect that the conference had already agreed the League would be an inseparable part of the treaty. None of his opponents could afford to defy publicly the popular Wilson at that point, so Clemenceau called off the plot. But the pliable Colonel House had already made so many concessions to the demands of the representatives of the old diplomacy that Wilson could never quite retrieve the strong position he had held at his departure. Weakened also by noisy opposition at home, the president had been required to compromise against his will and beyond his expectations.[23]

In 1928, Charles Seymour, professor of history and soon to be president of Yale University, brought out the fourth volume of his edition of *The Intimate Papers of Colonel House*.[24] Arranging the colonel's papers to form a running narrative, Seymour defended House against the aspersions cast on him by Ray Stannard Baker. Seymour, with House's aid, sought to demonstrate first that the Americans had had little choice but to accept the compromises required of them by their allies and, second, that those compromises had been the responsibility of Wilson, not House. For instance, House had advised Wilson against calling for the election of a Democratic Congress, an act which had helped to destroy bipartisan support of Wilson's foreign policy.[25] House also had advised Wilson to appoint Elihu Root or William Howard Taft to the peace delegation to pacify the Republican opposition and to guarantee acceptance of the treaty and the League at home. Wilson rejected this advice.[26]

At the peace conference itself, House had favored a preliminary treaty of peace that would settle conditions in Europe and remove the pressure from the conference. Delaying discussions of the League

---

23. *Ibid.*, pp. 306–313.
24. Charles Seymour, ed., *The Intimate Papers of Colonel House*, 4 vols. (Boston and New York, 1926–1928).
25. According to Seymour, House expressed his disapproval in the manner he always did, not by direct contradiction, but by silence (*ibid.*, IV, 68, n. 1).
26. *Ibid.*, p. 221.

would not have endangered the world organization at all, House and Seymour argued. In fact, Wilson had dissipated his strength in fighting for the League so that when he finally confronted the discrepancies between the secret treaties and his Fourteen Points, popular pressure for a quick settlement and public abuse of Wilson for delaying it had undermined his negotiating position.[27] Thus, House and Seymour implied that the concessions made to the old diplomacy at Paris had been the consequences of Wilson's own actions.

Unfortunately, the necessity of making significant concessions to the Europeans did not become apparent until after Wilson had left for home. Then the need "suddenly" appeared.[28] Wilson had left House in charge and had specifically said that he did not want his absence to stall discussions of the major issues. The inclusion of territorial and economic issues in the preliminary military treaty was not part of a plot to exclude the League of Nations from the peace. It came about because delays in agreeing to military terms had allowed time for the negotiation of some of these other problems. With Europe in such turmoil, it seemed wise to include as much in the preliminary treaty as possible. House and Lansing had even inserted the words *inter alia* (translated as "among other things") into the preliminary agenda so that the list of issues to be discussed in the preliminary peace could be interpreted to include the League of Nations. Seymour and House included letters and memoranda from Arthur Balfour to buttress their argument, and they dealt with the issue so successfully that the idea of a plot against the League was not taken seriously by historians from then on.

Since Seymour and House dismissed the plot theory, they did not even mention Wilson's "bombshell" announcement on his return to Paris that despite rumors to the contrary, the League would be part of the peace treaty. Moreover, they asserted, House had committed Wilson to no compromises in his absence. Yet they had to admit that negotiations were far advanced on several critical issues. House had at least implied agreement to refer reparations to a commission without any upper limit on the amount to be demanded from Germany and had allowed that the Saar and Rhine should be separated from Germany for at least a period of time.[29] Nonetheless, House clearly felt he had not committed Wilson to these compromises, and throughout the

27. *Ibid.*, pp. 202–204, 321.
28. *Ibid.*, p. 379.
29. *Ibid.*, pp. 382–383.

book House and Seymour spoke of any concessions as "Wilson's compromises."[30]

Once the treaty had been completed, House advised Wilson to approach the Senate in a conciliatory manner. He was disturbed that Wilson seemed in more of a fighting than a statesmanlike mood.[31] Then, after Wilson's relations with Colonel House had soured, House tried to relay a message from the British to the bedridden president that Wilson should instruct his Democratic followers to accept the treaty, with reservations if necessary, in order to get it ratified. Again Wilson had spurned House's advice.[32]

Seymour and House professed to be puzzled by the termination of the close relations between Wilson and House, something they termed a "lapse" rather than a break. Certainly they saw nothing in House's conduct to justify it, nor did the "lapse" come immediately after some conflict on an issue that could make it understandable. Since Wilson had maintained his affectionate relationship with House for some time after his return to Paris, it could not have been that Wilson believed House had bowed before a European intrigue or made unnecessary concessions.[33] In fact, House said he was distraught over all the concessions Wilson had made. "While I should have preferred a different peace, I doubt whether it could have been made, for the ingredients for such a peace as I would have had were lacking at Paris," he wrote. "And yet I wish we had taken the other road, even if it were less smooth, both now and afterward, than the one we took. We would at least have gone in the right direction and if those who follow us had made it impossible to go the full length of the journey planned, the responsibility would have rested with them and not with us."[34]

Thus, even House concluded the treaty was a bad one. The sense of tragic failure permeated his memoir although House could not restrain himself from defending his own role and, however gently, sliding responsibility for the concessions made in Paris back onto the shoulders of President Wilson. This tendency to apportion guilt for the lost peace bothered R. C. Binkley, who paused in 1929 to survey the historiography of the problem in an article for the *Journal of Modern History* entitled "Ten Years of Peace Conference History."[35] The naïveté

30. See, *e.g.*, *ibid.*, pp. 408–409.
31. *Ibid.*, p. 487.
32. *Ibid.*, pp. 508–511.
33. *Ibid.*, pp. 512–517.
34. *Ibid.*, pp. 488–489.
35. Robert C. Binkley, "Ten Years of Peace Conference History," *Journal of Modern History*, 1 (1929): 607–629.

of historical attempts to assign guilt for the outbreak of World War I should provide a warning to historians of Versailles, he said, but unfortunately, peace conference history seemed to be developing the same way.[36]

Despite Binkley's warning, the questions of guilt for the failed peace raised by Keynes, Lodge, Baker, and House continued to form the interpretive framework for later historical treatments of the treaty issue. But the emphasis shifted somewhat. The defenders of Wilson turned their major attention from the peace treaty itself to the Senate fight over ratification. One of the most important of these works was *The United States and the League of Nations* by D. F. Fleming.[37] Fleming blamed the shortcomings of the treaty as well as its Senate defeat on the Republicans, especially Henry Cabot Lodge, rather than on Wilson. He thought Lodge had been determined from the first to undermine Wilson's diplomacy and had formulated the Lodge amendments to the League Covenant with Theodore Roosevelt even before Wilson had negotiated that part of the treaty. The two conspirators had reasoned that if Wilson accepted the amendments, his prestige would be diminished and credit for the peace would be shared by the Republicans; if the amendments led the stubborn president to resist and kill the treaty, all well and good.[38] By insisting that Wilson secure amendments to the League Covenant on his return to Paris, they had forced the president into a position in which he would have to pay the price of other concessions to get agreement from the Allies. His enemies then had condemned him for the concession they themselves had made inevitable while belittling the amendments he had secured as worthless.[39]

Even so, Fleming insisted the peace had not been that bad. But Lodge was implacable, veiling his true intentions from even his relatives and close associates.[40] Fleming believed that Lodge wanted to

36. *Ibid.*, p. 607.
37. D. F. Fleming, *The United States and the League of Nations, 1918–1920* (New York, 1968; originally published 1932).
38. *Ibid.*, pp. 63, 74–75.
39. *Ibid.*, p. 174.
40. Theodore Roosevelt's sister, as a guest in Lodge's home on the day of the final vote on the League, recalled Lodge's saying to her that he had just been set to get the Republicans and Democrats to take the United States into the League with reservations when the White House drew back the Democrats and destroyed the two-thirds majority (Mrs. Corinne Roosevelt Robinson, quoted in *ibid.*, p. 475). Lodge's daughter, on the other hand, wrote that Lodge's "heart was really with the irreconcilables. But it was uncertain whether this league could be beaten straight out in this way, and the object of his reservations was so to

defeat the League, not merely amend the Covenant. Lodge plotted to pack the treaty with just enough amendments or reservations to make Wilson kill the treaty himself and thus take the responsibility for the death of his own dream.[41] Fleming believed Wilson would have compromised enough to win the Senate battle if he had remained healthy. Rejection of the League with its reservations in the hope of a favorable referendum on the peace in the 1920 election was a tragic mistake.[42]

Throughout his book, Fleming spoke almost exclusively of the conservative and opportunistic opposition to the treaty. He ignored the opposition of the disillusioned liberals and claimed that it was Republican partisanship and a recalcitrant Senate that destroyed the dream. The same theme dominated another book published at about this time, W. Stull Holt's *Treaties Defeated by the Senate*.[43] Convinced that the Versailles Treaty had been defeated by unworthy motives, such as Republican partisanship, personal hatred of Wilson, and the defense of senatorial prerogatives, Holt looked back at the whole history of the "anomoly" of requiring two-thirds of the Senate to consent to any treaty. This arrangement "had so increased the opportunities for political warfare unconnected with the merits of the question that many treaties had been lost," Holt concluded.[44]

In the 1930s none of the conservative critics of Wilson produced a significant work defending their position and conduct against the attacks of Wilsonians like Fleming and Holt. There was no need, as the disillusioned liberals did it for them. Once again the speaker for these liberals was an Englishman, this time Harold Nicolson. In his brilliant, witty, and vicious best seller, *Peacemaking, 1919*, Nicolson ridiculed

---

emasculate the Wilson pact that if it did pass it would be valueless, and the United States would be honorably safeguarded" (letter from Mrs. Clarence C. Williams, originally published in the *New York Herald Tribune*, March 7, 1930; quoted in *ibid.*, p. 476). Lodge's grandson and namesake insisted that Lodge had wanted the treaty ratified with reservations and that his heart was not with the irreconcilables. Later, however, as we have already noted, the elder Lodge was glad fate had kept the United States out of the League (Henry Cabot Lodge, *New York Herald Tribune*, March 25, 1930; quoted in *ibid.*).

41. *Ibid.*, pp. 482–484.

42. *Ibid.*, pp. 488–499. Fifty years later, surveying his own book in the light of later scholarship, Fleming was even more convinced that Wilson had had good reason to resist the Senate reservations although he was still willing to concede that it had been a mistake to reject them in the last extremity (*ibid.*, pp. 555–557).

43. W. Stull Holt, *Treaties Defeated by the Senate: A Study of the Struggle Between President and Senate over the Conduct of Foreign Relations* (Baltimore, 1933).

44. *Ibid.*, pp. 306–307.

Wilson and his principles, mocking the compromises Wilson had accepted at Versailles. But in the end, Nicolson hinted that a harsher rather than a milder treaty would have been preferable.[45]

In many ways, Nicolson's book paralleled that of John Maynard Keynes. Like Keynes, Nicolson saw Wilson as a fanatical and obsessed Presbyterian true believer who could convince himself that he had not compromised his principles and that the League embodied all he had sought.[46] Nicolson conceded that Wilson's program was better than a continued dependence on the dangerous and provocative balance of power in the European system.[47] But, in a major departure from Keynes, Nicolson felt in retrospect that Wilson's hopes had been impossible from the beginning. The American election of 1918 and the conduct of the Senate afterward made it clear his work might not be ratified, a fact that Wilson could never bring himself to face during the Paris negotiations.[48] If Wilson did not face it, his European adversaries did. They also knew that the principles Wilson advocated and expected the Americans to protect in Europe often merely were paid lip service in the United States.

> They observed, for instance, that the United States in the course of their short but highly imperialistic history, had constantly proclaimed the highest virtue while as constantly violating their professions and resorting to the grossest materialism. . . . Can we blame them if they doubted, not so much the sincerity as the actual applicability of the gospel of Woodrow Wilson? Can we blame them if they feared lest American realism would, when it came to the point, reject the responsibility of making American idealism safe for Europe? Can we wonder that they preferred the precisions of their own old system to the vague idealism of a new system which America might refuse to apply even to her own continent?[49]

So the European allies used Wilson's weaknesses against him. They whittled away at his proposals, seeking a middle way between Wilson's theology and the needs of a distracted Europe. This was not iniquitous, Nicolson said, but it was unintelligent. "They should have realized that there was no middle path between a Wilsonian and a Carthaginian peace. They should have realized that either was better

45. Harold Nicolson, *Peacemaking, 1919, Being Reminiscences of the Paris Peace Conference* (Boston and New York, 1933).

46. *Ibid.*, pp. 52–53, 202–203.

47. *Ibid.*, p. 192.

48. *Ibid.*, pp. 206–207, 94.

49. *Ibid.*, pp. 194–195.

than a hypocritical compromise."[50] Since Nicolson implied that a Wilsonian peace was impossible, this left only the Carthaginian option.

Nicolson's work had a tremendous impact in the United States. It marked a turning point in the historiography of Versailles and the League. Historians stopped berating Wilson for the compromises he had made in Europe. The concessions to European security were now accepted as inevitable. In the face of the rise of Hitler and fascism in Europe, concessions even seemed desirable. Wilsonians like Fleming and Holt might see in this a vindication of Wilson, a recognition that his concessions were minimal and the treaty was worthy of ratification. But other critics now agreed with Nicolson that Wilson had raised excessive expectations for a millennial peace when he should have let the European allies impose a treaty harsh enough to have prevented Germany from rising again. Post-World War II "realists" would argue in addition to this that Wilson should have compromised sufficiently with the moderate revisionists in the Senate to allow America to join the League and bear at least limited responsibility for enforcing the peace against a revanchist Germany. But in the 1930s, most anti-Wilsonians thought Nicolson's analysis an excellent reason for avoiding European intervention. If Wilson's ideals were seen to be hopeless in Europe and the German problem to be worked out within the old balance-of-power system, probably with war, then America was well out of it. So, whatever Nicolson's intention, his book contributed to the antiinterventionist outlook in America.

In the face of this growing isolationist sentiment, Wilsonian historians fought a rear-guard action on the treaty and the League. Perhaps they actually continued to command a majority of the historical community. But Wilson and his defenders did not fare even this well in the historiographical battle that developed over America's original intervention into World War I. The historiographical attack on America's entry into the war came later than the attack on the Treaty of Versailles. Politics had demonstrated the failure of Wilson's peace effort well before disillusionment with the war itself began to settle in. Soon, however, World War I revisionism was in full swing, reaching its peak about the same time that Harold Nicolson's book was being read in the United States.

50. *Ibid.*, pp. 7, 94–95.

NINE

America's Entry into World War I

One of the most debatable provisions of the Treaty of Versailles was the so-called German war guilt clause. In order for the Allies to justify their demands for war reparations, Germany had been compelled to accept full responsibility for beginning the war. While the debate over the terms of the Treaty of Versailles and the League Covenant raged in the United States and abroad, the debate over the war guilt clause had a life of its own.

Historical materials for a reassessment of war guilt were readily available. The Bolshevik regime in Russia had published much of the secret correspondence in the Czarist government files. These documents had revealed some of the more sordid Allied war motives, motives which many Americans saw reflected in the negotiations and which led to disillusionment about the whole "war to make the world safe for democracy." In the face of this, rival statesmen rushed their own versions of the war into print, and governments published an unprecedented range of documents shortly after the war ended to defend their own positions. The stage was set for a new battle of the books.

In the United States, Sidney Fay was the first major historian to question Germany's supposed responsibility for the war.[1] In a series of

1. Sidney Fay, "New Light on the Origins of the World War," published in three parts, *American Historical Review*, 25–26 (1920–1921).

articles, Fay exploded the myth that the Kaiser had plotted war in a conference at Potsdam. Fay admitted that Germany had given Austria a free hand to do whatever it wished to Serbia in response to the assassination of the Archduke Ferdinand. But Russia had mobilized before Germany had, in full knowledge that this would compel a German countermobilization. Fay's article made a convert of Clark University Professor Harry Elmer Barnes. Barnes was an accomplished polemicist as well as a man with respectable academic credentials, and he challenged the German war guilt thesis in a far more vigorous and extreme fashion than Fay. In his book, *The Genesis of the World War*, he stood the German war guilt thesis on its head. He assigned France and Russia the primary guilt for the war, saw Austria as a distant third, and assigned the least guilt to Germany and Great Britain.[2]

Barnes thus became the central American figure in a harsh and wide-ranging debate on the causes of World War I. Albert Bushnell Hart attacked Barnes and the revisionists. Arthur Schlesinger wrote that Hart's rejoinder was the best argument for Barnes's position. Other historians, whether specialists in this question or not, joined the fray. Finally, Sidney Fay's long-awaited book, expanding his earlier articles, was published in 1928. His work, unlike that of Barnes, was based on vast research in the original documents and so won a greater prestige among historians if not within the general public.[3] Fay's revisionism was far more moderate than Barnes's, but it demonstrated to the satisfaction of many that responsibility for the outbreak of World War I was borne far more equally by the Allies and the Central Powers than wartime America had allowed.

The destruction of the myth of Germany's sole responsibility for World War I took with it the conviction of many Americans that Germany had posed a threat to the United States. The belief in that threat had rested largely on the idea that the Central Powers had started the war purposely as the first step toward world conquest. Many Americans had been convinced that Germany was a ruthless and brutal military autocracy that would turn on the United States if it won the war. The leading wartime histories had cited this threat as the basic reason for American intervention and had seen submarine warfare as providing only the occasion for fighting Germany. Yet now it was clear that Germany had not planned the war. It was also clear that

2. Harry Elmer Barnes, *The Genesis of the World War: An Introduction to the Problem of War Guilt*, 2nd rev. ed. (New York and London, 1927; originally published 1926).

3. Sidney Fay, *The Origins of the World War*, 2 vols. (New York, 1928).

many of Germany's supposed atrocities in Belgium had been figments of British propaganda. The idea that American participation would make the world safe for democracy had been exploded by the conduct of the Allies at Versailles. Why, then, should the United States have intervened? The war guilt controversy thus triggered a separate debate on America's intervention into World War I.

The first major revisionist account of American intervention, John Kenneth Turner's *Shall It Be Again?*, was published in 1922. This was probably too early to have been affected by the war guilt controversy, but Turner had not needed the work of Sidney Fay or Harry Elmer Barnes to fan his opposition to American intervention. Turner was a journalist of strong Socialist leanings. Like Scott Nearing, he saw the war as a clash of rival imperialisms with which America was best unaffiliated. He thought Woodrow Wilson a willing servant of Wall Street which had taken America into the war to save the pocketbooks of the bankers and merchants dependent on Allied trade. Turner unaccountably omitted from his list of villains the munitions makers denounced by Senators Norris and LaFollette during the war. In omitting the munitions makers, in his strong Socialist leanings and in his denunciations of Wilson as the primary source of America's misfortunes, Turner differed from the main body of revisionists that would follow him. Nonetheless, his history presaged much that would appear in the more extensive and more thoroughly researched revisionist histories to come.[4]

By 1926, the war guilt controversy had reached a crescendo, and revisionist histories of American intervention began to appear as a direct outgrowth of that controversy. In that year, Harry Elmer Barnes presented an account of American intervention as a concluding section of his book on the origins of World War I, *The Genesis of the World War*. That same year, Judge Frederick Bausman contributed his version of American intervention, *Facing Europe*.[5] Barnes and Bausman represented two differing streams of revisionist history. Barnes was a former interventionist, a disillusioned liberal like so many of those who had contributed to the historiographical controversy over the Treaty of Versailles.[6] In contrast, Bausman represented those conserva-

4. John Kenneth Turner, *Shall It Be Again?* (New York, 1922).
5. Frederick Bausman, *Facing Europe* (New York and London, 1926).
6. Barnes did maintain some sympathy for Wilsonian internationalism, however. He favored the League of Nations but balked at military intervention as a weapon of enforcement. See Warren I. Cohen, *The American Revisionists: The Lessons of Intervention in World War I* (Chicago, 1967), pp. 86–87. Cohen's book is an

tive nationalists who had retained the nineteenth-century isolationist resentment of Great Britain, an attitude they shared with members of the German and Irish ethnic groups in the United States.[7] Bausman had published an earlier account of the origins of World War I, denouncing France and praising the Germans for attempting to hold back the Slavic tide of Russia.[8] He disclaimed any ethnic bias, pointing out that although his father had been of German extraction, his mother had been Ulster Irish and had "early taught him that nothing was so glorious as the British crown or so reverend as the Anglican bishop in his lawn sleeves."[9] Yet Bausman's books breathed hostility toward Britain, France, and Russia, and he was one of the chief witnesses in the 1920s campaign led by the Hearst press to eliminate supposed pro-British bias in school textbooks.[10]

Most revisionist historians were, however, disillusioned liberals. C. Hartley Grattan, who was moving increasingly toward socialism in the postwar decades, published the first documented revisionist history of American intervention in 1929, entitled *Why We Fought*.[11] In 1936 he followed this with *Preface to Chaos*, summarizing the conclusions of his earlier book and drawing lessons from it to warn America away from the new conflict looming in Europe.[12] Charles Beard waffled on the issue of American intervention throughout the 1920s but finally emerged on the revisionist side in the 1930s with his book *The Devil Theory of War*.[13] Perhaps the most influential of the revisionists was the liberal columnist for the *New York Herald Tribune*, Walter Millis. His fast-paced and sparklingly written book, *Road to War*, was a best seller in the 1930s.[14] Millis separated himself somewhat from the other revisionists. In the introduction to his book, he acknowledged availing himself of Grattan's *Why We Fought* but said, "my own approach has been a rather different one."[15] In later years, Millis professed surprise and some indignation that his book should have been a

---

excellent one that has greatly aided and influenced the account contained in this chapter.

7. *Ibid.*, pp. 43–45, 92–97.

8. Frederick Bausman, *Let France Explain* (London, 1922).

9. Bausman, *Facing Europe*, p. vi; see also his *Let France Explain*, p. 7.

10. Cohen, *American Revisionists*, pp. 95–97.

11. C. Hartley Grattan, *Why We Fought* (Indianapolis and New York, 1969).

12. C. Hartley Grattan, *Preface to Chaos* (New York, 1936).

13. Charles A. Beard, *The Devil Theory of War* (New York, 1936).

14. Millis, *Road to War*, p. 385.

15. *Ibid.*, p. vii.

bible to isolationists in the 1930s, and he even wrote an article on behalf of interventionism entitled "1939 Is Not 1914."[16]

Millis differed from the other revisionists in that he did not argue directly that America should have stayed out of the war. Instead, he said that the United States should have made its decision for war or peace on rational grounds rather than stumbling blindly into it. Yet Millis described the coming of war to the United States in a debunking style that left little doubt of his belief that intervention was stupid if not malign. Thus, his book closely resembled the rest of the revisionist histories, whatever his intentions.[17]

Joining Bausman to approach the war from the conservative nationalist viewpoint was Charles Tansill, a vehemently segregationist Southerner of Irish descent. His *America Goes to War* was this era's most complete and best-researched of all books on America's intervention into World War I, revisionist or otherwise.[18] Strangely enough, despite the differences in political orientation between the conservative revisionists like Bausman and Tansill and the liberal revisionists like Barnes, Grattan, Beard, and Millis, none of the interpretive conflicts between them can be traced to whether they were liberal or conservative. Charles Tansill denounced the influence of big business on the decision to intervene as ardently as did the liberals, and they in turn denounced the unneutral and pro-British ethnic biases of Americans as thoroughly as did the conservatives.

Thus, all revisionists condemned the British propaganda campaign for prejudicing the United States against Germany and criticized earlier historians for ignoring this British duplicity while dwelling on the far less extensive and far less effective German propaganda effort.[19] Revisionists also saw economic greed as the major factor in bringing about American intervention. But within this general agreement on the importance of the economic factor there were some differing emphases.

The Senate's Nye Committee and the popular press propagated an extreme version of the idea found among the earliest revisionists

16. Cohen, *American Revisionists*, pp. 152, 228.
17. *Ibid.*, pp. 122–123.
18. Tansill, *America Goes to War*, pp. 30–31.
19. Grattan, *Why We Fought*, pp. 35–39; Millis, *Road to War*, pp. 39, 42–43, 58; Bausman, *Facing Europe*, pp. 68–93; and Tansill, *America Goes to War*, pp. 16–31, 297–300, 599–600n. Even revisionists like Grattan, who acknowledged that Americans were predisposed toward Britain well before the British propaganda campaign, dwelt on the evils of British activities for many pages, implying that propaganda had drawn the Americans further and further from true neutrality.

that bankers and munitions makers were largely responsible for influencing America's decision to intervene. Supposedly these businesses had felt it necessary to save the Allies because their narrow economic interests had become thoroughly tied to those of England and France. But when antirevisionists like Charles Seymour attacked the Nye Committee findings by pointing out that the prosperity of the entire nation, not just a few greedy capitalists, had been bound up in the trade with the Allies, revisionists writing later in the era altered their emphasis somewhat.

Charles Beard led the revisionist shift. While conceding that there had been some pressure from narrow business interests, he denied that the war had been caused simply by "wicked politicians, perhaps shoved along by wicked bankers."[20] The whole citizenry had demanded the prosperity brought by the war trade. Thus, the American people had accepted Allied trade and supported loans to the Allies to maintain overseas demand without fully considering how this might entangle America in the war. The key factor, as Beard saw it, was the Wilson administration's reversal of its original decision to prohibit private loans to the belligerents. Wilson was "informed by bankers and by his official advisers that a domestic crash would come" if loans were not permitted, so "perhaps there was no choice," Beard mused.[21] But this decision had tied the welfare of the American economy to the survival of the Allies.

Then had come the crisis, as explained in a telegram dated March 5, 1917, from America's ambassador to Great Britain, Walter Hines Page. Page warned that unless the United States made a direct government loan to Britain, the Allied war effort would collapse. A loan from the American government itself would be an act of war, but America's leaders knew that "a domestic crisis would flow, in all probability, from the defeat of the Allies or a stalemate that thwarted their ambitions. . . ."[22] This had led ultimately to the decision for war.

Wilson's defenders might insist that Germany's submarine warfare had been a primary cause of the war, but Beard thought it only a minor one. As proof, Beard quoted a conversation between Wilson and Senator McCumber that had taken place shortly before the United States had entered the war. McCumber had asked Wilson if America would have become involved in the war even if Germany had com-

20. Beard, *Devil Theory of War*, pp. 18–19.
21. *Ibid.*, pp. 57–59.
22. *Ibid.*, pp. 93–97, esp. pp. 96–97.

mitted no act of war or injustice against American citizens. Wilson had replied, "I think so."[23] The other revisionists were not so quick to denigrate Germany's resumption of submarine warfare as a cause of American intervention. They also did not make so direct a connection between the bankers, Page's telegram, and Wilson's decision to intervene. They thought Wilson and his advisers had already learned to discount Page's advice because he was so blatantly pro-Allied. Page's telegram "contained nothing which was not familiar to the administration, and it had little influence in shaping the decisions of the president," wrote Charles Tansill.

> Despite all the efforts of the Nye Committee, there is not the slightest evidence that during the Hundred Days that preceded America's entry into the world war the president gave any heed to demands from "big business" that America intervene in order to save investments that were threatened by possible Allied defeat.[24]

But this did not mean that Tansill and the other revisionists had let the bankers off the hook. Greedy economic interests had indeed played a part in bringing about American intervention, but a less direct one than Beard had claimed. Big business had influenced Wilson and the American government to violate America's neutral commitments for the sake of the Allies, permitting Britain to stop all trade with the Central Powers while America supplied the Allied war effort. This had forced Germany to resort to submarine warfare, which in turn had brought American intervention. Given the unneutrality of America, Germany had been perfectly justified in using the submarine, the revisionists thought. After all, Great Britain had violated international law earlier and more flagrantly than Germany had. The British had laid mines in the open seas and then gradually instituted a blockade of Germany that starved thousands of civilians. Certainly this was a policy as inhumane as submarine warfare.

23. *Ibid.*, pp. 98–101.
24. Tansill, *America Goes to War*, pp. 133 (including n. 70), 657. Grattan had at first considered Page a major devil in bringing about intervention, initiating the revisionist attack on the ambassador to Britain in an article for the *American Mercury* in 1925 and convincing Barnes so sufficiently that Barnes called Page's activities reminiscent of Benedict Arnold's. But by 1929, Grattan had changed his mind, and so had most of the close students of the issue. "That Page played a part in bringing about the [intervention] cannot be doubted," wrote Grattan in 1929, "but that his position was the determining factor, no one can maintain. His letters were mere pin pricks when compared to the subtle and powerful forces at work on the president" (Grattan, *Why We Fought*, p. 372). See also Barnes, *Genesis of the World War*, pp. 598, 603.

American protests were strictly verbal and thereby totally ineffectual. All the United States had had to do to enforce its neutral rights was to embargo loans and weapons to the Allies or to convoy merchant ships to Germany. Had the United States done so, the revisionists were convinced that America would not have been drawn into the war. Instead, the United States had fallen back on the outdated international law it had used to justify its neutral rights for over a century. It was apparent that modern warfare had rendered many of these neutral rights obsolete, but Wilson's administration had insisted that to change the rules in the midst of a war would undoubtedly redound to the favor of one belligerent or the other and thus in itself be unneutral.[25]

In its response to Britain's illegal blockade, Germany was to be faulted not for immorality but for stupidity. The German government began the submarine campaign too early, before there were sufficient U-boats to make it effective. This gave Britain warning to prepare for a later campaign. It also triggered a confrontation with the United States at a time when the amount of damage the submarines were capable of inflicting on the Allies was too meager to justify the risk of war with America, leaving Germany little option but to retreat in the face of Wilson's protests.[26]

So for a time it looked to some as though Wilson's hard line against the submarine had preserved both the peace and American prosperity. Actually, Wilson had fused a time bomb. He refused to take simple, precautionary measures like forbidding Americans to travel aboard belligerent ships or accepting the right of submarines to sink armed merchant men without warning. He demanded that submarines provide for the safety of passengers and crews aboard defensively armed belligerent ships, thus protecting the lives of Americans who might be aboard. By declaring that he would hold Germany to "strict accountability" for any losses of American ships or lives to submarines that did not obey the obsolete rules of visit and search, Wilson set the stage for the *Lusitania* crisis.

The revisionists considered America's response to the sinking of the *Lusitania* a gross overreaction. The Germans had warned passengers in a newspaper advertisement not to board. The *Lusitania* carried weapons and was listed as an auxiliary cruiser in the British

25. Barnes, *Genesis of the World War*, pp. 596–599; Grattan, *Why We Fought*, pp. 144, 172, 209, 281; Tansill, *America Goes to War*, pp. 37, 40, 64, 144–146, 176–177, 234; Bausman, *Facing Europe*, p. 173; and Millis, *Road to War*, pp. 89, 177.
26. Tansill, *America Goes to War*, p. 244; and Millis, *Road to War*, pp. 136–137.

navy. It flew the American flag as a ruse on occasion, and the captain failed to take reasonable evasive maneuvers even though informed of submarine activity in the vicinity.[27] Grattan claimed in 1936: "At the present time there is no one conversant with such matters who disputes the right of Germans to sink the *Lusitania*."[28] Tansill, quoting Samuel Flagg Bemis, even speculated that the British might have exposed the *Lusitania* purposely to a submarine's torpedoes in hopes of bringing the United States into the war on a wave of indignation.[29]

In any case, Wilson's protest made clear that Germany would either have to abandon effective use of the submarine or face war with America. Wilson's threat, reiterated upon the later sinkings of the *Arabic* and the *Sussex*, did force Germany to back down temporarily. But this fleeting victory had been purchased at an inordinate price. Unless the British respected neutral rights and modified their blockade, Germany might be forced to renew submarine warfare when it had produced enough U-boats to make such warfare effective. In that case, America would be committed to war.[30]

Harry Elmer Barnes believed that Wilson had purposely maneuvered the submarine issue to bring about American intervention. He thought Wilson a willing conspirator with the bankers, munitions makers, Allied propagandists, and pro-Allied advisers Ambassador Walter Hines Page, Secretary of State Robert Lansing, and Colonel Edward House to drag the United States into the war. In this, Barnes was alone among the revisionists. For Barnes, the proof of Wilson's treachery was the president's acceptance of the House-Grey Memorandum of February 1916. According to the memorandum, President Wilson would wait until France and England agreed that a peace conference was desirable and then issue a call for one. If the Allies accepted and Germany refused, America would *probably* enter the war against Germany. If all nations accepted and the peace was not achieved because of German recalcitrance, the United States would leave the conference a belligerent on the side of the Allies. After Wilson inserted another "probably" so that the memorandum read that given German resistance, the United States would "probably" leave

27. Barnes, *Genesis of the World War*, pp. 616–617; Bausman, *Facing Europe*, pp. 222–223; and Grattan, *Why We Fought*, pp. 291–296.

28. Grattan, *Preface to Chaos*, p. 42.

29. Tansill, *America Goes to War*, pp. 288–289. This speculation derived from wartime newspaper theorizing.

30. Grattan, *Why We Fought*, pp. 42–43; Tansill, *America Goes to War*, pp. 238–239, 252–253, 267; Millis, *Road to War*, pp. 187–191; and Bausman, *Facing Europe*, p. 203.

the conference a belligerent on the side of the Allies, he accepted the memorandum. According to Barnes, the terms America had in mind for Germany were such that only a defeated nation would accept them. Despite this, the British and French refused to signal for the peace conference that would trigger American intervention.

> But this British rebuff did not lead Mr. Wilson to lose courage in his efforts to put the country into the War. His next step was taken in this country. Early in April, 1916, Wilson called into consultation Champ Clark, Congressmen Claude Kitchin and H. D. Flood, and sounded them out to see if they would support him in a plan to bring the United States into the War on the side of the Allies. This was the famous "Sunrise Conference" described later by Gilson Gardner in *McNaught's Monthly* for June, 1925. These men sharply refused to sanction any such policy, and Mr. Wilson allowed the campaign of 1916 to be fought out on the slogan, "He kept us out of war." Wilson did not dare to risk splitting the Democratic Party over entry into the War before the campaign of 1916 was success-fully ended. Once elected, he could count on even virulent Republican enemies like Lodge to offset any Democratic defection in Congress over the war problem.[31]

Barnes saw all Wilsonian peace initiatives after 1916 as sheer hypocrisy.[32] Germany was ready for peace on very moderate terms in 1916 and 1917. If the American people had known of these terms, there was no chance that Wilson or anyone else could have forced the United States into the war.[33] But Germany was convinced "quite correctly, that the United States had in practice given up the pose of neutrality and intended to get into the War as soon as possible." Therefore, the Germans began unrestricted submarine warfare as a last hope to force an honorable peace. Even at this, there was little probability that Germany would have conquered the Allies, with or without American intervention. Nevertheless, Wilson now had his excuse for intervention, Barnes concluded.[34]

None of the other revisionists attributed such Machiavellian intentions or actions to Wilson. Bausman and Grattan believed that Wilson had opposed intervention until the very eve of war, not even wavering in 1916 despite the evidence of the House-Grey Memorandum and the Sunrise Conference. Bausman and Grattan argued that Wilson had inserted the word "probably" into the House-Grey Memo-

31. Barnes, *Genesis of the World War*, pp. 626–630.
32. *Ibid.*, pp. 634–635.
33. *Ibid.*, p. 640.
34. *Ibid.*, pp. 632, 640.

randum to escape the binding commitment House had made, although Millis and Tansill disagreed and thought the insertion insignificant. Bausman and Grattan also doubted that the Sunrise Conference had taken place or that Wilson had indicated his intention to intervene at such a meeting. Grattan cited a personal letter from Ray Stannard Baker stating that no records of such a conference existed in Wilson's papers.[35]

Tansill and Millis both accepted the House-Grey Memorandum and the Sunrise Conference as proof that Wilson had moved toward intervention in 1916. But they contended that whatever Wilson's intentions had been at that time, he had quickly abandoned thoughts of intervention and returned to his search for neutrality and peace. They reminded their readers that in early 1916, Germany had been conducting its submarine warfare, and it appeared that this might bring the United States in. But when Germany gave its *Sussex* pledge, ending submarine warfare for an indefinite time, Wilson was able to back away from intervention. At this stage he had also become irritated with the British for their failure to invoke the House-Grey agreement and call a peace conference.[36] Thus, until Germany resumed its submarine warfare in 1917, Wilson had striven sincerely for peace. Unfortunately, the same could not be said for America's businessmen, bankers, and munitions makers, nor for those of Wilson's advisers who were beholden to these interests. "For the first time since the outbreak of the World War, [Wilson] was really neutral in his attitude towards the belligerents," Tansill wrote. "Surrounded by advisers who were eager for war, rebuffed by diplomats who had no thought of peace, President Wilson strove desperately to find some compromise which not only would put an end to the war then raging but would serve as the basis for a new world order."[37] Tragically, his advisers had brought Wilson to commit himself so strongly against Germany's use

35. Bausman, *Facing Europe*, pp. 118–119, 253–256, 258–259, 265, 283–288; and Grattan, *Why We Fought*, pp. 360, 362–364, 367, 372, 380–399, 400, 405–407.

36. Tansill disagreed with the others on the reasons for Wilson's retreat from intervention, however. He said that the Sunrise Conference had taken place during the congressional fight over the Gore-McLemore resolutions, intended to bar Americans from traveling aboard belligerent ships. When Wilson saw the extent of support for these resolutions, he realized how much domestic opposition truly existed to any war over Germany's use of the submarine (Tansill, *America Goes to War*, pp. 465–486, 496–497).

37. *Ibid.*, p. 631.

of the submarine that when Germany resumed submarine warfare, Wilson had to abandon his attempts at mediation and join the fray.[38]

It was at this point that Millis separated himself from the rest of the revisionists. He did not overtly criticize American intervention. He merely argued that Wilson had allowed himself to be maneuvered into a position of leaving the decision for American intervention in Germany's hands. Wilson had lost control. At the beginning, Wilson had had several options; "strict and effective neutrality, impartial intervention to force a peace, intervention in alliance with the Entente, even intervention on the side of Germany, for that matter—might, if consistently pursued, have been made to yield relatively satisfactory

---

38. Among Wilson's advisers, the revisionists had great respect for William Jennings Bryan, whom they considered the only true neutral in Wilson's administration. We have already seen their opinion of Walter Hines Page. Robert Lansing brought some debate among the revisionists. As counselor to the Department of State before succeeding Bryan as secretary, Lansing had formulated some rather strong protests against British violations of American neutral rights. Yet a 1915 memorandum published soon after the war had Lansing saying, "America's task was to save democracy, and . . . she must eventually take part in the war if that course was necessary to prevent a German victory" (quoted in Grattan, *Why We Fought*, p. 208n.).

Bausman and Millis consequently praised Lansing for following legal principles contrary to his pro-Allied sympathies, at least for a while. But Grattan discounted Lansing's protests as "burlesque," and Tansill took an even more jaundiced view. Whatever lawyerlike noises Lansing might have made in protesting British actions, "He was quick to perceive how deeply devoted Colonel House was to the cause of the Allies, and he was keen enough to realize that complete agreement with the colonel's viewpoint was the royal road to official promotion." While most of the other revisionists discounted Lansing's influence as that of a mere lawyer, Tansill noted that a memorandum from Lansing had been the basis for Wilson's reversal of his earlier decision to discourage private loans to the Allies. "This inspired decision of the president clearly indicates how important banking interests were using Mr. Lansing as a mouthpiece of their propaganda," Tansill wrote. "It also shows that Mr. Lansing had far more influence with the president than is generally believed" (Tansill, *America Goes to War*, pp. 162, 77). See also Bausman, *Facing Europe*, pp. 205–206; and Millis, *Road to War*, p. 197).

But even Tansill agreed that House was the most important and insidious of Wilson's advisers. All the revisionists saw House as the *éminence grise* behind Wilson and a man whose one great quality, tact, carried him to tasks far beyond the range of his abilities. Thus, House's inexperience and strong pro-Allied prejudices brought him to shape U.S. peace missions and proposals to favor the Allies and offend the Germans. Barnes, *Genesis of the World War*, p. 598, sees House as purposefully treacherous whereas the rest see him as a dupe of the Allies. See Bausman, *Facing Europe*, pp. 121, 176–190; Grattan, *Why We Fought*, pp. 183, 243–247; and Millis, *Road to War*, pp. 80–87.

results."[39] Unfortunately, Millis concluded, Wilson did not choose a course of action but blundered into war on the peripheral issue of neutral rights.

The revisionists had a tremendous impact on American opinion. Even Wilson's defenders now retreated from the near unanimity of opinion among wartime historians that America had gone to war to protect its own security from a ruthless Germany hell-bent on world conquest. Wilsonians came to agree that the president had asked for war merely to defend America's neutral rights against submarine warfare, not to defeat a real threat to America's security and national existence. Still they thought that Wilson's decision for war had been right and that Germany had no adequate justification for its use of the submarine against America's neutral trade.

In the forefront of the Wilsonian historians was Charles Seymour, whose works on Colonel House had played such a significant role in the historiographical controversy over the Treaty of Versailles. Seymour published three books on American intervention. The earliest was a slim volume for the Chronicles of America Series, *Woodrow Wilson and the World War*, published in 1921.[40] The second was an extensive narrative history of intervention, entitled *American Diplomacy During the World War*, originally given as the Albert Shaw Lectures in 1933 and published a year later.[41] His third book was a collection of interpretive essays designed to refute the Nye Committee and the revisionists, *American Neutrality, 1914–1917*.[42] Seymour was by far the most influential of the Wilsonian historians, being cited as the major authority for the accounts of many textbooks and surveys of the period.

Closely paralleling Seymour's outlook were two other major works of the period, Frederic Paxson's *Pre-War Years, 1912–1917*, itself based heavily on Seymour, and former Secretary of War Newton Baker's memoir, *Why We Went to War*.[43] Standing somewhat apart from this trio, as he had from Seymour during the Versailles controversy, was Wilson's biographer, Ray Stannard Baker. With harsh

---

39. Millis, *Road to War*, pp. 122, 391.
40. Charles Seymour, *Woodrow Wilson and the World War* (New Haven, 1921).
41. Charles Seymour, *American Diplomacy During the World War* (Baltimore, 1934).
42. Charles Seymour, *American Neutrality, 1914–1917* (New Haven and London, 1935).
43. Frederic L. Paxson, *Pre-War Years, 1912–1917* (Boston, 1936); and Newton D. Baker, *Why We Went to War* (New York, 1936).

words for Colonel House, Baker excused but did not defend American intervention, in volumes 5 and 6 of his *Woodrow Wilson: Life and Letters*.[44] Although a Wilsonian, he stood surprisingly close to the revisionists.

Seymour, Paxson, and Newton Baker denigrated the role of British propaganda in American intervention. The genuine brutality of the Germans, reflected in such episodes as the invasion of Belgium and the sinking of the *Lusitania*, had been responsible for the pro-Allied bias of the Americans.[45] But America had not intervened to prevent German victory, these Wilsonians now agreed. If Germany had not renewed its submarine warfare, America would have stayed out.[46]

Seymour, Paxson, and Newton Baker were quick to dismiss extreme revisionist contentions that submarine warfare merely furnished the excuse to save the Allies for the benefit of special interests like bankers or munitions makers.[47] Seymour saw nary a scrap of evidence for this theory. Wilson had made the decision for intervention, and he of all people was least likely to be influenced by the special interests of bankers. Page's cable regarding the financial straits of the Allies had had little effect. Wilson distrusted Page's excessive pro-Allied sentiments, and the cable was left unanswered. In any case, that cable dealt only with problems of future loans, and there was no concern in America about the safety of loans already outstanding.[48] Meanwhile, Newton Baker laughed at the supposed influence of munition makers, remembering how few and weak they were during his tenure as secretary of war.[49]

But if special interests had not directly brought intervention, had they manipulated America's neutrality policy in such a way as to

44. Ray Stannard Baker, *Woodrow Wilson: Life and Letters*, 8 vols. (Garden City, N.Y., 1927–1939).

45. Seymour, *American Neutrality*, pp. 19–22; 149–150; Paxson, *Pre-War Years*, pp. 124, 178–179; and Newton Baker, *Why We Went to War*, p. 24.

46. Newton Baker, *Why We Went to War*, p. 20n.; Paxson, *Pre-War Years*, p. 397; and Seymour, *American Neutrality*, pp. 51–54.

47. Interestingly, in 1933, when Seymour gave the Albert Shaw Lectures, he spent more time refuting charges from the British and French that Wilson had been too dilatory and insincere in his actions against the Germans than Seymour did refuting the revisionists. It was not until 1935 and the Nye Committee that Seymour considered the primary attacks on Wilson to come from those who criticized Wilson for intervening at all rather than those who criticized him for intervening too late. See Seymour, *American Diplomacy During the World War*, pp. 154–157.

48. *Ibid.*, pp. 18, 49, 207–210; and his *American Neutrality*, pp. 1–3, 85–87.

49. Newton Baker, *Why We Went to War*, pp. 118–131.

invite and justify German retaliation via submarine, as other revisionists maintained? Seymour, Paxson, and Newton Baker answered a resounding "No." "The general consensus of historical opinion, with which even [Count Johann von] Bernstorff [the German ambassador to the United States] and the more thoughtful Germans agree," claimed Seymour, "is that while the President may not have been personally impartial, he maintained a technical neutrality in circumstances of greatest difficulty."[50] America was perfectly within its rights to ship arms and allow private credits to the Allies, as even the Germans and revisionists admitted. Also American citizens were entitled to ride aboard belligerent merchant or passenger ships under the protection of international law which prohibited those ships from being sunk without warning and without provision for the safety of crew and passengers. To have accepted changes in those laws, however logical in the face of submarine warfare, would itself have been unneutral.[51]

When Wilson chose to exercise America's traditional neutral rights, he did not expect that this would lead to war, even when he decided to permit private loans to the belligerents.[52] But when the Allies instituted their illegal blockade of the Central Powers, insuring that America's "neutral" trade would benefit only the Allies and inviting German retaliation, why did Wilson not respond with an embargo of war materiel rather than mere written protests?[53] Seymour claimed that such an arms embargo would have done no good. Germany's submarine warfare was designed to stop all Allied trade, not just that in arms. So nothing but a total embargo of Great Britain would have kept American ships and goods out of harm's way.[54] If Wilson had instituted such an embargo, destroying American prosperity while risking a war with Britain on the side of Germany, "he would have provoked something like a revolt against his administration."[55] He

50. Seymour, *American Diplomacy During the World War*, p. 18.

51. Newton Baker, *Why We Went to War*, pp. 26–29.

52. Seymour, *American Neutrality*, pp. 98–109.

53. Seymour, *American Diplomacy During the World War*, p. 17; and Newton Baker, *Why We Went to War*, pp. 46–53.

54. Seymour, *American Neutrality*, pp. 57–61. Of course that misstated the revisionists' point. The revisionists believed that an embargo of war materiel would have reduced benefits of submarine warfare to the point that the risk of driving America into the war with the submarine would not have been worthwhile.

55. Seymour, *American Neutrality*, pp. 8, 98–109; and Newton Baker, *Why We Went to War*, pp. 126–131.

had been correct to rely on written protests that could await the end of the war for settlement.[56]

Even so, British offenses at times tempted Wilson to stronger measures. Each time a crisis was brewing with England, however, a more horrendous incident involving German submarines would divert him.[57] Wilson responded differently to Germany's violations of American neutral rights than he did to those of Great Britain not because he was purposely unneutral but because submarine warfare was far more destructive of American interests, not to mention lives, than the British blockade. Since American shippers could be reasonably assured of safe passage and some legal protection or hope of postwar compensation for a cargo confiscated by the British blockade, Allied policies would not stop American trade entirely. Submarine warfare, on the other hand, would result in "an almost complete blockade of American commerce, since shippers would not dare send cargoes and crew out to destruction." In this case, America could not afford to rely on protests designed to await settlement at the end of the war.[58] Thus, Wilson quickly made clear that continuation of submarine warfare would inevitably lead to American intervention.[59]

By late 1915, according to Seymour, the unwillingness of the Germans to add to the *Arabic* pledge against sinking unarmed passenger liners an overt recognition of the illegality of all submarine warfare had convinced Wilson that war with Germany was inevitable.[60] Consequently, the president had chosen to risk the possibility of an earlier intervention in a last, desperate gamble to jar the belligerents into peace. The House-Grey Memorandum was the key to his effort at "armed mediation." He would call a peace conference and let it be known that if either side rejected it, America would intervene against the obdurate nation. Thus, Seymour accepted revisionist contentions that Wilson had been ready for war more than a year before America actually joined the conflict.[61] But he insisted that this was not a sign of Wilson's supposed warmongering unneutrality. Instead it was a last-gasp effort to avoid war by forcing a peace.

---

56. Seymour, *American Neutrality*, pp. 6–9; and Newton Baker, *Why We Went to War*, pp. 46–50.

57. Seymour, *American Neutrality*, pp. 6–7, 137–138.

58. *Ibid.*, pp. 9–10. See also Newton Baker, *Why We Went to War*, pp. 46–53.

59. Seymour, *American Diplomacy During the World War*, pp. 90–93.

60. *Ibid.*, pp. 100–106.

61. *Ibid.*, pp. 130, 138–140, 156.

Wilson, indeed, had assumed that if intervention did become necessary, it would and should take place on the side of the Allies. The Allies were more likely to accept conditions "which would facilitate a future international organization for preserving peace, whereas an undefeated Germany would always remain a menace to world peace."[62] Besides, America's interests were bound up with those of the Allies.[63] Thus, Wilson and House had agreed in the House-Grey Memorandum to wait until Great Britain indicated readiness for the peace conference before calling it. Wilson's insertion of the word "probably" was not a renunciation of House's commitment but an "unimportant verbal change," regarded as insignificant by both House and Grey[64] despite Lloyd George's later claim that it had been the fatal cause of Britain's refusal to invoke the agreement and call for a conference.[65] Seymour thought Britain's rebuff a terrible tragedy, for Wilson and House would have shortened the war either through a peace of understanding or through intervention.[66]

After this, Wilson had fallen "back into distrust of both sides and a fervid determination to maintain American neutrality," Seymour said.[67] But resumption of submarine warfare would bring America into the war. Germany's leaders knew this, but they resumed anyway in the belief that they could defeat Britain before America's power could be mobilized.[68] Wilson decided to await an overt act before declaring war, but the die was cast. Politically, the delay helped crystallize American opinion behind the president, as the Zimmermann telegram and the destruction of American trade persuaded even the most pacifistic areas of the United States of the necessity for war.[69] The revisionists had maintained that Wilson's decision for war had been a betrayal of the vast majority of Americans who, in the election of 1916, had voted for Wilson as the man who "had kept us out of war." The Wilsonians, however, pointed to the vote in Congress for war as demonstration that the majority supported Wilson's decision.[70]

Ray Stannard Baker agreed with most of the contentions of the

62. *Ibid.*, p. 140; see also pp. 154–161.
63. *Ibid.*
64. *Ibid.*, pp. 143–144, 150–155.
65. *Ibid.*, pp. 154–155.
66. *Ibid.*, p. 171.
67. *Ibid.*, p. 208.
68. *Ibid.*, p. 197.
69. *Ibid.*, p. 203.
70. Seymour, *American Neutrality*, pp. 24–25; and Paxson, *Pre-War Years*, p. 420.

other Wilsonians but differed at several vital points. He considered the roles of House and Lansing to have been as destructive in the prelude to intervention as they had been at Versailles. Wilson alone in the administration had been truly committed to peace and neutrality. Among his advisers, only William Jennings Bryan had shared this devotion, and Bryan's resignation had left Wilson under undivided and unrelenting pressure for intervention from those who remained. Baker's chief assistance on volume 5 of his Wilson biography had come from Jospeh Fuller, who, it emerged, had been the anonymous author of the revisionist sketch of William Jennings Bryan written for Samuel Flagg Bemis's monumental and influential project, *The American Secretaries of State.*[71]

Ray Stannard Baker thought that Wilson had maintained his commitment to neutrality even during the House-Grey conversations. "Whatever his hopeful dalliance with House's scheme as a means of exploring the possibilities in Europe, it is to be noted that he did not at any time change the broad objectives of his own policy," Baker wrote. "He never committed himself on the military interventionist aspect of the scheme, as the British clearly perceived, guarding his freedom of action [by inserting the word "probably"] even in this desperate bid for peace." He never should have placed so much confidence in House, whose "well-intentioned bungling" and confident assurances of support to the Allies had encouraged their relentless prosecution of the war. As a result, the Germans had been driven by desperation to extreme counteraction.[72]

Thus, Wilson had not been ready for intervention in 1915. Baker, too, dismissed the Sunrise Conference as a myth.[73] What, then, had brought the war? On this, Baker was both eclectic and ambiguous. On the one hand, he blamed Germany's submarine warfare, for America's trade had flowed to one side only "by force of circumstances, and in consequence of the fortunes of war. Any measures to redress it after it had developed would thus appear inequitable."[74] Yet Baker clearly wished the United States had used an embargo early in the war to force British respect of America's rights. By the time such a policy was considered, America had become too dependent on its trade with Britain, and an embargo "would have resulted in an eco-

71. R. S. Baker, *Woodrow Wilson*, V, v; and Tansill, *America Goes to War*, p. 165, n. 15.

72. R. S. Baker, *Woodrow Wilson*, VI, 147, 153.

73. *Ibid.*, V, 170–171n.

74. *Ibid.*, p. 180.

nomic shock that America was unprepared to withstand either by knowledge, or vision, or fortitude."[75]

Thus, Baker excused, if he did not defend, Wilson's decision for war. Obviously he regretted it. When the Nye Committee hearings and the work of the revisionists inspired the 1930s movement for congressional legislation to prevent a repetition of 1917 by embargoing arms and loans to belligerents and keeping American passengers off belligerent ships, Baker was thoroughly sympathetic. In his Wilson biography, he had written, "There was no way then to remain truly neutral, there will be no way in future world wars unless we are prepared for the self-discipline and the economic losses resulting from embargoes and other restrictions."[76]

The other Wilsonian historians were not so enamored of embargoes. Newton Baker sympathized with a group, led by John Bassett Moore, who thought that America's best chance for staying out of future wars lay in the historic policy of asserting American neutral rights rather than abandoning them for isolation.[77] Seymour sympathized with still another group skeptical of the rigid Neutrality Acts and instead favoring a large measure of executive discretion. "Automatic embargoes are apt to prove dangerous as well as futile," wrote Seymour. "They withdraw from the Executive a power which may be of great value in his efforts to preserve peace." The power to impose or withhold an embargo was a potent diplomatic weapon, necessary because any European war would affect America. If America abandoned its economic weapons for isolation, it would be driven to build an armament of such size as to stand alone against any invasion of America's vital rights. Instead, the United States should cooperate with other states to stamp out the immediate threat of war whenever it appeared.[78]

Thus, under the pressure of revisionism, Wilson's historical defenders had divided over the way the lessons of World War I should be applied in fashioning the Neutrality Acts that commanded such wide popular support in the period preceding World War II. Some like Ray Stannard Baker would abandon neutral rights for the more cautious policy of isolation from Europe. Others like Newton Baker advocated vigorous but impartial enforcement of American neutral rights against any belligerents, aggressors or victims. Still others like Charles

75. *Ibid.*, p. 181.
76. *Ibid.*, pp. 362–363.
77. Newton Baker, *Why We Went to War*, pp. 26–27.
78. Seymour, *American Neutrality*, pp. 175–180.

Seymour remained interventionists. They sought some executive discretion for the president to apply the rules of neutrality in such a way as to favor the victims of aggression over their opponents.[79]

The revisionists were not so divided. Walter Millis moved toward the interventionists, claiming that "1939 is not 1914."[80] But the other revisionists strongly supported a passive neutrality over intervention in World War II. Tansill and Barnes later wrote virulent attacks on the Roosevelt policy that had taken America into the Second World War. Grattan's *Preface to Chaos* also opposed intervention. Charles Beard not only joined Barnes and Tansill in their postwar attack on America's entrance into World War II but in the 1930s furnished some of the most important work upon which the Neutrality Acts were based.

Beard had been driven by his analysis of America's decision for war in 1917 into a consideration of the entire basis of American foreign policy. While he might agree with antirevisionists like Seymour that America had been drawn into war by the economic interest of the entire people in trade with the Allies, Beard could not agree with Seymour that this was reason enough. He decided that the United States should reshape its economy to avoid dependence on foreign trade, the defense of which would inevitably lead the nation into more foreign wars. He spelled out his views in congressional testimony and in two major published works, *The Idea of National Interest* and *The Open Door at Home*.

In these books, Beard argued that America's resources should be invested at home, encouraging domestic purchasing power among the lower classes to create the demand that would in turn bring increased profits and production. This economic democracy joined to political democracy would be supported by fair commodity exchanges and defended by military force if necessary. Meanwhile, America could cooperate with Europe, the League, and the World Court in minor matters but make no commitments it was not ready and able to enforce by arms, avoiding giving other nations moral advice. Beard's suggestions for implementation of this scheme included embargoes on arms and loans and prohibitions of American passengers aboard belligerent ships, along with some other ideas borrowed from an article

79. For a description of these positions in the struggle over the Neutrality Acts, see Robert A. Divine, *The Illusion of Neutrality: Franklin D. Roosevelt and the Struggle over the Arms Embargo* (Chicago, 1962), pp. 17–22, 69–71.

80. Cohen, *American Revisionists*, pp. 159, 160, 167–169, 217–218.

by Charles Warren. It was these prescriptions of Beard and Warren that served as the basis for the Neutrality Acts of the 1930s.[81]

Perhaps at no other time has American historiography had so direct an impact on American politics. But the effects of these interpretations of the American role in World War I and the Treaty of Versailles were not limited to the realm of politics. Quite naturally, the reaction against interventionism influenced the historiography of earlier American diplomacy as well.

81. Charles A. Beard, with the collaboration of G. H. E. Smith, *The Idea of National Interest: An Analytical Study in American Foreign Policy* (New York, 1934); Charles A. Beard, with the collaboration of G. H. E. Smith, *The Open Door at Home: A Trial Philosophy of National Interest* (New York, 1934); and Charles A. Warren, "Troubles of a Neutral," *Foreign Affairs*, 12 (April 1934): 377–394.

TEN

World War I and the Historiography of American Neutrality

The searing experiences of World War I and the tragedy of Versailles had enormous impact on histories written in the postwar era. Books which examined issues sensitized by the Great War flooded the presses—books on past embargoes, earlier neutrality policies, the effects of propaganda, and previous struggles between the president and the Senate over treaties. Historians compared wars of the past with World War I and found them to be products of similar factors—not idealism or national survival but blundering and rapacity. The so-called imperial school of American revolutionary historiography received a boost from this change in atmosphere. Composed of such historians as Herbert Osgood, George Beer, Charles McLean Andrews, Claude Van Tyne, and Lawrence Henry Gipson, the imperial school derided the supposed idealistic motives of the American patriots. This school's sympathy for the British side of the Revolution drove supernationalists like the Hearst press, the American Legion, and elements of the Knights of Columbus into a rage. The theme of "a blundering generation" also infused a host of new books on the Civil War by such men as Avery Craven and J. G. Randall.

Diplomatic historians were no less affected. But surprisingly little of their reaction was apparent in the diplomatic textbooks of this era. Texts for students always were inclined to be less critical of American history for fear of disillusioning young minds. Also, most of the texts of the era were written in the mid-1920s, before revisionism had gained its full potency. Finally, the writers of texts tended to be older scholars whose ideas had been formed in the prewar era and had been less influenced by the war. In any case, many of these older scholars, and young ones too for that matter, continued to admire Wilson and his dreams and were therefore unimpressed by the mood of the revisionists.

One of the best-selling texts of this era, Carl Russell Fish's *American Diplomacy*, had been written before the war and was only slightly revised in 1929. Obviously, it would not be much affected by postwar revisionism. Even in the text's later editions, Fish gave a strongly prointerventionist account of the events leading to American participation in World War I, basing his narrative on the wartime works of John Spencer Bassett and John Bach McMaster. As he also favored the Treaty of Versailles,[1] it is not surprising that Fish made no sweeping revisions of his earlier interpretations of America's diplomatic past.[2]

Most of the other authors of diplomatic history texts published between 1920 and 1939 differed little from Fish in their attitudes toward World War I and Versailles. Randolph Greenfield Adams, custodian of the Clements Library at the University of Michigan, who published a college text in 1924, was, if anything, still more of an interventionist, complaining primarily about the delay in America's decision for war.[3] He wrote his book with the express purpose of teaching Americans that the policy of neutrality and isolation, however valuable for earlier times, was now thoroughly outmoded and pernicious.[4] John Holladay Latané's text, *A History of American Foreign Policy*, followed in this same pattern.[5]

One might have expected otherwise from Louis Martin Sears. His text, *A History of American Foreign Relations*, was written with considerable assistance from Charles Tansill.[6] In addition, Sears was

1. Carl Russell Fish, *American Diplomacy*, 5th ed. (New York, 1929), pp. 500–504, 514–519, 530–546.
2. In 1915, he did add a brief example to his account of the War of 1812, asserting that neutrality had failed in this case. He also said that America had made a mistake in the Jay Treaty by changing its legal attitude in a way that affected the belligerents unequally. Otherwise, the text remained as it had been in the previous Age of Imperialism.
3. Randolph Greenfield Adams, *A History of the Foreign Policy of the United States* (New York, 1924), pp. 372–376.
4. *Ibid.*, pp. 1–3, 412, 438–439.
5. Latané, *A History of American Foreign Policy*, p. 599.
6. Louis Martin Sears, *A History of American Foreign Relations* (New York, 1927 and 1935), pp. vii–viii; citations are from the 1935 edition.

the author of a monograph which cheered Jefferson's embargo as a valiant attempt to protect American neutrality and maintain the peace.[7] Yet even Sears followed the trail blazed by Fish, Adams, and Latané. He had harsher words for Theodore Roosevelt and imperialism than had the other text writers, and he was a bit more blatant in his admiration of Wilson's attempt to "combat and purify capitalism" with a new "liberal righteousness."[8] Yet Sears too disowned the revisionists and differed from his fellows only in that he defended Wilson against the charges that he had been too slow to intervene.[9]

These historians, like the vast majority of history text writers who had published in the Age of Imperialism, praised the growing intimacy of the United States and Great Britain, while doing their best to minimize, or at least fully explain, both sides of all the earlier historic Anglo-American conflicts. This tendency had reached its peak during World War I when many historians, including Latané and Fish, had helped propagandize the war. During the war, German- and Irish-Americans had had to suppress their anger at the pro-British interpretations that dominated the texts and popular histories. But once the war was over, the Hearst press and some elements of the Knights of Columbus led a campaign against what they deemed an excessive and unpatriotic pro-British bias. This attack took place in the early 1920s, before revisionism had made it respectable to condemn American intervention into World War I. So these groups concentrated on earlier episodes they felt were being distorted, particularly the American Revolution and the War of 1812. For instance, a New York committee of the board of education wrote in 1922 that authors should "refrain from such characterizations as 'War Hawks' or from cynical, sarcastic or sneering remarks" about the War of 1812. It feared that such statements would generate unfortunate attitudes in pupils.[10]

Ironically, some of the historians who had abandoned their attempts at objectivity to assume the role of patriotic propagandists during the war now found themselves attacked for endangering the patriotism of America's school children. Elementary texts by Albert Bushnell Hart, Claude H. Van Tyne, and Andrew C. McLaughlin were condemned by one group or another, and Carl Russell Fish's elementary school text was investigated but cleared by a California commit-

7. Louis Martin Sears, *Jefferson and the Embargo* (Durham, 1927).

8. Sears, *History of American Foreign Relations*, pp. 511–512.

9. *Ibid.*, pp. 522–527, 532–535.

10. Quoted in Bessie Louise Pierce, *Public Opinion and the Teaching of History in the United States* (New York, 1926), p. 279.

tee.[11] Perhaps it was this campaign that inspired Randolph Greenfield Adams, a good friend of Van Tyne, to assert defiantly that "Pro-German and Irish-Americans and other Americans who carried a perpetual chip on their shoulders as far as England was concerned" had hounded the State Department into protesting British actions prior to 1917 and kept America from intervening in a timely manner.[12]

But there was at least one diplomatic text writer of whom these anti-British groups approved, one author who broke the mold of pro-interventionist, pro-British, pro-League historians. He was the greatest of all historians of early American diplomacy, Samuel Flagg Bemis. The Knights of Columbus, in a campaign to encourage propaganda-proof history, offered a prize for monographs in American history. Bemis's *Jay's Treaty*, already near completion when the prize was announced and thus written independent of this campaign, was "the only scientific study submitted" and was awarded first prize in 1922.[13]

Whatever reasons the Knights of Columbus may have had for awarding their prize to Bemis in 1922, Bemis was certainly not influenced in his opinions by pro-German or pro-Irish sympathies. He was not even Catholic. He had been born in Worcester, Massachusetts, on what he considered "the wrong side of the hedge."[14] Like John and John Quincy Adams, whom he so much admired, and like his Harvard mentors, Frederick Jackson Turner and Edward Channing, Bemis was fiercely individualistic and nationalistic, with a thorough distrust of Great Britain, indeed of all European nations. These tendencies would remain constant in Bemis's thought over the years although his specific policy advice would change rather dramatically with the coming of World War II and the Cold War. Perhaps his pre-World War II ideas can best be understood by examining the 1936 edition of his textbook for his interpretations of contemporary events like World War I and Versailles and then by studying the way in which those ideas were embodied in his monographic works on early American diplomacy,

11. *Ibid.*, pp. 209, 306.
12. R. G. Adams, *History of the Foreign Policy of the United States*, p. 372.
13. Pierce, *Public Opinion and the Teaching of History*, p. 234, n. 82.
14. Samuel Flagg Bemis, *American Foreign Policy and the Blessings of Liberty* (New Haven, 1962), p. 297. For biographical information on Bemis, consult H. C. Allen, "Samuel Flagg Bemis," in *Pastmasters: Some Essays on American Historians*, ed. Marcus Cunliffe and Robin W. Winks (New York, 1969); also excerpts from his autobiography, published in the Society for Historians of American Foreign Relations, *Newsletter*, 7 (September and December 1976); also Russell H. Bostart and John A. DeNovo, "Samuel Flagg Bemis," Massachusetts Historical Society, *Proceedings*, 85 (1973): 117–129.

the area to which he devoted most of his research and upon which he became the world's foremost authority.

Although Bemis leaned a bit toward revisionism and isolationism, he did not fall conveniently into either category. He had been aboard the *Sussex* when a German submarine had torpedoed it and had testified to that effect before an American investigatory body. Shortly after the war, Bemis wrote an article for the popular news magazine, *Outlook*, entitled "Shall We Forget the *Lusitania*?" in which he declared that America's cause had been righteous "as no one now will deny."[15] In his textbook, published fourteen years later in 1936, Bemis still seemed to regard American intervention as proper. He based his account primarily on Charles Seymour, whose work he called "the most adequate analysis of American problems of neutrality."[16] In his detailed and straightforward narrative, Bemis presented submarine warfare as the primary cause for American intervention and warned that revisionists like Walter Millis had to be read with the greatest care.[17] Nonetheless, the revisionist movement obviously carried some weight with Bemis. His text treated with respect those revisionists like Joseph Fuller, who had argued that America might have avoided the war if it had used the embargo to compel British respect for neutral rights.[18] He even went so far as to suggest that the British might have exposed the *Lusitania* and the *Sussex* deliberately to German torpedoes to bring America into the war.[19]

Wilson's primary mistake, however, was not intervention as such, but intervention without conditions, Bemis believed. America should have devoted its efforts to maintaining freedom of the seas, intervening only with a maritime force, and avoiding the dispatch of armies or loans to Europe. Bemis thought Wilson should have had an explicit understanding with the Allies about the terms of peace to be required of Germany, thus avoiding the problems that the secret treaties posed for the Treaty of Versailles.[20]

In spite of his proclivities for isolationism, Bemis did not consider the Treaty of Versailles a bad one. It was imperfect, but not Carthaginian. It violated the principle of self-determination in a few

15. Samuel Flagg Bemis, "Shall We Forget the *Lusitania*?" *Outlook*, August 30, 1922, p. 710.
16. Samuel Flagg Bemis, *A Diplomatic History of the United States* (New York, 1936), p. 585n.
17. *Ibid.*, pp. 584–587.
18. *Ibid.*, pp. 588–589.
19. *Ibid.*, p. 610.
20. *Ibid.*, p. 613.

places but extended it to millions who had never known it before. It weakened Germany but left the living core of the nation untouched.[21] As a young man, Bemis had favored the treaty's ratification. "To many of us who lived through those war years and who ardently hoped for a better world to follow the tragedy of the nations," it had seemed that the vicious partisanship of Lodge and the irreconcilables had combined with Wilson's refusal of "essential reservations" to "foolishly throw away the victory."

> Those of us who have lived on into two decades after must now see things in a different light. The League of Nations has been a disappointing failure. . . . It has been a failure, not because the United States did not join it; but because the great powers have been unwilling to apply sanctions except where it suited their individual national interests to do so, and because Democracy, on which the original concepts of the League rested for support, has collapsed over half the world.[22]

Thus, the European powers, unwilling to apply sanctions themselves, would ask the United States to apply them and in areas of no vital interest to America. America was well out of the League, Bemis believed. But in the end, the League would prevail or civilization might collapse. Wilson's steadfastness to that ideal might transfigure his political mistakes.[23]

Although Bemis was against American participation in the League, he did not advocate the rigid neutrality that isolationists were devising in the Neutrality Acts of the 1930s. He agreed that America should remain uninvolved in European hostilities but thought that the United States should not frustrate League action in situations where the League had been able to unify and apply sanctions. This discretionary use of neutrality was the stance advocated by many pre-World War II interventionists.[24]

Bemis regarded modern American diplomacy as drastically inferior to earlier American diplomacy. This attitude is the key to understanding Bemis's interpretations in those model monographs on early American foreign policy which have furnished the basis of his reputation. "The United States made no serious mistakes in its diplomacy and committed few minor errors, from 1775 to 1898," Bemis wrote in his text. It took advantage of Europe's quarrels and its own detached

21. *Ibid.*, p. 634.
22. *Ibid.*, p. 651.
23. *Ibid.*, pp. 652–653.
24. *Ibid.*, pp. 806–807.

geographical situation to achieve objectives that were perfectly compatible with America's interests and character.[25] But after 1898, Americans decided that they would have to take their proper place in the world by acquiring an overseas empire. "Actually," said Bemis, "the United States had already taken its proper place in the world before 1898. That was in North America." Acquisition of the Philippines involved the United States in "precisely the improper place, where it was most likely to become entangled in international rivalries alien to its interests." Then followed a long succession of "deplorable diplomatic blunders." The Open Door policy helped the British more than the Americans, and China actually would have furnished more trade to the United States had it been partitioned or brought under British or Japanese protection. Since Americans never would fight to maintain the Open Door, Bemis asked, why try to maintain it by words? The Washington Naval Conference of 1922 was a success to the degree that it marked a retreat from unilateral American commitments in Asia, but much of the good will so won had been shattered by the Immigration Act of 1924 which excluded Orientals.[26]

Bemis regarded Theodore Roosevelt's imperial meddling as a unalloyed danger. Roosevelt's mediation of the Russo-Japanese War had alienated both sides. His participation in the Morocco settlement had endangered America's noninterventionist role there. Roosevelt's corollary and his taking of Panama had been thoroughly unnecessary. The liberation of Cuba and the acquisition of Puerto Rico could have secured American interests in the Caribbean without further intervention. But at least Roosevelt had avoided full involvement in Europe. Wilson's "unconditional" intervention into World War I had been a disaster.[27] Now, however, America's policies were to be clarified. Imperialism was being liquidated. The Monroe Doctrine would be restored to its pristine condition by abandonment of the Roosevelt Corollary and of American intervention in areas where the doctrine prevented European intervention. Bemis saw a new neutrality in the works and rejoiced that the incompatibility of being a creditor nation while maintaining high tariff was being recognized.[28]

While many of these attitudes, expressed in the mid-1930s, may have been somewhat different when Bemis began writing his monographs on early American history in the 1920s, they do throw some

25. *Ibid.*, p. 802.
26. *Ibid.*, pp. 803–804.
27. *Ibid.*, p. 804.
28. *Ibid.*, p. 805.

valuable light on otherwise puzzling interpretations that emerged from those earlier works. Here it should be emphasized that Bemis's interpretations were not the crux of his monographs. The influence of Bemis's works derived from the intensity of research that lay behind them, especially his exhaustive use of the archives of all nations involved in a given diplomatic situation. Although all historians in the field admired his books, and his multiarchival approach became the *sine qua non* of diplomatic history research, his interpretations persuaded few even in his own day.

Bemis's *The Diplomacy of the American Revolution,* published originally in 1935, is still the standard work on the subject.[29] It emphasized the danger of American entanglement in European quarrels. European diplomacy in the eighteenth century was "rotten, corrupt, and perfidious," warned Bemis.[30] America's diplomatic success had resulted from staying clear of European politics while reaping advantage from European strife.[31] Franklin, Jay, and Adams had done just this during the Revolution and as a consequence had won the greatest victory in the annals of American diplomacy.[32] Bemis conceded that the French alliance had been necessary to win the war. Yet he regretted that it had brought involvement with "the baleful realm of European diplomacy." Vergennes was quite willing to lead America to an "abbatoir" where portions of the United States might be dismembered if this would advance the interests of France.[33]

Bemis lauded Franklin for being the first to break congressional instructions when he had held secret from Vergennes his suggestion to the British that they cede Canada to the United States.[34] Still, Jay had been wise to insist on a more explicit recognition of independence prior to negotiations. While other historians had claimed that this stubbornness had been hurtful and unnecessary, delaying matters until the failure to capture Gibraltar had strengthened the British hand, Bemis argued that it had been Jay's eventual weakening on this point rather than his original hard line that had hurt the United States. "If Franklin and Jay had stood firm," they might have gotten an ad-

29. Samuel Flagg Bemis, *The Diplomacy of the American Revolution,* 2nd ed. (Bloomington, Ind., 1957).
30. *Ibid.,* p. 13.
31. *Ibid.,* p. viii.
32. *Ibid.,* p. 256.
33. *Ibid.,* pp. 255, 184.
34. *Ibid.,* pp. 208–209.

vance recognition of independence, and the peace preliminaries might have been signed before the news of Gibraltar had arrived.[35]

Thus, Bemis indicated his preference for diplomats who aggressively asserted American rights and remained defiantly independent of European politics. His *Jay's Treaty* applied the same values. In this book, Bemis pictured Great Britain as a ruthless and unscrupulous adversary. He described the activities of British secret agents in Kentucky and Vermont, implying that they represented a serious British desire to see the United States dismembered.[36] He demonstrated that Britain's decision to hold the Great Lakes posts, in violation of the peace treaty of 1783, had preceded the American offences by which the British had justified keeping the forts. Bemis maintained it had been British interest in the fur trade that had led to this decision.[37] A more benevolent concern for the Indians of the area, which some later historians found to be the most significant British motivation, Bemis relegated to secondary status.[38] The British policies of closing the West Indies to American ships, pressing for compensation for the Loyalists, and agitating for payment of private debts were roundly condemned by Bemis.

Jefferson and Madison won Bemis's praise for trying to stand up to the British. Their attempts to retaliate commercially against Britain, however futile, were at least spirited and manly.[39] But Federalist appeasement of Britain undermined any hope of winning America's rights. The most significant incident of Federalist appeasement was the Jay Treaty itself, Bemis believed. When John Jay arrived in England in 1794 to negotiate his treaty, "a shrewd diplomatist . . . would have . . . pronounced [the situation] favorable for the United States."[40] Yet Jay's susceptibility to flattery and his anxiety to obtain a settlement, combined with treachery of Hamilton in revealing to the British minister America's unwillingness to join the armed neutrality against Britain, had thrown away America's advantages. Jay had secured terms far less favorable than an "abler negotiator" might have won. Nevertheless, in a somewhat surprising conclusion, Bemis decided that the Jay Treaty

35. *Ibid.*, pp. 212–213.
36. Samuel Flagg Bemis, *Jay's Treaty: A Study in Commerce and Diplomacy*, new rev. ed. (New Haven and London, 1962), pp. 23–27.
37. *Ibid.*, pp. 4–9.
38. *Ibid.*, pp. 10–22.
39. *Ibid.*, p. 140 *et passim*.
40. *Ibid.*, p. 316.

could have been improved only marginally and was necessary to America's survival. War would have been disastrous to America's credit and perhaps to its hold on the back country.[41]

While he reluctantly conceded the necessity of accepting half a loaf in Jay's negotiations with England, Bemis was much happier describing American diplomatic successes. In his classic article, "Washington's Farewell Address: A Foreign Policy of Independence," Bemis extolled not only Washington's advice to remain independent of European quarrels but also his warnings against toleration of foreign influence in American domestic matters. Bemis gloried in Americans' attention to Washington and their resistance to French influence on behalf of Jefferson over Adams in 1796.[42] Adams had rewarded the American people by preventing the Federalists from rushing America into war with France, doing so without loss of honor and in the process clinching "the independence of American diplomacy by cutting loose from the entangling French alliance."[43]

Bemis also relished America's diplomatic success against Spain in 1795, when the Pinckney Treaty won the right of navigation of the Mississippi by exploiting Spain's insecure position between the belligerents in the Anglo-French war. In his *Pinckney's Treaty*, Bemis claimed that Spain also had been frightened by Jay's Anglo-American negotiation and had envisioned the spectre of an Anglo-American alliance aimed at the conquest of New Orleans and Florida. Fortunately, according to Bemis, the Spanish negotiators had not known the full text of the Jay Treaty and so had been unaware of how little they had to fear from Jay's weak bargain.[44]

Bemis was not alone in his praise for America's early policy of

41. *Ibid.*, pp. 368–373.
42. Samuel Flagg Bemis, "Washington's Farewell Address: A Foreign Policy of Independence," in his *American Foreign Policy and the Blessings of Liberty*, pp. 240–258; originally printed in the *American Historical Review*, 39, no. 2 (1934).
43. Bemis, *Diplomatic History of the United States*, pp. 124–125.
44. Samuel Flagg Bemis, *Pinckney's Treaty: A Study of America's Advantage from Europe's Distress, 1783–1800*, rev. ed. (Westport, Conn., 1960; originally published 1926), pp. 218–244; see also note in 1960 edition, pp. 284–293. Arthur Whitaker challenged Bemis on this point in *The Spanish American Frontier: 1783–1795: The Westward Movement and the Spanish Retreat in the Mississippi Valley* (Boston, 1927), and in his two articles, "New Light on the Treaty of San Lorenzo; An Essay in Historical Criticism," *Mississippi Valley Historical Review*, 15 (March 1929): 435–454; and "Godoy's Knowledge of Jay's Treaty," *American Historical Review*, 35 (July 1939): 804–810. Whitaker tried to show that Spanish minister Manuel de Godoy had full knowledge of the Jay Treaty and its contents. Whitaker agreed with Bemis that the Jay Treaty was weak and that Godoy's knowledge of it had

neutrality. World War I inspired a profound interest in earlier American efforts to avoid involvement in European wars. The policies of George Washington and his cabinet toward the wars of the French Revolution received the attention of two excellent monographs, Charles Thomas's *American Neutrality in 1793* and Charles Hyneman's *The First American Neutrality*.[45] Both commended Washington's administration for its definition of neutrality as true impartiality toward warring nations rather than a mere abstention from combat.[46]

Meanwhile, Louis Sears wrote a monograph treating Jefferson's embargo more favorably than had any historian since Henry Adams.[47] Thus Jefferson's reputation received a considerable boost in this era. Bemis had praised him for taking a more independent stance against Britain than had Hamilton, and Charles Thomas lauded him for being more neutral than his Federalist rival. Now Sears considered his embargo a worthy precedent for modern America, and William Kirk Woolery devoted an entire monograph to his diplomatic contributions in the period between 1783 and 1793.[48]

Civil War diplomacy also offered an opportunity for comment on the issue of American neutrality. Historians of the imperial era, borrowing from Minister Charles Francis Adams, had considered the Civil War a step forward in America's battle for neutral rights. America had permitted the British a wide range of neutral rights, exemplified in the *Trent* affair, thus giving the United States some precedents to enlist

---

made Pinckney's task more difficult. But Whitaker argued that Spain's separate peace with France had triggered hostile British preparations for an invasion of Spanish territory, perhaps Mexico, and this, plus the pressure of American frontiersmen, had brought Godoy to sign the treaty anyway (Whitaker, *Spanish-American Frontier*, pp. 206–207).

45. Charles Marion Thomas, *American Neutrality in 1793: A Study in Cabinet Government* (New York and London, 1931); and Charles S. Hyneman, *The First American Neutrality: A Study of the American Understanding of Neutral Obligations During the Years 1792–1815* (Urbana, Ill., 1934).

46. Thomas credited the United States exclusively with developing the idea of an impartial neutrality whereas Hyneman said that the Italian city-states were the first to practice it in 1778–1779 but that America's precedent was more important and undertaken in ignorance of the Italian precedents.

47. Sears, *Jefferson and the Embargo*. An earlier monograph by Walter Wilson Jennings, entitled *The American Embargo, 1807–1809: With Particular Reference to Its Effect on Industry* (Iowa City, 1921), took the harsher line of Henry Adams. It was not so influential as Sears's work, however. Jennings was an economist and assistant professor of commerce rather than a historian of foreign policy and dealt far more with the economics than with the diplomacy of the issue.

48. William Kirk Woolery, *The Relation of Thomas Jefferson to American Foreign Policy, 1783–1793* (Baltimore, 1927).

in any future dispute with Britain.[49] But Frank Owsley disagreed vehemently. He thought the Civil War had hurt America's neutral precedents.

Owsley was one of the Vanderbilt agrarians who promoted the old virtues of the South in the face of the industrial age.[50] His sympathies were clearly with the Confederacy in his *King Cotton Diplomacy: Foreign Relations of the Confederate States of America*. Owsley blamed the Union for undermining America's consistency on the issue of neutral rights. At the first "opportunity to make use of her superior sea power against an inferior maritime belligerent," he wrote, the North had

> abandoned all her former principles and occupied the British position at one grand stride. She laid a paper blockade, adopted the practice of search and seizure of vessels hundreds of miles from the blockaded coast, stretched the doctrine of continuous voyage, . . . and ferociously denied the right of England to sell either cannon or ships to the enemy. When the Civil War was over, the body of principles upholding neutral rights on the seas gained by American and European struggle against British practices had been sadly altered. . . .[51]

Owsley also sneered at the increasingly favorable treatment historians had been giving British Civil War diplomacy. He assumed that if England had refused to intervene to save its cotton industry, another economic motive must have been involved, in this case "war profits."[52] Owsley discounted as "too good to be true" the "idealistic theory" of older historians that the democratic, antislavery sympathies of Britain's common people had prevented British intervention on the side of the Confederacy. Owsley complained that historians had noted mass meetings supporting the North but had discredited similar meetings favoring the South. Neither side's meetings were spontaneous in any case but were "drummed up by well-subsidized leaders and were frequently packed by the liberal use of small coin." Owsley thought the population of industrial England ignorant and politically apa-

49. Frederic Bancroft had dissented somewhat from this position, saying that Seward's dispatch on the *Trent* affair, while releasing the Confederate envoys, had made other wild claims about neutral and belligerent rights that could undermine later legal positions (Bancroft, *Life of William H. Seward*, II, 243–253).

50. Frank L. Owsley, *King Cotton Diplomacy: Foreign Relations of the Confederate States of America*, 2nd ed. (Chicago, 1959; originally published 1931).

51. *Ibid.*, p. 411. See also Owsley, "America and the Freedom of the Seas," in Avery Craven, ed., *Essays in Honor of William E. Dodd* (Chicago, 1935), pp. 194–256.

52. Owsley, *King Cotton Diplomacy*, pp. 549–558.

thetic, and he suspected popular opinion was actually divided where it existed at all. It was doubtful that the common people had any influence on Britain's nonintervention policy anyway, he concluded.[53]

Despite the fact that Owsley's interpretations were consonant with the rising tide of revisionism, many historians discounted his opinions on Civil War diplomacy because of his caustic pro-South sympathies. In addition, his dissenting view was overwhelmed by other significant books which continued the earlier movement toward a more favorable view of British diplomacy. Historians of the pre-World War I era like James Ford Rhodes, Frederic Bancroft, James Morton Callahan, and James Kendall Hosmer had offered progressively more sympathetic interpretations of British actions. During World War I two Englishmen, Brougham Villiers and W. H. Chesson, wrote a brief and impressionistic book, *Anglo-American Relations, 1861–1865*, that carried this movement to new heights of praise for British policy.[54] The movement was capped by the publication of two well-researched and highly influential monographs, Ephraim Adams's *Great Britain and the American Civil War*[55] and *Europe and the American Civil War* by Donaldson Jordan and Edwin Pratt.[56]

Ephraim Adams was the first historian to base a study of Civil War diplomacy on wide research in the British archives and on private papers. Despite some clarifications made possible by his multiarchival research, he told a familiar story. Continuing the tradition of his earlier books on British activities in Texas and California, he gave a very sympathetic view of British motives. Adams found no evidence of the hostile motive previously ascribed to the British that they desired the breakup of the United States and the introduction of balance-of-power diplomacy in North America. The British simply believed that the North could never force the South back into the Union and hoped the North would accept the inevitable before the war worked too great a hardship on America and its trading partners like England.[57]

As a confirmed Anglophile, Ephraim Adams did not deal extensively with the neutral rights issue. Since he presumed that America should have joined World War I earlier to support Britain and the

53. *Ibid.*, pp. 545–546.

54. Brougham Villiers (Frederick J. Shaw) and W. H. Chesson, *Anglo-American Relations, 1861–1865* (London, 1919).

55. Ephraim Adams, *Great Britain and the American Civil War*, 2 vols. (Gloucester, Mass., 1957; originally published 1925).

56. Donaldson Jordan and Edwin J. Pratt, *Europe and the American Civil War* (Boston, 1931).

57. Ephraim Adams, *Great Britain and the American Civil War*, I, 31–53.

democracies instead of holding to its broad definition of neutral rights, he did not make much of Civil War precedents. Owsley's view that the Civil War had marked a setback for neutral rights ultimately prevailed among historians.

Jordan and Pratt told much the same story as Ephraim Adams. But their book's introduction, written by Samuel Eliot Morison, produced an unfortunate historiographical result. Jordan and Pratt as well as Adams had accepted and elaborated the long-standing idea that Britain's upper classes had sympathized with the South whereas the lower classes and the nonconformists had favored the North. But here Morison misread their conclusions, and attributed an influence to popular opinion that neither Adams nor Jordan and Pratt asserted. "There is a curious legend in American history," wrote Morison, "that England as a whole was hostile, positively and mischievously so, to the Union. Professor Ephraim Adams has already proved this to be unfounded on the diplomatic side; Professor Jordan shows that it has little foundation in public opinion." The governing classes of Europe thought in terms of balance of power and had an obvious interest in seeing two republics instead of one between the Rio Grande and the 49th parallel. "If neither government hailed the Stars and Bars as equal to the Stars and Stripes, public opinion was the fundamental reason," Morison declared. Never before had large masses of opinion exerted such weight in foreign policy.[58]

Actually neither Adams nor Jordan (who wrote on English opinion while Pratt covered the French) had said that popular opinion had prevented British intervention. Adams, who discussed the issue most thoroughly, said that the British had been tempted to intervene only to hasten the North's acceptance of the inevitable separation and to end the needless suffering in America and England. The British leaders had drawn back not because of public resistance to support of a Confederacy based on slavery but because they saw that the North would not yet accept the inevitable and would fight a meddling England. The British actually decided to continue neutrality before the Emancipation Proclamation had had a major effect in England. Of course, once the proclamation had raised the issue of slavery, thoughts of intervention were totally abandoned, but this came after the major crisis had passed.[59] Morison's unfortunate exaggeration would inspire much useless revisionist rhetoric in later years.

58. Jordan and Pratt, *Europe and the American Civil War*, pp. xi–xii.
59. Ephraim Adams, *Great Britain and the American Civil War*, II, 73–74. See also Jordan and Pratt, *Europe and the American Civil War*, pp. 119–124, 156–158.

Thus, World War I had revived interest in earlier episodes of American history when they had involved the issue of neutrality. Almost all authors writing about these episodes explicitly noted their relevance to contemporary foreign policy. But although World War I sensitized the neutrality issue, historians still divided quite evenly in their attitudes toward it. Pro-British sympathies softened the praise for early American isolationism in the works of many of the leading diplomatic history textbooks and monographs. But World War I revisionists and those still not enamored of the British Empire could find considerable comfort in the interpretations of the greatest of all historians of early American foreign policy, Samuel Flagg Bemis, not to mention the monographs of Louis Sears, Frank Owsley, Charles Thomas, and Charles Hyneman. The advance to parity of the neutralist-isolationist view marked a significant change from the previous era when activist, interventionist attitudes had been so predominant.

ELEVEN

World War I and the Historiography of Nineteenth-Century American Expansionism

The postwar age of disillusionment and revisionism saw a renewed popularity come to the old policies of neutrality and isolation. So also did it see more caustic treatments of the sort of assertiveness and expansionism that the revisionists partially blamed for America's mistaken intervention in World War I. Revisionists and Wilsonians could agree that American treatment of Mexico and other neighbors to the South had been callous and aggressive. Both revisionists and Wilsonians condemned the exuberant interventionism of Theodore Roosevelt, and all segments of the American public seemed to welcome the development of the Good Neighbor policy under Hoover and Franklin Roosevelt. Everyone cheered a more cooperative approach to Latin America and abandonment of the Roosevelt Corollary. Meanwhile, the country seemed agreed that the United States should grant independence to the Philippines in short order.

Still, it is not clear how much of this movement was a direct result of disillusionment with World War I. As we have seen, historians had been urging somewhat greater restraint and more cooperation in U.S. policy toward Latin America even during the Age of Imperialism. Imperialist sentiments had not overcome completely criticisms of some of the earlier instances of American expansion such as the Spanish-American War, the Mexican War, and the acquisition of

Florida. Many imperialists also had come to doubt the wisdom of holding the Philippines, and this well before World War I.

So World War I's contribution to the swing of the historiographical pendulum on issues of expansionism is in doubt. In addition, the pendulum met strong counterpressures from other directions. Frederick Jackson Turner's frontier thesis, still tremendously influential in the 1920s and 1930s, emphasized the positive characteristics of the frontier to the extent that it helped to offset the many pointed criticisms of frontier expansionism inspired by postwar disillusionment. Many students and readers of Samuel Flagg Bemis also continued to share his belief that America's contemporary diplomatic ills were the product of the Spanish-American War and the interventionist spirit it had generated, not results of earlier diplomacy which had held fast to neutrality and intracontinental expansion.

An excellent example of Turner's influence was the early career of Arthur Preston Whitaker. A student of Turner, he published two superb books on early Spanish-American diplomacy, *The Spanish-American Frontier, 1783–1795*, and *The Mississippi Question, 1795–1803*.[1] Whitaker combined the European archival research recommended by Bemis with the attention to developments on the frontier inspired by his mentor, Turner. He treated American expansionism matter-of-factly and without indignation, admitting the aggressiveness and acquisitiveness of the frontiersmen without moralizing or condemning them. Whitaker might differ with Bemis in detail,[2] and his tone might not be as chauvinistic as Bemis's, but he was no more willing than Bemis to condemn this expansionism as greedy and unwarranted imperialism.

Many historians, however, were willing to condemn expansionism in this way. One of their most influential books was Albert Weinberg's *Manifest Destiny: A Study of Nationalist Expansionism in American History*.[3] Weinberg took a caustic look at the means by which the American government and people justified their growth at the expense of other and usually weaker peoples. Although Weinberg insisted that the story of American expansionism was "perhaps the most

1. Whitaker, *The Spanish-American Frontier*; and his *The Mississippi Question, 1795–1803: A Study in Trade, Politics, and Diplomacy* (New York and London, 1934).

2. See account of the controversy over the Pinckney Treaty recounted in previous chapter, n. 44.

3. Albert K. Weinberg, *Manifest Destiny: A Study of Nationalist Expansionism in American History* (Chicago, 1963; originally printed in Baltimore, 1935).

cheerful record of such perilous ambitions that one can find," his portrait of it was devastating.[4]

As Weinberg recited the variety of moralistic excuses the United States had used to justify its expansion, such as geographical predestination or the white man's burden, he took pains not to question the sincerity of those who offered the rationales. But his sarcastic tone and his attention to the speedy abandonment of these rationales whenever they conflicted with new desires made America's expansionist justifications sound absurd if not hypocritical.[5]

Interestingly, Weinberg was attacking expansion from a position of Wilsonian idealism, not revisionist cynicism. After puncturing the moralistic justifications for American expansion and intervention, he still strongly supported international collaboration and collective security. Totally noninterventionist policies were impractical, he believed, and collective rather than unilateral intervention was often just and necessary.[6]

Weinberg was one of the few historians chronicling American diplomacy who included the treatment of the Indians as part of the United States' diplomatic record. To the extent that he and other historians did so, they contributed to the increasing disapproval of expansionist and imperialist diplomacy. Their accounts reflected awareness of anthropological studies which dealt with Indian culture on its own terms and which demanded new respect for tribal ways being submerged in the American melting pot. These anthropological studies challenged the time-honored assumption that Anglo-American civilization was inherently superior to supposedly "primitive" Indian culture.

Historians who joined the anthropologists to condemn the record of U.S. diplomacy toward the Indians especially attacked previous reformers' attempts to rectify past aggression by redistributing Indian lands and integrating Indians into the mainstream of Anglo-American life under the Dawes Severalty Act of 1887. A flood of articles and books denounced the Dawes Act as just another cynical land-grab scheme in line with the earlier policy of displacement and destruction.[7] This movement culminated in a reversal of Indian policy.

4. *Ibid.*, p. 8.
5. *Ibid.*, p. 41.
6. *Ibid.*, pp. 451–485. See also Weinberg's article urging collective security on the eve of World War II, "The Historical Meaning of the American Doctrine of Isolation," *American Political Science Review*, 34 (June 1940).
7. See Randolph C. Downes, "A Crusade for Indian Reform, 1922–1934," *Mississippi Valley Historical Review*, 32 (December 1945): 331–354. Straight historical

The New Deal encouraged tribal land-holding and a new respect for Indian culture, all of which was embodied in the Indian Reorganization Act of 1934. But most historical writing on the Indians took place outside of the literature of American diplomacy. Other expansionist episodes received far more attention and carried far more weight in the developing diplomatic historiography of the era. One of the most significant of these developments concerned the War of 1812. Formerly, it had been treated as part of America's praiseworthy, if at times stumbling, defense of neutrality. But as the World War I revisionists argued that American intervention had marked the triumph of economic greed over America's better instincts for peace and neutrality, so diplomatic historians now saw the same tendencies at work in 1812. The influence of westward expansion on the war, a minor theme in all diplomatic histories except for the brief articles which Howard Lewis and Dice Anderson had published in the previous era, now became the central issue. A number of articles on this theme appeared in the 1920s, capped by Louis Hacker's "Western Land Hunger and the War of 1812."[8] Hacker used the same arguments as Lewis and Anderson to discredit the maritime explanation of the war, and, like Lewis, he emphasized land hunger over the Indian threat as the primary motivating force in the West.

With a more thorough and well-documented presentation than Lewis, Hacker argued that the Indians were too few and too weak to pose a credible threat to any but the smallest, most isolated towns. Western farmers were far more interested in the virgin lands of the St. Lawrence valley than in eliminating British support of Tecumseh and

---

works were not suffused with the same degree of indignation that the polemical articles were but, nonetheless, leaned more toward Helen Hunt Jackson than toward Theodore Roosevelt. See, *e.g.*, Ralph Henry Gabriel, *The Lure of the Frontier: A Story of Race Conflict* (New Haven, 1929); Grant Foreman, *Indians and Pioneers: The Story of the American Southwest Before 1830*, rev. ed. (Norman, Okla., 1936); and Grant Foreman, *Indian Removal: The Emigration of the Five Civilized Tribes of Indians*, new ed. (Norman, Okla., 1953).

8. Louis M. Hacker, "Western Land Hunger and the War of 1812: A Conjecture," *Mississippi Valley Historical Review*, 10 (1924): 365–395. Earlier articles included Christopher B. Coleman, "The Ohio Valley in the Preliminaries of the War of 1812," *Mississippi Valley Historical Review*, 7 (1920): 39–50; and John F. Cady, "Western Opinion and the War of 1812," *Ohio Archaeological and Historical Quarterly*, 33 (1924): 427–476. For an excellent historiographical article covering these developments, see Warren H. Goodman, "The Origins of the War of 1812: A Survey of Changing Interpretations," *Mississippi Valley Historical Review*, 28 (1941–1942): 171–186.

the Prophet. Frontier farmers were so crude and wasteful in their methods that they had to keep moving to virgin land to survive. The great plains of the Louisiana Purchase seemed a desert to them, and Canada looked to be their only alternative. Thus, it had been greed, not Indian threats, and certainly not national honor or neutral rights, that had impelled America to war in 1812.

Although Hacker's attention to the West received much support in the post-World War I era, his land-hunger thesis was immediately attacked. His challenger was to become one of America's most influential diplomatic historians, Julius Pratt. When Pratt was studying for his Ph.D. at the University of Chicago, the idea struck him that the Northwest's desire for Canada might have had more influence on the War of 1812 than commonly had been supposed. Encouraged by William Dodd, who already had written on the role of the West in the Mexican War, Pratt wrote a dissertation that was published as *The Expansionists of 1812*. In this book and in a subsequent article, "Western Aims in the War of 1812," Pratt elaborated the western causes of the war and vigorously criticized the failings he saw in Hacker's land-hunger thesis.[9] Where Hacker had dismissed the Indian threat as a motivation for the war because the Indians had been too few to pose a serious danger, Pratt insisted that the actual danger was less crucial than the Westerners' perception of the Indian threat. Clearly exhibiting the impact of World War I, Pratt wrote:

> Now and then comes a danger which actually threatens the existence of a nation or a people, but most international friction and most wars arise from marginal irritations akin to that which existed in 1812 in the Ohio Valley. . . . Certainly no one threatened "the existence of the white civilization" in the colonies from 1765 to 1775; it was an accumulation of small annoyances upon the fringes of society that brought on revolution. The existence of civilization in the South—or the existence of slavery—can hardly be said to have been threatened in 1860. Spain did not threaten our national existence in 1898, nor did Germany in 1917. [These and other events] might have suggested to Mr. Hacker that a danger to national existence is not necessary to the production of a belligerent state of mind.[10]

9. Julius W. Pratt, *The Expansionists of 1812* (New York 1925); and his "Western Aims in the War of 1812," *Mississippi Valley Historical Review*, 12 (June 1925): 36–50. Biographical information is from Donnie Lee Dennis, "A History of American Diplomatic History," unpublished dissertation, University of California, Santa Barbara, 1971, pp. 145–147.

10. Pratt, "Western Aims in the War of 1812," p. 38.

Thus, Pratt aligned his interpretation of the War of 1812 with the imperial view of the Revolution and the "blundering generation" interpretation of the Civil War. But his work on the War of 1812, like the rest of his studies of American expansionism, was hardly the indictment of America's aggressive diplomacy that Hacker's and Weinberg's had been. Pratt insisted that the West's interest in Canada stemmed from a sincere though mistaken desire for security. Hacker had argued that the Westerners had run out of wooded land in the Northwest and, having exhausted their own land, were confronted with either moving onto the plains they considered "the great American desert" or acquiring the rich Canadian bottom land along the St. Lawrence. Pratt showed that vast amounts of wooded land did remain unpopulated in the Old Northwest. Thus, fear of Indian attacks rather than "agrarian cupidity" accounted for western desires to conquer Canada. Pratt admitted that the Indian friction itself was the product of American expansion into Indian lands, however. "If the whites had not coveted the lands of the Indians, possibly even if they had gone about getting them by more moderate and fairer means, Indian hostility might have been avoided and with it the 'British-Indian menace.' "[11]

Although the Northwest wanted Canada, Pratt said, some Southerners feared it would upset the balance between slave and free territory. Southerners wanted Florida, not Canada. By a clever but thoroughly circumstantial argument, Pratt tried to demonstrate that the South and Northwest had struck a bargain to seek the conquest of both Canada and Florida. This explained the support of both sections, including some seaboard sections of the South, for the War of 1812. It also provided another reason for the Northeast, which feared expansion, to oppose the war.[12]

Although Pratt did not claim that western war aims were the primary cause of the war, the depth of his research and the subtlety of his argument elevated the importance of those aims in the minds of most historians of his time.[13] This tended to increase disillusionment with American foreign policy because it diverted attention from the more easily justified American resentment of Britain's arrogant conduct on the high seas.

Pratt continued to study and criticize American expansionism throughout this postwar era. In a 1934 article for the *American Mer-*

---

11. *Ibid.*, p. 50.
12. Pratt, *Expansionists of 1812*, pp. 66–70, 140–152.
13. Goodman, "Origins of the War of 1812," pp. 174, 182–183.

cury, Pratt examined "The Collapse of American Imperialism," rejoicing that the American people had "no stomach for further colonial ventures."[14] The following year he contributed an essay on "The Ideology of American Expansionism," in which he sarcastically examined American rationales for conquest. He concluded that Americans seemed unable to do wrong knowingly and had to find pious justifications for deviance from or abandonment of principle.[15] Yet Pratt's work did not ring with the indignation of many of the historians of this era. He admitted the aggressiveness of some American diplomatic actions, yet he resisted the idea that these actions were born of mere greed and rapaciousness. Fear, ignorance, and legitimate security needs had played some part, along with a not wholly unattractive activist frontier spirit. Pratt seemed to defend American expansionism against economic determinists and other indignant critics almost as often as he criticized it for its aggressiveness. These tendencies were even more apparent in his 1936 book, *The Expansionists of 1898*, to be discussed later. They were magnified tenfold by the effects of World War II and the Cold War on his general account of American imperialism published in 1950, *America's Colonial Experiment*.[16]

Pratt's downgrading of economic motivation among Westerners bothered George Taylor. Taylor added to the general acceptance of the significance of western war aims by showing that Westerners had suffered a severe depression in the years prior to the declaration of war. Westerners blamed British ship seizures for their hard times since the British blocked western exports and forced prices to plummet. Thus, even maritime explanations came to rest on the West and on selfish economic interests rather than on more noble motives of national honor.[17]

But the growing attention given western causes did not revive the formerly discredited legend that a Republican caucus of war hawks had forced an unwilling Madison to support war in exchange for his renomination. In an article examining "War Guilt in 1812," Theodore Clark Smith concluded that this legend had no more validity than did

14. Julius W. Pratt, "The Collapse of American Imperialism," *American Mercury*, 31 (March 1934): 269.

15. Julius W. Pratt, "The Ideology of American Expansionism," in *Essays in Honor of William E. Dodd*, ed. Avery O. Craven (Chicago, 1935).

16. Julius W. Pratt, *The Expansionists of 1898: The Acquisition of Hawaii and the Spanish Islands* (Chicago, 1964; originally published in Baltimore, 1936); and his *America's Colonial Experiment: How the United States Gained, Governed, and in Part Gave Away a Colonial Empire* (Englewood Cliffs, N.J., 1950).

17. George R. Taylor, "Agrarian Discontent in the Mississippi Valley Preceding the War of 1812," *Journal of Political Economy*, 39 (1931): 471–505.

the German war guilt thesis of World War I. Madison had already been advancing toward war, and the meeting which Federalists maintained had subverted Madison had been intended merely to inform him that he could now expect a majority of Congress to support his actions, Smith said.[18]

The major studies of the Florida question published in this era also adopted a moderate rather than an indignant tone. Philip Coolidge Brooks's *Diplomacy and the Borderlands* specifically rejected Herbert Fuller's angry 1906 work *The Purchase of Florida* as too thinly researched to justify "a lamentation over our sins of aggrandizement."[19] He noted that unlike the Spanish, Americans had conducted a campaign of extermination against the Indians of the border area[20] and that the United States had acquired Florida through a blatant use of its superior power,[21] but he did so without censure. Charles Carroll Griffin's *The United States and the Disruption of the Spanish Empire, 1810–1822* adopted a similar stance. Griffin admitted the United States had no legal right to Florida and that despite America's rhetoric, it had taken the province from self-interest rather than some "ideal love of justice." Yet he could still say that John Quincy Adams had restrained anti-Spanish feeling in America, maintained a high level of civilized intercourse between nations, and consulted principles rather than expediency in his diplomacy toward Spain.[22]

The dispassionate tone which marked these books, as well as those of Pratt and Whitaker, also predominated in the work of another of the truly significant diplomatic historians of this era, Dexter Perkins. Born in New England, Perkins forsook his family's moderate republicanism to become a liberal Democrat with a great admiration for Woodrow Wilson. He campaigned avidly for the League of Nations and repeatedly sang its praises on the editorial page of the Rochester *Times-Union*.[23] His great contribution to diplomatic history was a multivolume history of the Monroe Doctrine.[24]

18. Theodore Clark Smith, "War Guilt in 1812," Massachusetts Historical Society, *Proceedings*, 64 (June 1931): 319–345.

19. Philip Coolidge Brooks, *Diplomacy and the Borderlands: The Adams-Onis Treaty of 1819* (Berkeley, 1939), p. 245.

20. *Ibid.*, pp. v, 192.

21. *Ibid.*, pp. v–vi, 196.

22. Charles C. Griffin, *The United States and the Disruption of the Spanish Empire, 1810–1822: A Study of the Relations of the United States with Spain and with the Rebel Spanish Colonies* (New York, 1937), pp. 21, 276, 18 n. 18, 284–285.

23. Dexter Perkins, *Yield of the Years: An Autobiography* (Boston and Toronto, 1969).

24. Dexter Perkins: *The Monroe Doctrine, 1823–1826* (Cambridge, Mass., 1927); *The Monroe Doctrine, 1826–1867* (Baltimore, 1933); and *The Monroe Doctrine,*

In a mildly debunking tone, Perkins set out to disabuse Americans of what he considered to be the myths they believed about the doctrine. First, he dismissed the controversy over the Doctrine's authorship as essentially barren. Although he was a good internationalist, he resisted the temptation to use the authorship question to condemn isolationism.[25] He believed it wise to have avoided a joint Anglo-American declaration at the time, as there had been no immediate emergency and because America and Britain had different approaches to South America. He said Adams had supplied this cautionary, two-spheres attitude, but Monroe should share credit for the overall policy of the doctrine. Monroe had furnished the doctrine's all-pervasive passion for republicanism and he had offered no resistance to a unilateral approach once Adams had suggested it. And both partners were too astute to close the door irrevocably on cooperation with Britain in case the new nations won British recognition or in case a true emergency materialized.[26]

After brushing this authorship question aside, Perkins turned the historical profession's attention to the European aspects of the doctrine. From his exhaustive search of European archives he concluded that the threats against which the doctrine had been aimed, Russian expansion in the Northwest and an attempt by the Holy Alliance to restore Spain's former colonies, were almost wholly il-

---

1867–1907 (Baltimore, 1937). This series was capped by a book summarizing the previous volumes and bringing the story up to date, orginally titled, Hands Off: A History of the Monroe Doctrine (Boston, 1941). It was later revised and the title changed to A History of the Monroe Doctrine (Boston, 1955).

25. In fact, despite Perkins's dismissal of the authorship issue, the debate continued. Interestingly, the partisans of Jefferson and Monroe were once again trying to get their heroes back square with the isolationists. William A. MacCorkle, former governor of West Virginia, took Worthington Ford's article as an affront to the South and wrote The Personal Genesis of the Monroe Doctrine (New York and London, 1923) to restore credit for authorship to Monroe, the Virginian. His analysis was based heavily on Schouler. In 1934, seven years after the publication of Perkins's first volume, T. R. Schellenberg tried to demonstrate "The Jeffersonian Origins of the Monroe Doctrine" (Hispanic American Historical Review, 12 [February 1934]: 1–31). He showed Jefferson's continual concern for the separation of the two spheres and bewailed the fact that Jefferson's willingness to accept a joint declaration with Britain had deprived him of credit for the two-spheres idea, despite the fact that Jefferson had only wanted to enlist Britain's support of the principle, not violate it. Besides, he said, Adams only prevented a joint declaration. It had been Monroe and Jefferson who had decided to actively present a unilateral declaration in the president's address to Congress.

26. Perkins, Monroe Doctrine, 1823–1826, pp. 8, 43–44, 74–76, 93–94, 96–103.

lusory. The comforting myth that the Monroe Doctrine had saved Latin America from European despotism was totally false. In fact, the doctrine had been an exercise in futility until revived by Polk in the 1840s.[27] Yet Perkins still had great respect for the originators of the doctrine. Their stand had been both idealistic and courageous. With access to the European archives, modern historians could know what Adams could only suspect, that the threat was not serious. But the doctrine's originators had had no way to be certain of this. Canning had taken the threat seriously, and his communications, combined with the direct statements of the czar, had convinced all the American leaders but Adams that there was a real threat from the Holy Alliance. In the face of this, the Americans had made a unilateral statement because the British had refused to accept the full independence of the Latin American republics. The American officials had done so knowing that the British might then try to embarrass them by remaining neutral if the Holy Alliance attacked Latin America, thus forcing the United States to put up or shut up. Nor had the United States been motivated by greed and a desire to stake out its own empire in Latin America. The United States had far more trade with Spain and its colony of Cuba than with the rest of Latin America. The doctrine, by alienating Spain, promised more losses than benefits. Although the doctrine became an instrument of intervention in later years, Perkins concluded that its originators had not intended it as such.[28]

Other historians searching the European archives came to similar conclusions. Samuel Eliot Morison, in his article "Les origins de la Doctrine de Monroe" had already suggested that the threat of the Holy Alliance had been nonexistent.[29] British historians C. K. Webster and H. W. V. Temperley agreed in their accounts of Castlereagh and Canning,[30] as did William Spence Robertson, who investigated the French side in *France and Latin American Independence*.[31] But one significant historian took strong exception to writing the history of the Monroe Doctrine from the archives of Europe. Edward Tatum, in his *United States and Europe, 1815–1823*, said that this angle sadly distorted the

27. *Ibid.*, pp. 104–121, 260.

28. *Ibid.*, pp. 40–41, 53–59, 70–78, 104, 259–260.

29. Samuel Eliot Morison "Les origins de la Doctrine de Monroe," *Revue des Sciences Politiques*, 47 (1924): 52–84.

30. C. K. Webster, *The Foreign Policy of Castlereagh*, (London, 1925); and H. W. V. Temperley, *The Foreign Policy of Canning* (London 1925).

31. William Spence Robertson, *France and Latin American Independence* (Baltimore, 1939).

real intent of Adams and Monroe. An examination of American as opposed to European sources showed that the object of the declaration had not been the hollow threat of Russia in the Northwest or the Holy Alliance in Latin America. Its target, according to Tatum, had been Great Britain itself, the only nation that posed a true threat to the United States. Thus, Adams and Monroe had avoided the joint declaration because a unilateral warning against European intervention would include Great Britain, whose activities in Cuba, Puerto Rico, and Colombia had offended America and its leaders.[32]

Tatum's anti-British and anti-European view of the doctrine fit well with his support of the isolationism of the 1920s and 1930s. Like Samuel Flagg Bemis, he spoke approvingly of extracting benefits from the strife of Europe while avoiding "enthusiastic tilting at windmills in the Old World." Unfortunately, Tatum thought, time had made strange interventionist and entangling additions to the doctrine's principles. "Never did a statesman more nearly fill the role of seer than did Adams when he warned his countrymen that a departure from these fundamental ideals would mark the end of the America he loved so well."[33]

Tatum found some support for his emphasis on Anglo-American rivalry in the Western Hemisphere from J. Fred Rippy. Rippy, an admirer of Franklin Roosevelt and the New Deal, did caution that his purpose in writing *Rivalry of the United States and Great Britain over Latin America, 1808–1830* was not "to furnish explosives for those who would like to destroy the foundation of Anglo-Saxon harmony." But as World War II approached, Rippy became more isolationist, and his later works did not reflect this same concern for the preservation of Anglo-American cooperation.[34]

Rippy and Tatum had both been students of another anti-British isolationist and nationalist, Eugene McCormac of the University of California. Rippy remembered that McCormac had expressed a thor-

32. Edward Howland Tatum, Jr., *The United States and Europe, 1815–1823: A Study in the Background of the Monroe Doctrine* (Berkeley, 1936).

33. *Ibid.*, pp. 277–278.

34. J. Fred Rippy, *Rivalry of the United States and Great Britain over Latin America, 1808–1830* (Baltimore, 1929), pp. vii–viii. See also his *The United States and Mexico*, rev. ed. (New York, 1931; originally published 1926); *The Capitalists and Colombia* (New York, 1931); *Latin America in World Politics: An Outline Survey*, 3rd ed. (New York, 1938; originally published 1928); and *America and the Strife of Europe* (Chicago, 1938). This last work incorporated an earlier brief work, Rippy and Angie Debo, "The American Policy of Isolation," *Smith College Studies in History*, 9, nos. 3–4 (April–July 1924), which traced isolationist sentiments from 1775 to 1793.

ough dislike of the pro-British Hamilton, praised Jefferson and Jackson, and denounced the path of empire America had taken after 1898.[35] McCormac's biography of James K. Polk, one of the few important studies of the Mexican War written in this era, reflected these values. McCormac admired Polk and was in full agreement with Justin Smith on the question of Mexican War diplomacy. The United States' actions had been fully justified by Mexican intransigence and British interference, he claimed.[36] It is not surprising that McCormac's interpretation of the Mexican War also received the approval of Bemis in his diplomatic history text since the two shared such similar political views.

This nationalist, expansionist, anti-British view of the Mexican War did not go unchallenged in the wake of World War I, however. N. W. Stephenson produced a little survey, *Texas and the Mexican War*, the major point of which was that Polk's imperialism had been the cause of the war.[37] Richard Stenberg gave yet a stronger critique of Polk. Stenberg accepted the testimony of Anson Jones, the one-time president of the Texas republic, that Polk had masterminded a conspiracy to involve Texas and Mexico in a war that could be used to justify further expansion. Jones had claimed that Commodore Robert Stockton and others had approached him with this scheme, asking approval to have the Texas militia move into the area between the Nueces and the Rio Grande and clear it of Mexican troops. This would provoke a war, according to Stenberg. Stockton's scheme failed because Jones refused to support it. But Polk successfully triggered the war of conquest later by other means, such as annexing Texas without further negotiation and ordering Taylor to the Rio Grande. Such a picture of an intriguing Polk also "invites one to accept fully" the contention that Polk had sent Frémont secret instructions to seize California, Stenberg said.[38]

35. J. Fred Rippy, *Bygones I Cannot Help Recalling: The Memoirs of a Mobile Scholar* (Austin, 1966), p. 99.

36. Eugene Irving McCormac, *James K. Polk: A Political Biography* (Berkeley, 1922), pp. vi–vii.

37. N. W. Stephenson, *Texas and the Mexican War* (New Haven, 1921), pp. 260–261.

38. Richard Stenberg, "The Failure of Polk's Mexican War Intrigue of 1845," *Pacific Historical Review*, 4 (1935): 39ff. Stenberg seems to have been particularly attracted to conspiracy theories. He also claimed that John Quincy Adams had purposely yielded Texas to the Spanish negotiator, Luis de Onis in 1819. Stenberg used some vague references from Adams's letters to show that Adams knew Onis's instructions had permitted yielding Texas up to the Colorado River

The image of a grasping, imperialistic America was furthered by John Fuller's account of the All-Mexico Movement.[39] Similarly inclined was the historian who became the definitive authority on the acquisition of Oregon, Frederick Merk. Merk, another of Frederick Jackson Turner's students, began his long teaching career at Harvard in 1921. In a series of articles published in the 1920s and 1930s, Merk combined his frontier studies with extensive archival work in England to demonstrate that Polk's aggressive pressure tactics on Oregon had actually endangered rather than facilitated America's diplomatic success. The disputed territory between the 49th parallel and the Columbia River no longer seemed valuable to the British. The area had been "trapped-out" and the Columbia proved too difficult to navigate for commercial purposes. So the British Foreign Secretary Lord Aberdeen had been ready to accept America's demand for a border at 49 degrees latitude. However, Aberdeen could not let the settlement seem too much of a retreat because he would be open to attack from his Whig opponents, especially Lord Palmerston. Ultimately he had elicited a promise from the Whigs not to oppose the concession. Polk's blustering had hurt rather than helped this process, for it had made the British compromise seem more humiliating. However, Merk claimed that neither Polk nor the 54°40' fanatics were typical of the American people, the majority of whom had supported the peaceful inclinations of the Senate.[40]

Thus, the pendulum of historical opinion swung away from the more approving histories of expansionism written in the Age of Imperialism to a more disapproving stance in the aftermath of World War I. These histories of nineteenth-century America expansionism fall into three general, none-too-neat categories. First were the historians who attacked expansionist diplomacy as imperialistic, greedy, brutal, and hypocritical. This group, whose disillusioned attitudes were similar to those of the World War I revisionists, included Albert Weinberg, Louis Hacker, and Richard Stenberg.

A second group was composed of those with leanings toward Wilsonian internationalism. While refuting the harshest charges

---

(Richard Stenberg, "The Boundaries of the Louisiana Purchase," *Hispanic American Historical Review*, 14 [1934]: 54).

39. John Douglas Fuller, *The Movement for the Acquisition of All Mexico, 1846–1848* (Baltimore, 1936).

40. Merk's essays are conveniently collected in Frederick Merk, *The Oregon Question, Essays in Anglo-American Diplomacy and Politics* (Cambridge, Mass., 1967). See particularly "Snake Country Expedition, 1824–25" (published in

against America's expansionist diplomacy, especially those of the economic determinists, they did agree that American expansion had enough imperialistic characteristics to make the idealistic rationales offered for it seem slightly ridiculous. Still, they were willing to believe these ideals were sincerely held and contained a germ of truth sufficient to allow American statesmen to rationalize pursuit of economic or strategic interests in idealistic terms. The accounts of Wilsonian historians were generally matter of fact but often contained ironic, debunking, or apologetic tones. Dexter Perkins, Julius Pratt, Frederick Merk, and Arthur Whitaker were of this ilk.

Finally, there was a group of more nationalistic, isolationist, and anti-British historians. They distinguished sharply between early American expansionism in North America, of which they heartily approved, and the extracontinental imperialism that followed the Spanish-American War, which they detested. They tended to favor the old assertive neutrality policies, and their outlook bore some resemblance to that of the conservative revisionists of World War I. But their isolationist and anti-British tendencies seemed to derive from a nativist outlook rather than an Irish or German resentment of Great Britain. Among these historians were Samuel Flagg Bemis, Edward Tatum, and Eugene McCormac.

Ironically, as much as these groups might disagree in their attitudes toward America's early continental expansion, they were in substantial accord concerning the imperialist movement. They all denounced it. Expansion still had many defenders among post-World War I historians, but imperialism had almost none.

1934), "British Party Politics and the Oregon Treaty" (1932), "British Government Propaganda and the Oregon Treaty" (1934), and "The British Corn Crisis of 1845–1846 and the Oregon Treaty" (1934).

TWELVE

World War I and the Historiography of America's Imperial Age

The imperialist crusade which had so entranced the United States at the turn of the twentieth century fell into disrepute during the post-World War I era. Historians generally berated the Spanish-American War as one of brutal aggression and the acquisition of the Philippines as a serious mistake. They denounced the Roosevelt Corollary, the taking of Panama, and Dollar Diplomacy. They even stripped the halo from the Open Door policy. They also revived the reputation of the anti-imperialist.[1]

Perhaps the most significant indication of the unpopularity of imperialism in the 1920s and 1930s was the one already mentioned, that conservatives like Samuel Flagg Bemis, the most ardent defenders of America's nineteenth-century expansionism, were in the forefront of the attack on the Spanish-American War and the imperialism to which it had led. These conservatives based much of their rhetoric on James Ford Rhodes's *The McKinley and Roosevelt Administrations, 1897–1909*.[1] This concluding volume of Rhodes's great history appeared in 1922. Rhodes was a close friend of John Hay, and so his account of the Spanish-American War and its imperial aftermath, while critical, was not overly hostile.[2] Rhodes bemoaned McKinley's collapse in the face

1. Fred Harvey Harrington, "Anti-Imperialist Movement in the United States." *Mississippi Valley Historical Review*, 22 (1935): 211–230.
2. James Ford Rhodes, *The McKinley and Roosevelt Administrations, 1897–1909* (New York, 1922), p. 122.

of prowar pressure and claimed that the president could have resisted without destroying the Republican party.[3] Rhodes disliked the acquisition of both the Philippines and Hawaii, but his antiimperialism was mild and conservative. He was no cultural relativist; he did not advocate national self-determination for less-developed peoples.[4] He thought that the proper alternative for the Philippines had been to leave them with Spain, not turn them loose.[5]

Rhodes's attitude toward imperialism was based on his fear of entanglements with great powers, not the effects of American imperialism on native peoples. He thought the inhabitants of American dependencies had benefited tremendously from American rule.[6] He saw American imperialism as a sincere though misguided attempt to live up to a religious duty to protect the nation's security, not a product of sordid economic interest.[7] He was careful to point out that business had opposed the Spanish-American War.[8] He also belittled the roles of imperialists such as Roosevelt, Mahan, and Lodge. They were merely jingoes spoiling for a fight and motivated by a desire to see Cuba independent, not conspirators searching for a means to grab overseas colonies.[9] Here was the major distinction between conservative isolationist treatments of the Spanish-American War and those of leftist isolationists. Those on the Left had come to believe that the war was an imperialist maneuver, designed from the outset to secure an American empire.[10]

The most significant left-revisionist account was Walter Millis's *The Martial Spirit*, published in 1931.[11] Like Rhodes, Millis believed that McKinley had succumbed to popular pressure and gone to war

3. *Ibid.*, p. 61.
4. *Ibid.*, pp. 188, 114.
5. *Ibid.*, pp. 108, 114, 118, 130–131, 270–275, 366.
6. *Ibid.*, pp. 112, 364–366.
7. *Ibid.*, pp. 108–111, 364–366.
8. *Ibid.*, p. 55.
9. *Ibid.*, pp. 57–59.
10. For an account closely paralleling the one of Rhodes, see that of another Republican, Alfred L. P. Dennis, *Adventures in American Diplomacy, 1896–1906* (New York, 1928). Neither Dennis nor Rhodes was as disenchanted with the British as Bemis. Both were admirers of John Hay and impressed with the Open Door as a successful nonentangling policy based on diplomacy rather than force. Otherwise, their opinions seem quite consistent with those of Bemis. See *ibid.*, pp. 63–64, for the Spanish-American War; pp. 10–12, 23, 32, 35 for Dennis's emphasis on a restrained interpretation of Monroe Doctrine; p. 32 for his sympathy with Rhodes; and p. 15 for his attitude toward the Open Door.
11. Walter Millis, *The Martial Spirit: A Study of Our War with Spain* (Cambridge, Mass., 1931).

when Spain had "definitely yielded everything which we had asked and a cause for war no longer existed."[12] Unlike later left-revisionists, Millis lacked sympathy for the Cuban rebels; they were little better than bandits whose actions created more suffering than the Spanish reconcentration policy. But Cuban propaganda and America's own unscrupulous yellow press had convinced the American people otherwise.[13] Millis did not accuse Wall Street or other American business interests of promoting the war to secure new colonial markets, but he implied a stronger connection between economic interests and the war than Rhodes had done. The frontier had disappeared, industrialism had fully developed, and the nation needed new markets and outlets for national energy. Politicians had sensed this and raised new expansionist issues as a consequence.[14]

If Millis only implied some vague connection between business and the war, he emphasized far more strongly and explicitly the responsibility of imperialists like Roosevelt, Lodge, and Admiral George Dewey. Roosevelt and Dewey had plotted a war on the Philippines, and Roosevelt had maneuvered Dewey's appointment as commander of the Far Eastern fleet. Then Roosevelt and Lodge had taken advantage of the absence of Roosevelt's superior, Secretary of the Navy John D. Long, to reposition ships, requisition ammunition, and order Dewey to undertake offensive operations in the Philippines in case of war with Spain. Millis implied that the "two conspirators" had acted contrary to the wishes of Long and the McKinley administration.[15] Ultimately they had attained their goal, annexation of the Philippines.

Millis condemned the annexation. He believed the Filipinos had been competent to rule themselves and should have been left free to do so.[16] Millis was influenced in this belief by his era's rising cultural relativism which increasingly affected studies of the American Indian

12. *Ibid.*, pp. 137, 160.

13. *Ibid.*, pp. 10, 36, 40–41, 75–76. The yellow-press theme was elaborated later in this era in two important monographs: Joseph E. Wisan, *The Cuban Crisis as Reflected in the New York Press, 1895–1898* (New York, 1934); and Marcus M. Wilkerson, *Public Opinion and the Spanish-American War: A Study in War Propaganda* (Baton Rouge, 1932).

14. Millis, *Martial Spirit*, pp. 8–9.

15. *Ibid.*, pp. 85–87, 112–113.

16. *Ibid.*, p. 333. In the revisionist movement to rehabilitate Germany, Lester Burrell Shippee had investigated the German documents made available by World War I and had found that German ambitions in the Philippines were less threatening than had been believed in the Age of Imperialism (Shippee, "Germany and the Spanish-American War," *American Historical Review*, 30 [July 1925]: 754–777).

and of Latin American and Asian countries with which the United States had diplomatic dealings. But Millis's acceptance of cultural relativism had its limits. As we have already noted, he considered the Cuban rebels to be little better than bandits. Thus, although he condemned the attempts of the imperialists to abandon the Teller Amendment and annex Cuba along with the Philippines, he approved of the sense of decency behind America's acceptance of a protectorate. At least this allowed Cuba a limited measure of self-rule, "an act of fairly evident justice which, in the piratical times of thirty years ago, we were to pride ourselves upon as remarkable."[17]

But what Millis saw as an act of "fairly evident justice" toward Cuba, revisionists more radical than he saw as simply a disguised form of imperialism. Scott Nearing, whose book *The Great Madness* had been one of the first to condemn World War I, joined with Joseph Freeman in 1925 to denounce American imperialism in a book entitled *Dollar Diplomacy: A Study in American Imperialism.*[18] A doctrinaire socialist and economic determinist, Nearing saw the Spanish-American War as part of a history of imperialism dating from the first moments of America's existence. Thus, he said that Jefferson had been "a lifelong antiexpansionist on principle," forced by growing economic demands to take Louisiana. Nearing believed that the Monroe Doctrine had been originated primarily to protect the Western Hemisphere for U.S. expansion. Manifest Destiny he saw as a function of the economic interests of the slave oligarchy.[19]

Modern American imperialism differed from earlier expansionism only in the type of economic interests that stood behind it, according to Nearing and Freeman. In America's early days, those interests had been territorial. Later, commercial interests became dominant. Now financial investments were the primary force behind American foreign policy. American investments had been the leading cause of the Spanish-American War although these interests had been reinforced by the commercial value of the Philippines and the imperial motivations of men like Theodore Roosevelt.

Nearing and Freeman stopped short of calling the Spanish-American War a conscious plot to acquire new colonies. However, they believed colonial wars the inevitable consequence of capitalism, and, therefore, regardless of the intent of America's policy makers at

17. Millis, *Martial Spirit*, p. 404.
18. Scott Nearing and Joseph Freeman, *Dollar Diplomacy: A Study in American Imperialism* (New York, 1925).
19. *Ibid.*, pp. 233–239, esp. p. 234.

the outset of the war, America had been foredoomed to expand wherever the opportunity arose. It still was. But the form of American expansion was changing. Outright conquest and possession of colonies, as undertaken in the Philippines, Guam, and Puerto Rico during the Spanish-American War, were "a mode of imperialist acquisition which began to go out of existence at the end of the nineteenth century." America had followed Europe in turning to the new imperialism—protectorates and spheres of influence. The Open Door was an example of this. Meanwhile, "an intensification of the Monroe Doctrine has served as the diplomatic facade of the economic conquest of Latin America. . . ."[20]

None of these books seemed to have more than a nodding acquaintance with and respect for the foreign cultures they discussed. They based their opposition to American intervention on strategic, economic, and ideological factors. But Leland Jenks's *Our Cuban Colony* was a more subtle and accurate radical assessment of American imperialism in the Caribbean.[21] Jenks's book appeared under the auspices of the organization behind the book by Nearing and Freeman, the Fund for Public Service. This fund sponsored a series of studies of American imperialism edited by Harry Elmer Barnes. Barnes himself took something of the same meat-ax approach that Nearing and Freeman had taken. His introduction to Jenks's book was far less subtle than the text of the book itself.

Barnes argued that imperialist territorial expansion had changed to financial capitalism as the frontier had closed and an excess of capital had demanded new markets abroad. Thus, America had entered the Spanish-American War under a party that was to a peculiar degree dominated by industry and finance. America's Cuban policy had developed out of a clash of "ostensible benevolence with economic realities." The result had been a revised economic imperialism in which investors eschewed political and military force for economic ascendency. "This is less repulsive and more aesthetic than wholesale slaughter by marines, but it may also be much more potent than physical force in the establishment of a permanent economic hegemony," Barnes warned.[22]

Jenks himself was more guarded. He stated flatly that businessmen had opposed the Spanish-American War and that America's treat-

20. *Ibid.*, pp. xiii–xiv, 250–255, esp. pp. 258–260.
21. Leland H. Jenks, *Our Cuban Colony: A Study in Sugar* (New York, 1928).
22. Barnes, introduction to Jenks, *Our Cuban Colony*, pp. viii–xv.

ment of Cuba had been well intended even if much of it had proved to be "inappropriate and unwise." American investments had made Cubans more prosperous but also had made them less free. Cuba was at least as competent to govern itself as Alabama or Cook County, said Jenks, and should be left free to do so. The Platt Amendment had outlived its usefulness. The United States was powerful enough to have no fear of other nations, and the amendment hurt America's reputation in the rest of Latin America. But while Jenks was willing to offer this advice against the old imperialism of political domination, he was unsure about the answer to the new imperialism, the economic ascendency of American investors in Cuba. Cuba needed those investments, yet they rendered Cuba dependent upon export crops and reduced the island's national independence. Jenks offered no solution to this dilemma, but he implied that America should expect Cuba to nationalize foreign investments sometime in the future.[23]

Liberal internationalists were hardly more favorable to the Spanish-American War and its imperial aftermath than conservative or radical isolationists. The best example of this was Julius Pratt's *Expansionists of 1898*. Pratt simply assumed throughout his book that the Spanish-American War and imperialism had been mistakes. He softened the charges of radical isolationists like Millis and Nearing somewhat by absolving business of responsibility for the Spanish-American War. Radicals had implied business responsibility by theorizing that one of the major motives for the war had been the new markets and resources that a resulting empire might bring. Pratt's careful survey of business magazines, stock market reactions, chamber of commerce resolutions, and business lobbying in the State Department convinced most post-World War I historians that business had indeed opposed the Spanish-American War.[24]

Yet Pratt had not absolved business of all responsibility for the evils the post-World War I generation saw in the imperial crusade. Business might have opposed the war at the outset, but Pratt went on to say that business had been converted en masse to the acquisition of overseas colonies once the war was under way. The European threats to partition China had pushed businessmen into imperialism, Pratt said. Thus, they fell in behind the historians, politicians, and journalists who had discovered earlier the need for new markets and investments and had mounted the imperial crusade.[25]

23. *Ibid.*, pp. 1, 41, 57, 304–313.
24. Pratt, *Expansionists of 1898*, p. 232, n. 8.
25. *Ibid.*, pp. 22, 230–278.

It was the ideas of these imperialist historians, politicians, and journalists that occupied most of Pratt's study. "Far-fetched and fallacious" as their ideas might seem, they were sincerely held and widely influential. Contrary to the fashion of his time, Pratt said these ideas owed little to economics and much to the strategic theories of Mahan, the Social Darwinism of John Fiske, the moral uplift of Josiah Strong and of various churches, and the racial theories of John W. Burgess, who "planted the seed of expansionist policy only to abjure the ripened fruit."[26] But if Burgess had "abjured the ripened fruit," Theodore Roosevelt had not. Having absorbed the ideas of the expansionists of 1898, Roosevelt had maneuvered to include Philippine operations in the war. But here Pratt refused to make as direct a connection as some revisionists had made between expansionists like Roosevelt and the Spanish-American War. "Whether Roosevelt was at this time contemplating the actual conquest of the Philippines or merely the most effective means of waging war against Spain is not entirely clear," he hedged.[27]

In any case, Rooseveltian imperialism was under a cloud. The taking of Panama was pronounced arrogant and unnecessary by Wilsonian internationalists like Dexter Perkins and J. Fred Rippy, radicals like Scott Nearing and Leland Jenks, and conservative isolationists like Samuel Flagg Bemis and James Ford Rhodes. Most of them portrayed Roosevelt himself as a bellicose adolescent, comic and menacing at the same time. Such an image was etched indelibly on the American mind by the acid biography of Roosevelt by Henry Pringle.[28] This disparate group of historians could also agree that military interventions under the Roosevelt Corollary had been excessive and counterproductive.

All but the radical authors assumed that the result of American interventions had been somewhat beneficial to the indigenous peoples, especially in Cuba, and they did see some strategic imperative to preventing the chaotic conditions in the Caribbean that might tempt European intervention. Still they thought that American intervention had not done enough good to compensate for the anti-American feeling it had generated. Thus, they welcomed the Good Neighbor policy's renunciation of unilateral American intervention. Such views had begun gathering strength toward the end of the Age of Imperialism,

---

26. *Ibid.*, pp. 3–33, 279–316; for comment on Burgess, see p. 11.
27. *Ibid.*, p. 222.
28. Henry F. Pringle, *Theodore Roosevelt* (New York, 1931).

and they continued to increase in popularity after World War I until the Good Neighbor policy was welcomed by all.[29]

But while everyone seemed to accept the Good Neighbor policy, they did so for slightly different reasons. Liberal internationalists like Perkins and Rippy emphasized the cooperative aspects of Good Neighborism. They admitted that intervention had sometimes been essential to American interests and security. Now, they thought, the ill effects of such necessary intervention would be negated because a majority of Western Hemisphere nations would agree to joint operations.

The more conservative isolationists ignored or opposed cooperative intervention, emphasizing instead simply more restraint in unilateral intervention. They were willing to accept restraint not because American rule had been oppressive but because they felt that the United States was strong enough to tolerate some disorder on its borders while warning off European intervention. In addition, they believed that Latin America was maturing to the point that disorders were becoming fewer and less dangerous.

In this area, some old admirers of Theodore Roosevelt were still willing to make a few tepid gestures of defense. One of these was Chester Lloyd Jones, professor of commerce and political science at the University of Wisconsin. In 1916 Jones had written *Caribbean Interests of the United States*, in which he had called the Platt Amendment and the Roosevelt Corollary "farsighted." In addition, he had said that Dollar Diplomacy conferred a favor on both foreign investors and the weaker nations that the American government protected from exploitation.[30]

By 1936, when Jones published *The Caribbean Since 1900*, he had altered this view somewhat. American intervention had been beneficial although "not uniformly happy." Now the United States should seek to increase Latin American stability so that intervention would no longer be necessary, a process he thought was going well. He urged greater caution in intervention saying that America had underestimated the difficulties and overestimated the benefits in the past. Still,

---

29. Perkins, *Monroe Doctrine, 1867–1907*, pp. 396–455; Rippy, *Latin America in World Politics*, pp. 235–291; Dennis, *Adventures in American Diplomacy*, pp. 10–12; and Rhodes, *McKinley and Roosevelt Administrations*, pp. 130–131, 268–275, 366. See also Dana G. Munro, *The United States and the Caribbean Area* (Boston, 1934). Although Munro's later works clearly placed him with people like Perkins and Rippy, this earlier book was so bland as to make it almost impossible to determine his attitude toward U.S. intervention.

30. Chester Lloyd Jones, *Caribbean Interests of the United States* (New York and London, 1916), pp. 325, 328–329.

the joint responsibility for intervention contemplated by the Good Neighbor policy could not be expected to work well for a while. Some short-term extranational control of weaker states "seems unavoidable," he concluded.[31]

Russell Fitzgibbon was another significant historian of the Caribbean area. He was a friend and follower of Jones, to whom he dedicated his *Cuba and the United States, 1900–1935.*[32] Like Jones, Fitzgibbon saw America's previous intervention in Cuba as beneficent, but he too urged greater restraint and praised Franklin Roosevelt for "abrogating the Platt Amendment." Yet his reasoning showed that he was not entirely reconstructed. Even without the Platt Amendment, Fitzgibbon pointed out, the United States had the right to protect its interests and the lives of its citizens. Thus, abrogation of the Platt Amendment would not mean the end of all American intervention in Cuba.[33]

A similar attitude could be seen in Howard Hill's *Roosevelt and the Caribbean.*[34] Hill too commended Theodore Roosevelt's policies, particularly toward Cuba, saying that his cautious intervention there and the alacrity with which he had withdrawn afterward contrasted strikingly and pleasingly with the admittedly brutal and arrogant way Roosevelt had treated Colombia over the Panama Canal. Most of Roosevelt's interventions had been benevolent, motivated by security needs rather than economic greed, and "promotive of international amity and peace." Yet Hill's tone made it seem that he too would welcome greater restraint.[35]

The progress of Rooseveltian imperialists from pride to doubt appeared in the historiography of the Far East as well as that of the Caribbean. The prime exhibit was Tyler Dennett. A minister and journalist who had made two trips to the Orient before becoming a historian, Dennett had been hired by the State Department to undertake an examination of American Far Eastern policy for the benefit of the American delegation to the Washington Naval Conference of 1921.

31. Chester Lloyd Jones, *The Caribbean Since 1900* (New York, 1936), pp. 463, 471, 476–480.
32. Russell Fitzgibbon, *Cuba and the United States, 1900–1935* (New York, 1935).
33. *Ibid.*, pp. 24–27, 32–33, 122–123, 144–148, 252–263.
34. Howard C. Hill, *Roosevelt and the Caribbean* (Chicago, 1927).
35. *Ibid.*, pp. 68, 69, 102, 174, 207–209, 213.

The outcome was his significant and influential book, *Americans in Eastern Asia,* published in 1922.[36]

At this point in Dennett's career, he was strongly interventionist. He was not uncritical of America's policies toward the Orient, saying that the United States shared the guilt with all other nations, East and West, for the "welter of evil which now comprises the Far Eastern question." But generally he considered America's aim of an open door beneficial for both the United States and Asia.[37] It was not America's goal but its means that he disliked. He thought the United States should have cooperated more with Britain and Japan rather than operating unilaterally. Unilateralism required excessive belligerence and military expenditures, such as Perry's show of force in Japan and the acquisition of strategic bases such as Hawaii and the Philippines. The support of powerful friends like Japan and Great Britain would have permitted Perry and McKinley to have accomplished their goals more decorously through patient negotiations rather than urgent and forceful measures.[38] And if cooperation with these friendly nations would have been helpful, the official alliances desired by John Hay would have been better yet.[39]

By 1925, when Dennett published his dissertation, *Roosevelt and the Russo-Japanese War,* he was even more in favor of firm alliances and threats of coercion and less hopeful that informal cooperation would be adequate. As proof he compared the futility of Hay's verbal victories and clever diplomacy in combatting Russian aggrandizement in China with the success of Theodore Roosevelt's supposed threat to use force against Russia if a third power came to its aid, a gesture worth "a thousand diplomatic notes."[40] Unfortunately, however, the American people would support neither such forceful measures in the Far East nor the European alliances necessary to aid them. Had America only stood in 1914 where Roosevelt had stood in 1904–1905, Dennett wondered whether Germany would ever have marched into Belgium. He thought it a tragedy that the United States had reverted to its old policy in the Far East, "expecting something for nothing, . . . standing back

36. Tyler Dennett, *Americans in Eastern Asia: A Critical Study of the Policy of the United States with Reference to China, Japan and Korea in the 19th Century* (New York, 1922).

37. *Ibid.*, pp. vi–viii.

38. *Ibid.*, pp. 626, 631, 634.

39. *Ibid.*, pp. 648, 644–645.

40. Tyler Dennett, *Roosevelt and the Russo-Japanese War* (New York, 1925), pp. 330, 333.

until some other Power made the effort, and then demanding a share in the fruits of victory."[41]

By the 1930s, Dennett had become considerably more disillusioned with American policy in the Far East. His Pulitzer Prize-winning biography, *John Hay*, dwelt on the same theme as his previous books, that diplomatic notes and clever diplomacy, however successful they might be temporarily, were "mere flap-doodle" unless backed by force. But Dennett was no longer sure that the American people had been misguided in their refusal to approve the exercise of force in the Orient. Probably America would have been no more entangled there than it was in Dennett's time if Hay and Roosevelt had been permitted to use adequate measures. Yet this

> involved intervention in a region where American interests were actually very small. The best that could be hoped for, the preservation of the undiminished historical relation of Manchuria to the Chinese Empire, promised to the United States no benefit proportionate to the responsibilities which would have had to be assumed.[42]

In addition, Theodore Roosevelt, the unsullied hero of his earlier book, emerged somewhat tarnished from the Hay biography. Dennett found him often reckless, unnecessarily brutal in Panama, and willing to play "the demagogue on an international scale for the sake of winning a presidential nomination."[43]

As the 1930s advanced, Dennett's disillusionment increased. By 1939 he declared that he had "somewhat reluctantly . . . reached an almost completely isolationist point of view."[44] His retreat from interventionism was noted by many in his articles and speeches of the late 1930s. Bemis even wrote him that his own textbook, just published in 1936, had "much in common . . . with many of your ideas."[45] Thus, although Dennett would later support American entry into World War

---

41. *Ibid.*, pp. 332, 335, 337. Dorothy Borg has traced Dennett's changing ideas in her "Two Histories of the Far Eastern Policy of the United States: Tyler Dennett and A. Whitney Griswold," in Dorothy Borg and Shumpei Okamoto, eds., *Pearl Harbor as History: Japanese-American Relations, 1931–1941* (New York and London, 1973), pp. 551–573. But I think she overestimates the magnitude of change between Dennett's two early books.

42. Tyler Dennett, *John Hay: From Poetry to Politics* (Port Washington, N.Y., 1963), pp. 323, 334–335, 403.

43. *Ibid.*, pp. 363, 382, 401.

44. Quoted in Borg, "Tyler Dennett and A. Whitney Griswold," p. 730, n. 23.

45. *Ibid.*, ns. 23, 26.

II, at this point he had joined the march of his colleagues away from America's past interventionist diplomacy.

Another historian of United States-Far Eastern relations who showed the influence of the movement against imperialism was Foster Rhea Dulles. But disillusionment never struck so deep with him as it did with Dennett. Dulles was a cousin of the two Dulles brothers who would later become secretary of state and head of the CIA, John Foster Dulles and Allen Dulles. The Dulles family had strong ties to missionary activities in China, and Foster Rhea Dulles began his newspaper career as a correspondent for the *Christian Science Monitor* in Peking. He wrote several books on America's Far Eastern relations during his days as a newspaperman and carried this interest with him into a career as a diplomatic historian at Ohio State University. His most important book in the prewar period was *America in the Pacific: A Century of Expansion.*[46] Dulles generally favored America's expansion to the Pacific and beyond. But he criticized the taking of the Philippines, saying that it "clearly broke with the tradition that the United States was a nation in which self-government, democracy, and equal rights were the basic principles of national life." He claimed: "In no other instance of our expansion could this charge be sustained."

Thus, he rejoiced that the United States was no longer seeking commercial and naval bases once considered essential to American interests in the Pacific. Instead of harboring ambitions for absolute supremacy, America now stood for peace and stability in the Far East. "None but the most aggressive of imperialists will regret this change in attitude," Dulles said.[47] But beyond this, Dulles resisted the antiinterventionist currents of the age. He praised the Open Door policy and said that Secretary of State Henry Stimson could have done no less than he did in his famous Stimson Doctrine, refuse to recognize Japan's conquest of Manchuria. Dulles further warned that force might be required to maintain the Open Door.[48]

Since Dulles advocated intervention to preserve the Open Door and Dennett's conversion to isolationism came well after the production of his three major works, the presentation of the full isolationist view of American policy in the Far East was left to the period's other great historian in this field, A. Whitney Griswold. Griswold was a junior colleague of Bemis at Yale. He shared many of Bemis's ideas, but

---

46. Foster Rhea Dulles, *America in the Pacific: A Century of Expansion* (Boston and New York, 1932).
47. *Ibid.*, p. ix.
48. *Ibid.*, pp. ix–xiii.

Griswold based his isolationism on a liberal, Beardian view of politics rather than the conservative, anti-New Deal attitude shared by Bemis and Dennett. Griswold was also like Beard in the present-minded and purposeful way he used his history to promote his political opinions. His blatant advocacy brought even the opinionated Bemis to comment in the margin of Griswold's manuscript that Griswold should stick closer to the facts and stop preaching.[49]

Griswold published his *Far Eastern Policy of the United States* in 1938 with the avowed hope that it would keep the United States from "jumping into" a war in the Far East.[50] He traced America's relations with the Orient from 1898 to 1937, arguing that 1898 had marked a turning point in those relations. Until that time the United States had sought only trade and the protection of its citizens in the Far East. It had indeed used river patrols, extraterritoriality, and the most-favored-nation principle to do so, but it had acquired these privileges through suasion rather than force, and its refusal to participate in carving up China gave American policy a "moral ascendency" over that of its European rivals.[51]

John Hay had changed that policy after America acquired the Philippines. Hay had tried to commit other powers to the Open Door and even had tried to protect the territorial integrity of China.[52] It was a far different proposition to preserve rather than merely respect the integrity of China, Griswold said.[53] If Hay's notes contained no formal commitment to such preservation, they mobilized popular opinion behind the idea that there was one. This Griswold thought a grievous error. Administration after administration had tried to enforce the doctrine aggressively, endangering America's peace and security, only to admit defeat and fall back.[54]

Griswold urged a more conciliatory policy toward Japan. He was sure that such conciliation had been responsible for Japan's willing-

49. Jamie W. Moore, "East Asia, the Historian, and the Burden of A. Whitney Griswold," unpublished paper in my possession, p. 30, n. 46.
50. Quoted in Borg, "Tyler Dennett and A. Whitney Griswold," p. 567.
51. A. Whitney Griswold, *The Far Eastern Policy of the United States* (New York, 1938), pp. 6–8.
52. Griswold followed Pratt on the Spanish-American War, saying that business and most of the nation were converted to keeping the Philippines only after the battle of Manila. The instigators of the idea were Roosevelt and Lodge, and their motives were simply expansion. The idea of keeping the Philippines to protect America's position in China was an afterthought—a rationalization, not a motive, Griswold said (*ibid.*, pp. 8–14, 34).
53. *Ibid.*, pp. 80–81.
54. *Ibid.*, pp. 305–332, 380–438, 440–443.

ness to settle the Panay incident so quickly and reasonably. Neither the Open Door nor the territorial integrity of China was worth a war. Attempts to maintain them obstructed "the most profitable trend of American commerce and investment in the Far East which, since 1900, had been toward Japan, not China." Besides this, they threatened to involve "the United States in European politics via the back door of Eastern Asia."[55]

Griswold implied that the United States had been lured into overcommitment in Asia by Great Britain. He recounted the story Dennett had told of how the Open Door notes had come to be written by John Hay. Alfred Hippisley, a British subject employed by the Chinese customs service, had urged an American declaration of policy in communications to his friend William Rockhill, Hay's chief adviser on Asian affairs. Rockhill had used Hippisley's language verbatim in drafting the Open Door notes. Thus, Britain had secured overt American support for its own interests against the powers seeking to carve up China. Griswold did not think cooperation with Britain had been devoid of value. At least it had eliminated rivalry between America and England. "Yet many an American diplomatic venture had foundered on the too casual assumption that British and American interest in that quarter of the globe were identical."[56]

Griswold's book represented many of the trends among historians who had reacted strongly against the experiences of World War I and the Treaty of Versailles. His anti-British, antiinterventionist outlook was shared by conservative isolationists such as Bemis, McCor-

55. *Ibid.*, pp. 466–467.

56. *Ibid.*, pp. 67–87, 472. Griswold rejected Dennett's suggestion, advanced previously in Bertah A. Reuter, *Anglo-American Relations During the Spanish-American War* (New York, 1924), that the United States had issued the Open Door notes as prior payment in a deal to secure Britain's retreat from the Caribbean. Griswold based this rejection on lack of any specific evidence of such an arrangement and on a specific denial from Hippisley himself. See Griswold, *Far Eastern Policy of the United States*, p. 85; and Dennett, *John Hay*, p. 296. One other work on Asia in this period which deserves mention is Payson J. Treat's *Japan and the United States, 1853–1921* (Boston and New York, 1921). It was written early in the era and bore no marks of World War I revisionism. Treat wrote a reasonably balanced account, urging better understanding between Japan and the United States. "Thoughtful Americans recognize the peculiar necessities of Japan—the pressure of a rapidly increasing population dwelling in a small area with limited natural resources," he said. But he warned that Japanese economic growth must not come at the expense of the rights and liberties of neighboring states. Japanese-American relations would be increasingly unsatisfactory if Japan "should endeavor to extend her special interests in China by force or intrigue" (*ibid.*, pp. 243–244).

mac, and Rhodes as well as liberal isolationists like Charles Beard and Harry Elmer Barnes. His hard-boiled, disillusioned, iconoclastic tone was also more common in this era, even among Wilsonian internationalists, than it had been. Wilsonians did not abandon the field of historical interpretation. They even joined in the general condemnation of the territorial acquisitions and excessive interventions abroad that had characterized the Age of Imperialism. Still, in their primary concern for American involvement in Europe, they were clearly on the defensive. Meanwhile, conservatives had all but abandoned Theodore Roosevelt's brand of foreign policy activism and retreated to isolationism. However, they remained strong defenders of earlier continental expansion, and with the support of liberals still enamored of Turner's frontier thesis, the diplomacy of westward expansion fared better in historical interpretation than did the later imperialist movement.

By the end of the 1930s, the storm of World War II was approaching. It would scour the old historiography and change the assumptions of a whole generation.

PART FIVE

The Age of Munich
1939-1965

The outbreak of World War II brought yet another drastic change to historical outlooks on American diplomacy. The failure of appeasement at Munich indicated to isolationist and interventionist alike that a peaceful demeanor and decent intentions were not always adequate to maintain peace, security, and justice in international affairs. The Japanese attack on Pearl Harbor drove the lesson home and destroyed isolationism almost as thoroughly as it did the American battleships anchored there. The lesson of Munich came to be applied not only to the Axis during the war but also to the Soviet Union and the communist movement in the war's aftermath. Appeasement brought war as surely as aggression, Americans decided. Military force was a necessary and legitimate tool of foreign policy. War might well be the lesser of evils in certain situations.

These attitudes were formulated into a highly influential philosophy of foreign relations by a group of political theorists who called themselves "realists." World War II and the Cold War led them to believe that the basis for a successful foreign policy had to be balance-of-power politics. They scathingly denounced American policies, past or present, that they thought had failed to take proper account of the role of national self-interest and power, especially when these policies included utopian goals such as the spread of democracy throughout the world or when they failed to balance more limited goals with the power available to achieve them. Facing the threat of nuclear holocaust, Americans had to concern themselves less with ideology and more with establishing a balance of power to preserve the peace. This meant an activist, interventionist policy, one no longer hamstrung by old phobias against foreign alliances and standing armies.

But it also meant restraint. Interventions vital to American security were justified. Intervention in areas that were not vital or in pursuit of mere economic as opposed to strategic interests was to be condemned. Restraint toward the nation's enemies was necessary as well. Realists detested crusades, whether against the Nazis or the communists, and urged that the balance of power, not moral indignation, be the guiding principle even in the heat of war. Naturally the realists had a significant impact on historical interpretations of America's entry into World War II and the development of the Cold War. But they also affected interpretations of earlier events in American diplomacy, as they commended the realism of men like Alexander Hamilton or Theodore Roosevelt while deriding the utopianism of Thomas Jefferson or Woodrow Wilson.

Most historians of this era accepted the general theoretical structure of the realists. But many still insisted that there was a greater role for ideals in foreign policy than the realists would allow, and they defended leaders and policies that the realists had criticized. Far outside the debate that took place within this consensus, a few radicals chipped away at the sacred assumptions of the Munich generation but for the present received scant attention.

THIRTEEN

World War II and the Creation of the Munich Analogy

Pearl Harbor instantaneously united America behind Franklin Roosevelt and the war against the Axis. In the process it also discredited the isolationists, the World War I revisionists, and the idea that a peaceful national demeanor, neutrality, and the oceanic moat surrounding the United States could shelter America from the clash of great powers abroad. A new way would have to be found to keep America's peace, the vast majority of Americans decided, and this new way might best be gleaned by investigating the failure of former policies to prevent World War II or America's entry into it.

Two books representing this trend were published during the war, Walter Lippmann's *U.S. Foreign Policy: Shield of the Republic* and Dexter Perkins's *America and Two Wars*. Both of these books argued that American entry into World War II had been thoroughly justified and necessary but that the war itself might have been prevented if America had not followed such misguided policies in the prewar years. Americans had forgotten what the Founding Fathers had known so well, that American interests and commitments, in the final analysis, had to be protected by force. The United States had been lulled into complacency by the vast oceans that separated it from the great powers abroad. Americans also naïvely had come to assume that their intentions were so obviously peaceful and good that no nations could find cause to attack them. Thus, the United States had failed to intervene against the Axis threats in Europe and Asia until too late to stop the conflagration of World War II. If only America had cooperated with England, France, and Russia in the interwar years, World War II might have been avoided.[1] Naturally, Perkins and Lippmann regarded America's rejection of the League of Nations as a tragedy.[2] The Washington Naval Conference and the Kellogg-Briand Pact seemed instances of appeasement that had invited aggression.[3] The Stimson Doctrine had been "wholly inadequate."[4] Finally, the Neutrality Acts had capped two decades of foolish isolationism.[5]

The only significant difference between Perkins and Lippmann concerned the diplomacy of Franklin Roosevelt. Both praised him for leading the United States into the war, but they disagreed over the pace of American intervention. Perkins thought Roosevelt's march toward war had been necessarily slow. It was essential that the enemy strike the first blow before America's inherent isolationism and skepticism would be reduced sufficiently to allow a unified country to enter the war.[6] Lippmann, however, drew the opposite conclusion from the fact that "the illusions of a century" stood between the American people and their ability to understand the imbalance between their commitments and their war readiness. It required dramatic and vigorous action to overcome such delusions. Roosevelt's policies were too timid to be successful, and America entered the war unprepared, unable to reach full mobilization until 1944.[7] This dispute over the pace and vigor of Roosevelt's interventionism would emerge as one of the most significant lasting historiographical debates concerning the diplomacy of World War II.

Perkins and Lippmann agreed, however, that World War II had provided a vital lesson for the United States. America would have to increase its military preparedness and give up its isolationist policies. Potentially aggressive nations had to be faced with greater power than their own. America would have to cooperate or ally with Great Britain

1. Walter Lippmann, *U.S. Foreign Policy: Shield of the Republic* (Boston, 1943); and Dexter Perkins, *America and Two Wars* (Boston, 1944).

2. Perkins, *America and Two Wars*, pp. 31–52, esp. pp. 52–56, 98–100, and Lippmann, *U.S. Foreign Policy*, pp. 32–37.

3. Perkins, *America and Two Wars*, pp. 104–106; and Lippmann, *U.S. Foreign Policy*, pp. 104–105.

4. Perkins, *America and Two Wars*, p. 114; and Lippmann, *U.S. Foreign Policy*, p. 43.

5. Perkins, *America and Two Wars*, p. 115. See also Lippmann, *U.S. Foreign Policy*, pp. 41–42.

6. Perkins, *America and Two Wars*, pp. 148–149, 154–155.

7. Lippmann, *U.S. Foreign Policy*, pp. 43–45, 110.

and, if possible, Russia. A breach between the Allies would present the danger of "a war which might be more dreadful and more prolonged than that in which we now find ourselves," said Perkins.[8] Lippmann added that peace could be maintained only if one side had a preponderance of power. A mere balance of power invited aggression and war. America must organize the peace by becoming a member of an alliance with such overwhelming power that no outside nation would dare challenge it.[9]

Thus, the lessons of World War I had been overthrown. Peace required power, not neutrality, isolation, or appeals to morality without force. Lippmann himself apologized for being one of the vast majority of Americans who had forgotten these basic principles.[10] His rediscovery of them probably was encouraged not only by the events of World War II but also by the writings of two other men who were profoundly affected by the same events and whose reactions to them were highly influential throughout America's intellectual community—Reinhold Niebuhr and Nicholas Spykman.[11]

Reinhold Niebuhr was a Protestant theologian who spearheaded the revival of neo-Calvinism in America. An activist egalitarian and socialist in his early days, Niebuhr came to believe that the Axis's demonic drive toward world conquest was a more overwhelming problem than the inequitable distribution of wealth in the United States. The Nazis demonstrated in historical terms the Calvinist emphasis on the ineradicable power of evil in men. The Christian realist could not counter this evil with flaccid appeals to some utopian future, be it earthly or heavenly. Earthly power for evil must be met with organized power on behalf of good even though the use of such power for good inevitably partook of the corruption of fallible and finite man.

Niebuhr thought that American liberals had unfortunately derived too optimistic a view of mankind from the French philosophes and Founding Fathers like Thomas Jefferson. One of the worst of these moralistic illusions was that generosity toward dictators would assuage their appetites "instead of merely giving them occasion for regarding 'liberal' democracy as a craven and corrupt form of

---

8. Perkins, *America and Two Wars*, p. 190.
9. Lippmann, *U.S. Foreign Policy*, pp. 146–147.
10. *Ibid.*, pp. vii–x.
11. Lippmann may also have been influenced by the work of the British scholar, E. H. Carr, *The Twenty Years' Crisis, 1919–1930, An Introduction to the Study of International Relations* (New York, 1939).

government which they have a mission to destroy." Actually even America's most benevolent intentions were tainted with self-love and self-interest, and its hegemony would therefore fail to produce the utopia that its liberals and pacifists seemed to think it would, Niebuhr concluded.[12]

Nicholas Spykman, professor of international relations at Yale and an advocate of geopolitics, shared these sentiments and applied them in specific terms to a structural analysis of international affairs.[13] He admitted that power was not the only aspect of foreign policy. International relations were also "influenced by love, hate, and charity, by moral indignation and the hope of material gain, by the moods and psychological abnormalities of rulers, and by the emotional afflictions of peoples." However, international society was without a central authority to preserve order or protect nations in their rights. "The result is that individual states must make the preservation and improvement of their power position a primary objective of their foreign policy." The United States had to "accept this basic reality" if it wanted a sound policy.[14]

For Spykman, all other aspects of foreign policy, including wealth, ideology, and propaganda, were weapons in the power struggle rather than independent motives. He saw America's participation in World War II simply as a necessary attempt to restore the balance of power in Europe and Asia. The threat of Germany and Japan was their potential hegemony in Europe and Asia, not their evil ideology. Self-consciously applying the dictums of the German geopolitical school, he said that America's geographical position required it to seek a balance in Europe and Asia because a united Europe or Asia had had the resources to cross the oceans and threaten the Western Hemisphere. He was certain that this was the intention of both Japan and Germany, and therefore he supported American intervention in both theaters.[15]

Spykman believed that America's proper strategy in Europe was alliance with England. Britain sat astride America's line of communications to the Continent, controlling the North Sea, the Channel, and the Mediterranean. Since it was also in Britain's interest to support a bal-

---

12. Reinhold Niebuhr, *Christianity and Power Politics: Discerning the Signs of the Times* (New York, 1940), pp. 47, 54, 102, 108–109. See also his *The Children of Light and the Children of Darkness* (New York, 1944).

13. Nicholas Spykman, *America's Strategy in World Politics: The United States and the Balance of Power* (New York, 1942).

14. *Ibid.*, pp. 7–8.

15. *Ibid.*, pp. 166–176, 194–199.

ance in Europe, an Anglo-American alliance was natural. But Spykman warned against any attempt to establish an all-European federation. If America had had an interest in an integrated Europe, it should have supported Hitler.[16] Spykman also warned against any attempt to establish an Anglo-American hegemony throughout the world as some were urging. It would be no more welcome than a German-Japanese hegemony and would cause Russia, Germany, and China, the great land powers, to band together to counteract it.[17]

Thus, contrary to Lippmann, and perhaps more like Niebuhr, Spykman thought a balance of power more likely to keep the peace than hegemony, however benevolent the intentions of the Americans and British, let alone the third potential power, Russia. The British probably would want Germany left strong enough to balance Russia at the end of the war, and America should agree. A Russia stretching from the Urals to the North Sea was no better than a Germany stretching from the North Sea to the Urals.[18] Spykman had similar ideas about Asia. He thought Europe was a more powerful entity and therefore more important to the United States, but Asia was rising and soon would be of almost equal significance. As long as Japan sought hegemony there and certainly as long as it was allied in its purpose with Germany, America had to fight the Japanese. But Spykman saw Japan as similar to Britain in its geographic relationship to the United States. Like Britain, it was a naval power in a position to determine American communications with a vast continental area. America could exert real power in Asia only in alliance with Japan just as it could exert power in Europe only in alliance with Great Britain. In any case, the long-run danger to the balance of power in Asia was China not Japan, Spykman thought. Sooner or later, the United States would have to remedy the "present inconsistency" toward Japan, and help that nation establish the balance of power in Asia. But this could happen only after Japan was cleansed of its militaristic ambitions.[19]

Spykman probably overestimated the World War II generation's newly awakened interests in balance-of-power politics. The emotional

16. *Ibid.*, pp. 98–99, 463.
17. *Ibid.*, pp. 458–459.
18. *Ibid.*, p. 460. In fact, Spykman thought that as long as the Allies had not stopped German rearmament before the war, they would have been wiser not to have opposed Germany in Eastern Europe. They could not defend Eastern Europe, it would not have added much to Germany's strength, and once Russia had had a common border with Germany, Russia would have quickly become a firm Western ally (*ibid.*, pp. 115–116).
19. *Ibid.*, p. 470.

and ideological response to Nazi Germany and militaristic Japan was too strong to permit this sort of detachment or consideration of the future manipulation of present allies. Even Spykman, while casting furtive glances at the problem China and Russia might pose to the future balance of power, was more concerned with the question of whether America would retreat to isolationism after the war was over. On this point realists and idealists agreed that the experience of World War I and World War II showed the folly of isolationism. Both America's interest in the balance of power and its idealistic hope of preventing a new rise of fascism after the war necessitated an interventionist policy for postwar America.

Yet the end of World War II found a new wave of isolationism and revisionism waiting in the wings, led by the key figures of the old World War I revisionism. Charles Beard published a brief attack on Franklin Roosevelt and his diplomacy only a year after VJ Day.[20] Charles Tansill once again contributed the most fully researched of the revisionist tomes, *Back Door to War*.[21] Harry Elmer Barnes put together a series of essays written by Tansill and other leading revisionists, entitling his book, *Perpetual War for Perpetual Peace*, and dedicating it to the memory of the recently deceased Beard.[22] Among the revisionists who contributed the gist of their books to Barnes's collection were George Morgenstern,[23] William Henry Chamberlin,[24] Frederick Sanborn,[25] and William Neumann.[26]

The revisionists regretted America's entry into World War II. American security had not been even remotely threatened, they argued, nor had there been any compelling moral issue involved. They admitted that Hitler was a dangerous neurotic, but his major goal had been the destruction of Soviet Russia. Only the folly of Roosevelt and

20. Charles A. Beard, *American Foreign Policy in the Making, 1932–1940: A Study in Responsibilities* (New Haven, 1946). He followed this with a much thicker volume, *President Roosevelt and the Coming of the War, 1941* (New Haven, 1948).

21. Charles Callan Tansill, *Back Door to War: The Roosevelt Foreign Policy, 1933–1941* (Chicago, 1952).

22. Harry Elmer Barnes, ed., *Perpetual War for Perpetual Peace: A Critical Examination of the Foreign Policy of Franklin Delano Roosevelt and Its Aftermath* (New York, 1969; originally published in Caldwell, Idaho, 1953).

23. George Morgenstern condensed his *Pearl Harbor: The Story of the Secret War* (New York, 1947).

24. William Henry Chamberlin had written *America's Second Crusade* (Chicago, 1950).

25. Frederick C. Sanborn had just published his *Design for War: A Study of Secret Power Politics 1937–1941* (New York, 1951).

26. Some ten years later William L. Neumann would publish *America Encounters Japan: From Perry to MacArthur* (Baltimore, 1963).

the leaders of Western Europe had drawn Hitler away from his goal. Far better to have left Hitler and Stalin to destroy one another. Instead, the Americans and Western Europeans had allied themselves with Stalin. Then, by demanding unconditional surrender on the part of both Germany and Japan, they had created a vacuum of power in Europe and Asia that Stalin naturally had exploited. Thus, America faced a ruthless empire stronger than Germany and Japan combined.[27]

Ironically, for all their anger at America's entry into World War II, the revisionists reinforced the lesson of Munich. They argued that the sacrifice of Czechoslovakia at Munich by Chamberlain and Daladier, egged on by Roosevelt, was a tragic and stupid move. War in 1938 would have meant a crushing defeat for Hitler, said Tansill and Barnes. Hitler was not yet prepared for war. Russia, France, and Britain were still acting in concert. The Czechs had strong defensive positions in the Sudetenland, and Britain and France together had more tanks and planes than Germany. Besides, the German military had been prepared to overthrow Hitler if he had been humiliated and forced to back down over the Sudeten issue.[28]

After helping to destroy the Allied defensive potential, Roosevelt later had urged resistance to Hitler's aggression. Why would Roosevelt have supported appeasement when the Allies were strong and resistance when they had been weakened? Tansill and Barnes maintained that Roosevelt had feared war in 1938 over the Sudeten "would lead to so rapid a termination of the war (in the defeat of Germany) that he would not have time to involve this country in the great conflict. By the end of August 1939, with the Czech army immobilized and Russia aligned with Germany, it looked like a long war, well suited to Mr. Roosevelt's interventionist program."[29] And just why would Roosevelt want a gratuitous war for America? It would ensure his own election, preserve the British Empire, and secure American control of markets abroad.[30]

With these nefarious secret plans, Roosevelt undertook to "lie

27. Beard, *President Roosevelt and the Coming of the War*, pp. 576–577; Barnes, *Perpetual War for Perpetual Peace*, p. 6; Chamberlin, in *ibid.*, p. 495; and Tansill, *Back Door to War*, p. 574.

28. Tansill, *Back Door to War*, pp. 406–428.

29. Barnes, *Perpetual War for Perpetual Peace*, p. 202n.; Tansill, in *ibid.*, p. 171. Morgenstern agreed that appeasement at Munich had been a mistake but argued that Roosevelt had favored it because he thought Germany too strong in 1938 and that Allied strength was greater in 1939 (Morgenstern, in *ibid.*, pp. 201–203).

30. Barnes, *Perpetual War for Perpetual Peace*, pp. 14, 635; Sanborn, in *ibid.*, p. 193; and Tansill, *Back Door to War*, pp. 561, 652.

America into war." Having urged the British and French to resist Hitler, he steadily moved America away from the neutrality he was by law bound to uphold and by his own words pledged to maintain. He gave direct government aid in the form of armaments to the Allies, he ordered the navy to convoy their ships, and he had American vessels fire at German submarines. He knew he could not win the support of the American people for war unless Germany directly threatened or attacked the United States. This Hitler refused to do. "After a lengthy and minute ransacking [of German records after the war], it transpired that nowhere in these papers was there to be found any evidence of any German plans to attack the United States," wrote Frederic Sanborn. "Quite to the contrary, the embarrassing fact developed from the secret papers that for many months prior to Pearl Harbor Chancellor Hitler was doing all that he could to avoid conflict with the United States!"[31]

Since Roosevelt could not lure Germany to create an incident that would bring the United States into the war, he decided to take the "back door to war" by provoking Japan. This tragic anti-Japanese policy had begun with Henry Stimson. He had wanted to use economic weapons to stop the Japanese invasion of Manchuria, a policy resisted by a wiser Herbert Hoover. Still Stimson had managed to issue a moral condemnation of Japan by refusing to recognize the outcome of the Manchurian incident. Roosevelt and his secretary of state, Cordell Hull, had then taken over Stimson's policies and continued to oppose Japanese expansion in an attempt to maintain the Open Door and the territorial integrity of China. To the revisionists, this was pure stupidity. China was a rotting hulk that the Chinese Nationalist government was incapable of putting to rights. American profits from the China trade were one third less than those garnered from trade with Japan, and American investments in China were also minimal. Stimson, Hull, and Roosevelt ignored the historical ambitions of Russian expansionism in China and disregarded the role a strong Japan played in the Far Eastern balance of power. "Gross errors were also made in calculating that Japan could be coerced by economic pressure and naval force to follow American bidding in its relations with China," wrote William Neumann.[32]

31. Sanborn, in Barnes, *Perpetual War for Perpetual Peace*, pp. 191–192, 216–217. See also Chamberlin, in *ibid.*, pp. 490–491; and Barnes, in *ibid.*, pp. 9, 40.
32. Neumann, in Barnes, *Perpetual War for Perpetual Peace*, pp. 234–241, esp. p. 235.

Until Roosevelt found he could not manipulate his way into the European war by squeezing Hitler, his Far Eastern policy was merely foolish. Afterward it was satanic. Brushing aside Japanese peace feelers transmitted through two Maryknoll priests, the Roosevelt administration froze all Japanese assets in the United States and embargoed Japanese-American trade. Roosevelt and his advisers knew that this would bring war. Japan would have to move into Indo-China and the East Indies to insure the supplies of oil and metals that America had denied to them.

Despite American hostility, Prince Konoye, the Japanese prime minister, sought a summit meeting between himself and Roosevelt as a "last-ditch" effort to prevent war. Roosevelt turned him down. This brought the fall of the moderate Japanese cabinet and the installation of a more hawkish one under General Hideki Tojo. Yet even Tojo sought peace. He offered a modus vivendi that would end Japanese military movements in Southeast Asia and permit the Japanese an honorable withdrawal to Manchuria once a reasonable agreement had been made with China. However, he set a deadline of late November for negotiations to be concluded. After that Japan would resort to forceful measures.

Roosevelt and Hull knew of the Japanese moves because the "Magic" project had broken a "top-secret" Japanese code. Yet Hull rejected the modus vivendi and sent back instead an ultimatum, admitting that he had washed his hands of the issue and had turned it over to the military. Secretary of War Stimson concluded: "The question was how we should maneuver them into firing the first shot without allowing too much danger to ourselves."

Roosevelt had already anticipated this, claimed the revisionists. He had ordered the Pacific fleet to leave San Diego and station itself permanently at Pearl Harbor, against the wishes of the high naval command. There he offered the fleet as a sacrifice to guarantee America's entry into the war. He made sure, however, that only the obsolete battleships were in the harbor and that the indispensable aircraft carriers were out to sea at the time of the attack. He saw to it that Hawaii did not have a decoding machine for the American commanders there to read Japan's intentions for themselves and allowed only vague information to reach them. Then, while Japanese planes butchered three thousand Americans, "In the quiet atmosphere of the oval study in the White House, with all incoming telephone calls shut off, the Chief Executive calmly studied his well-filled stamp albums while

[Harry] Hopkins fondled Fala, the White House scottie. At one o'clock, Death stood in the Doorway."[33]

The venomous characterizations of Roosevelt, along with the horrifying charges of the revisionists, naturally excited many replies. These replies were so extensive and convincing to the post-World War II generation that the revisionists were quickly discredited. The revisionists complained that they were being unfairly treated, that their publications were blacked out by a conspiracy of eastern establishment publishing houses while so-called "court historians" received special access to government documents denied their opponents.[34] It was indeed true that certain historians who had connections with the government, Herbert Feis, who had worked for the State Department, and William Langer, late of the Office of Strategic Services (OSS), did get special access to documents earlier than other historians. The other accusations of the revisionists were strained and implausible. In any case, Americans of the postwar era found it hard to believe the basic contention of the revisionists that the Axis had posed no direct threat to the United States. It was this skepticism, above all else, that made World War II revisionism a historiographical dead end.

Certainly there was no doubt in the minds of most historians that Hitler's Germany had posed a major threat. This was the conclusion of the American historian who studied the German documents most closely in this period, Hans Trefousse. Trefousse did not find any evidence of a specific Nazi plan to invade the Western Hemisphere. But he was sure that Hitler would have formulated such a plan if he had been able to defeat Britain and Russia, eliminating the opposition of the British fleet and giving him control of the vast resources of all Europe.[35] Trefousse believed that Roosevelt had conducted American foreign policy brilliantly, leading America slowly but surely toward intervention.

Basil Rauch had reached the same conclusions without benefit of

---

33. Tansill, *Back Door to War*, pp. 648, 652. In addition to the revisionists already cited, see Robert A. Theobold, *The Final Secret of Pearl Harbor: The Washington Contribution to the Japanese Attack* (New York, 1954); Husband E. Kimmel, *Admiral Kimmel's Story* (Chicago, 1955); and Anthony Kubek, *How the Far East Was Lost: American Policy and the Creation of Communist China, 1941–1949* (Chicago, 1963).

34. Barnes, *Perpetual War for Perpetual Peace*; see particularly Barnes's own introductory and concluding essays.

35. Hans L. Trefousse, *Germany and American Neutrality, 1939–1941* (New York, 1951). Saul Friedländer published a similar study in Germany in 1963, but it was not published in English until 1967: *Prelude to Downfall: Hitler and the United States, 1939–1941* (New York, 1967).

Trefousse's research in the German documents. Assuming that Hitler had indeed posed a threat to American security, he answered Charles Beard's revisionism almost line by line in his *Roosevelt: From Munich to Pearl Harbor*.[36] He justified Roosevelt's actions at every turn, making his book more a lawyer's brief than a critical work of history. He, too, contended that Roosevelt had moved at just the right pace to allow circumstances to convert isolationists and bring a unified America to the aid of the Allies. Rauch went so far as to argue that Roosevelt had been consistent throughout in his interventionist policies and in his explanations to the American public. Donald Drummond's survey, *The Passing of American Neutrality, 1937–1941*,[37] was more balanced and better researched, and he admitted that Roosevelt had been purposely vague to conceal at least partially the direction of his policy. Still, he agreed with Rauch that Roosevelt's pace had been about right. Drummond felt that the unwillingness of isolationist public opinion to face the full realities of the situation justified Roosevelt's reluctance to spell out the full implications of his policies.[38]

But the most definitive and well researched of all the books on American entry into World War II disputed Rauch and Drummond. The magisterial two-volume work of William Langer and S. Everett Gleason argued that Roosevelt had been too cautious in his march toward intervention. Documenting Roosevelt's vacillating policy with massive evidence, Langer and Gleason pointed to public opinion polls taken during the years before 1941 to show that the public had been far less isolationist than Rauch and Drummond assumed. If Roosevelt had provided clear and vigorous leadership instead of hesitant, limited actions covered by devious and uncandid remarks, America might have been much better prepared for war when it came and might have aided the Allies before they had teetered dangerously on the brink of collapse.[39] Langer and Gleason found support from another prominent historical authority on World War II, Robert Divine, whose shorter, textlike survey, *The Reluctant Belligerent*, was widely used in college classes.[40]

36. Basil Rauch, *Roosevelt: From Munich to Pearl Harbor* (New York, 1950).

37. Donald F. Drummond, *The Passing of American Neutrality, 1937–1941* (Ann Arbor, 1955).

38. *Ibid.*, pp. 178–181.

39. William L. Langer and S. Everett Gleason, *The Challenge to Isolation, 1937–1940* (New York, 1952), pp. 5–6. See also their *The Undeclared War, 1940–1941* (New York, 1953).

40. Robert A. Divine, *The Reluctant Belligerent: American Entry into World War II* (New York, 1965), pp. 91–92, 100–101, 158.

Historical monographs on specific episodes in American diplomacy of the 1920s and 1930s reflected this dispute over whether America should have intervened earlier. Almost all agreed that the isolationism and appeasement of the interwar period had been a tragic mistake. But some historians saw reasons to excuse American decision makers for what all agreed to be mistakes whereas others chose to berate them. John Chalmers Vinson chose to berate. In a close study of the naval limitation treaties of 1921, he derided the treaties as providing a "parchment peace." His biography of William E. Borah portrayed Borah's efforts to outlaw war as naïve and silly.[41]

Robert Ferrell, a student of Bemis and one of the outstanding scholars of the interwar period, was somewhat less vehement. He called the American public's faith in the Kellogg-Briand Pact "appallingly naïve" and hoped that by the 1950s American public opinion had "become truly sophisticated and will give its unwavering support to a realistic American foreign policy."[42] Nevertheless, he gave high marks to the intelligence and understanding of prewar secretaries of state like Frank Kellogg and Henry Stimson, portraying them as helpless before the ill-informed and isolationist American people.[43] L. Ethan Ellis was not so gentle with Kellogg,[44] but Robert Divine agreed with Ferrell's favorable assessment of Stimson. Divine's book, *The Illusion of Neutrality*, was the key work on Franklin Roosevelt's early foreign policy, and Divine praised Stimson as the leader of the movement to give the president some discretion in applying the Neutrality Laws so as to distinguish between aggressor nations and their victims. Such executive discretion would allow the United States to cooperate with the League of Nations and the Allied powers in applying sanctions. Divine found such intelligent and vigorous action a welcome contrast from what he considered Roosevelt's mushy and indecisive conduct at critical times.[45]

But Stimson was also the subject of the one significant revisionist

41. John Chalmers Vinson, *The Parchment Peace: The United States Senate and the Washington Conference, 1921–1922* (Athens, Ga., 1955); and his *William E. Borah and the Outlawry of War* (Athens, Ga., 1957).

42. Robert H. Ferrell, *Peace in Their Time: The Origins of the Kellogg-Briand Pact* (New Haven, 1952), p. 265.

43. *Ibid.*; see also Robert H. Ferrell, *American Diplomacy in the Great Depression: Hoover-Stimson Foreign Policy, 1929–1933* (New Haven, 1957), and Ferrell's handling of Kellogg and Stimson in the American Secretaries of State Series which Ferrell was coediting at this time with Bemis.

44. L. Ethan Ellis, *Frank B. Kellogg and American Foreign Relations: 1925–1929* (New Brunswick, N.J., 1961).

45. Divine, *The Illusion of Neutrality*.

monograph on a pre-World War II subject, Richard Current's *Secretary Stimson.*[46]Although Current rejected the "plot" theory of Pearl Harbor, he accepted the rest of the revisionist view, ridiculing Stimson as militaristic and imperialistic. He criticized not only the Stimson Doctrine but also Stimson's later career as secretary of war, particularly his badgering of Roosevelt to take a stronger stand in Europe. Stimson's ideas were "peace through force, imperial responsibility, [and] law unilaterally interpreted and applied. . . ."[47]

But Current's assessment stood almost alone. Stimson's policy toward the Far East raised questions among some nonrevisionists, but his interventionist policies toward Europe were almost unanimously acclaimed. Isolationism was discredited by being branded a product of what Basil Rauch called "inert conservative forces."[48] This popular image of Neanderthal isolationism was furthered by Walter Johnson's *Battle Against Isolation,* written during the war to extol the activities of William Allen White's Committee to Defend America by Aiding the Allies.[49] More careful studies of isolationism pointed out that many liberals as well as conservatives had favored that policy in the interwar period. But the significance of that was dismissed. As Selig Adler wrote: "[By the spring of 1940,] the liberals moved out of the isolationist camp, [and] left the bitter right in almost complete control. . . . Old-time progressives, like Senators Gerald P. Nye and Burton K. Wheeler, who remained intransigent isolationists, became more conservative in domestic policy. . . . Henceforth isolationism was to become the seminal power of the reaction against twentieth-century changes in American life."[50]

Wayne Cole's studies of isolationism were less judgmental than any of the previously mentioned works. His book on the America-First Committee and his biography of Gerald P. Nye noted the same conservative trend in isolationism. But Cole emphasized more heavily than other historians the influence of midwestern liberal populism on isolationism. He noted that the continuing influence of populism was masked by the fact that the America-First Committee, with its strongly conservative, big business, anti-New Deal bias, became the leading

46. Richard N. Current, *Secretary Stimson: A Study in Statecraft* (New Brunswick, N.J., 1954).

47. *Ibid.,* p. 247.

48. Rauch, *Roosevelt: From Munich to Pearl Harbor,* pp. 9–10.

49. Walter Johnson, *The Battle Against Isolation* (Chicago, 1944).

50. Selig Adler, *The Isolationist Impulse: Its Twentieth-Century Reaction* (New York, 1957), p. 298.

advocate of isolationism, obscuring other more liberal isolationist organizations.[51] But even a sympathetic Cole gave no hint that he thought the isolationists had been right. Cole complimented Franklin Roosevelt's cautious movement toward interventionism, saying Roosevelt operated so cleverly that he never gave the isolationists a concrete issue on which to defeat him. Nor did Cole's emphasis on the midwestern Populist component of isolationism help rescue its popularity, for at this very time Richard Hofstadter and others were noting some anti-Semitic, antiintellectual, and paranoid tendencies within the Populist movement. The Populists were being cited as the harbingers of the plot mentality that had dominated the Pearl Harbor revisionists and the McCarthy witch hunters of the 1950s.[52]

Other historians noted different components of isolationism. Samuel Lubell argued that ethnic origins were the primary determinant of isolationism, with those ethnic groups most antagonistic to the British Empire, the Germans and Irish, forming its backbone. Other historians thought that conservative Republican partisanship was dominant. One historian even detected a strong correlation between isolationism and authoritarian personalities.[53] But almost all historians writing in this era tended to study isolationism as a kind of pathology, whatever motives or make-up they assigned to the movement, until the word itself became so charged with derogatory overtones that even its proponents avoided its use.[54]

Thus, historians favoring America's intervention in Europe

51. Wayne S. Cole, America First: The Battle Against Intervention, 1940–1941 (Madison, Wis., 1953), pp. 69–79; and his Senator Gerald P. Nye and American Foreign Relations (Minneapolis, 1962), pp. 3–4. John Wiltz published a study of the Nye Committee that was more favorable to the committee's work ironically because the committee had helped disprove the "merchants-of-death" thesis by failing to uncover evidence for it. Wiltz was far less kind to Nye's own tub-thumping public speeches than to the conduct of the committee inquiry; however, Wiltz also doubted that the inquiry influenced the passage of the Neutrality Acts to the extent maintained by Divine and others (John E. Wiltz, In Search of Peace: The Senate Munitions Inquiry, 1934–1936 [Baton Rouge, 1963]).

52. Richard Hofstadter: The Age of Reform: From Bryan to F.D.R. (New York, 1955); Anti-Intellectualism in American Life (New York, 1963); and The Paranoid Style in American Politics and other Essays (New York, 1965).

53. Samuel Lubell, The Future of American Politics (New York, 1952); Leroy M. Rieselbach, "The Basis of Isolationist Behavior," Public Opinion Quarterly, 24 (Winter 1960): 645–657; and Bernard Fensterwald, "The Anatomy of American 'Isolationism' and Expansionism," Journal of Conflict Resolution, 2 (June–December 1958): 111–139, 280–309.

54. Alexander DeConde, "On Twentieth-Century Isolationism," in Alexander DeConde, ed., Isolation and Security (Durham, 1957), p. 5.

swept all before them. The revisionists were dismissed contemptuously by most, and the only significant debate remaining was whether Roosevelt could or should have moved more rapidly to aid the opponents of Hitler in Europe. Revisionist accusations that Roosevelt had purposely provoked the Japanese attack at Pearl Harbor were just as thoroughly discredited within the historical profession as was the revisionist position on European intervention. The major surveys of American entry into World War II by Rauch, Drummond, and Langer and Gleason dealt very harshly with the plot thesis. They were supported by Samuel Eliot Morison's exhaustive study of the U.S. Navy in World War II. Admiral Morison's attitude toward the plot thesis was encapsulated in the scathing title of an article on the subject he drew from his study of the navy, "Did Roosevelt Start the War—History Through a Beard."[55] Many other prominent historians joined the attack on the Pearl Harbor revisionists, including Robert Ferrell and Herbert Feis, culminating in the definitive study, Roberta Wohlstetter's *Pearl Harbor: Warning and Decision*.[56]

These historians found the plot theory totally implausible on its face. It would have required the connivance of too many people, including all of America's major governmental and military leaders. Indeed, Roosevelt would not have needed to sacrifice the fleet to enter the war by the back door. He could have sent the fleet to sea just before the attack. An unsuccessful Japanese attack on an empty harbor would have united the American people behind the war as effectively as the successful one did. In any case, the government had sent "war warnings" to the military commanders in Hawaii, and these should have been sufficient to alert them to the possibility of an attack in the near future.

Why, then, was Pearl Harbor caught unprepared? Roberta Wohlstetter gave the most complete and convincing answer. America's breaking of the Japanese diplomatic code had given the government a general idea of when the attack would come but not where. Roosevelt and his lieutenants had expected the attack to come in

55. Samuel Eliot Morison, *History of United States Naval Operations in World War II*, 15 vols. (Boston, 1947–1962), and esp. his *The Rising Sun in the Pacific* (Boston, 1948). Morison condensed this multivolume history into *The Two-Ocean War* (Boston, 1963). His article, "Did Roosevelt Start the War—History Through a Beard," appeared in *Atlantic Monthly*, 162 (August 1948).

56. Roberta Wohlstetter, *Pearl Harbor: Warning and Decision* (Stanford, 1962); Robert Ferrell, "Pearl Harbor and the Revisionists," *Historian*, 17 (Spring 1955); and Herbert Feis, "War Came at Pearl Harbor: Suspicions Considered," *Yale Review*, 45 (Spring 1956).

Southern Asia, on the colonies of Britain, France, and the Netherlands. The administration worried that the American people might not support a war to resist attacks on such foreign colonies and so neglected to concentrate attention on America's own vulnerable territories. Roosevelt had no idea that Japan would be so foolish as to eliminate the American government's dilemma and guarantee America's forcible resistance to Japanese expansion.

There had been some clues that might have led Americans to expect an attack on Pearl Harbor, but these had been drowned out by other information. A report from the Peruvian Embassy in Japan had warned of an attack on Hawaii, but American Ambassador Joseph Grew had called it unreliable and far-fetched when he relayed it to Washington. America had intercepted Japanese messages requesting and transmitting ever more detailed information about the location of the fleet in Pearl Harbor. But reports about American fleet activities in other ports disguised the importance of this, and intelligence specialists surmised that the Japanese wanted such information to protect their move south, not to sink the American fleet in its home harbor. In any case, very little of the information provided by "Magic" pointed to Pearl Harbor. America had broken a diplomatic rather than a military code, and so information about military movements was scarce and indirect. The Japanese kept the secret of the coming attack very well, hiding it from many of the highest officials in their own government.

By the time Wohlstetter had finished, in 1962, no more was to be heard of the plot thesis in historical circles. But while historians had concluded that Roosevelt's policies toward Japan had not been purposely provocative, many remained unconvinced of the wisdom of those policies. Here was the second major lasting debate over American intervention into World War II.

Roosevelt's Far Eastern policy had strong and prominent defenders. The surveys of Rauch, Drummond, and Langer and Gleason all had indicated that Roosevelt and Secretary of State Hull had just cause to draw the line against further Japanese expansion. Herbert Feis agreed in his *The Road to Pearl Harbor*, which was the most complete analysis of America's policy toward Japan and, like the work of Langer and Gleason, was based on special access to State Department manuscripts.[57] Roosevelt and Hull also received strong support from re-

---

57. Herbert Feis, *The Road to Pearl Harbor: The Coming of the War Between the United States and Japan* (Princeton, 1950).

search on the Japanese side. Robert Butow reached beyond the accessible records published by the Far East war crimes tribunals, into the Japanese archives themselves. His *Tojo and the Coming of the War* portrayed Japanese policy very harshly, concluding that nothing short of war could have halted the Japanese conquest of all Asia.[58] Edwin Reischauer's survey of United States-Japanese relations concluded the same although from far less thorough research.[59]

All of these historians regretted America's mild responses to earlier Japanese aggression. American restraint had been motivated by hopes that Japanese moderates might regain control of their government and restrain the aggressive militarists. But the moderates had differed from the militarists only in their methods, not in their goals. All influential Japanese coveted control of China and the resources of Southeast Asia. American policies calculated to appease the moderates in hopes of staving off the militarists were thus fruitless and fore-doomed.[60] Once Japan had signed the Axis Pact, the Japanese became a threat to America's very existence, not just its economic or sentimental interests in China. Japanese conquest of China and of the European colonies of Southeast Asia would mean not only the loss of Asia's resources to the Allies but their active employment in the destruction of the forces opposing Hitler. America would be left to stand alone against the Axis. Unless the United States wanted a Far Eastern Munich, it could do no less than apply economic sanctions to prevent this calamity.

These historians agreed that such a move was risky. Japan might retreat to regain America's supply of oil and vital raw materials, but it might also drive forward into Southeast Asia to acquire its own sources of these supplies, enabling it to continue the war in China. Roosevelt and Hull tried to postpone any confrontation since the United States was unprepared for war and since in the meantime Japan was using up irreplaceable oil. Nevertheless, these historians agreed that Hull and Roosevelt had correctly refused Japanese Premier Konoye's request for a meeting with the American president. Konoye was duplicitous and weak, and "Magic" intercepts showed that the rest of the Japanese government and the army had no intention of making major

58. Robert J. C. Butow, *Tojo and the Coming of the War* (Princeton, 1961).

59. Edwin O. Reischauer, *The United States and Japan* (Cambridge, Mass., 1950).

60. Feis, *Road to Pearl Harbor*, pp. 7–8; Reischauer, *United States and Japan*, pp. 24–29; and Langer and Gleason, *Challenge to Isolation*, pp. 301–302.

concessions.[61] Later Japanese proposals also demonstrated that even a temporary truce would require America to supply oil that would be used to perpetuate the war against China.[62] Some of these historians did wonder if a bit more flexibility on the part of the Americans would have delayed the inevitable clash a few more weeks, but they concluded that the United States could not have afforded the concessions needed to avoid war indefinitely.[63]

At this point, historical supporters of Roosevelt's policies ran into considerable opposition. This time it was not limited to discredited revisionists or isolationists. It came instead from interventionists who thought that Roosevelt should have accepted some sort of modus vivendi with Japan to free America's hand for an all-out effort against Hitler in Europe.These interventionist critics of Roosevelt borrowed much of their historical outlook on Asia from the old isolationist, A. Whitney Griswold, but patterned their view of world politics in general upon Lippmann, Niebuhr, Spykman, and another addition to the realpolitik line-up, George Kennan. Kennan, in his highly influential book, *American Diplomacy, 1900–1950*, had made his Europe-first inclinations more pointed and specific than had the other realpolitikers who had written during the war itself.[64] Emphasizing power and interest over abstract morality and ideology, Kennan wished that the United States had found a way to propitiate Japan, even at the sacrifice of Chinese interests. This would have avoided the two-front war that had limited America's effort in Europe. Kennan did not analyze the events leading to World War II closely enough to determine whether such propitiation had been possible, but other so-called realists did.

These realists based their suppositions about avoiding war with Japan on the dispatches and writings of Joseph Grew, American am-

61. Feis, *Road to Pearl Harbor*, pp. 259, 274–281; Langer and Gleason, *Undeclared War*, pp. 706–709; and esp. Butow, *Tojo and the Coming of the War*, pp. 243–260.

62. There is some confusion over the exact number of tons of oil Japan decided to require. Feis said four million from the United States and one million from the Dutch East Indies; Butow said Tojo remembered the figure as six million tons (Feis, *Road to Pearl Harbor*, p. 311; and Butow, *Tojo and the Coming of the War*, p. 335).

63. Langer and Gleason, *Undeclared War*, pp. 872–902; Feis, *Road to Pearl Harbor*, pp. 302–319; Butow, *Tojo and the Coming of the War*, pp. 337–343; Drummond, *Passing of American Neutrality*, pp. 379–380; and Rauch, *Roosevelt: From Munich to Pearl Harbor*, pp. 455–477.

64. George F. Kennan, *American Diplomacy, 1900–1950* (Chicago, 1951); page citations are from the paperback (Mentor Publishers).

bassador to Japan during the crisis. Grew made public many of his dispatches and conclusions in two works, *Ten Years in Japan*, published in 1944, and *Turbulent Era*, published in 1952.[65] He argued that Germany's attack on Russia in July of 1941 had given the United States a chance to negotiate a settlement with Japan. The Japanese militarists who had concluded the Tri-Partite Pact with Germany and Italy had counted on the nonaggression pact between Germany and Russia to keep the Soviets friendly to the Axis. Japan wanted to move south without fear of attack from the rear by the Russian army. Now the militarists were discredited, and Konoye might have been willing to compromise the China situation and to abandon Germany if Roosevelt and Hull had met with him. A dramatic settlement at the meeting might have roused the moderates and allowed them to overcome the military opposition which Grew admitted did exist. Had Hull not been so fearful of appeasement and so trapped by the memory of Munich, a more flexible policy might have prevented war with Japan.[66]

Grew's analysis was accepted and expanded by several close studies of Japanese-American relations. F. C. Jones, a British scholar who received his Ph.D. at Harvard, wrote *Japan's New Order in East Asia*, in which he chastised the British for supporting Hull's rigid policy instead of Grew's more flexible one.[67] Paul Schroeder and David Lu scrutinized the Tri-Partite Pact. They insisted that after the German invasion of Russia, Japan had made as clear as it could, without a dishonorable open repudiation of the alliance, that it had the right to exercise independent judgment as to when and if it would declare war on the United States should the latter enter the war against Hitler. Thus, said Schroeder and Lu, Konoye's promised concessions would have accomplished America's major goals. The threat of Japanese-German cooperation was ended and Japan was ready to abandon its expansion southward. America would be safe from attack in the Pacific, and the British and French supply lines from their colonies

65. Joseph C. Grew, *Ten Years in Japan* (New York, 1944); and his *Turbulent Era: A Diplomatic Record of Forty Years, 1904–1945*, 2 vols., ed. Walter Johnson (Boston, 1952).

66. Grew, *Turbulent Era*, II, 1244–1270, 1314–1315, 1361–1374. In Hull's memoirs, as Grew noted, Hull had written: "As for me, I was thoroughly satisfied that a meeting with Konoye, without an advance agreement, could only result either in another Munich or in nothing at all. I was opposed to the first Munich and still more opposed to a second Munich" (quoted in *ibid.*, p. 1334, n. 69).

67. F. C. Jones, *Japan's New Order in East Asia: Its Rise and Fall, 1937–45* (London, 1954).

would be secure. Britain, France, and the United States could direct their energies solely against Hitler.

Instead, Hull abandoned the diplomatic gains brought on by this enormous gamble of economic sanctions and preferred war to allowing some Japanese control over China. Schroeder and Lu regarded this as foolish. China was currently incapable of unifying itself and controlling its own destiny even with American help. Elimination of the Japanese presence would create a vacuum into which Russia would move unless the United States expended tremendous amounts of manpower and materiel to hold it off. The diversion of resources from the European theater not only prolonged the war there but permitted the Soviet Union to move further west than it might have done had the Allies invaded Normandy earlier. Borrowing many of these insights from George Kennan's realist tract, *American Diplomacy*, Schroeder especially derided this policy as excessively moralistic because it refused to leave China to some Japanese control and too legalistic because it insisted on the applicability of earlier treaties. In addition, the policy was too beholden to an emotional and uninformed public opinion. Policy makers were unwilling to be seen as appeasers of the unpopular Japanese.[68]

Such criticisms did not convince Herbert Feis. In his introduction to David Lu's book, he specifically took issue with Lu and by implication with Schroeder and Jones. Japan was willing only to give ambiguous hints that it might not be faithful to the obligations of the Axis Pact. For this America would have had to divert from its own war effort supplies of oil and critical metals for Japan to use against China and perhaps even against the United States itself. Certainly past Japanese duplicity discouraged reliance on a few vague Japanese reservations about the Axis Pact.[69]

But realist ideas of a flexible policy toward Japan and a concentration on Europe had a strong influence elsewhere. Armin Rappaport looked back on earlier policies and found Stimson's nonrecognition of Japan's conquest of Manchuria unnecessarily unre-

68. Paul W. Schroeder, *The Anglo-American Alliance and Japanese-American Relations, 1941* (Ithaca, 1958), pp. 38, 179–199, 208–215; Jones, *Japan's New Order in East Asia*, pp. 459–468; and David J. Lu, *From the Marco Polo Bridge to Pearl Harbor: Japan's Entry into World War II* (Washington, D.C., 1961), pp. 244–246. Lu's book and conclusions were marred by his unconvincing attempt to portray Japanese foreign minister Yosuke Matsuoka as much more consistent and friendly to the United States than any reasonable reading of the evidence will allow. See also Kennan, *American Diplomacy, 1900–1950*, pp. 44–48.

69. Lu, *From the Marco Polo Bridge to Pearl Harbor*, pp. iv–v.

alistic, provocative, and ineffective.[70] William Neumann, who earlier had contributed to Barnes's revisionist *Perpetual War for Perpetual Peace*, published a survey of American-Japanese relations in which he chastised the United States not for entry into World War II but for needlessly fighting a two-front war. A pacifist and a conscientious objector during World War II, he came to criticize Tansill as well as Rauch, thus moving away from the revisionist position and closer to the realists.[71]

And so the historical debate over American entry into World War II had been reduced to rather narrow issues. Revisionist arguments against American intervention had been thoroughly discredited as had accusations that Roosevelt had plotted to sacrifice the fleet at Pearl Harbor. Almost everyone agreed that America's security and survival had required intervention. The isolationist sentiments of the 1920s and 1930s were widely denounced and generally considered the product of right-wing narrowness and popular delusion. The only significant debates remaining among historians were whether Roosevelt had led the country toward intervention against Hitler too cautiously, and whether a more flexible policy in the Far East might have delayed war there, allowing America to concentrate its forces in the more critical European theater. The widespread rejection of isolationism and appeasement engendered by the experience of World War II would play a significant role in both the diplomacy and the historiography of the Cold War.

70. Armin Rappaport, *Henry L. Stimson and Japan* (Chicago, 1963).
71. Neumann, *America Encounters Japan*, pp. 282–289, 309–313, 336, 340.

FOURTEEN

The Cold War

In the years before World War II, especially during the tenure of the Russo-German Pact, many Americans were inclined to regard Nazi Germany and Stalinist Russia as two peas in a pod. Fascism and communism were equally totalitarian and equally to be reviled. "The American people know that the principal difference between Mr. Hitler and Mr. Stalin is the size of their respective mustaches," editorialized the *Wall Street Journal* in 1941.[1] After Germany's attack on Russia, Roosevelt extended Lend-Lease aid and began the process of wartime collaboration that finally brought the Axis to its knees. Gradually the image of Stalin and the Soviets softened in the minds of most Americans, only to be hardened once again as the clash of interests between the United States and Russia destroyed hopes for a peaceful and stable postwar world. Memories of Stalin's ruthless prewar purges revived as horror stories of Russian suppression leaked out of Poland and the other Eastern European nations liberated by Soviet troops. Once again Stalin and Hitler, communists and Nazis, were lumped together as totalitarians in America's public mind. Naturally enough, the "lessons" learned in the earlier march toward World War II were

1. Quoted in Les K. Adler and Thomas G. Paterson, "Red Fascism: The Merger of Nazi Germany and Soviet Russia in the American Image of Totalitarianism, 1930s–1950s," *American Historical Review*, 75, no. 4 (April 1970): 1051.

applied to the Cold War. Shortly after Churchill's famous speech decrying Soviet imposition of an "Iron Curtain" across Europe, H. V. Kaltenborn warned his listeners that the Soviet Union was "a ruthless, totalitarian power which is seeking domination in both Europe and Asia." "Remember Munich!" he cried.[2] The American government underwent a similar conversion slightly in advance of the people at large. As Harry Truman moved with trepidation into the presidency, he naturally turned to the State Department for advice and information on foreign affairs. The State Department was ready and waiting; Roosevelt had all but ignored the department, relying primarily on the military for advice on international diplomacy and making the significant decisions himself. Now the State Department's turn had come.

At first the department itself was none too certain of the course of action it should recommend regarding the Soviet Union. Memorandums by state department officers Cloyce K. Huston and "Chip" Bohlen circulated within the agency in late 1945, promoting an extension of Roosevelt's cooperative policy toward the Russians. They suggested tactics for winning Stalin's confidence and cooperation such as praising Russia's goals (but not its means) in Eastern Europe and offering to share unconditionally America's atomic technology. But when Russia refused to withdraw its troops from Iran and Stalin verbally attacked the capitalist states in a February 1946 preelection speech, these suggestions failed to command much enthusiasm. The advice that swept the department and crystallized American policy came instead from America's Moscow Embassy, where George Kennan composed his famous "long telegram" recommending containment of Russia rather than cooperation.[3]

America's Russian Embassy personnel had long looked askance at Roosevelt's attempts to get along with the Soviets during World War II. The secretive and hostile atmosphere American diplomats encountered at all levels of the Russian government made them skeptical of Roosevelt's plans for a postwar world that depended on the close cooperation of Russia with Great Britain and the United States. Kennan, military attaché General John Deane, and Ambassador Averell Harriman all advocated a tougher bargaining stance toward Russia. After years of plucking fruitlessly at the sleeves of Roosevelt and his

2. *Ibid.*, p. 1056.
3. Robert L. Messer, "Paths Not Taken: The United States Department of State and Alternatives to Containment, 1945–1946," *Diplomatic History*, 1, no. 4 (Fall 1977): 297–319.

military advisers, suddenly Kennan and the State Department were heeded. Kennan's analysis not only explained Soviet belligerence, his containment policy followed lessons the World War II generation had learned from Munich.

In the "long telegram," revised and published a year later in *Foreign Affairs* under the pseudonym "X," Kennan warned that the Soviet government was implacably hostile toward the capitalist West. Communist ideology pushed it in this direction. So did the rigid internal tyranny of the Soviet system, for it required a continual conjuring of an outside enemy to reconcile the people to the material and spiritual sacrifices demanded of them by their government. Thus, Moscow could never assume any community of aims between itself and the capitalist world. Any softening of Russian policy could be only tactical and illusory. Soviet hostility to the West was "basic to the internal nature of Soviet power, and will be with us ... until the internal nature of Soviet power is changed." The main concern of such a regime was invariably to fill "every nook and cranny available to it in the basin of world power."[4]

Did this mean inevitable war between America and Russia? Kennan thought not. Russian communism set no rigid timetable for the overthrow of capitalism and decried "premature adventurism." Although weakness and disunity would invite Russian aggression and perhaps war, a firm containment, "the adroit and vigilant application of counterforce at a series of constantly shifting geographical and political points," would forestall Soviet aggression. Containment had a better chance of preserving peace with Russia than such a policy would have had with individual aggressive leaders like Hitler or Napoleon. "The Soviet Union [was] more sensitive to contrary force, more ready to yield on individual sectors of the diplomatic front when that force [was] felt to be too strong, and thus more rational in the logic and rhetoric of power." Ultimately, Kennan said, even a fanatic movement like Soviet communism would either break apart or mellow as its attempts to expand and bring about the world revolution were continually frustrated.[5]

Kennan's "X" article was printed in the wake of the announcement of the Truman Doctrine and the advent of the Marshall Plan. By that time, Kennan was director of the Policy Planning Section of the State Department. His identity as the author of the "X" article was

4. George F. Kennan, "The Sources of Soviet Conduct," reprinted in his *American Diplomacy, 1900–1950*, pp. 89–98, 105.
5. *Ibid.*, pp. 98–106, esp. pp. 98–99.

quickly discovered and his article regarded as the philosophical basis for America's suddenly renewed intervention in Europe. Contemporaries viewed the wide popularity of this intervention with dumbfounded amazement. All at once, America seemed to have reversed its sacred policy of avoiding European entanglements during peacetime. Liberals and radicals who continued to advocate propitiation of Russia were ostracized. Henry Wallace was fired by Truman for criticizing the increasingly hard line against Russia, and Wallace's campaign for the presidency on a third-party ticket in 1948 was crushed. Most liberals took the line of the newly formed Americans for Democratic Action, led by Reinhold Niebuhr, which combined progressive domestic policies with anticommunism abroad. The fall of Czechoslovakia, the Berlin blockade, and the Korean War solidified the impetus for confrontation with the Soviet Union, and the need for containment was almost universally accepted in the United States.

The containment policy required a renewed appreciation of the role of force and the balance of power in foreign affairs. The lessons in realpolitik taught by Spykman, Niebuhr, and Lippmann during World War II were now applied to Russia. The defeat of Germany and the collapse of France had left a vacuum of power in Europe. The hopes held by Franklin Roosevelt and encouraged by Lippmann for cooperation between Russia and the Western Allies had proved unfounded. The Soviet Union had rushed into the vacuum, and without a powerful Germany or France to check its advance, the whole of Europe might fall into Russian hands, shifting the balance of power ominously against the United States. Britain had emerged from World War II dangerously weakened. It was in no position to resist Russia unaided. America promptly had shifted its armed forces out of Europe and into the Pacific once Germany had been defeated. With the victory over Japan, the American army had been rapidly demobilized. The vacuum in Central Europe stood as an irresistible temptation to Russia and its communist dream, it was now feared. The United States would have to add its power to that of Great Britain and the weakened states of Western Europe if the balance of power that so long had formed an important a part of America's security was to be maintained.

A highly influential group of political scientists, historians, and columnists preached this gospel with great effectiveness in the postwar era. Aside from Lippmann and Niebuhr, Kennan himself was one of the most influential of these so-called realists. His book, *American Diplomacy*, was read by a whole generation of college students in the 1950s as a primer in American foreign policy. In that book, Kennan inveighed against the moralism and legalism he believed to have permeated American foreign policy since 1900 and called for a policy directed by a candid analysis of America's national interest rather than a vague and unrealistic plan for world democracy and peace. Such idealism had led America alternately to withdraw from the evil of a Europe unprepared to accept American ideals or to conduct devastating crusades to recreate the world in America's image. Kennan called for a calm and steady application of America's limited power to achieve limited goals essential to America's interests and security. Containment was such a policy. It avoided Munich-like appeasement that would invite aggression and war while abjuring provocative actions that might themselves produce war.[6]

Serving with Kennan on the State Department's planning staff was another significant author and promulgator of realist thought, Louis Halle. In two important books, *Civilization and Foreign Policy* and *Dream and Reality*, Halle warned against hopes of cooperation with Russia and urged a more realistic view of power just as Kennan had.[7] Another leading realist was University of Chicago political scientist Hans Morgenthau. As a German immigrant educated in Europe, a foreign policy based on national interest and power probably seemed to him more natural than it did to home-grown American realists. Like Kennan's writings, Morgenthau's books were widely read in American classrooms and at large. As head of the Center for the Study of American Foreign and Military Policy at the University of Chicago, Morgenthau also influenced significant graduate work and publications in American foreign policy. Historians and political scientists like Robert Osgood, Kenneth Thompson, Gerald Stourzh, Tang Tsou, and Norman Graebner wrote important works on American diplomacy under his auspices or influence.[8]

6. In addition to the historical essays condemning legalism and moralism in the Spanish-American War, World War I, and World War II, this book carried the reprint of the Mr. X article discussed above (*ibid.*). See also Lloyd C. Gardner, *Architects of Illusion: Men and Ideas in American Foreign Policy, 1941–1949* (Chicago, 1970), pp. 270–300, esp. p. 293.

7. Louis J. Halle, *Civilization and Foreign Policy* (New York, 1955); and his *Dream and Reality: Aspects of American Foreign Policy* (New York, 1959).

8. Hans Morgenthau's most important books were *In Defense of the National Interest: A Critical Examination of American Foreign Policy* (New York, 1951), and *Politics Among Nations: The Struggle for Power and Peace* (New York, 1948). Robert Osgood's major work was *Ideals and Self-Interest in America's Foreign Relations: The Great Transformation* (Chicago, 1953); see also his *Limited War: The Challenge of American Strategy* (Chicago, 1957) and *NATO: The Entangling Alliance* (Chicago, 1962). Kenneth W. Thompson analyzed the realist school in *Political Realism and the Crisis*

The conversion of Americans to balance-of-power politics vis-à-vis the Soviet Union was almost universal. The inspiration of the realists permeated almost every survey of the Cold War and every general textbook on diplomatic history. Perhaps the mildest of the surveys of the Cold War, omitting for the moment those of the Left, was one of the earliest—William Hardy McNeill's *America, Britain, and Russia*. Stalin might have considered attempts by the West to achieve democratic government in Eastern Europe deliberate threats to the Soviet Union, McNeill thought, since it should have been clear that any popularly elected government in that area by nature would have been unfriendly to Russia. Yet McNeill believed Stalin had no real reason for feeling threatened and noted that Russian documents were unavailable to scholars to test Stalin's true motives. He denounced Stalin's "duplicity and ruthlessness" in Poland and Eastern Europe. "Only by accepting Stalin on his own terms, only by unreservedly espousing the amorality of power could more durable agreements have been reached."

What made McNeill's version milder than most other Cold War accounts was his implication that acceptance of Stalin's terms might still have been best although it was probably impossible because it would have seemed a betrayal to Roosevelt, Churchill, and their peoples. McNeill argued that Stalin had become more a nationalist and less a revolutionary and thus might have been reasonably content with a secure protective sphere in Eastern Europe. Naturally he would move into a vacuum of power, but if Britain and the United States had strengthened Western Europe, a measure of peaceful stability might have emerged. Nevertheless, some conflict was inevitable. McNeill castigated Roosevelt for naïvely believing that the Grand Alliance could hold together, calling this "an absurdly superficial view of international relations." Given the impossibility of winking at Stalin's conduct in Eastern Europe, perhaps Churchill's policy of hard bargaining

---

of World Politics: An American Approach to Foreign Policy (Princeton, 1960). Gerald Stourzh applied realist principles to the diplomacy of the Revolution in his *Benjamin Franklin and American Foreign Policy* (Chicago, 1954); Tang Tsou applied them to *America's Failure in China, 1941–50* (Chicago, 1963); and Norman Graebner applied them to the diplomacy of Manifest Destiny in his *Empire on the Pacific* (New York, 1955). Graebner also edited and wrote works more directly relevant to the Cold War, including *Cold War Diplomacy: American Foreign Policy, 1945–1960* (Princeton, 1962); *The New Isolationism: A Study in Politics and Foreign Policy Since 1950* (New York, 1956); *An Uncertain Tradition: American Secretaries of State in the Twentieth Century* (New York, 1961); and *Ideas and Diplomacy: Readings in the Intellectual Tradition of American Foreign Policy* (New York, 1964).

from a strong military position was the best. At least both sides would know where they stood. In any case, McNeill approved the Truman Doctrine and resistance to "international communism" in Greece, where he had served with U.S. Army Intelligence after World War II.[9] McNeill's book was part of a series of British historical studies and not widely distributed in America. It was well known to scholars and much cited by them, but its length and limited accessibility made it less influential than some of the shorter surveys published in softback covers and commonly used in college classes dealing with the Cold War. Among these studies were John Spanier's *American Foreign Policy Since World War II*,[10] John Lukacs' *A History of the Cold War*,[11] and William Carleton's *The Revolution in American Foreign Policy: Its Global Range*.[12] These, along with more obscure surveys like Richard Van Alstyne's *American Crisis Diplomacy*[13] and Desmond Donnelly's *Struggle for the World*,[14] took a harsher view of the Cold War. Their attitude was typified by that of John Lukacs, who asserted that "Stalin, not Truman, was the principal architect of the Iron Curtain and the Cold War" and that Truman had halted the "eventual spread of Russian Communist tyranny" with his Truman Doctrine and Marshall Plan.[15]

This assumption underlay the general diplomatic history texts of this era as well. Perhaps the most notable and significant convert to this view of the Cold War in the historical community was Samuel Flagg Bemis. In the editions of his textbook published after World War II, he dropped all hints of World War I revisionism and all admonitions against political involvement outside the Western Hemisphere. Praising the views of his Yale colleague, Nicholas Spykman, Bemis warned that Europe's distresses were no longer America's advantage. "The North American continent, the Western Hemisphere, were no longer secure. Thenceforth the United States would strive to unite the free

9. William Hardy McNeill, *America, Britain, and Russia: Their Cooperation and Conflict, 1941–1946* (New York, 1970; originally published in London, 1950), pp. 28–31, 47, 64, 313–328, 405–409, 564–565, 576–579, 583, 609–610, 736, 740–741.

10. John Spanier, *American Foreign Policy Since World War II* (New York, 1960).

11. John Lukacs, *A History of the Cold War* rev. ed. (New York, 1962).

12. William G. Carleton, *The Revolution in American Foreign Policy: Its Global Range* (New York, 1963).

13. Richard W. Van Alstyne, *American Crisis Diplomacy: The Quest for Collective Security, 1918–1952* (Stanford, 1952).

14. Desmond Donnelly, *Struggle for the World: The Cold War, 1917–1965* (New York, 1965).

15. John Lukacs, *A New History of the Cold War* (New York, 1966), pp. 63, 67.

nations of the globe to resist the landmass of imperialistic Soviet power and/or the new might of Communist China."[16]

Rivaling Bemis's book as the most popular and influential text-book on the history of American foreign policy was *A Diplomatic History of the American People* by Thomas Bailey. Published first in 1940, it went through numerous editions, its sales spurred on by the witty prose that contrasted so markedly with the heavy-handed approach of Bemis. The opportunities for humor were far greater in Bailey's approach, it must be admitted, because Bailey ignored much of the tortuous detail of diplomatic negotiations that had fascinated Bemis and emphasized instead the influence of public opinion on American diplomacy. As far as Bailey was concerned, most of American public opinion was ignorant and short-sighted, exerting a harmful effect on American diplomacy. Bailey found no dearth of hilarious anecdotes with which to illustrate this thesis, which made him an enormously popular lecturer on the Stanford campus as well as a best-selling text writer.[17]

Bailey was somewhat more critical of American foreign policy than Bemis's later work. But Bailey thoroughly supported the American side of the Cold War. He attacked the gullibility and slothfulness of the isolationists and the "myths" with which they had supported themselves since World War I. Not all Americans were bearing the Cold War burdens cheerfully, he complained. "Not all of them are prepared to recognize that their very way of life is jeopardized by the communist menace. Many are grumbling over defense expenditures, not realizing that to Moscow the most eloquent language is that of force. Many are in a mood to be taken in by Soviet smiles and wiles."[18] Bailey even wrote a survey of Russian-American relations to demonstrate the basic antagonism of the two superpowers.[19]

The other major texts of this period were almost all as strident in their advocacy of the Cold War. Julius Pratt published one similar in interpretation to those of Bailey and Bemis, as did Robert Ferrell,

16. Samuel Flagg Bemis, *A Diplomatic History of the United States*, 5th ed. (New York, 1965), pp. 879, 907, 1009.

17. His view of public opinion is spelled out comprehensively in Thomas A. Bailey, *The Man in the Street: The Impact of American Public Opinion on Foreign Policy* (New York, 1948).

18. Thomas A. Bailey, *A Diplomatic History of the American People*, 7th ed. (New York, 1964), p. 897.

19. Thomas A. Bailey, *America Faces Russia: Russian-American Relations from Early Times to Our Day* (Ithaca, 1950).

Bemis's student.[20] Somewhat less strident, but still supportive of the American side in the Cold War, were the texts by Richard Leopold, a student of early twentieth-century diplomacy and a professor at Northwestern, and Alexander DeConde, whose major field of interest was early American diplomacy.[21]

As the vast majority of Americans rallied around the policy of confrontation with Russia, some historians and politicians began to ask whether the United States had placed itself at a disadvantage in the Cold War by its cooperation with the Soviet Union during World War II. Many of these questions were inspired by the publication of Churchill's memoirs. The British prime minister recounted instances in which he had sought to shape British and American strategy to limit Russia's war gains but had been frustrated by Roosevelt's desire to avoid political decisions and concentrate strictly on the military defeat of the Axis.[22] Churchill's criticisms of Roosevelt's policy were taken up by several other widely read histories, including Hans Morgenthau's prominent realist tract, *In Defense of the National Interest*, and Hanson Baldwin's *Great Mistakes of the War*. These books were not deeply researched, and their conclusions did not win general approval among historians, but their charges did receive much public attention and popular acceptance.

Roosevelt's critics argued that he should have treated Stalin as a rival from the beginning. Roosevelt should have extracted solid guarantees for national independence and democracy in Eastern Europe by using the second front as a bargaining lever. Instead, Roosevelt had tried to preserve Eastern European independence by wooing Stalin, showing him that there was no reason to fear the Western Allies and therefore no reason to impose his rule on his neighbors. Thus, Roosevelt offered for Stalin's confidence a premature promise of a second front for Europe in 1942. When the invasion failed to materialize until 1944, Stalin became less rather than more trustful and used the failure

20. Julius W. Pratt, *A History of United States Foreign Policy* (Englewood Cliffs, N.J., 1965; originally published 1955); and Robert H. Ferrell, *American Diplomacy, A History* (New York, 1959).

21. Richard W. Leopold, *The Growth of American Foreign Policy* (New York, 1962); and Alexander DeConde, *A History of American Foreign Policy* (New York, 1963).

22. Winston S. Churchill, *The Second World War*, 6 vols. (Boston, 1948–1953); and Robert E. Sherwood, *Roosevelt and Hopkins: An Intimate History* (New York, 1948). An earlier critic of this sort was William C. Bullitt, "How We Won the War and Lost the Peace," *Life*, 25 (Aug. 30 and Sept. 6, 1948) 83–97, 86–103.

as moral leverage to win more concessions from Roosevelt and Churchill.

These critics also argued that Roosevelt should have followed Churchill's advice and invaded Europe through the Balkans rather than across the Channel. A Balkan invasion might have placed British and American troops in Eastern Europe ahead of the Russians and thus prevented the tier of Eastern European states from falling behind the Iron Curtain. But Roosevelt ignored such political considerations in his military strategy and pushed for the Normandy invasion strictly on military grounds. Invasion of France rather than of the Balkans guaranteed that Soviet troops would be occupying much of Eastern and Central Europe by the time the Western Allies could meet them.

This error was compounded, according to these critics, by Roosevelt's unwavering demand for the unconditional surrender of the Axis. Roosevelt hoped to prevent the dissension among the Allies that might be produced by a specific discussion of war aims. Unconditional surrender also would remove the temptations for an individual nation to negotiate a separate compromise peace with the Axis. Thus, the problems that had plagued Wilson in World War I, problems of which Roosevelt was very conscious, could be avoided.

Unfortunately, the unconditional surrender formula not only increased German and Japanese resistance; it insured that the power of the Axis nations would be thoroughly eradicated. This removed their contributions to the balance of power that had formerly restrained the Soviet Union, which left a vacuum Russia was quick to exploit.

As World War II came to a close in Europe, the United States had one last chance to attend to the political effects of its military decisions. With German resistance crumbling faster in the East than in the West, the Western Allies could have raced to take Berlin before the Russians. Instead, on military grounds, Eisenhower ordered his armies to attack southward toward Czechoslovakia and leave Berlin's liberation to the Russians. Even then the Americans could have gone beyond the military demarcation line between the Russians and the West, which had been determined at Yalta, and taken Prague. Churchill urged that they do so. When frustrated in that, he asked that at least the British and Americans remain in the positions they had taken beyond the demarcation line, pulling back only when it was clear that the Soviet Union was going to live up to its side of the Yalta agreement and stop some of its high-handed actions in Central Europe. But again the Americans decided otherwise. They moved their troops out of Europe and, after the defeat of Japan, demobilized them. Russia then exploited the vacuum America had created.[23]

Some substantial monographs supported this indictment of Roosevelt's policies. Anne Armstrong's study, *Unconditional Surrender: The Impact of the Casablanca Policy upon World War II*, concluded that the policy had indeed stiffened German resistance and had given the Germans time to reinforce Italy after Italy's Marshal Badoglio had indicated his willingness to surrender.[24] The memoirs of Robert Murphy, who had represented the State Department with Eisenhower's command headquarters, argued that America's position in Eastern Europe would have been substantially improved if Roosevelt had accepted Churchill's advice.[25] Edward Rozek blamed the fall of Poland to Russia largely on Roosevelt's unconditional surrender policy and on the Lend-Lease aid to Russia that gave the Red Army the ability to move quickly into Eastern Europe. Unlike most other historians, Rozek did not consider Churchill a heroic resister of Roosevelt's naïveté. Churchill himself had been too accommodating to the Russians. "The road of appeasement to Moscow leads not to relaxing by good will and faith the tensions, Moscow-made, but to surrender and to slavery," Rozek warned.[26]

Almost all American historians came to accept the contention that Roosevelt and his advisers had neglected the political dimension of the war. Roosevelt had indeed ignored State Department advisers like Averell Harriman and Joseph Grew, who took account of these political factors, and relied instead on military advisers like George Marshall and Dwight Eisenhower, for whom crushing the enemy was the primary concern. Yet the majority of historians who studied America's wartime diplomacy closely began to doubt that this neglect of the political consequences of military matters had had a significant effect on the Cold War that followed.

The most important of these historians, and the one upon whose work so many later surveys and texts were based, was Herbert Feis. With his special access to State Department archives, Feis covered America's wartime diplomacy in three significant volumes: *Church-*

23. Morgenthau, *In Defense of the National Interest*, pp. 95–112; and Hanson Baldwin, *Great Mistakes of the War* (London, 1950).

24. Anne Armstrong, *Unconditional Surrender: The Impact of the Casablanca Policy upon World War II* (New Brunswick, N.J., 1961), pp. 50–100.

25. Robert Murphy, *Diplomat Among Warriors* (New York, 1964), pp. 211, 252–256, 273, 440.

26. Edward J. Rozek, *Allied Wartime Diplomacy: A Pattern in Poland* (New York, 1958), pp. viii–x, 441–443.

ill—Roosevelt—Stalin, Between War and Peace: The Potsdam Conference, and Japan Subdued.[27] Feis admired Churchill's political acumen and chastised Roosevelt although he did not believe that unconditional surrender had had a serious impact. He showed that even though Churchill and Stalin had expressed doubts about the formula from time to time, neither had seriously challenged it. Each of the Big Three had made clear that unconditional surrender did not require the destruction of the population or national existence of the Axis nations. The Nazis fought to the last not because of the demand for unconditional surrender but because they feared the Russians and knew retribution awaited them for their atrocities. Thus, there was no hope of making a peace that would leave Germany powerful enough to check Russia.

American popular opinion would not have stood much compromise with the Nazis, in any case. Neither would it have accepted the rapid turnabout of attitude necessary to keep American troops in Europe forward of the Yalta line to extort Russian cooperation in Poland and the Balkans. As long as America's military leaders thought that Russian help was necessary to pin down the Japanese Manchurian army after victory in Europe, Roosevelt had to avoid a confrontation with the Soviet Union. This left Feis criticizing Roosevelt not so much for specific actions during World War II but for raising false hopes of Russian postwar cooperation. Failing to educate the American people to the inevitable postwar rivalry with Russia meant that demands to "bring the boys home" left the American government with no option but to withdraw its troops from Europe and demobilize. Since Stalin knew this would come about, a temporary occupation of Eastern Europe by the Western Allies would have provided little leverage, Feis concluded.[28]

While Feis reduced the significance of the unconditional surrender formula and the dispute over Churchill's suggestion to hold positions beyond the Yalta line, America's military historians undercut the importance of the British-American quarrel over the second front in the coming of the Cold War. Maurice Matloff, Forrest Pogue, and

27. Herbert Feis, *Churchill—Roosevelt—Stalin: The War They Waged and the Peace They Sought* (Princeton, 1957); *Between War and Peace: The Potsdam Conference* (Princeton, 1960); and *Japan Subdued: The Atomic Bomb and the End of the War in the Pacific* (Princeton, 1961). Feis also wrote *The China Tangle: The American Effort in China from Pearl Harbor to the Marshall Mission* (Princeton, 1953), which will be discussed later.

28. Feis, *Churchill—Roosevelt—Stalin*, pp. 125, 357, 371, 633–638.

Kent Greenfield were participants in the U.S. Army-sponsored study of World War II. Samuel Eliot Morison wrote a comparable study of the navy. In their measured and thoroughly researched works, they recalled that when Roosevelt offered the Russians a second front in 1942, no one thought that Russia would emerge from the war as strong as it did. Most thought the Russians were on the verge of losing to Germany. Even the Poles expected to be stronger than the Russians by the end of the war. With this perception of Russian weakness, it seemed unnecessarily dangerous to the anti-German war effort to use the second front as leverage in a confrontation with Stalin over a postwar settlement, at least until well after Stalingrad.

Yet the military historians agreed with Churchill that an attempt at a cross-Channel invasion in 1942 or 1943 was premature and that Churchill's peripheral Mediterranean strategy was better for that stage of the war. Perhaps the Russians did not understand the delay. They scoffed at British and American claims that the casualty rate of an invasion attempted before the Germans had been softened would be intolerable. The Russians were already receiving tremendous losses on the Eastern front, and they regarded men as more expendable than scarce materiel. But Churchill rightly feared that a premature invasion would bog down into the murderous and static trench warfare seen in World War I. His small nation could not accept such casualties again, and an early invasion would inevitably be a British operation because it would come before America was fully mobilized. Given the shortage of landing craft, a second European front appeared to be militarily impossible in 1942. An invasion of North Africa seemed the best alternative. Roosevelt realized the political importance of involving American troops immediately against Germany. Without that involvement, popular pressure would inevitably force increased effort in the Pacific theater where Pearl Harbor rankled the American psyche even more than Hitler.

However, the military historians agreed that the cross-Channel invasion was the proper course in 1944. Certainly it was correct militarily, they said. But they also thought that the political benefits of such an invasion were greater than those of Churchill's Balkan strategy. A Balkan campaign might have become mired in the rough and mountainous terrain of Southern Europe as had the invasion of Italy. The Red Army might have driven right over the top of the British and American thrust to the Northeast, liberating all of Germany and France. Even if the Balkan campaign had reached far enough north to block the Russians, it could not have arrived in Poland or Czechoslovakia before them, and the Russians might have trampled on those countries all the harder if the British and Americans had occupied the Balkans. In addition, the military historians found that Churchill's opposition to a cross-Channel invasion had been exaggerated by earlier historians. Churchill was primarily anxious to delay the invasion until the bombing campaign and Allied attacks in the Mediterranean weakened the Germans sufficiently to prevent a fiasco like the Gallipoli campaign of World War I, which had nearly destroyed Churchill's political career. Thus, Churchill's Balkan invasion would still have been a limited one, not a complete substitute for a cross-Channel invasion.

Under these circumstances, the military historians doubted that Churchill's strategy could have done more than adjust the military line of demarcation slightly and this at tremendous political and military risks. The military historians joined the rest of the historical community to doubt the wisdom of Roosevelt, Marshall, and Eisenhower when they had ignored the political effects of military actions. But military historians went far to remove the second front issue as evidence that American policy had cost the United States heavily in the early stages of the Cold War. And, they pointed out, Roosevelt and Marshall had supported the critical and most politically dangerous decision of all, to make the major effort in Europe and relegate the Pacific to a secondary theater. The minor losses the Western Allies might have suffered from Roosevelt's naïveté paled before the consequences of that courageous decision.[29]

Briefer surveys of World War II diplomacy, designed for classroom use, followed this same general pattern. They all spoke harshly of Roosevelt's naïve optimism toward the Russians and his refusal to consider the political implications of military decisions, but most saw this as making little difference in the long run. William Neumann, in *Making the Peace*, written in 1950, took a slightly different tack. He believed that Roosevelt had wanted a settlement of postwar arrange-

29. Kent Roberts Greenfield, *American Strategy in World War II: A Reconsideration* (Baltimore, 1963); Maurice Matloff and Edwin M. Snell, *Strategic Planning for Coalition Warfare, 1941–1942* (Washington, D.C., 1953); Maurice Matloff, *Strategic Planning for Coalition Warfare, 1943–1944* (Washington, D.C., 1959); Forrest C. Pogue, *The Supreme Command* (Washington, D.C., 1954); and Samuel Eliot Morison, *Strategy and Compromise* (Boston, 1958). For further qualifications and debate, see Trumbull Higgins, *Winston Churchill and the Second Front, 1940–1943* (New York, 1957), in which Higgins approves America's military strategy of an early European second front but then supports Churchill's political strategy once it was clear the war was won.

ments early rather than at the end of the war.[30] But he was orthodox on other points, complaining about Roosevelt's blindness to Russia's ambition in Eastern Europe. He made less distinction than most historians did between Roosevelt's naïveté and Churchill's realism, blaming both Allied leaders for accommodating Russia. Gaddis Smith, a student of Bemis, published a far more widely read survey entitled *American Diplomacy During the Second World War, 1941–1945*,[31] in which he restored the distinction between Churchill and Roosevelt, with Churchill winning the benefit of the doubt. "In retrospect it seems clear that Roosevelt's basic assumption was false," he wrote. "The evidence indicates that Soviet leaders believed that their state and ideology could never be secure as long as the world contained any large concentration of noncommunist power. . . . Russian security and expansion were two sides of the same coin."[32] But neither Smith nor Neumann argued that a more realistic attitude on the part of Roosevelt and his advisers, however much to be desired, would have made a substantial difference in the position of Russia and the Western Allies after the war. And John Snell made this the major point of his influential book, *Illusion and Necessity: The Diplomacy of Global War, 1939–1945*.[33]

If there was no way short of World War III to prevent Russia from moving into the vacuum of power inevitably created by World War II, was there a third alternative to Roosevelt's overly sanguine cooperation with the Soviets and Churchill's fruitless attempts to reach Eastern Europe before the Russians? Some of the very realists who had praised Churchill's policies thought so. Perhaps this was not surprising since Churchill himself suggested the alternative and sporadically followed it during World War II.

30. William L. Neumann, *Making the Peace, 1941–1945* (Washington, D.C., 1950), p. 7.

31. Gaddis Smith, *American Diplomacy During the Second World War, 1941–1945* (New York, 1965).

32. *Ibid.*, pp. 5–6, 10–11, esp. p. 16.

33. John Snell, *Illusion and Necessity: The Diplomacy of Global War, 1939–1945* (Boston, 1963).

FIFTEEN

Cold War Dissenters: Realists, Right-Wingers, and the New Revisionists

In October of 1944, Winston Churchill knew that the invasion of Normandy had precluded any major American or British effort in the Balkans. Trying to salvage something in that area, he had come to an agreement with Stalin to divide the Balkans into spheres of influence. Greece was to be in the British sphere, Rumania, Hungary, and Bulgaria in the Russian sphere, while Britain and the Soviets would "go fifty-fifty" in Yugoslavia. This idea came to little in the long run because Roosevelt and Hull strenuously objected to a spheres-of-influence approach. They accepted the agreement only as a temporary military expedient. In any case, the spheres-of-influence agreement did not extend to the more vital areas of Poland and Germany. When Allied unity broke down over these more important issues, the Balkan agreement passed into limbo.[1]

Taking this cue from Churchill, some of America's realists suggested that if the Western armies really had been unable to beat Russia to Eastern Europe, then the spheres-of-influence policy would have been less provocative to the Soviets and offered a better chance to

1. Confusion over the exact percentages of influence each country was supposed to have permeates most Cold War histories, for the percentages changed as negotiations went on, and Churchill gave an inaccurate account of the substance and significance of the agreement in his memoirs. See Albert Resis, "The Churchill-Stalin Secret 'Percentages' Agreement on the Balkans, Moscow, October 1944," *American Historical Review*, 83, no. 2 (April 1978): 368–387.

diminish the Cold War than Roosevelt's naïve attempts to win Stalin over to democratic policies in Eastern Europe with a friendly demeanor. Hans Morgenthau concluded that if unconditional surrender and the cross-Channel invasion were indeed products of inescapable military necessity, then the Yalta concessions to Russia in Eastern Europe were the price required to win the war. In that case a legalistic insistence on free elections in the area was foolish, and moral indignation at Russia's violations of the principle was fatuous. The United States simply should have accorded Russia its sphere of influence where the Red Army was in occupation and put itself in a condition to resist any extension of that sphere.[2] Herbert Feis agreed: "Either of two other courses [besides Roosevelt's] might have saved more freedom for the Polish people: a fixed stance of opposition, backed by American and British armies in Europe; or a complete dissociation, after spoken protest, from the Soviet course in Poland."[3] We have already seen that William McNeill had considered these same alternatives in 1950.

This "softer" spheres-of-influence approach to the Russians had received a major endorsement from Walter Lippmann. Lippmann was one of the earliest critics of Kennan's "X" article. He did not deny that the time had come to check Russian expansion, despite his earlier hopes for cooperation with the Soviet Union. "I agree entirely that Soviet power will expand unless it is confronted with power, primarily American power, that it must respect," he wrote.[4] But the United States should not have gone to the lengths it had to pressure Russia to allow free elections in Eastern Europe. It should have protested and then withdrawn from the Soviet sphere of interest, leaving Stalin to bear the onus of his own actions. That would have been the proper time to ally with Great Britain and Western Europe to contain Russian expansion. Kennan's containment policy went wrong by trying to contain Russia everywhere. Alliances with disorganized and backward nations like Greece, Turkey, or Nationalist China would destroy the Atlantic community. The United States should not undertake commitments in areas where it could not exert real control, that is the Middle East and Asia. If America risked war in these areas, European nations would back out of the Atlantic alliance because they would be the battleground in any war involving the United States and the Russians. Thus, Lippmann approved of the Marshall Plan's economic aid to Europe and condemned the Truman Doctrine's universal-

2. Morgenthau, *In Defense of the National Interest*, pp. 109–112.
3. Feis, *Between War and Peace*, p. 38.
4. Walter Lippmann, *The Cold War* (New York, 1947), p. 10.

ist commitment to defend any nation threatened by invasion or internal overthrow by armed minorities.

Lippmann recommended instead that the United States redress the balance of power, then negotiate a mutual withdrawal of American and Soviet troops from Europe. Kennan was wrong to imply that the Soviet Union had ambitions of conquering the world for its communist ideology. Russia was motivated less by ideology than by the same national ambitions that had dominated Russian foreign policy since long before its Revolution. Thus, its ambitions were limited, predictable, and negotiable. Waiting for the Soviet government to collapse or moderate before America negotiated with it was also a mistake. Contrary to Kennan's analysis, Lippmann felt sure that the Soviet regime was here to stay.[5]

Ironically, according to Kennan's later writings, he had agreed with much of Lippmann's criticism of the containment doctrine. In the debates within the State Department, Kennan had argued against the universalist aspirations of the Truman Doctrine. He had urged concentration on the vital nations of Europe rather than on Third World nations. He had advocated a policy aimed at disengagement in Europe rather than a permanent division of the territory. He was skeptical of using military force as the primary agent of containment. Russia had no intention of launching a military invasion of Western Europe; the Soviet danger was not military but political. America should strengthen the independent nations of Europe with economic aid, not station masses of troops on the borders of the Russian sphere. Military support might be given to Western Europe to quiet its unreasoning jitters about the danger of a Russian invasion and to underline America's commitment to its defense, but no more.

Kennan was probably neither so clear nor so consistent in his agreement with Lippmann's ideas as his later *Memoirs* made him seem.[6] Yet he did resign from the State Department because of his disagreement with the increasingly hard line of American foreign policy, and his publications subsequently dissented from that line

5. *Ibid.*, pp. 24–25, 30–38, 42–43, 52–53. For Lippmann's progress toward this view from his earlier insistence on a joint United States/British/Russian hegemony, see his *U.S. War Aims* (Boston, 1944), pp. 131–142, 157–160.

6. Compare George F. Kennan's *Memoirs, 1925–1950* (Boston, 1967), pp. 260–264, 270–271, 334–339, 370–372, 430–431, 488–491, with Herbert Feis, *From Trust to Terror: The Onset of the Cold War, 1945–1950* (New York, 1970), pp. 222–224. See also Gardner, *Architects of Illusion*, pp. 279–299; and John W. Coogan and Michael H. Hunt, "Kennan and Containment: A Comment," Society for Historians of American Foreign Relations *Newsletter*, 9, no 1 (March 1978): 23–25.

more and more overtly. How did Kennan reconcile his support for Lippmann's "softer" approach with his strong criticism of Roosevelt's cooperative policy toward the Soviet Union in World War II? He gave his answer in his influential 1951 book, *American Diplomacy*. Although he had opposed what he considered Roosevelt's unilateral concessions to win Soviet collaboration in the war, he thought Roosevelt's mistakes had made little difference in the postwar situation. Britain and the United States could not have won the war without Russia, and so the peace was mortgaged to Russian purposes from the start. Yalta merely ratified the inevitable. "There was nothing the Western democracies could have done to prevent the Russians from entering [Eastern Europe] except to get there first, and this they were not in a position to do." The United States could and should have withheld aid and encouragement, stopping Lend-Lease once it was clear what Stalin intended in East Europe, but the short-run advantages of this would have been minimal.

> We might have arrived in the center of Europe slightly sooner and less encumbered with obligations to our Soviet allies. The postwar line of division between East and West might have lain somewhat farther east than it does today. . . . But we were still up against the basic dilemma that Hitler was a man with whom a compromise peace was impracticable and unthinkable and that, while "unconditional surrender" was probably not a wise thing to talk a lot about and make into a wartime slogan, in reality there was no promising alternative but to pursue this unhappy struggle to its bitter end, whether you were acting in agreement with your Russian allies or whether you were not; and this meant that sooner or later you would end on some sort of a line in eastern or Central Europe, . . . with ourselves on one side and Soviet forces on the other, and with the understanding between us just about what it has proved to be in these six years since the termination of hostilities.[7]

Kennan's best alternative was the spheres-of-influence approach. After the Russians had spurned cooperation in the relief of the Warsaw uprising, he would have confronted them with a choice. They could change their policy and agree to collaborate in the establishment of truly independent countries in Eastern Europe, or they could forfeit Western support for the remaining phases of their war effort. He was convinced that the Russians were overextending themselves by trying to control Eastern Europe. Without the blessing and assistance of the West in maintaining control there, they would have to retreat somewhat. Fulsome collaboration with Russia was not necessary to the

7. Kennan, *American Diplomacy, 1900–1950*, pp. 74–77.

preservation of world peace, despite what Roosevelt had taught most Americans—"a reasonable balance of power and understanding on spheres of influence would do the trick."[8] As a reputed hard-liner against Russia during the war and as author of the containment doctrine, most Americans assumed Kennan was in full agreement with the policies of Truman and his secretary of state, Dean Acheson. The scope of his disagreement was slow to emerge. His 1951 book, *American Diplomacy*, did not specifically apply his criticisms to the postwar era but only to the period between 1900 and 1945. He was slightly more explicit in his 1954 publication, *Realities of American Foreign Policy*,[9] and quite specific in his 1956 article, "Overdue Changes in Our Foreign Policy."[10] Finally, in 1957, he created a storm when, delivering the Reith Lectures in Great Britain, he suggested negotiations with the Soviet Union for disengagement in Central Europe. Acheson indignantly claimed that Kennan had "never grasped the realities of power relations." Even Lippmann said it was too late because neither the East nor the West now wanted a unified and neutralized Germany.[11]

Nevertheless, other realists moved toward the Kennan-Lippmann position as the Cold War continued. They, too, came to accept the contentions of Feis and the military historians that holding the Russians farther east during World War II had been impracticable. The beginnings of détente after the Cuban missile crisis of 1962 made them wonder whether coexistence on the basis of spheres of interest might have melted the Cold War earlier. Ultimately, Vietnam brought a widespread disillusionment with the Cold War. As more and more Americans came to wonder whether the confrontation with Russia had been necessary after all, the realists increasingly would emphasize their attachment to the spheres-of-influence alternative that would have left Stalin unthreatened in his Eastern European security zone. Also, they would minimize their previous denunciations of Roosevelt's "soft" policy toward Russia during World War II.[12]

8. Kennan, *Memoirs, 1925–1950*, p. 250. See also his *American Diplomacy, 1900–1950*, pp. 66–77.

9. George F. Kennan, *Realities of American Foreign Policy* (Princeton, 1954).

10. George F. Kennan, "Overdue Changes in Our Foreign Policy," *Harper's*, 253 (August 1956): 27–33.

11. See George F. Kennan, *Memoirs, 1950–1963* (Boston, 1972), pp. 229–266, esp. pp. 250, 254–255. His Reith Lectures were later published as *Russia, the Atom, and the West* (New York, 1958).

12. Compare Morgenthau's 1951 book, *In Defense of the National Interest* with his essay on the Cold War in Lloyd C. Gardner, Arthur Schlesinger, Jr., and

But even before the escalation in Vietnam made clear the gap between the Truman-Acheson hard-line containment policy and the policy of the Kennan-Lippmann realists, several significant differences became apparent. First of all, the realists tended to apply the Munich analogy less rigidly than did those supporting Truman and Acheson. They were more willing to negotiate and compromise with their enemies as long as negotiations reflected a real balance of power. Kennan had found it difficult "to get the Pentagon to desist from seeing in Stalin another Hitler and fighting the last war all over again in its plans for the next one."[13]

Part of the realists' willingness to negotiate was based on their denigration of the role of ideology in foreign policy. Although they recognized that Russian motivation was part ideology and part national interest, they thought that the latter was paramount to Stalin. Being concrete and limited, national interest could be negotiated whereas ideology and morality were more absolute and less susceptible to negotiation.[14] The realists decried ideological considerations in American as well as Russian foreign policy. This did not mean that they disapproved of American democracy. They were devoted to the American system. Several were profoundly religious and therefore hostile to the Russian communists on that score. But the realists tended to be deeply conservative in outlook toward human nature, acutely aware of human fallibility and the limitations of American power. What could not be defeated must be tolerated; goals must be balanced with the power available. Many realists were well-traveled cosmopolitans. To them, a modicum of civility and humanity was all they could hope for in this world. Crusades and fanaticism were more harmful than the evils they sought to extirpate. Thus, realists preferred eco-

---

Hans J. Morgenthau, *The Origins of the Cold War* (Waltham, Mass., 1970); Louis Halle's 1955 *Civilization and Foreign Policy* with his *The Cold War as History* (London, 1967); and William Neumann's *Making the Peace, 1941–1945*, published in 1950, with his *After Victory: Churchill, Roosevelt, Stalin, and the Making of the Peace* (New York, 1967).

13. Kennan, *Memoirs, 1950–1963*, p. 90.

14. For this emphasis on national interest in Russia's motivation, see Norman Graebner, *The Cold War: Ideological Conflict or Power Struggle?* (Boston, 1963); Isaac Deutscher, *Stalin: A Political Biography* (New York, 1949); Barrington Moore, Jr., *Soviet Politics—The Dilemma of Power* (Cambridge, Mass., 1950); and Marshall D. Shulman, *Stalin's Foreign Policy Reappraised* (Cambridge, Mass., 1963). For emphasis on ideology, see Raymond Dennett and Joseph E. Johnson, eds., *Negotiating with the Russians* ([Boston], 1951); Zbigniew Brzezinski, *The Soviet Bloc: Unity and Conflict* (Cambridge, Mass., 1960); and Zbigniew Brzezinski, *Ideology and Power in Soviet Politics* (New York, 1962).

nomic and political to military measures in dealing with the Russians. They urged reliance upon conventional over atomic weapons where military measures might be necessary, and they advocated limited wars for limited political ends rather than total wars for total victory. In attempting to keep the Soviet Union contained, they were more willing than Truman and Acheson to accept neutralist and even communist regimes in strategic areas as long as these regimes were truly independent of Russia.

The realists were also more Europe-centered than their opponents. Their concepts were derived from a close study and appreciation of European balance-of-power philosophers. They regarded the areas of great industrial productivity as the prizes of the Cold War since only those areas were able to sustain large military forces. American interests in Africa were too few and too remote to justify major intervention there, and the same was true of all but the most strategically vital geographical features of Latin America. Japan was the only Asian nation of industrial strength. Therefore, realists were much more reluctant to intervene in the rest of Asia than were most other Americans. Like Paul Schroeder, they regretted that the United States had not avoided war with Japan in 1941 since they regarded the European conflict as the real threat to America. They accepted what they considered the inevitable collapse of Chiang Kai-shek's regime in China with greater equanimity than most. They did not regard China as a power capable of threatening America's security. They railed against the idea that America had "lost" China, and the two most significant works on the collapse of Nationalist China were written by realists, Herbert Feis and Morgenthau's student, Tang Tsou.[15] Kennan later wrote that he had not opposed China's entrance into the United Nations after the Chinese Revolution but that he had not been anxious to have the United States establish formal diplomatic relations with Mao Tsetung's regime. He distrusted the Chinese as a people. Even in their weakness, the Chinese had always been able to take advantage of Western diplomats and had never had any real interests in common with the United States.[16]

Naturally, the realists approached the Korean War somewhat skeptically. Kennan said that the United States had to bear some of the blame for North Korea's invasion because the Japanese peace treaty made provision for permanently stationing American troops in Japan. This was regarded by the North Koreans and Chinese as a threat.

15. Feis, *China Tangle;* and Tsou, *America's Failure in China.*
16. Kennan, *Memoirs, 1950–1963,* pp. 56–58.

Kennan supported resistance to the North Korean invasion but urged limited goals and particularly warned against provocations like pushing beyond the 38th parallel or bombing close to the Russian and Chinese borders in the North.[17]

Specific realist criticisms of Truman and Acheson made little impact on popular opinion, however. General realist theories were incorporated into the very books that praised the policies of Truman and Acheson. Only Lukacs' History of the Cold War, of all the major diplomatic texts and Cold War surveys, took the realist criticisms of Truman and Acheson seriously and spoke approvingly of disengagement. Probably the reason the realist criticisms made so small a dent was that they were very subtle and minute compared with the criticisms coming from the right-wingers, who were charging that Roosevelt, Truman, and Acheson were appeasers who had betrayed Eastern Europe, sold out China, and harbored communists in the State Department. After all, in the basic decisions which Roosevelt, Truman, and Acheson had made, they had followed most of the realist prescriptions. They had put Europe first in World War II. They had refused to send American forces to rescue Chiang Kai-shek. They had redressed the balance of power in Europe; and if Kennan and Lippmann had criticized this policy for being too militarily oriented, there were other realists like Morgenthau and Robert Osgood who considered NATO vital.[18] The Truman-Acheson policy was the realist one of containment, not the liberation of Eastern Europe that was being urged by Republicans and right-wingers. And, most importantly, even though Truman and Acheson had approved of the invasion of North Korea beyond the 38th parallel, they had kept the war limited, firing MacArthur when the popular general demanded total victory.

It is not surprising, then, that the realists' subtle differences from the Truman-Acheson policies would be submerged by the far more dramatic differences between Truman and his right-wing critics. Although the right-wingers made little impact on the scholarly world, their criticisms had a far more potent influence on lay public opinion than those of the realists. Right-wing ideas were reflected even in the Republican platform of 1952, in some of the proposals of Eisenhower's secretary of state, John Foster Dulles, and later, in Barry Goldwater's 1964 presidential campaign against Lyndon Johnson.

17. Kennan, Memoirs, 1925–1950, pp. 524–526; Memoirs, 1950–1963, pp. 56–58.

18. See esp. Osgood, NATO: The Entangling Alliance.

Until World War II, right-wing conservatives had been leaders of isolationism. By the 1950s many were hard-line interventionists supporting a global anticommunist crusade. The transition was a difficult and interesting one. Prominent conservative isolationist writers who became hard-line interventionists included John Chamberlain, William Buckley, and Russell Kirk. But not all became converts. When right-winger James Burnham urged military resistance to communism in a book entitled, *The Struggle for the World*,[19] Harry Elmer Barnes called it "the most dangerous and 'un-American' book of the year" and "a blueprint for aggressive war."[20] The pain of the transition was obvious in the writings of William Buckley, an enthusiastic America-firster in 1941 who had gloomily concluded by 1952 that he would have to acquiesce in big government and interventionism as long as the communist threat existed.[21]

How did right-wing conservatives rationalize their isolationist sentiments prior to World War II with interventionism against the Soviet Union in the postwar era? The process can be most easily traced in William Henry Chamberlin's book, *America's Second Crusade*, one of the few semischolarly histories of both World War II and the origins of the Cold War written by a right-winger.

At the time of the Munich agreement, Chamberlin as an isolationist had praised the Allied leaders for accommodating Germany. But in his postwar book Chamberlin now joined the other World War II revisionists in berating Britain and France for appeasing Hitler. Had the Allies stood firm at Munich, Germany and Russia would have become embroiled and perhaps destroyed one another. The mistake was compounded when the British and French foolishly guaranteed Poland against Hitler's invasion. With Germany and Russia having made the infamous pact dividing Poland between them, the guarantee forced Hitler to turn his military might westward. If Britain and France had stood aside, Germany and Russia would inevitably have clashed over Eastern Europe, leaving the West to pick up the pieces.[22]

Even with Germany attacking west, America should have

---

19. James Burnham, *The Struggle for the World* (New York, 1947).

20. Quoted in George H. Nash, *The Conservative Intellectual Movement in America Since 1945* (New York, 1976), p. 124.

21. *Ibid.*, p. 125.

22. Chamberlin, *America's Second Crusade*, pp. 40–70, 346; and Justus D. Doenecke, *Not to the Swift: The Old Isolationists in the Cold War Era* (Lewisburg, Pa., 1979), p. 39.

stayed out of World War II, asserted Chamberlin. Neither Germany nor Japan had plans to extend their conquests into the Western Hemisphere. Russia was far more dangerous than either of them and at least equally objectionable morally because Stalin wanted to conquer the world for communism. Russia's espionage system was much more efficient than Germany's or Japan's, and its industrial and military power had become greater as well. Even if Germany and Japan had won their war, Europe and Asia would have been divided between those two powers. But as a consequence of World War II and the fall of Nationalist China to the communists, a single nation, Russia, ruled almost the entire heartland of Euro-Asia.[23]

America's entry into World War II had been a disaster not only in itself but also because America's conduct of the war had ensured Russia's postwar dominance of Euro-Asia. Chamberlin thought unconditional surrender a terrible mistake and believed that America should have made peace with Germany and Japan when they were still strong enough to be useful partners in the coalition against Russia.[24] He thought the Balkan strategy would have held the Russians farther east and that the territory the British and American armies took at the end of the war should have been held. He was particularly critical of "The Munich Called Yalta." Without Yalta, the United States and Britain could have saved both Poland and China. A Balkan strategy, sending Polish exile troops into Poland ahead of the Soviets, would have succeeded, he believed. Even Western disapproval of Russia's program in Poland might have stirred sufficient resistance there to make Russia's task of consolidation impossible.[25] Yalta's concessions to Russia in Manchuria permitted Stalin to aid the Chinese communists with captured Japanese arms and a base from which to overrun the rest of China.[26]

Thus, Chamberlin's analysis of America's World War II strategy was simply a more extreme and strident version of some of the earlier realist critiques. But Chamberlin and the right-wing saw something more than naïveté behind America's errors. They blamed at least some of them on the disloyalty of American policy makers. In the "one-sided appeasement which was followed at Teheran and Yalta," men "who secretly or openly sympathized with communism were at least acting logically," Chamberlin wrote. "But the majority erred out of

23. Chamberlin, *America's Second Crusade*, pp. 179, 337–345.
24. *Ibid.*, p. 342.
25. *Ibid.*, pp. 217–218.
26. *Ibid.*, pp. 215, 218–220.

sheer ignorance and wishful thinking about Soviet motives and intentions."[27] He included Roosevelt and Marshall among the merely naïve, noting that Roosevelt had stiffened against the Russians somewhat in the last weeks of his life. But he thought that "extreme New Dealers and fellow travelers," not to mention communist spies, had been vicious and effective in disarming the United States against Soviet aggression. Chamberlin accused Henry Wallace of being one of the leading exponents of the "Russia can do no wrong" theory and of permitting disloyal men to serve on almost every commission he chaired. Chamberlin accepted the idea that Alger Hiss had been a spy and recalled that Hiss had served at Yalta. He also said that the responsibility of fellow travelers for the China debacle should not be obscured by the obvious exaggerations of Senator Joseph McCarthy. "On the basis of what is known beyond reasonable doubt, . . . it may be said that in no previous war was the United States so plagued with infiltration of government agencies and warping of policies in the interest of a foreign power," he concluded.[28]

Since the Roosevelt adminstration had refused to let the Germans and Russians consume one another and instead had created a vacuum of power into which Russia could enter to dominate the heartland, Chamberlin saw no alternative but to confront Russia with superior power. Regarding Russia as ideologically driven to world conquest, Chamberlin and most of the right-wing were converted to interventionism. This conversion was aided and joined by other conservatives who had been less isolationist but whose interventionism was directed more toward Asia than toward Europe. These "Asia-firsters," for whom General Douglas MacArthur served increasingly as a symbol and leader, had resented the Europe-first strategy of Roosevelt and Marshall. They came to form the "China lobby" that advocated liberal aid to Chiang Kai-shek and the Nationalists. They accused Roosevelt of betraying China at Yalta and Dean Acheson of "losing" China to the Reds.[29] Right-wingers blamed Acheson for "inviting" North Korea's invasion of the South when he left Korea out of America's announced defensive perimeter. They supported MacArthur's demands for bombing communist sanctuaries beyond the Yalu River when the Chinese entered the war and pushed United Nations forces

---

27. *Ibid.*, p. 343.
28. *Ibid.*, pp. 251–257.
29. The right-wing version of this story was written by the old isolationist Kubek, *How the Far East Was Lost.*

back to the 38th parallel. Right-wingers were enraged at Truman's dismissal of MacArthur and the president's willingness to accept a compromise peace in Korea. They echoed MacArthur's cry that there was "no substitute for victory."

The Republican party made effective use of these issues in the 1950s. Robert Taft, the conservative Republican leader of the Senate, was only a reluctant Cold Warrior in Europe and voted against the formation of NATO. But he avidly denounced the Democrats' "appeasement" policy in Asia. The Democratic party's vulnerability on Asian issues, dramatized by Senator McCarthy's campaign against the State Department officials who had "lost" China, was significant to the Republican victories in the election of 1952. The Republican platform tried to appeal to both isolationists and interventionists by condemning the Democrats first for getting into Korea without the consent of Congress and then for not fighting to total victory. But, clearly, anti-communist global interventionism was smothering isolationism among right-wingers.

Although right-wing attitudes toward the Cold War had a strong "Asia-first"tinge, conservatives ultimately promoted a strong interventionist position in Europe, too. Eastern European émigrés like Robert Strausz-Hupé, Stefan Possony, and Gerhart Niemeyer emphasized the importance of their former homelands. James Burnham agitated against any abandonment of Europe for Asia in a book highly influential in Republican party councils, *Containment or Liberation?*[30] Burnham argued that the Democrats' policy of containment would lead to America's defeat. Russia already occupied the heartland. Western Europe could not continue to exist without economic access to Eastern Europe and China. The Asia-first policy of Taft and MacArthur would not work either because Russia and China were already too strong in Asia to be contained by the remainder of the nations there, even with America's help. The only alternative was to liberate Eastern Europe and drive Russia back from the heartland. This was to be done not by invasion since America and Western Europe would always be weaker than their opponents on land. Instead, political warfare would stir revolt there, to be protected by the West's superior air power and atomic weapons.[31]

Much of this right-wing policy found its way into the Re-

30. James Burnham, *Containment or Liberation? An Inquiry into the Aims of United States Foreign Policy* (New York, 1952, 1953).

31. *Ibid.*, pp. 27, 39–41, 77–78, 101–116, 117–140, 150.

publican platform and the pronouncements of John Foster Dulles. The platform taunted the Democrats for the "tragic blunders" of Yalta, Teheran, and Potsdam and for selling out China and Poland. It contrasted Russia's "Asia-first" policy with Truman's "Asia-last" policy and said the Republicans would not sacrifice the Far East to gain time for the West. Dulles and the platform denounced the containment policy as defensive and immoral. It left captive peoples subject to what Chamberlin had called Soviet "slave labor" and "genocide." Dulles went on to advocate the "liberation" of Eastern Europe and warned of "massive retaliation" with nuclear weapons if communists committed aggression anywhere. The Republicans cut the budget for the army as they preferred to concentrate on air power. Meanwhile, Dulles tried to shore up America's defenses in Asia and the Third World by negotiating alliances such as the South East Asia Treaty Organization and the Baghdad Pact.

Nevertheless, many conservatives became disillusioned over the actual performance of the Republicans once they took office. Conservatives enjoyed the vigor demonstrated by Dulles and Eisenhower in the overthrow of a left-leaning government in Guatemala and in their refusal to abandon Quemoy and Matsu in the Formosa Straits. Chamberlin thought the Quemoy-Matsu issue sufficiently important and Dulles's action there sufficiently strong to dedicate his 1962 book, *Appeasement: Road to War*, "To the Memory of John Foster Dulles, Patriot, Statesman and Unflinching Warrior in the Struggle Against Appeasement."[32] But the administration's inactivity in the face of the Hungarian Revolution showed that Dulles and Eisenhower were not really going beyond containment. The compromise peace in Korea negotiated under Eisenhower, the toleration of the Cuban Revolution, the refusal to intervene at Dienbienphu, and the administration's opposition to Britain, France, and Israel in the Suez crisis added to right-wing disillusionment. "The net balance of 1959, after six years of an administration brought into power by the basic backing of conservative votes, registers an immense slippage in our will to resist communism and in our position vis-à-vis communism," wrote conservative Frank Meyer.[33] John Birch Society founder Robert Welch even went so far as to accuse Eisenhower of being a conscious agent of the communist conspiracy.

32. William Henry Chamberlin, *Appeasement: Road to War* (New York, 1962).
33. Quoted in Nash, *The Conservative Intellectual Movement in America Since 1945*, p. 254.

The right-wing found few adherents in the historical community. No major text accepted the ideas that the Democrats had "lost" China or should have bombed beyond the Yalu. None thought Yalta the product of treason. None saw containment as a disguised surrender to communism or held out strong hopes for liberation, though several texts were vehemently anticommunist. Postwar editions of Bemis's *Diplomatic History of the United States* came the closest to the right-wingers. Bemis called Yalta another Munich and said it had unhinged the balance of power in both Asia and Europe. But he admitted that it would have been difficult to turn on the Russians in the middle of the war, and he considered Yalta a mistake rather than treason. He admired MacArthur's military accomplishments in Korea but was noncommittal on the general's plans to bomb China. He argued that Russia was indeed seeking world conquest. He applauded Dulles's anticommunist stands, saying that "each time Soviet leadership had temporized when confronted with actual force."[34] Less strident but still conservative and strongly anticommunist were Thomas Bailey and Julius Pratt. Robert Ferrell was near the center of the Truman-Acheson position whereas Richard Leopold and Alexander DeConde were somewhat softer in tone, approaching but not quite reaching the Kennan-Lippmann realist posture.[35]

By the early 1960s these texts, along with the special studies of the Eisenhower-Dulles era and the more general surveys of the Cold War, had formed a fairly broad consensus as to the record of the Eisenhower administration and the needs of the future.[36] Within this

34. Samuel Flagg Bemis, *A Diplomatic History of the United States*, 5th ed. (New York, 1965), pp. 904–905, 922–927, 940, 992–993, esp. p. 988.

35. See Thomas A. Bailey, *A Diplomatic History of the American People*, 7th ed. (New York, 1964), pp. 760, 766, 818, 821–824, for support of Truman rather than MacArthur on Korea; pp. 826, 830, for support of overturning Arbenz in Guatemala; pp. 831–832, for disquiet at French defeat in Indo-China; and pp. 897–899, for strong anticommunism. See also Julius W. Pratt, *A History of United States Foreign Policy*, 2nd ed. (Englewood Cliffs, N.J., 1965), pp. 430–431, for Yalta as mistake; p. 549, for support of worldwide containment; pp. 549–550 for strong anticommunism; p. 472, for criticisms of liberation; p. 476, for opposition to disengagement; and pp. 500–502, for opposition to neutralism in Southeast Asia. See also Robert H. Ferrell, *American Diplomacy: A History* (New York, 1959), pp. 540–547; Richard W. Leopold, *The Growth of American Foreign Policy* (New York, 1962), pp. 620, 634–642, 711–713, 802–803; and Alexander DeConde, *A History of American Foreign Policy* (New York, 1963), pp. 632–633, 653–654, 656, 729–730, for opposition to Guatemala; p. 712, for limited war policy in Korea; and p. 787, for opposition to liberation.

36. Bemis was considerably to the right of this consensus and the right-wing completely beyond the pale. The right-wing was derided for its McCarthyism and its conspiracy theories especially, with devastating portraits of

consensus, the Kennan-Lippmann realists and the Truman-Acheson advocates were brought closer together by a common opposition to Dulles and by changing conditions. Russia's tactics had altered, these historians claimed. Stalin was dead, and his successors were bound to be more reasonable than that paranoid tyrant. In addition, the de-Stalinization campaign had weakened the bonds between Moscow and communists in other nations, including China and some Eastern European satellites. Communism was no longer monolithic.

The strategic situation also had changed. Both Russia and the United States had developed the hydrogen bomb, and any adventurous policy that brought an all-out clash between the two superpowers meant mutual destruction. The Soviets, recognizing this, had shifted their emphasis from the conventional capability to invade Europe, supposing they had ever had that intention, to "wars of national liberation," most historians claimed. Thus, the United States had to shift its strategy too. Wars of national liberation could not be countered by threats of massive retaliation. Instead, America should increase its foreign aid to relieve conditions which might foster revolution in noncommunist countries. The United States had a natural advantage in this contest, for America could encourage truly independent nationalism whereas the Soviets would seek domination through communist parties subservient to them. Thus, Dulles's refusal to tolerate neutralism in the Third World had been as wrong-headed as his plan for massive retaliation. In case revolutions were stirred in noncommunist countries by forces that were beholden to Soviet or Chinese communism, the United States should be prepared to meet such "brush-fire" wars with limited counterforce appropriate to the situation. Since wars of national liberation were likely to be guerrilla wars, the United States should rebuild its ground forces and train them and those of its allies in counterguerrilla tactics. The consensus was that failure to do this in Indo-China had cost the United States heavily. If America could shift its Cold War strategy in this way, communism could be contained, and the mellowing of the Soviet regime that Kennan had predicted might well continue. Ultimately it might be possible to arrive at a truce with the Soviet Union and ease the Cold War.

Perhaps the most influential book promoting this historical consensus was Walt Whitman Rostow's historical survey and analysis of

---

this set of mind being chronicled by historians like Richard Hofstadter in books such as Hofstadter's *The Paranoid Style in American Politics* and *Anti-Intellectualism in American Life*.

the Cold War, *The United States in the World Arena*.[37] The other standard surveys of the Cold War, including those of Spanier, Lukacs, Carleton, and Donnelly, agreed. They supported their ideas by citing numerous special studies that encouraged the same conclusions. The major books on the Korean War all upheld the concept of limited war and reviled MacArthur's demands for total victory.[38] Army officers like Maxwell Taylor, Matthew Ridgway, and James Gavin offered strategic plans and rationales for decreasing America's dependence on nuclear weapons and providing a flexible response to threats posed by limited communist aggression.[39]

This consensus found expression even in sympathetic studies of the Eisenhower administration. Emmet John Hughes tried to excuse Eisenhower for the errors of his administration by claiming that Dulles had been the hard-liner and had dominated Eisenhower in foreign policy.[40] Hughes argued, and almost all other historians agreed, that Dulles had not lived up to his hard-line rhetoric but that even Dulles's continuation of the Truman-Acheson policies was inappropriately rigid in the changed conditions of the Eisenhower era.

In this common opposition to the Dulles-Eisenhower policies, the differences between the Kennan-Lippmann realists and the Truman-Acheson advocates seemed to narrow. The conflict over the extent to which ideals should play a part in American foreign policy, a dispute which had led to some bitter words on both sides, was shunted aside by people like Walt Rostow, who insisted that the job of a statesman was to shape the diplomatic situation so that ideals and interests were brought into line with one another.[41] John F. Kennedy helped to narrow the gulf between them somewhat as well, although in the first year or two of his administration, Kennedy's policies were confused

37. Walt Whitman Rostow, *The United States in the World Arena* (New York, 1960).

38. See David Rees, *Korea: The Limited War* (New York, 1964); John Spanier, *The Truman-MacArthur Controversy and the Korean War* (Cambridge, Mass., 1959); Trumbull Higgins, *Korea and the Fall of MacArthur* (New York, 1960); and Allen Whiting, *China Crosses the Yalu* (New York, 1960).

39. Maxwell Taylor, *The Uncertain Trumpet* (New York, 1960); Matthew Ridgway, *Soldier* (New York, 1956); and James M. Gavin, *War and Peace in the Space Age* (New York, 1958).

40. Emmet John Hughes, *The Ordeal of Power: A Political Memoir of the Eisenhower Years* (New York, 1963).

41. For a bitter attack on the realists' deprecation of idealism, see Frank Tannenbaum, *The American Tradition in Foreign Policy* (Norman, Okla., 1955). Reinhold Niebuhr had also criticized fellow realists like Kennan and Morgenthau for too rigorously ignoring idealism.

and contradictory. Chided as soft on communism when he suggested abandonment of Quemoy and Matsu during the campaign of 1960, he tried to compensate by taking a harder line on Cuba than Nixon and the Eisenhower administration had done. The resulting Bay of Pigs invasion was universally regarded as a disaster, though Right and Left divided over whether the mistake was support of the invasion in the first place or allowing it to fail once it had been undertaken. To compound the confusion that realists and Truman-Acheson advocates of limited war felt about Kennedy, the new president placed much emphasis on strategic weapons to overcome a supposed "missile gap" between Russia and the United States.

But as time went on, Kennedy seemed to be moving in the direction to which the realists and Truman-Acheson advocates had pointed him. He emphasized a "flexible response" rather than massive retaliation and strengthened America's limited war capability by building U.S. ground forces and instituting antiguerrilla training. He appointed George Kennan ambassador to Yugoslavia, accepted a neutralist regime in Laos, and in other ways demonstrated an increasing willingness to tolerate neutralist and even communist regimes that were truly independent of Russia. The handling of the Cuban missile crisis seemed the final proof to many historians that Kennedy and the Democrats were reliably realistic. By taking a firm yet flexible stand, leaving the Soviet Union a face-saving way of climbing down, and winning Khrushchev's praise, Kennedy had paved the way for the Nuclear Test Ban Treaty and seemed to have brought Russia and the United States close to a détente.[42]

But one major area of difference between the realists and the Truman-Acheson advocates still remained prominent. How much should the United States intervene in the Third World? To what extent was America's security bound up in the existence of friendly regimes in Asia and Latin America? That difference would become critical in Vietnam and Santo Domingo during President Johnson's term of office.

Vietnam had already become something of an embarrassment during Kennedy's administration. Some policy makers and historians saw Vietnam as a test of America's ability to fight a limited war against

42. See the later editions of the textbooks and Cold War surveys already mentioned in this chapter. See also Arthur M. Schlesinger, Jr., *A Thousand Days: John F. Kennedy in the White House* (Boston, 1965); Theodore C. Sorensen, *Kennedy* (New York, 1965); and Henry M. Pachter, *Collision Course: The Cuban Missile Crisis and Coexistence* (New York, 1963).

communist wars of national liberation. Others, particularly the realists who had had little use for Asian containment from the beginning, objected to any major expenditures there and thought that if the South Vietnamese could not maintain themselves with moderate economic and military aid, it was not worth much American effort. Although realists became increasingly uncomfortable over the growing American intervention in Vietnam, it was not until Johnson began bombing the north under the Tonkin Gulf Resolution and sending vast numbers of American military men there that they became alarmed. Until then, indications that Kennedy might reduce America's effort and withdraw, along with Lyndon Johnson's 1964 presidential campaign platform of limiting America's involvement, kept the issue from exploding.

Certainly Johnson's rhetoric sounded reasonable when compared with his opponent Barry Goldwater's right-wing views as put forth in his revealingly titled book, *Why Not Victory?* In this book, Goldwater supported the intervention against Arbenz in Guatemala, regretted that the United States did not aid the Hungarian revolutionaries in 1956, agreed with MacArthur on Korea, and said that America should have knocked down the Berlin Wall.[43] With Johnson's defeat of Goldwater, in 1964, it therefore seemed that the realist and Truman-Acheson consensus had triumphed. Few saw the disaster that Vietnam would bring to that viewpoint. Nor did many foreign policy intellectuals and historians foresee that Vietnam would catapult the small and generally ignored group of radical historians into prominence. Some of these radical historians had won notoriety in the era of Munich, but few had won much respect in the historical community.

The Munich era's most comprehensive leftist revisionist history of the Cold War—in this case the liberal rather than the socialist left— was D. F. Fleming's *The Cold War and Its Origins*.[44] Fleming, the historian and advocate of Wilsonian internationalism in the aftermath of World War I, "kept the faith" throughout World War II, despite the movement of the bulk of his compatriots toward Cold War balance-of-power politics. Fleming believed that only international cooperation, not balance-of-power diplomacy, could prevent World War III. He insisted that Roosevelt's cooperative policy toward the Russians had been right. Stalin's demands on Eastern Europe were understandable given the terrible destruction the German invasion had caused in

43. Barry M. Goldwater, *Why Not Victory?* (New York, 1962), pp. 44–45.
44. Denna Frank Fleming, *The Cold War and Its Origins: 1917–1960*, 2 vols. (Garden City, N.Y., 1961).

Russia. Fleming accused the Western Allies of purposely inviting Hitler eastward with the Munich pact. No wonder Stalin insisted on friendly regimes on his western border. Roosevelt's only mistake had been his refusal to acquiesce in Russia's East Europe claims at the beginning of the war. If the Russians imposed tyrannical police states in their sphere, the British and Americans were equally guilty for installing unjust conservative regimes in Italy and Greece.[45]

Fleming rejected the charge that Russia had broken its Yalta pledges to hold free elections in Poland and Eastern Europe. Stalin simply had a different interpretation of free elections. Fleming agreed with William McNeill that Stalin probably had not anticipated the depth of anti-Russian feelings in Eastern Europe and had hoped that he might be able to establish majority-based regimes that would still be friendly to the Soviet Union. Roosevelt had understood this predicament and, contrary to the claims of many Cold Warriors, had not turned against the Russians in the last weeks of his life.

Unfortunately, Roosevelt's successor had not been so understanding. Truman vacillated for a few months but finally decided that Russia was an enemy. He had tried to use America's possession of the atomic bomb along with Russia's need for Western economic aid to secure democracy in the Balkans. But this pressure had only hurried Russian consolidation of the East European sphere. So Truman had withheld the atomic bomb secret and had demanded inspection prior to relinquishing the technology to the United Nations. Thus, he made himself guilty of starting the arms race. Meanwhile, he was pressuring Russia out of Iran, thus inciting the Cold War. Even then, if the United States had put forth the Marshall Plan before announcing the militaristic Truman Doctrine, the Cold War might have been averted. Despite the "strained interpretations" that made Stalin's February 9, 1946, speech into Russia's declaration of Cold War, Fleming asserted that Stalin had actually avoided a harsh policy toward the West until after the Truman Doctrine.[46]

In 1965, Fleming's mild revisionism was supplemented by a book of similar structure and assumptions but of far harsher tone and argument—Gar Alperovitz's *Atomic Diplomacy*.[47] Alperovitz was a socialist, but he did not condemn all of America's diplomatic history as

45. *Ibid.*, I, xii–xiii, 84–87, 107, 148, 173–187, 252, 331.

46. *Ibid.*, pp. 207–211, 216, 218, 249–262, 267–269, 315–331, 339, 348, 476–478; II, 1048.

47. Gar Alperovitz, *Atomic Diplomacy: Hiroshima and Potsdam* (New York, 1965).

unvarying capitalist aggression.[48] Like Fleming he found much to admire in Franklin Roosevelt's World War II policy and blamed the Cold War on Harry Truman and his hard-line advisers. But unlike Fleming, Alperovitz did not see Truman's contradictory actions early in his presidency as vacillation. Alperovitz believed that Truman had decided almost immediately after taking office to face down the Russians on Eastern Europe. At first he accepted Ambassador Averell Harriman's idea of using American economic strength to do so. Thus, he talked tough to Russian Foreign Minister V. M. Molotov and cut off Lend-Lease abruptly. But Secretary of War Henry Stimson advised Truman to delay the showdown until the atomic bomb had been dropped on Japan. With American troops leaving Europe, Stimson did not think America's economic power capable of forcing the Red Army back behind Russian borders. According to Alperovitz, Truman accepted this advice and embarrassingly reversed his initial hard line, sending Harry Hopkins to talk with Stalin and restoring Lend-Lease. He also tried to delay the start of the Potsdam Conference until the bomb had been dropped. At the conference itself he referred matters to commissions for later decisions so as to make maximum use of atomic diplomacy.

By this time Truman knew that the bomb was unnecessary to defeat Japan. Without the bomb, even without Russia's entry in the war, Japan was ready to surrender. Many of his military advisers had concluded that there would be no need for the blood-curdling invasion of the home islands they earlier had thought would be necessary. While orthodox historians like Herbert Feis had admitted this, they thought that such conclusions had never reached the president in a form to be taken seriously and that Truman had dropped the bomb to save the American lives that he thought would be lost if the war was prolonged. But Alperovitz insisted that Truman had been well informed that no invasion would be necessary. Thus, he must have dropped the bomb for its effect on Russia, not Japan. The demonstration of the power of the bomb might make Russia more manageable in Eastern Europe and end the war with Japan before Russia had acquired all it had been promised in Asia at the Yalta Conference. Thus, the Americans had actually rushed to demolish two Japanese cities before the war could end so that the bomb would have a maximum impact on Russia.

48. See Staughton Lynd and Gar Alperovitz, *Strategy and Program: Two Essays Toward a New American Socialism* (Boston, 1973).

Until this time, Russian policy in Eastern Europe had not been as harsh as it might have been, Alperovitz pointed out. For example, Stalin permitted elections in Hungary that resulted in a noncommunist government. But when Truman began his post-Hiroshima campaign for more democratic regimes in the Balkans and violated the spheres-of-influence agreement that Alperovitz said Roosevelt had accepted, Stalin responded by toughening his position. Thus, Truman's atomic diplomacy had caused the Cold War.[49]

There was another group of Cold War revisionists with a tone milder than Alperovitz's but assumptions considerably more radical. This group came to be known as the Wisconsin school, many of its members having been students there of Fred Harvey Harrington. One of this group, William Appleman Williams, returned to the University of Wisconsin as a professor and trained still more students who would become prolific historians. Williams and the Wisconsin school formulated an interpretation of all American diplomatic history that they called "Open Door Diplomacy." It was an amalgam of the ideas of Charles Beard, Frederick Jackson Turner, and Karl Marx. They considered capitalist nations to be inevitably aggressive. As long as property was inequitably divided, there would be pressure from the less privileged for a redistribution of goods. The upper classes could stave off such demands only if they expanded the economy. This they could do by redistributing wealth to increase the purchasing power of the lower classes and thereby create greater demand, production, and employment. But this would diminish their own relative power and wealth. The only alternative was imperialism. By exploiting foreign resources and markets, they could pacify domestic labor without a drastic revision of the national social, economic, and political structure.

Imperialism was the tragic alternative to which the United States had turned since even democratically inclined statesmen like Jefferson and Madison had been too attached to the concept of private property to violate it in order to insure economic equality. At first America had relied primarily on territorial expansion, with Indians, Frenchmen, Spaniards, and Mexicans all suffering the consequences. The Industrial Revolution and the end of the frontier shifted the emphasis on expansion from territory to exports. America's power elite sought new markets to avoid depressions that would otherwise result from the growing gap between America's production and consump-

49. Alperovitz, *Atomic Diplomacy*, pp. 11–13, 19–26, 202–242. For an analysis similar to those of Alperovitz and Fleming, see David Horowitz, *The Free World Colossus* (New York, 1965).

tion. Thus, America turned to overseas imperialism to supplement its earlier territorial expansion.

But this was a "new imperialism," seeking markets rather than formal colonies. Such "Open Door Diplomacy" would require free trade and the breakdown of old imperial preference systems in the Third World. America would seek this not out of antiimperial sentiments but with the confidence that wherever there was a "free market and no favor," America's natural economic advantages would allow the United States to dominate. Natives might be nominal rulers, but America's economic power would dictate all essential decisions. The United States would have the benefits of colonialism without many of its drawbacks.

William Appleman Williams put forth this theory in a series of increasingly influential books.[50] His colleagues and students applied the theory to particular episodes in a harvest of monographs. Charles Vevier and Thomas McCormick dealt with America's Open Door policy in Asia; Walter LaFeber studied the rise of imperialism and the Spanish-American War; and Lloyd Gardner expanded the suggestions of Williams's *Tragedy of American Diplomacy* into a full-scale study of Franklin Roosevelt's diplomacy.[51]

Since the Wisconsin school saw America's imperialistic drive for markets as consistent throughout the nation's history, it did not emphasize contrasts among American leaders. Thus, Williams and Gardner did not acknowledge significant differences between Roosevelt and Truman in the way Fleming and Alperovitz had. Both presidents were advocates of the Open Door. Roosevelt had returned to the Open Door mainstream in 1935 after what Gardner identified as a brief flirtation with a nationally independent economy in the first New Deal. Roosevelt had then taken the United States into World War II to preserve American access to the markets of Europe and China as Japan and Germany moved to close the Open Door in those areas.[52] Once in the war, Roosevelt had struggled not only to preserve the Open Door in the areas threatened by the Axis but to hold it open in

50. William Appleman Williams: *American-Russian Relations, 1781–1947* (New York, 1952); *The Tragedy of American Diplomacy* (Cleveland, 1959); *The Contours of American History* (Cleveland, 1961); and *The Great Evasion* (Chicago, 1964).
51. Williams and Gardner will be treated in this section; the books of Vevier, McCormick, and LaFeber will be covered in a later chapter.
52. Ascribing far greater influence to Cordell Hull than other historians had, Gardner and Williams saw the essence of Roosevelt's policy to be the Reciprocal Trade Acts.

the areas dominated by America's allies as well. Thus, Roosevelt used America's economic and military might as leverage to open the British Empire, knowing that America's superior economy would soon replace British influence there. But the great tragedy was that Roosevelt and Truman tried to force open the door in Eastern Europe, the sphere Stalin had claimed as his own. Lend-Lease, offers of aid, the reparations question, the International Monetary Fund, and the Export-Import Bank, all were manipulated to bring Eastern Europe and even Russia into the liberal trade system Williams and Gardner saw as central to the conduct of American policy. Thus, the atom bomb was only a supplement to a policy as much Roosevelt's as Truman's. In "the debate over what would have happened if Roosevelt had lived," Williams wrote that

> little would have changed—there is actually very little evidence that Roosevelt seriously entertained the idea of, let alone a developed program for, initiating a fundamental reevaluation of America's conception of itself and the world. . . . In short, it is not possible to account for the continuance of the Open Door Policy simply by blaming Roosevelt's successors. . . . [53]

Although the theories offered by Williams and Gardner could have been couched in a virulently anti-American tone, they were actually stated very mildly. Williams and Gardner regarded America's policy as a mistake, a "tragedy," well intended but having sad consequences. They did not treat that policy as a vicious plot by an evil capitalist clique but as a product of general American ideology. Even though their critique was based on Lenin's theory that imperialism was an inevitable consequence of capitalism, they still seemed to imply that America could achieve a more humane and successful foreign policy by recognizing its former errors and only mildly reforming itself.[54] The tone of radical criticism would become far harsher after Johnson escalated the Vietnam conflict in 1965. It would also become far more influential. But for now, Williams saw little more than "the bared fangs of his reviewers," according to one historian.[55]

53. Williams, *Tragedy of American Diplomacy*, pp. 150, 157. See also Lloyd C. Gardner, *Economic Aspects of New Deal Diplomacy* (Madison, Wis., 1964), pp. viii, 134–141, 154, 172–193, 223, 262, 291, 294, 308–310.
54. See Williams, *Tragedy of American Diplomacy*, pp. 211–212.
55. Keith Berwick, review of Williams' *Contours of American History*, in *William and Mary Quarterly*, 3rd ser., 20, no. 1 (January 1963): 145.

SIXTEEN

The Age of Munich
and the Historiography
of American Interventionism

World War II almost instantaneously improved the reputation of earlier twentieth-century American interventionism. Revisionist writings on World War I and Versailles were all but completely overturned.[1] The shift of opinion on the Spanish-American War and subsequent imperialism was not so dramatic, but it was certainly noticeable. After World War II, no major historian argued that the United States should have refused to intervene in World War I. All agreed that it was crucial to American security that Germany be prevented from conquering the entire European continent and destroying the balance of power. The only question was whether Wilson had intervened for that pragmatic purpose or for some ephemeral, utopian reason.

Not surprisingly, Walter Lippmann signaled the changing attitudes of historians toward World War I. In various writings from 1941 onward, Lippmann claimed that Wilson and the American people had indeed entered the war to preserve the balance of power and the security of the United States. Lippmann conceded that the occasion of the war had been Germany's unrestricted use of the submarine, but the "substantial and compelling" motivation "was that the cutting of

1. In a 1939 poll, Americans approving U.S. intervention in World War I were outnumbered by dissenters 2 to 1. By April of 1941, they were in the majority (Neumann, *After Victory*, pp. 38–39).

the Atlantic communications meant the starvation of Britain, and, therefore, the conquest of Western Europe by imperial Germany." The destruction of the European balance would have left the United States to face "a new and aggressively expanding German empire which had made Britain, France, and Russia its vassals, and Japan its ally."[2]

Lippmann did not offer much evidence to prove that Wilson had entered the war for these realistic reasons. He said he knew from his own acquaintance with Colonel House that House had entertained these sentiments. He cited some columnists, himself included, who had offered security reasons for intervention in 1917. But ultimately he resorted to saying that Wilson and the American people had "intuitively" grasped the need to protect the European balance of power. Lippmann could not have thought that this intuition had run very deep. He said that Wilson had no foreign policy "which gave him the means of judging whether, why, when, where, how, and to what end, the United States must take its position in the war." Further, he said, Wilson avoided explaining his decision to intervene in terms of American security, basing it on legal and moral grounds. Thus, "the nation never understood clearly why it had entered the war."[3]

Realist historians like George Kennan and Robert Osgood accepted Lippmann's contention that America should have intervened in the war to protect Britain and the balance of power. But they disagreed as to whether Wilson and the American people had actually done so for that reason, intuitively or otherwise. Osgood admitted that some of Wilson's advisers had thought intervention necessary to American security, especially Colonel House, Robert Lansing, and Walter Hines Page. But they had not propounded security arguments in their discussions with Wilson, and Wilson had paid his advisers little heed anyway. Even less had the president heeded advice given him in print or from the political stump by outsiders and underlings like Theodore Roosevelt, Henry Cabot Lodge, Lewis Einstein, or Lippmann himself.

Most Americans of the pre-World War I era who demanded intervention for the protection of American security, including the leaders of the preparedness campaign, did not think of security in realistic terms. They did not speak of the subtle interest the United

2. Lippmann, U.S. Foreign Policy, pp. 33–34.

3. Ibid., pp. 32–38. See also Walter Lippmann, "The Atlantic and America," Life, April 7, 1941, pp. 85–92. For another book in this vein, see Forrest Davis, The Atlantic System: The Story of Anglo-American Control of the Seas (New York, 1941).

States had in the European balance of power but only of the chimerical threat of a direct German invasion of the United States or the Western Hemisphere. Yet few Americans accepted such propagandistic cries of "Wolf!" at face value. Certainly Wilson and the higher echelons of the American government did not. They did not even think Germany could defeat Britain and France, and they held to this belief despite Germany's commencement of unlimited submarine warfare in 1917. Thus, although "Armed intervention might well have been the wisest alternative from the long-run standpoint of American ideals and interests," Wilson and the American people had not chosen war "upon mature deliberation; they simply drifted into war, guided largely by impulses . . . with but a tenuous relation to broad and enduring national policy."[4]

Many historians came to agree with Osgood and Kennan in the early post-World War II period. Lippmann seemed disproven by the generally accepted fact that neither Wilson nor his advisers genuinely had feared a German victory when America intervened. Only later did the U-boat campaign bring England to the brink of starvation, and only later did the collapse of the Russian and Italian fronts permit Germany to come within an ace of breaking through French lines to Paris. Thus, it had been the narrow and relatively inconsequential issue of submarine warfare versus neutral rights that had drawn Wilson into the war. Otherwise, Wilson would have remained neutral and permitted a German triumph, with all of its consequences for the balance of power and American security.[5]

Worse yet, Wilson's failure to understand and explain America's self-interest in going to war helped destroy the hopes for national security that should have been fulfilled by the peace that followed. On this point, Walter Lippmann joined ranks with the other realists. Since the American people never clearly understood the nation's security interests in the war, they were "open to every suggestion and insinuation that the nation had fought for no good reason at all, that its victory

4. Osgood, *Ideals and Self-Interest in America's Foreign Relations*, pp. 153–194, 200, 223, 253–255, 262–263. See also Kennan, *American Diplomacy, 1900–1950*, pp. 64–73.

5. See Richard Leopold, "The Problem of American Intervention," *World Politics*, 2 (April 1950): 405–425; Edward M. Earle, "A Half-Century of American Foreign Policy: Our Stake in Europe, 1898–1948," *Political Science Quarterly*, 64 (June 1949): 182; and Thomas A. Bailey, *Woodrow Wilson and the Lost Peace* (New York, 1944), pp. 13–14.

was meaningless, that it had been maneuvered into a non-American war by the international bankers and the British diplomats."[6] Attacks on Wilson's lack of realism were very common in the historical community in the early post-World War II years. This was most dramatically exemplified by the appearance of a plethora of psychohistorical biographies of Wilson which attempted to explain the strange quirk of character that had led him to deal in rigid moralistic and legalistic terms with matters better handled flexibly and realistically in terms of power and self-interest.[7] A plausible defense of Wilson against this realist onslaught was slow to emerge. The most prominent Wilsonian scholar of this era, Arthur Link, at first accepted the realist analysis. In his 1954 volume for the New American Nation Series,[8] he admitted that Wilson had ignored the balance of power and taken America to war only because submarine warfare was a gross violation of American neutral rights. Link rejected the idea that Wilson had been influenced by the supposedly realistic advice of Lansing and House. If Germany had adhered to the *Sussex* pledge, Wilson would have pursued his neutral course relentlessly, Link said. "The German decision to gamble on all-out victory or complete ruin . . . alone compelled Wilson to break diplomatic relations . . . and finally to ask for a declaration of war— because American ships were being sunk and American citizens were being killed on the high seas, and because armed neutrality seemed no longer possible."[9] Link differed from the realists only in his belief that this was good and sufficient reason for war.

But another of Wilson's defenders, Edward Buehrig, was not so ready to concede that Wilson had ignored the balance of power in deciding to intervene. In his 1955 book, *Woodrow Wilson and the Balance of Power*, Buehrig detected a subtle indication of realism in the president's hopes that a negotiated peace would avoid total defeat of

6. Lippman, *U.S. Foreign Policy*, pp. 37–38.

7. The best of these biographies were Alexander L. George and Juliette L. George, *Woodrow Wilson and Colonel House: A Personality Study* (New York, 1956); and John M. Blum, *Woodrow Wilson and the Politics of Morality* (Boston, 1956); the worst was a hatchet job by Sigmund Freud and William C. Bullitt, *Thomas Woodrow Wilson, Twenty-Eighth President of the United States; A Psychological Study* (Boston, 1967).

8. Arthur S. Link, *Woodrow Wilson and the Progressive Era, 1910–1917* (New York, 1954).

9. *Ibid.*, pp. 276–281.

either the Allies or the Central Powers.[10] All of Wilson's defenders, including Link himself, quickly adopted this formulation of Wilsonian realism. At first Link phrased his adoption of this view a bit carelessly by asserting in the 1956 Albert Shaw Lectures (later published as *Wilson the Diplomatist*) that the president had called for a declaration of war because of his "apparent fear that the threat of German victory imperiled the balance of power and all his hopes for the future reconstruction of the world community."[11] But almost all historians had come to agree that Wilson and his advisers had not feared an imminent German victory when they had intervened, so this statement of Wilson's realist concerns proved untenable. Link admitted it[12] and reverted to his earlier contention. If Germany had avoided American ships in its resumption of submarine warfare, Wilson might have contented himself with armed neutrality and stayed out of the war even if this had meant a German victory. But Link agreed with Buehrig that when Germany began sinking American ships, Wilson's decision for war had been more than a defense of neutral rights. Only a strong reaction to the German provocation would preserve America's prestige and leverage abroad and its chance to influence the peace. With what Link called a "higher realism," Wilson was determined that the peace be a just one, not one which sowed the seeds of future wars by crushing either of the belligerents, inciting revenge, and disrupting the balance of power.[13]

The works of two other prominent historians, Ernest May and Daniel Smith, supported Buehrig and Link. Ernest May was the author of what is still the best one-volume study of American intervention. His judicious analysis of the structure of American neutrality showed how few Wilson's alternatives were, and his research in the German archives demonstrated clearly that Germany had decided for unlimited submarine warfare expecting fully that America would declare war but gambling that it could starve the Allies into total surrender before America's intervention could be militarily effective. With even

10. Edward H. Buehrig, *Woodrow Wilson and the Balance of Power* (Bloomington, Ind., 1955), p. 144.

11. Arthur S. Link, *Wilson the Diplomatist: A Look at His Major Foreign Policies* (Baltimore, 1957), p. 88.

12. See Link's comments on the reprinting of a segment of his *Wilson the Diplomatist* in Herbert J. Bass, ed., *America's Entry into World War I: Submarines, Sentiment or Security?* (New York, 1964), p. 92n.

13. Arthur S. Link, "The Higher Realism of Woodrow Wilson," *Journal of Presbyterian History*, 41 (March 1963): 1–13; and his *Wilson: Campaigns for Progressivism and Peace, 1916–1917* (Princeton, 1965).

Germany expecting its actions to inspire a declaration of war, American retreat indeed would have rendered the United States impotent abroad and unable to protect its interests or the power balance after the war.[14] Daniel Smith's biography of Robert Lansing, along with his shorter survey of the war and an excellent historiographical article on the controversial subjects surrounding it, took a line similar to that of May and Link.[15] But Smith and May attributed more of Wilson's realism to the influence of Lansing and House than did Link. For Link, House was a dupe of the Europeans and Lansing was disloyal for inviting the British to think that Wilson would welcome extreme demands from them when they were asked for their peace terms.

The historiographical debate over the Treaty of Versailles took the same path as the debate over American intervention into World War I. After the elimination of those revisionists opposed to both, the debate was left to the realists and the Wilsonians, and their disagreements were as narrow over Versailles as they were over American intervention. Just as they agreed that America's intervention into World War I was proper but differed over Wilson's motives and explanations for that action, so they agreed that the Treaty of Versailles, whatever its shortcomings, should have been ratified, and they differed only on the degree to which Wilson could be blamed for the treaty's shortcomings and for its failure in the Senate.

In retrospect, the narrowness of this disagreement seems rather surprising. All admitted that the Treaty of Versailles should either have been more lenient toward Germany, to win a grateful nation's support, or harsher so that Germany would have been stripped of the power to act on its resentment. One might have expected some realists to take up Harold Nicolson's implied approval of a harsher treaty. Yet none did. The two leading realist critiques, those by George Kennan and Robert Osgood, both concluded that the treaty should have been more lenient.

George Kennan was the more emphatic of the two. He thought that once America had entered the war, Wilson had abandoned any hopes for a negotiated peace and fought for total victory to make the world safe for democracy. This had shattered the equilibrium of Eu-

---

14. Ernest May, *The World War and American Isolation, 1914–1917* (Cambridge, Mass., 1959).

15. Daniel M. Smith: *Robert Lansing and American Neutrality, 1914–1917* (Berkeley, 1958); *The Great Departure: The United States and World War I, 1914–1920* (New York, 1965); and "National Interest and American Intervention, 1917," *Journal of American History,* 52 (June 1965): 5–24.

rope. Russia had exhausted itself and thereby fallen victim to revolution, removing its strength at least temporarily from the concert of Europe. The Austro-Hungarian Empire had been shattered, to be replaced by successor states based on ethnic identity and self-determination, as Wilson had insisted. Germany, mortally offended but not mortally wounded, was in a position to exploit this vacuum, and World War II was the result. Impractical idealism had lain down with war hysteria, producing a peace "too mild for the hardships it contained."

According to Kennan, Wilson should have avoided quarrels over the technicalities of neutrality, armed the United States earlier, and used military power rather than idealistic appeals as his leverage for peace. If intervention had become necessary to save England, he could have made clear that this was in the national interest, not a product of American altruism. The American people then would have understood the necessity for America to maintain its presence in Europe following the peace and would have supported the League of Nations.[16]

Several of Kennan's specific criticisms of the peace were rejected by his fellow realist, Robert Osgood, in his longer, more detailed study. Perhaps this was because these arguments had been anticipated and effectively countered by the two most complete analyses of the peace published in the post-Munich era, those by Paul Birdsall and Thomas Bailey. Paul Birdsall's *Versailles: Twenty Years After* was a strong defense of Wilson. Published in 1941, it heralded the beginning of the historiographical movement to resurrect the treaty's reputation from the devastating criticisms of Keynes and Nicolson. Since it was published before the full development of the realist school, it was aimed primarily at the disillusioned liberals of the 1930s. Thus, Birdsall defended Wilson against liberal charges that the president had betrayed his principles. Like Ray Stannard Baker, Birdsall attributed many of the treaty's concessions to Colonel House (though he disowned the "plot" theory), and he especially blamed Lloyd George for failing to support Wilson's attempts to limit reparations. Still, Birdsall said, the treaty that emerged was not a bad one. It established at least some degree of international responsibility for colonial possessions and provided much self-determination for Europe. Deviations from self-determination for the sake of defensible borders had surely been justified.

16. Kennan, *American Diplomacy, 1900–1950*, pp. 56–65, esp. p. 61.

Munich had proved that Czechoslovakia could not exist unless its border was in the Bohemian mountains.

Birdsall also defended Wilson against some of the criticisms of the nascent realist school, anticipating several of the points Kennan would make in 1950. He implied agreement with Lippmann that Wilson had realistically considered the balance of power when he intervened in 1917 and then made the peace. The war itself, not Wilson, had been responsible for the plight of Russia and Austria. The Austro-Hungarian Empire already had been shattered when the Paris Conference met, and Wilson could do no more than move its borders around a bit. Birdsall even defended Wilson's idealism in terms similar to Link's later concept of higher realism. "Only in a stable world can democracy survive," he wrote.

> Those who decry idealism and justice as sentimental and unrealistic terms in world politics miss the point. For idealism and justice are the very rudiments of common sense. They amount to a practical realization of what the traffic will reasonably bear.[17]

Thomas Bailey was far more critical of Wilson. In his two-volume work, published in 1944 and 1945, he denied that Wilson had been realistic and said that he had entered the war without any thoughts for the balance of power since no one thought the Allies were losing at the time. Bailey also criticized Wilson for dismissing the realistic advice of Robert Lansing at the Paris Peace Conference and for ignoring House's warning to be flexible in his battle with the Senate. Yet Bailey's account did not fit the realist mold. Like Birdsall, he favored Wilson's idealistic plans for the peace treaty and criticized him for the blunders that had compromised his principles. He did not argue that Wilson's excessive idealism had helped undermine the European balance of power. Without reference to the nascent realist movement, however, he did note that Wilson had been far in advance of most of the Allies in seeking a peace that would leave Germany intact. In the face of this it seemed incongruous to blame Wilson for the destruction of the balance of power when his plans, whatever their motivation, were the most likely of all to preserve the power of the enemy states. Even Kennan had been forced to admit that the sort of actions necessary to save the Austro-Hungarian Empire would have been impossible under the protests of American public opinion.[18]

17. Paul Birdsall, *Versailles: Twenty Years After* (New York, 1941), pp. 4–12.
18. Kennan, *American Diplomacy, 1900–1950*, pp. 64–65.

Thus, despite his more caustic handling of Wilson's "blunders," Bailey's analysis of the Versailles treaty was not far from Birdsall's. Certainly both thought the treaty deserved to be ratified.[19]

The analyses of the peace conference by Birdsall and Bailey quieted most criticism of Wilson's concessions. Realist critics of Wilson, except for Kennan, turned away from that issue and attacked Wilson instead for his handling of the domestic debate over the peace. Here they found support from Thomas Bailey, who considered Wilson's blunders in the Senate fight far more serious than his mistakes at the peace conference itself. Bailey had little use for Henry Cabot Lodge but thought that he represented many of the doubts and nationalistic impulses the majority of Americans may have felt at the threatened transformation of their long-standing isolationism. In the end, Bailey blamed the Senate defeat of the treaty at least as much on Wilson as on Lodge.[20]

Robert Osgood spelled out the significance of this point for the realist view of American diplomacy. Unlike Kennan, he did not criticize Wilson's "inevitable" concessions in making the peace. He attacked Wilson for raising the people's expectations with excessive appeals to idealism, leading them to imagine that no deviations from American desires would be necessary. Since Wilson had gone to war for inadequate reasons, Osgood said, he had resorted to such idealistic appeals to sustain his course. "Consequently, he presented the League as a substitute for the balance-of-power system, not as a supplementation or extension of it."[21] In the absence of any explanation of the nation's self-interest in the League, the American people's enthusiasm for participation waned rapidly. For Osgood, this was the most damaging of Wilson's errors.

Wilsonians accepted much of this.[22] Still they charged the Senate defeat of the treaty mostly to the strength and vindictiveness of Wilson's enemies. Like Arthur Link, they thought Wilson's idealistic explanations of the treaties were a form of "higher realism" and fully credible. It was not Wilson's fault that the people's enthusiasm waned.[23]

19. Bailey, *Woodrow Wilson and the Lost Peace*, pp. 12–14, 252–253, *et passim*.

20. Thomas A. Bailey, *Woodrow Wilson and the Great Betrayal* (New York, 1945), pp. 10–15, 276–279, 356–357.

21. Osgood, *Ideals and Self-Interest in America's Foreign Relations*, pp. 284–285, 287.

22. Birdsall, *Versailles: Twenty Years After*, p. 5.

23. Link, "Higher Realism of Woodrow Wilson," pp. 1–13; and his *Wilson the Diplomatist*, pp. 91–98.

Several monographs came to Wilson's defense against realist critics. David Trask's study of America's role in strategic planning on the Supreme War Council during World War I showed Wilson's realistic understanding of the connections between military strategy, war aims, and the peace that would emerge. In World War I, Wilson had provided for a coordination of military and political aims that realist critics of Franklin Roosevelt would have welcomed.[24] Lawrence Gelfand concluded that Wilson had been more realistic than the supposed experts of the inquiry group that advised him on the peace.[25]

By 1965, the differences between the realists and the Wilsonians had narrowed considerably. The realists had abandoned many of the criticisms of Wilson's Versailles diplomacy whereas the Wilsonians accepted many of the criticisms of Wilson's tactics in the fight with the Senate. The differences remaining were subtle ones of shade and tone, dealing with the degree to which Wilson understood the realities of power politics and the degree to which he should be chastised or excused for his admitted errors.[26]

With revisionism on the run, the Left contributed little to the historiography of World War I and Versailles. William Appleman Williams offered brief, impressionistic sketches of World War I in his numerous surveys. He emphasized the role of America's drive for Open Door markets in both the coming of the war and the negotiating of the Versailles treaty. He included William Jennings Bryan with Wilson in the catalogue of Open Door imperialists. Bryan had lost much of his charm for the revisionist Left when Charles Beard disclosed that Bryan had approved the extension of loans to the belligerents. Williams also argued that the Versailles treaty was less a struggle between Wilson and the Allies over Germany than it was a struggle over the means to contain the communist revolution that had begun in Russia and was spreading through Eastern Europe.[27]

Thus Williams saw Wilson's purpose in joining the Allied intervention in the Baltic and Siberia as an attempt to strangle bolshevism. He considered this resistance to revolution the primary focus of Wil-

---

24. David F. Trask, *The United States in the Supreme War Council: American War Aims and Inter-Allied Strategy, 1917–1918* (Middletown, Conn., 1961).

25. Lawrence E. Gelfand, *The Inquiry: American Preparations for Peace, 1917–1919* (New Haven, 1963), p. 328.

26. See, e.g., Arthur Link's brilliant speculation on why Wilson refused to accept the treaty with the Lodge reservations when that was the last chance to save the League. Clearly it is an explanation, not an exculpation (Link, *Wilson the Diplomatist*, pp. 148–154).

27. Williams, *Tragedy of American Diplomacy*, pp. 46–90.

son as well as the other leaders of the Paris Peace Conference and so denied that Wilson or the Allies were supporting true national self-determination. In this, Williams stood quite alone.[28] Other students of the peace conference noted the way the threat of the revolutions had hastened the efforts of the Allied negotiators. But they assumed that these revolutions were not the true expression of the people's will in Eastern Europe and relegated the issue to the background. Their primary focus was still on the relations between the Allies and the Germans.

Almost all of the monographic studies of the Allied intervention into Russia regarded it as futile and ill advised, even the realists who might have been expected to praise any attempt to nip the Russian Revolution in the bud. These monographs all defended Wilson against charges that he and the Allies had made an intense effort to destroy the Revolution. They emphasized the half-heartedness of the Allied intervention and that Wilson had joined the effort very reluctantly after opposing it for months. American historians also insisted that Wilson's primary purpose had not been to oppose the Revolution. Cooperation with the Whites had come about almost inadvertently. George Kennan's prize-winning multivolume study argued that Wilson had sent troops into Siberia to save the Czech army as it tried to leave by way of the trans-Siberia railroad.[29] Betty Unterberger wrote that the Siberian intervention had been intended to restrain the Japanese and the other Allies.[30] Even a historian of the Left, Christopher Lasch, argued against the idea that Wilson had intervened to strangle the Revolution.[31]

Diplomatic history textbooks took a rather eclectic approach between the realist and Wilsonian views of the World War I period.

28. Arno Mayer, whose second volume on World War I diplomacy would give considerable legitimacy to Williams's assertions, had at this point completed only the first volume covering the period 1917–1918. Although this first volume did delineate the growing conflict between Wilsonian and Leninist ideas of the New Diplomacy, Mayer had not yet reached the peace conference period nor the critical times of conflict between Leninist and Wilsonian principles. Besides, at this time Mayer seemed quite favorable to Wilson although he gave a couple of brief hints that the Social Democrats who stood between Wilson and Lenin had the proper view of things. See Arno Mayer, *Political Origins of the New Diplomacy, 1917–1918* (New Haven, 1959), esp. pp. 329–333, 352, 358, 361–362, 367, 371, 387, 393.

29. George F. Kennan, *Russia Leaves the War* (Princeton, 1956); and his *The Decision to Intervene* (Princeton, 1958).

30. Betty Miller Unterberger, *America's Siberian Expedition, 1918–1920: A Study of National Policy* (Durham, 1956).

31. Christopher Lasch, *The American Liberals and the Russian Revolution* (New York, 1962).

Bemis dropped all hints of revisionism in the later editions of his text. Thomas Bailey followed suit. The 1940 edition of his text had implied that intervention was a mistake whereas the later editions saw intervention as necessary. Richard Leopold and Alexander DeConde leaned toward the Wilsonian interpretation of the period. Ferrell was Wilsonian on intervention and realist on Versailles, and Pratt was critical of Wilson's utopianism throughout his text.[32]

The lessons of Munich also brought some change in the historiography of the Spanish-American War and the imperialist movement of the early twentieth century, but here the impact was less and the range of divergence narrower. Most historians of the post-World War II era welcomed those aspects of the imperial age that revealed an America awakening to the responsibilities of a world power. Consequently, the Spanish-American War, the taking of the Philippines, the Open Door, and the activities of Theodore Roosevelt received a somewhat better press than they had in the previous era.[33] However, this stopped considerably short of a full rehabilitation of these episodes in American diplomacy.

Mitigation of the Spanish-American War did not begin in earnest until the late 1950s. Up to that time, post-World War II historians still wrote of the war in tones reminiscent of Walter Millis. Richard Hofstadter portrayed the war as a consequence of a "psychic crisis" among old-stock Americans who reacted irrationally and belligerently to the economic depressions, political radicalism, new immigration, and rising power of the industrial nouveau riche that undermined their long-established dominance of America's higher affairs.[34] He also dissected the brutal philosophy of Social Darwinism that the imperialists had used to support their dominance of weaker peoples.[35] The advocacy progressive liberals gave the "needless" Spanish-American War and the subsequent imperialist surge was critically noted by Hofstadter and emphasized by William Leuchtenberg in several

32. Compare the 1940 edition of Bailey's *Diplomatic History of the American People*, p. 595, with the 1942 edition, as well as the full chapters on World War I and Versailles. See Leopold, *Growth of American Foreign Policy*, pp. 336, 373–374; Ferrell, *American Diplomacy*, pp. 285–289, 299, 307, 312–313; Pratt, *History of United States Foreign Policy*, pp. 273–275, 293–295, 306; and DeConde, *History of American Foreign Policy*, pp. 459, 479, 480–486.

33. See, e.g., the wartime summaries already cited; Perkins, *America and Two Wars*, pp. 11–20; and Lippmann, *U.S. Foreign Policy*, pp. 28–30.

34. Richard Hofstadter, "Manifest Destiny and the Philippines," *America in Crisis*, ed. Daniel Aaron (New York, 1952).

35. Richard Hofstadter, *Social Darwinism in American Thought*, rev. ed. (New York, 1959; originally published 1944).

widely noticed works.[36] Theodore Roosevelt's "usurpation" of power to order Dewey's attack on the Philippines played a prominent role in these critiques, and the stress upon this episode received further confirmation in Foster Rhea Dulles' numerous influential surveys of the diplomacy of this period.[37]

By the end of the 1950s some careful historical studies began to modify this view. Two of Bemis' students, J. A. S. Grenville and George Berkeley Young, showed that the Navy Department had devised plans as early as 1896 to attack the Spanish fleet at Manila if war broke out over Cuba. The object was to deprive Spain of revenue from the islands and perhaps to trade control of the harbor for the independence of Cuba. There were no plans for a military occupation or for keeping the archipelago. Roosevelt's telegram had not been a decisive factor; the McKinley adminstration had intended the attack all along. Nor had business influenced the decision. Business interest in the Philippines had not appeared until after reports of the battle of Manila. Grenville and Young also emphasized McKinley's acumen and purposefulness in all of this. McKinley had not vacillated over the Philippines but had only waited until public opinion had jelled before announcing his determination to keep at least a portion of the islands.[38]

By denying that McKinley had operated weakly and indecisively, Grenville and Young were following the lead of two significant biographies of McKinley that appeared in this era, Margaret Leech's *In the Days of McKinley*[39] and H. Wayne Morgan's *William McKinley and His America*.[40] Leech and Morgan agreed that both the war and the decision to keep the Philippines had been inescapable. Although McKinley had made both decisions reluctantly, he had

36. Hofstadter, *Age of Reform*; William Leuchtenberg, "The Needless War with Spain," *Times of Trial*, ed. Allan Nevins (New York, 1958); and William Leuchtenberg, "Progressivism and Imperialism: The Progressive Movement and American Foreign Policy, 1898–1916," *Mississippi Valley Historical Review*, 39 (1952): 483–504.

37. Foster Rhea Dulles: *The Imperial Years* (New York, 1956); *America's Rise to World Power, 1898–1954* (New York, 1955); and *Prelude to World Power: American Diplomatic History 1860–1900* (New York, 1965).

38. J. A. S. Grenville and George Berkeley Young, *Politics, Strategy, and American Diplomacy: Studies in Foreign Policy, 1873–1917* (New Haven, 1966), esp. pp. 267–296; several of the articles collected in this book were written in the 1950s.

39. Margaret Leech, *In the Days of McKinley*, (New York, 1959).

40. H. Wayne Morgan, *William McKinley and His America* (Syracuse, 1963); see also his *America's Road to Empire: The War with Spain and Overseas Expansion* (New York, 1965).

made them purposefully and correctly.[41] Ernest May's *Imperial Democracy* denied that McKinley's actions had been all that consistent and purposeful and argued that McKinley had abandoned his sincere search for peace out of a cowardly fear for the fate of the Republican party.[42] But this did not bring him to agree with earlier critics that the war had been needless. May demonstrated more thoroughly than had any previous historian that McKinley's ultimatum to Spain had required Cuban independence if no other course would satisfy the Cuban rebels. McKinley had not included this directly in his ultimatum message because he had had to clear the message with conservative Republican Senators who would have objected and split the party. So McKinley had communicated the demand in other ways through Woodford, the American minister to Spain. Spain had understood this requirement and was determined to resist it. Woodford may have come to believe that Spain was ready to grant independence if given a little time. But May showed that Spain was manipulating Woodford by appealing to his hopes while desperately seeking aid from the other European powers. Since the rebels never would have stopped fighting unless granted full independence and Spain was neither capable of defeating them nor willing to grant independence, the war was bound to continue despite Spain's belated acceptance of a portion of McKinley's ultimatum. Whether May thought this adequate justification for American intervention he never made clear, but he wrote, "Rightly or wrongly, [McKinley] conceived that he had some justification for demanding a final end to the violence in Cuba. . . ."[43]

The imperialist surge that followed the Spanish-American War was not rehabilitated to the same extent as the war itself. Most historians still saw the acquisition of the Philippines, the assertion and protection of the Open Door in China, and the military interventions in Latin America as mistakes. This sort of apologetic criticism was typified by Julius Pratt's *America's Colonial Experiment,* a work considerably more defensive of American expansionism and imperialism than his prewar studies. Following the thesis of Bemis's "Great Aberra-

41. Leech, *In the Days of McKinley,* pp. 170, 180, 185, 328; and Morgan, *America's Road to Empire,* pp. ix–xii, 49–62, 87–90, 96–97, 111–112.

42. Ernest R. May, *Imperial Democracy: The Emergence of America as a Great Power* (New York, 1961), pp. 157–159.

43. *Ibid.,* pp. 151–154, 156–157, 159, 167–168. For Morgan's agreement, see Morgan, *America's Road to Empire,* p. 49. Margaret Leech did not discuss the independence issue, having written her book before May's was published. She still thought the war inevitable. See Leech, *In the Days of McKinley,* pp. 180–185.

tion," Pratt said that the acquisition of colonies and protectorates had been only a passing phase in American history. There was no reason for the United States to be ashamed for having tried the experiment. According to Pratt, some peoples needed guardianship until they could learn to govern and protect themselves. America's attempts to provide this had been benevolent and beneficial to the inhabitants, in the main. The United States had released most of its colonies and had kept only those of strategic importance. This was legitimate, and unselfish, because many of the colonies that were kept were economic liabilities. America had the power through the twentieth century to take and keep much more, gaining world dominion. Pratt argued that only then would it have deserved the charge of imperialism that Russia and its satellites were making without justification.[44]

The other major historian of American imperialism, Whitney Perkins, was somewhat impatient with the apologetics of the liberal internationalists like Pratt. Where strategic interests were concerned, some imperialism was inevitable, he thought. Yet the United States had tried to hide from this fact by claiming that it was only preparing its dependencies for self-government. "A nation which has tremendous economic strength and world-wide strategic concerns must develop a political philosophy which will take account of unavoidable dependency, whether it be economic or strategic, or, as it sometimes must, political as well." He hoped the illusion that there was some distinctively American way of avoiding the dilemmas and responsibilities of power was fading.[45]

Whitney Perkins was one of the few realists to face squarely the implications of his belief that American security and the balance of power had to take precedence over the ideal of national self-determination for all, and perhaps even over the physical and mental well-being of weaker peoples. Realist historians had managed to avoid this dilemma often because they saw few historical occasions where considerations of interest and power had contradicted a proper formulation of American ideals. Like their orthodox critics, they usually found their position supported by both interests and ideals.

Certainly this was the case with historians of diplomacy toward Latin America. Samuel Flagg Bemis, for instance, published a highly

44. Pratt, *America's Colonial Experiment*, pp. 1–3, 331–369, esp. pp. 352–353.
45. Whitney T. Perkins, *Denial of Empire: The United States and Its Dependencies* (Leyden, 1962), pp. 7, 9–10, 342–346, 351.

influential survey of *The Latin American Policy of the United States,* in which he justified almost all past U.S. interventions because Latin American instability had truly jeopardized American security. But Bemis, writing in the heat of World War II, was more convinced than most historians that these interventions had been beneficial to Latin America and that any resistance had been misguided. His exceedingly strong anticommunism also caused him to see any intervention against socialism as ultimately beneficial even to those witless enough to welcome revolution. Thus, he never saw American ideals and interests as conflicting. He denied that the interventions had been motivated by mere economic interest, which he agreed would have merited condemnation. He welcomed the Good Neighbor policy with its pledges of nonintervention but only because he thought Latin American stability had increased enough in the recent past to make nonintervention possible.[46]

Most American historians dissented from Bemis, however. They argued that Latin American instability had never posed a true security threat to the United States and that most intervention there had been mistaken overreaction. Adopting the "soft" realist outlook, most historians regarded Latin America as less vital to American security than the developed nations of Europe and urged restraint there. They welcomed the Good Neighbor policy in Latin America not because stability only recently had been established but because they thought the policy long overdue.

Most historians of United States-Latin American relations also shared the cosmopolitan outlook of the realists. Their knowledge and respect for Latin culture allowed them to see greater virtue and idealism in letting well enough alone than in missionary intervention to spread the supposed benefits of Anglo-American civilization. Thus, neither these historians nor Bemis saw any reason for a conflict between American ideals and American security interests in Latin America. Bemis previously had seen both pointing toward intervention. The rest saw both indicating a need for restraint and nonintervention. Still, this did not lead to wholesale and indignant criticisms of past American interventionist policies. If American interventions had involved some injustice and oppression, most historians agreed they had also conferred some benefits. Like Bemis, they condemned interventions

46. Samuel Flagg Bemis, *The Latin American Policy of the United States: An Historical Interpretation* (New York, 1943).

motivated by mere economic greed but insisted that many had been motivated by a sincere if often mistaken view of American security needs.[47]

One might have thought that the Cuban or Dominican crisis would force realist historians to choose between ideals and interests, but neither did. The Bay of Pigs invasion was easily condemned because it had so little chance of success and because the majority of Cubans seemed to support Castro. The missile crisis seemed at the time so direct a security threat that Kennedy's intervention, especially as it was successful and did not involve wholesale suppression of the Cuban people, was almost unanimously praised. The Dominican intervention triggered some debate. Walter Lippmann argued that intervention was justified by the possibility that a communist government there might invite the Soviets into America's Caribbean sphere of interest and upset the balance of power. George Kennan, on the other hand, continued to exclude Latin America from the circle of advanced powers necessary to America's security. But the discovery that the communists had never posed much of a threat in the revolution short-circuited the debate before it could foster much clarification in the thought of historians. The other incident that might have brought about clarification, the CIA-supported overthrow of the Arbenz government in Guatemala, was passed over by most historians without much comment at all.

The historiography of American intervention in Asia followed a similar pattern. The vast majority of historians thought American intervention in the Far East had been as excessive as it had been in Latin America and condemned it for the same reasons. They thought American security never had been involved in the Philippines or China's Open Door and that the imposition of American power on the unwilling Asians had been unnecessary. Thus, again American interests and ideals had pointed in the same direction, toward restraint, and again the realists were not forced to face the painful sacrifice of ideals

47. In this era, Dana G. Munro supported the security argument clearly, in contrast to his noncommittal prewar books; see his *Intervention and Dollar Diplomacy in the Caribbean, 1900–1921* (Princeton, 1964). See also Donald Dozer, *Are We Good Neighbors?* (Gainesville, Fla., 1959); Alexander DeConde, *Herbert Hoover's Latin American Policy* (Stanford, 1951); Edwin Lieuwen, *U.S. Policy in Latin America: A Short History* (New York, 1965); J. Lloyd Mecham, *A Survey of United States–Latin American Relations* (Boston, 1965); Wilfrid Hardy Callcott, *The Caribbean Policy of the United States, 1890–1920* (Baltimore, 1942); and Bryce Wood, *The Making of the Good Neighbor Policy* (New York, 1961).

to interests that theoretically they should have been prepared to accept.

H. Wayne Morgan was one of the few historians to defend the decision to keep the Philippines. He claimed it was the only possible course under the circumstances and judged America's subsequent colonialism wise and beneficent, part and parcel of America's necessary movement toward internationalism.[48] Most followed Ernest May, sympathetically portraying the dilemma in which McKinley had found himself but skeptical of the decision to keep the Philippines as a stepping stone to the China market. The China market never had proved as valuable economically as the Japanese trade, and the attempts of America to exploit the market had led to many instances of selfishness and insensitivity among American businessmen in China, as historians like John King Fairbank and Charles Campbell pointed out.[49] Fairbank's studies especially exhibited a knowledge and respect for Chinese culture, and in his hands the claims of Western businessmen, missionaries, and politicians that they were civilizing the backward Asians seemed ludicrous. Paul Varg, also acutely conscious of Chinese culture, defended the missionaries somewhat from the charges of historians like Fairbank. He credited the missionaries with restraining the American government and some business interests from too blatant an exploitation of China. Yet he had to conclude that the missionaries had done considerable harm to China as well by attempting to press the Chinese into a foreign mold.[50]

However, the impact of America's policy on Asians received less criticism from historians than the effect of Asian commitments on America's own security. These commitments had invited conflict with Japan. If America had been more restrained, Japan might not have joined the Axis Pact, war in the Pacific might have been avoided, and the chaos which permitted the triumph of the Chinese communists in 1949 might have been averted.

With such a view predominating in the historical community, A. Whitney Griswold's 1938 work, *The Far Eastern Policy of the United*

48. Morgan, *America's Road to Empire*, pp. 111–115.

49. John King Fairbank, *The United States and China*, new ed. (Cambridge, Mass., 1958); and Charles S. Campbell, Jr., *Special Business Interests and the Open Door Policy* (New Haven, 1951).

50. Paul A. Varg, *Missionaries, Chinese, and Diplomats: The American Protestant Missionary Movement in China, 1890–1952* (Princeton, 1958), pp. 321–322; see also his *Open Door Diplomat: The Life of W. W. Rockhill* (Urbana, Ill., 1952).

States, remained the standard work against which all later accounts of the subject were measured.[51] But as historians moved to adopt the realist view, Griswold was modified in two ways. First, his isolationist, anti-British outlook was rejected in favor of the idea that a reduction in Asian commitments would have permitted more effective intervention in Europe in conjunction with the British.[52] This pro-British outlook strengthened when historians reexamined Griswold's claims that a subtle and self-interested British influence had duped the United States into issuing the Open Door notes and beginning its excessively assertive policy in Asia. Studies by R. G. Neale and Paul Varg found no evidence that Alfred Hippisley had made his suggestions to William Rockhill under orders from the British government and pointed out that Hippisley's advice had run counter to actual British policy in several aspects.[53] John King Fairbank and Charles Campbell reminded Americans that the United States had not needed Great Britain to lure it into the Open Door policy. The United States had pursued the Open Door since the early nineteenth century and had always done so by riding on the coattails of the British.[54]

Historians of the Munich era made still another important modification of Griswold's thesis. Griswold had portrayed America's Asian policy as one that had progressed steadily toward full commitment to China and opposition to Japan, with each president since William McKinley sharing the blame. But postwar historians were kinder to John Hay and Theodore Roosevelt than Griswold had been. They recalled that John Hay's Open Door notes only announced a principle the United States had long followed and that for Hay the policy was strictly a diplomatic one, not a military commitment. He and Theodore

51. About the only monograph in the Age of Munich that gave unalloyed support to America's full commitment to China was Roy Curry, *Woodrow Wilson and Far Eastern Policy, 1913–1921* (New York, 1957).

52. Halle, *Dream and Reality,* pp. 216–233; and Kennan, *American Diplomacy, 1900–1950,* pp. 37–50.

53. R. G. Neale, *Great Britain and United States Expansion, 1898–1900* (East Lansing, Mich., 1966), pp. 168ff.; and Varg, *Open Door Diplomat,* p. 29. For the realists' agreement, see Halle, *Dream and Reality,* pp. 222–227; and Kennan, *American Diplomacy, 1900–1950,* pp. 31–32.

54. Campbell, *Special Business Interests and the Open Door Policy;* and Fairbank, *United States and China.* Contrary to most of the realists, Fairbank was trying to counter the accusations that Communist China was then hurling at the United States concerning past American exploitation of China rather than condemning the policies that had embroiled the United States with Japan. Thus, Fairbank did not criticize the United States for an excessive attachment to China but instead condemned the ineffectiveness of America's moral pronouncements on China's behalf.

Roosevelt both understood that the people of the United States would not support a major military intervention in Asia. Historians shifted the blame for the overcommitment in Asia to Roosevelt's successors, especially Taft and Wilson.[55] Yet despite the mild condemnations of American imperialism in the Philippines and of the Open Door in China, historians of Asian-American relations had the same difficulty as the historians of United States-Latin American relations. Most saw enough risk to American security in the area that absolute nonintervention seemed inadvisable. As alternatives, they could only suggest restraint toward Communist China, lowered expectations, and military and economic aid to the noncommunist nations of Southeast Asia and Japan to maintain the semblance of a balance of power.[56]

Theodore Roosevelt was one of the major beneficiaries of historians' new-found admiration for balance-of-power politics. Roosevelt's solicitude for the Japanese position in the Asian balance of power and his subtle contributions to the European balance at the Algeciras Conference, won him new respect as a shrewd realist rather than as a rambunctious adolescent. Still, he was not universally admired even by realists. Robert Osgood disowned him as a man whose "romantic national egoism" overbore his realism.[57] And Howard Beale, who produced the most extensive and best-researched study of Roosevelt's foreign policy, rendered a decidedly mixed verdict. Beale found worth-

---

55. John Blum, *The Republican Roosevelt*, 2nd ed. (Cambridge, Mass. 1954), pp. 126, 132–134, 137–141; William H. Harbaugh, *Power and Responsibility: The Life and Times of Theodore Roosevelt* (New York, 1961), pp. 288–289, 506; and George E. Mowry, *The Era of Theodore Roosevelt, 1900–1912* (New York, 1958), pp. 148, 163–164, 185–191, 196. See also Raymond A. Esthus, "The Changing Concept of the Open Door, 1899–1910," *Mississippi Valley Historical Review*, 46, no. 3 (1959): 435–454. For Wilson, see Link, *Wilson: Struggle for Neutrality* (Princeton, 1960). See also Burton F. Beers, *Vain Endeavor: Robert Lansing's Attempts to End the American-Japanese Rivalry* (Durham, 1962), which compares Wilson's pro-Chinese attitudes unfavorably with those of his secretary of state, Lansing. Akira Iriye matched this new perception of fluctuations in Griswold's straight line between the Open Door notes and Pearl Harbor by noting fluctuation in Japanese policy as well. As people like Mowry and Esthus denied that American policy had consistently become more anti-Japanese, Iriye said that the Japanese policy at times had tried for a restrained policy in China and accommodation with the United States in the period between 1921 and 1931 (Iriye, *After Imperialism: The Search for a New Order in the Far East, 1921–1931* [Cambridge, Mass., 1965]).

56. See, in addition to the books cited in n. 55, see Russell H. Fifield, *Southeast Asia in United States Policy* (New York, 1963), esp. pp. 37–38; and his *Woodrow Wilson and the Far East: The Diplomacy of the Shantung Question* (New York,

57. Osgood, *Ideals and Self-interest in America's Foreign Relations*, pp. 67–85.

while realism in Roosevelt's handling of the balance between the major powers. But he harshly condemned Roosevelt's imperialism and his cavalier treatment of weaker peoples. As a colleague and friend of Fred Harvey Harrington at the University of Wisconsin, Beale naturally thought Roosevelt should have supported the nationalist movements in the Third World, especially in China, instead of hitching American policy to the interests of the dying British Empire. Thus, his book was a puzzling combination of realist praise for balance-of-power politics and radical condemnation of imperialism, along with Griswoldian denunciations of the British Empire. The contradictions within Beale's work, being different from the dilemma hidden within the premises of most of the realists, confused many historians. One of Theodore Roosevelt's later biographers commented that Beale's book was the most exhaustive and balanced treatment of Roosevelt's foreign policy "Except for a set of neo-isolationist conclusions that seem curiously distended from the body of the work. . . ."[58]

Standing even further outside the post-Munich consensus than Beale was a small group of radicals who more directly challenged the realist perspective on Roosevelt, balance-of-power politics, and America's policies in the Far East. The realists had convinced most historians that World War II and the fall of China to communism might have been prevented if the United States had abstained more in China and been more tolerant of Japanese imperialism there. But William Appleman Williams, like Beale, argued that the United States never had been truly committed to China. Americans had sought only to exploit China, often in conjunction with the Japanese and other imperial powers. If the United States had supported the Nationalists in China in cooperation with the revolutionized Soviet Union in the 1920s, such a combination would have been sufficient to deter the Japanese imperialists, perhaps without a war. Instead, the United States had exploited China, opposed the progressive forces in Asia, and appeased Japan, all for the benefit of its Open Door empire.[59]

Expanding on the general outlook of Williams, Walter LaFeber challenged the whole conventional view of the rise of imperialism and the Spanish-American War. In *The New Empire*, LaFeber insisted that the Spanish-American War and subsequent imperialism were not a

58. Howard K. Beale, *Theodore Roosevelt and the Rise of America to World Power* (Baltimore, 1956). For the comment on Beale's book, see Harbaugh, *Power and Responsibility*, p. 534.

59. William Appleman Williams, "China and Japan: A Challenge and a Choice of the Nineteen Twenties," *Pacific Historical Review*, 26 (1957): 259–279.

sharp break from America's earlier policy but a continuation of it. He refused to make a distinction between continental expansionism and overseas imperialism, as they both stemmed from the need of a capitalist society to expand its economy and prevent a revolutionary redistribution of goods. He traced overseas expansionism back to the beginning of the Industrial Revolution prior to the Civil War. He examined and emphasized the economic roots of imperialist strategic thought, showing how Alfred Thayer Mahan, Josiah Strong, Theodore Roosevelt, and others had been affected by their fears of a radical response to industrial overproduction. Mahan, the most careful thinker of the group, had outlined a strategy of insular imperialism that would solve the situation. America would not colonize markets as the Europeans had done. It would merely acquire small, easy-to-govern islands as stepping stones to the Asian market. These would serve as naval bases not only to protect the colonies and America's trade routes but to insure that there was an Open Door to American trade in China. The American elite's assumption was that the United States' economy was becoming strong enough to undercut its rivals and dominate any underdeveloped nation that allowed America to trade with it on liberal terms.

Since America's colonial acquisitions of the early twentieth century followed this plan precisely, LaFeber could not believe that the United States had "stumbled" into empire. It had gone into the Spanish-American War and its imperialist crusade with a conscious and careful plan. Disputing Pratt's almost universally accepted thesis that business had opposed the Spanish-American War, LaFeber pointed to several expressions of business thought that were prowar. He insisted that business support for war had been the major factor in bringing McKinley to refuse Spain's hesitant but real steps toward a resolution of the Cuban issue. Yet in the end, even LaFeber had to admit that business was the last of the major interest groups to be converted to war and that its conversion, if there was a conversion before war broke out, simply made the American people's support for war unanimous.[60]

Thomas McCormick and Charles Vevier, two other students of Fred Harvey Harrington at Wisconsin, supplemented LaFeber's book with their own accounts of Open Door imperialism in early twentieth-century China.[61] Still other radicals applied the thesis to the antiim-

60. Walter LaFeber, *The New Empire: An Interpretation of American Expansion, 1860–1898* (Ithaca, 1963).
61. Thomas McCormick, "Insular Imperialism and the Open Door: The China Market and the Spanish-American War," *Pacific Historical Review*, 32, no. 2

perialists who had opposed acquisition of the Philippines. In contrast to Harrington's earlier favorable account, the radicals found the anti-imperialists to be motivated by racism and the confidence that the economies and politics of weaker nations could be dominated without the obligations or formal trappings of military imperialism. Thus, the antiimperialists joined William Jennings Bryan and Henry Wallace as deposed heroes of the Left. In seeking trade expansion rather than a radical internal redistribution of goods, the antiimperialists of the 1890s had shown themselves to be "free trade imperialists" like the vast majority of American liberals.[62]

Thus, America's abandonment of the Philippines and other formal imperial holdings merely meant the substitution of one kind of imperialism for another. Contrary to Julius Pratt's claim, America had never "given away" its empire. An example of this was the Good Neighbor policy as interpreted by Lloyd Gardner's *Economic Aspects of New Deal Diplomacy*. Gardner portrayed the Good Neighbor policy as a model of Open Door imperialism rather than as an advance from the dark days of the Roosevelt Corollary. The United States was using its economic leverage to dictate the foreign policies of Latin American nations and was still intervening when revolutions, justified though they might be, threatened the cozy relationship between U.S. economic interests and dictatorial governments in the Southern Hemisphere.[63]

(May 1963): 155–169; and Charles Vevier, *The United States and China, 1906–1913* (New Brunswick, N.J., 1955).

62. John W. Rollins, "The Anti-Imperialists and Twentieth Century American Foreign Policy," *Studies on the Left*, 3, no. 1 (1962); and Thomas McCormick's rebuttal in the same issue. See also Christopher Lasch, "The Anti-Imperialists, the Philippines, and the Inequality of Man," *Journal of Southern History*, 24 (1958): 319–335.

63. Gardner, *Economic Aspects of New Deal Diplomacy, passim*. Two other books by graduates of the University of Wisconsin followed the course of America's Open Door imperialism in Cuba: David F. Healy, *The United States in Cuba, 1898–1902: Generals, Politicians, and the Search for Policy* (Madison, Wis., 1963); and Robert F. Smith, *The United States and Cuba: Business and Diplomacy, 1917–1960* (New York, 1960). But the approach of Healy and Smith partook more of Fred Harvey Harrington's left liberalism than of Williams's neo-Marxism. Healy and Smith emphasized the role of economic interest in the policies of the United States toward Cuba and condemned the "ivory tower" or "chessboard" approach of the realists, who emphasized strategic factors. But they did not speak of imperialism as the inevitable product of capitalism, and they agreed that political factors and racism might have been more important than economics in pushing America toward continuing intervention in Cuba. Smith specifically supported the containment of Soviet imperialism and urged support for eco-

The views of this Wisconsin school were not exactly ignored. Walter LaFeber's book even won the Beveridge Award of the American Historical Association. But it was not until the Vietnam War had become a major issue in American politics that these views came into real prominence. Meanwhile, in the wake of Munich, the realists' insistence on the virtue of balance-of-power politics swept almost all before it. In defense of early twentieth-century American policies, some historians showed how these policies had maintained the balance whereas realist critics pointed to the ways they had undermined it. The Spanish-American War was no longer dismissed as unnecessary and foolish. Almost all historians also assumed American intervention into World War I had been proper and debated only whether Wilson had understood the correct reasons for it. The Treaty of Versailles was criticized less for its deviations from Wilson's utopian goals than it had been previously, and the failure of the Senate to accept it was denounced more vociferously. An active policy in Europe and cooperation with Great Britain were assumed to be necessary to American interests.

Interventionism in Asia and Latin America was not so highly regarded as European intervention, however. Most historians thought past intervention in Latin America had gone well beyond America's security requirements. Interventions in Asia were also thought to have been ill advised as they undermined the balance of power and provoked Japan, thus diverting the United States from concern for its primary security area in Europe. Certainly these historians did not believe that American interventions in Asia and Latin America had done much to further democracy and liberty. So even if such ideals were proper considerations for the making of foreign policy, as the realists doubted, this still did not contradict the policy of restraint demanded by American security and economic interests in the Third World. Similar attitudes underlay the shifts in the historiography of earlier American diplomacy as well.

---

nomic and social reform in Latin America as the only means of avoiding complete loss of U.S. holdings and communist domination of the area.

SEVENTEEN

The Age of Munich
and the Historiography
of Early American Diplomacy

The intellectual atmosphere of the Age of Munich affected historical interpretations of early American diplomacy in three significant ways. First, it inspired a more sympathetic treatment of the British side of Anglo-American relations. World War I revisionism had not inspired an overwhelming number of anti-British interpretations, but the few it did were of towering importance, especially those of Samuel Flagg Bemis. Post-World War II historians often wrote to correct what they thought had been Bemis's bias.

Second, the intellectual atmosphere inspired more lenient judgments of past American expansionism. The renewed appreciation of power politics made it seem inevitable that a strong nation should move into a vacuum of power. Axis aggression made American intentions and methods appear benevolent by comparison. As events transpired, the power America had gained ultimately had been essential to the defense of Europe's liberal democracies against the aggressions of dictatorships in the twentieth century.

Third, the rise of the realists exerted a significant influence on the historiography of early American diplomacy. The realists concentrated their study and commentary on twentieth-century American foreign policy. They made only a few casual observations about earlier periods, usually to show how inferior modern American policy was to previous diplomacy. Yet their brief comments set off a major historiographical battle over the comparative realism of the various Founding Fathers.

Major realist publicists like Kennan, Lippmann, and Morgenthau tended to categorize all of the Founding Fathers, Republican and Federalist alike, as realistic.[1] For instance, Hans Morgenthau conceded that Jefferson had often thought in idealistic terms and that his realist touch in foreign affairs had been far less sure than Hamilton's. But whatever Jefferson's motives, Morgenthau maintained that his actions had generally coincided with the realistic interests of the nation.[2]

This contention that liberals and conservatives alike had been realistic found considerable support in the major studies of the American Revolution. Gerald Stourzh, writing under the auspices of Morgenthau's Center for the Study of American Foreign Policy, defended Franklin's conduct as pragmatic and realistic. Franklin's attachment to the French alliance had been based on the genuine need to defend the United States against the British, not on mere gratitude. His conduct during the peace negotiations showed that he would have tossed aside the alliance if he had been able to acquire Canada and eliminate the British threat on America's northern border. Stourzh insisted that Franklin's subtlety and willingness to exploit intangibles such as good will were far more realistic than John Adams's "pretentious diplomacy of the big stick."[3]

Richard Morris, editor of the Jay Papers and author of the best seller *The Peacemakers* did not dispute Stourzh's contention that Franklin had been competent and realistic.[4] But he insisted that Jay had been even more so. He denied Bemis's assertion that a more obdurate stand would have substantially improved the peace terms. All in all, he thought the commissioners, particularly Jay, had nicely balanced their goals with the power available.[5]

While most historians followed Morgenthau, Stourzh, and Morris in believing that realism was the proper criterion by which to judge the respective performances of Franklin, Jay, and Adams, at least one

---

1. Kennan, *American Diplomacy, 1900-1950*, p. 11. For similar views, no doubt influential in Kennan's own formulation, see Lippmann, *U.S. Foreign Policy*.

2. Morgenthau, *In Defense of the National Interest*, pp. 4-24.

3. Gerald Stourzh, *Benjamin Franklin and American Foreign Policy* (Chicago, 1954), pp. 129-133, 143-166, 173-177, 180-182, 247-256.

4. Morris was a long-time advocate of his fellow New Yorker.

5. Richard B. Morris, *The Peacemakers: The Great Powers and American Independence* (New York, 1965), pp. 264, 270, 286-287, 307-309, 345-346.

historian dissented. Richard Van Alstyne thought that the commissioners' realism had contained large components of rapacious expansionism. Americans had been much offended by parliamentary restrictions on their westward expansion and had joined France to plunder the offending British Empire. Then when the French had refused to support this expansionism against the claims of Spain, the Americans had turned away from the alliance. Thus, Franklin, Jay, and Adams all had sought empire as well as independence.[6]

Van Alstyne's argument would gain many adherents as disillusionment with Vietnam increased. But for most historians writing in the Age of Munich, realism was still the test of competency. Among historians writing on the diplomacy of the Federalist era, the only question was whether or not to accept Morgenthau's contention that all of the Founding Fathers, liberal and conservative alike, had been truly realistic. Most rejected it. Pro-Federalist historians considered the Republicans excessively ideological, irrationally anti-British, and foolishly attached to France. Pro-Republican historians insisted that the Republicans had blended realism with a praiseworthy commitment to liberty, democracy, and equality whereas their Federalist opponents had masked their unpopular aristocratic and pro-British sentiments with contrived appeals to realistic principles. On the whole, the pendulum of historical opinion swung toward the Federalists, with Republican sympathizers fighting a defensive battle.

Federalist popularity was revived in part because of the pro-British tendencies of the Munich era. One factor in this was the carefully researched and authoritative book by A. L. Burt on relations between the United States, Great Britain, and Canada.[7] Burt covered much the same ground that Bemis had but interpreted British actions far less harshly.[8] In this climate, Alexander Hamilton's reputation received a considerable boost. Felix Gilbert's influential study of the ideas behind early American foreign policy applauded Hamilton as the major representative of European political realism in America.

6. Richard W. Van Alstyne, *Empire and Independence: The International History of the American Revolution* (New York, 1965), pp. 212–215, 219–222, 228–229.

7. A. L. Burt, *The United States, Great Britain, and British North America from the Revolution to the Establishment of Peace After the War of 1812* (New York, 1961; originally published 1940).

8. For instance, Bemis attributed British refusal to turn over the frontier posts after the Revolution primarily to a greedy desire to keep the fur trade whereas Burt said the primary factor was Britain's desire to avoid betraying its Indian allies and bringing on a massacre of thinly populated Canadian frontier settlements.

Gilbert praised Hamilton for basing his nonentanglement policy on America's geopolitical situation whereas others had based it upon the superiority of republicanism over monarchy or on the supposed peaceful proclivities of democracy and free trade.[9] These others, including Hamilton's Republican opponents, soon acquired a similar realism from their diplomatic experiences. But they and most Americans accepted power politics only with horror and resignation whereas Hamilton accepted them as an advocate. Clearly Hamilton was first among equals.[10]

Hamilton's reputation gained further respectability from two significant biographies published in this era by Broadus Mitchell and John Miller.[11] Broader surveys of the period also tended to favor Federalists over Republicans. John Miller did so in the volume he wrote on the Federalist era for the prestigious New American Nation Series, and Paul Varg published an influential study of the foreign policies of the Founding Fathers, commending Hamiltonian realism over the idealism of Jefferson and Madison.[12]

Although Jeffersonian historians were on the defensive in this era, they mounted a strong counterattack. Dumas Malone provided an authoritative and favorable assessment of Jefferson's diplomacy as secretary of state in the third volume of his definitive biography.[13] Irving Brant's multivolume biography of Madison was considerably more vehement than Malone's in its defense of Republican foreign policy.[14] But perhaps the most complete analysis and defense of Republican diplomacy was Alexander DeConde's *Entangling Alliance*.[15] DeConde was not overly enamored of either Republican or Federalist policies and denied realist contentions that the Founding Fathers had shaped a golden age of statesmanship. But he was far more critical of Hamilton than of Jefferson. Hamilton had not operated from some profound understanding of the realistic principles of foreign policy, DeConde

9. Felix Gilbert, *To the Farewell Address: Ideas of Early American Foreign Policy* (Princeton, 1961); reprinted in paperback, from which citations are taken, as *The Beginnings of American Foreign Policy: To the Farewell Address* (New York, 1965).

10. *Ibid.*, pp. 72–73, 86–89, 111, 136, 165.

11. Broadus Mitchell, *Alexander Hamilton*, 2 vols. (New York, 1957–1962); and John C. Miller, *Alexander Hamilton, Portrait in Paradox* (New York, 1959).

12. John C. Miller, *The Federalist Era, 1789–1801* (New York, 1960); and Paul A. Varg, *Foreign Policies of the Founding Fathers* ([East Lansing, Mich.], 1963).

13. Dumas Malone, *Jefferson and the Ordeal of Liberty* (Boston, 1962).

14. Irving Brant, *James Madison*, 6 vols. (Indianapolis, 1941–1961).

15. Alexander DeConde, *Entangling Alliance: Politics and Diplomacy Under George Washington* (Durham, 1958).

argued. He had simply disguised with high-sounding phrases his partisan and near-treasonous attempts to pacify the British while undermining the French alliance. DeConde implied that Jefferson and the Republicans had been at least as realistic as Hamilton and were certainly motivated by higher ideals.[16]

Julian Boyd, the editor of Jefferson's papers, was equally scornful of the Federalists. His essay, *Number 7: Alexander Hamilton's Secret Attempts to Control American Foreign Policy*, argued that Hamilton had been literally rather than figuratively treasonous, using his contacts with George Beckwith, the British agent, to undermine Jefferson's attempts to wring concessions from Great Britain.[17]

Another controversial interpretation of early American foreign policy was Stephen Kurtz's analysis, *The Presidency of John Adams*.[18] Kurtz denied that Adams had demonstrated unique integrity and courage by sacrificing his political career to make peace with France in 1798. Instead, Adams had been trying to rescue his administration since public opinion had already been moving strongly in the direction of peace before he made his decision. He was defeated not because he made peace but because of his support for the tax measures and restrictions on civil liberties that had accompanied the war scare. Most historians in this era rejected Kurtz's contentions, however.[19]

In the Age of Munich the War of 1812 underwent the most significant interpretive alterations of all the diplomatic episodes in early American history. An influential historiographical article by Warren Goodman published in 1941 questioned the adequacy of the dominant view that western influences had brought the war.[20] That same year, A. L. Burt published his survey of Anglo-American-Canadian relations, which fulfilled Goodman's prediction that historians would relegate western issues to a secondary status and return their attention to the maritime issues of impressment and ship seizures.

16. *Ibid.*, pp. 116–132, 465–471, 501–511.

17. Julian P. Boyd, *Number 7: Alexander Hamilton's Secret Attempts to Control American Foreign Policy* (Princeton, 1964).

18. Stephen G. Kurtz, *The Presidency of John Adams: The Collapse of Federalism, 1795–1800* (Philadelphia, 1957).

19. See, e.g., Page Smith, *John Adams*, 2 vols. (Garden City, N.Y., 1962). See also the college texts mentioned in the previous chapter. All of them, including DeConde's, praised Adams's courage.

20. Warren H. Goodman, "The Origins of the War of 1812: A Survey of Changing Interpretations," *Mississippi Valley Historical Review*, 28 (1941–1942): 171–186.

Over the years, Burt's interpretation was reinforced and elaborated until few historians or texts were left to promote the western view. This swing back to maritime issues was accompanied by two other trends more relevant to the general themes of diplomatic historiography in the Age of Munich: a more sympathetic view of Britain's position on these maritime issues, and the conviction that America's final decision for war in 1812 had been unrealistic, tragic, and unnecessary.

Burt's interpretation had hinted subtly at these conclusions, and his tendencies were made more overt and definite by another influential work on the War of 1812, Bradford Perkins's *Prologue to War*. In addition to offering a relatively sympathetic view of the British, Perkins helped undermine the western interpretation of the causes of the war by attacking its major prop, the geographical distribution of congressional voting on the war declaration. Perkins pointed out that most of the votes for war had come not from the thinly populated West, despite its unanimity for war. The populous East had cast far more votes for war, although admittedly it had also cast the vast majority of the votes against the war. Still, Perkins insisted it was necessary to explain the motivation behind the prowar eastern votes if the war were to be understood. Obviously, eastern votes had not been won by fears of Indians or bargains for Canada and Florida. Yet the maritime issues that might have motivated the East had been hanging fire for years. Why had they led to war in 1812 and not before?

Perkins offered two answers. First, citing works by Norman Risjord, he argued that the easterners as well as westerners had tired of the long string of humiliating failures America had suffered in its attempts to force concessions from the belligerents by commercial warfare. National honor and frustrated pride had led many to choose war rather than backing away from the embargo Madison had laid on Britain following acceptance of France's Cadore letter. Republicans, as authors of the commercial warfare policy, must have felt the embarrassment most acutely, for they would be humiliated as party members as well as Americans. This was borne out by the congressional vote on the war, Perkins said. The vote corresponded more closely to the party division between Federalists and Republicans than it did to the geographical division between East and West. Thus, the motivations for war had been maritime issues, national honor, and political partisanship rather than frontier grievances or ambitions.

Perkins acknowledged that the United States had adequate

provocation to declare war. But he did not conclude from this, as Henry Adams and other critics of the Republicans had, that Jefferson should have declared war earlier when America was united over the Chesapeake affair and better prepared militarily. Instead, he said the war should have been avoided altogether. America simply did not have the power to enforce its will, and the Republicans were foolishly unrealistic to attempt it. "Whereas Washington and Adams kept objectives and means in harmony with one another, their successors often committed the United States to seek absolute right with inadequate weapons," he wrote.[21]

Irving Brant led the Republican defense in his biography of James Madison, arguing that Madison had been in firm command of the diplomatic situation throughout the crisis. Madison had purposely used the Cadore letter as an excuse to direct America's diplomatic and economic efforts at Britain alone rather than at both belligerents simultaneously. When Britain refused any concession, Madison had rightly determined on war and led the way toward it. He had neither been forced into it by the war hawks nor succumbed to mere partisan interests. Thus Madison had shown himself to be "a hard realist."[22]

But Brant's defense was overwhelmed by other significant works on the War of 1812 that followed the interpretive lines laid down by Burt and Perkins. Almost all agreed that America should have avoided the war. Roger Brown softened the indictment of Republican partisanship somewhat by showing how fearful the Republicans had been that if they fell victim to another humiliation, the Federalists would not only win the following election but destroy the republican system in favor of a monarchy or aristocracy. But with this elaboration and qualification, he supported Perkins's view fully.[23] Reginald Horsman contributed further to the undermining of the western interpretation by arguing persuasively that Canada had not furnished an aggressive, expansionist motive for the war but had been seen as a tactical target to be exchanged for an end to Britain's maritime offenses.[24] These conclusions were summarized and popularized by two short summaries widely used as college texts, Harry Coles's *The War of*

21. Bradford Perkins, *Prologue to War: England and the United States, 1805–1812* (Berkeley, 1961), pp. 408–415, 424–437.

22. Brant, *James Madison*, V, 478–483.

23. Roger H. Brown, *The Republic in Peril: 1812* (New York, 1964).

24. Reginald Horsman, *The Causes of the War of 1812* (Philadelphia, 1962); see also his "Western War Aims, 1811–1812," *Indiana Magazine of History*, 53 (1957): 9–18.

1812[25] and Patrick White's *A Nation on Trial: America and the War of 1812.*[26]

As historians assessed the origins of the Monroe Doctrine in this era, the same influences were at work: the increased sympathy for England, defensiveness against charges that American expansionism had been pervasive and morally culpable, and the measurement of America's actions against the standards of realism. These tendencies were displayed in somewhat exaggerated form in Walter Lippmann's hasty account of the formulation of the Monroe Doctrine. Lippmann described the doctrine as a wise and realistic attempt to protect American security, not an attempt to stake out an empire for the United States. It had been realistic because America's leaders had balanced their goals with the power available. Knowing the United States could not defend the Western Hemisphere alone, these leaders had relied on the British fleet, to resist European intrusion. They could do this because they had had an "agreement" with the British despite the unilateral announcement of the doctrine. Unfortunately, that agreement had not been made "permanent [and] binding," Lippman said. Thus, later generations of Americans forgot the role of the British in the Monroe Doctrine and deluded themselves that America had defended the hemisphere with its own unaided power. This misjudgment of the nation's power and influence had led to further far-flung commitments unsupported by military force, ultimately inviting World War II.[27]

Lippmann's argument that the original doctrine had been justified by America's desire to avoid the intrusion of great powers in areas where this would pose a threat to U.S. security found considerable acceptance in the historical community in this era. So did his charge that later generations had forgotten to balance the doctrine's commitment with adequate power (that is, a British alliance).[28] But Lippmann's contention that the doctrine's original authors had had an "agreement" with the British was quickly dismissed. Not surprisingly, Samuel Flagg Bemis led the assault. In his prize-winning biography of John Quincy Adams, he pointed out that there had been no agreement with the British and that the British had actually denounced the doc-

25. Harry L. Coles, *The War of 1812* (Chicago, 1965).

26. Patrick C. T. White, *A Nation on Trial: America and the War of 1812* (New York, 1965).

27. Lippmann, *U.S. Foreign Policy*, pp. 9–10, 16–22, esp. p. 21.

28. See, e.g., John A. Logan, Jr., *No Transfer: An American Security Principle* (New Haven, 1961).

trine because it barred them as well as the rest of Europe from expansion in Latin America. But the postwar era had softened even Bemis on the British. He now thought an agreement might have been desirable and said it was Britain's own blindness that had turned aside American efforts in that direction. The British had prevented the settlement of the issues between the two nations and the formation of a "satisfying Anglo-American entente worthy of the rights of man." Lippmann was attempting to gloss over that failure, Bemis said,

> as if it were necessary to support the cause of 1940 by a perverted historical dialectic. It is despite their former differences that the British people and the American people have grown to look with common concern upon the tyrants of the world. That, rather than any pleasing historical fiction, is the most powerful testimony to their solidarity.[29]

Bemis's moderation toward the British may well have been influenced by another outstanding work on the Monroe Doctrine written in the 1940s, Arthur Whitaker's *The United States and the Independence of Latin America*.[30] One of Whitaker's purposes was to dispute Edward Tatum's contention that the Monroe Doctrine had been primarily anti-British in its intent. According to Whitaker, John Quincy Adams actually had been pursuing cooperation with Britain by this time. Adams's main point in urging a unilateral declaration was not to challenge Britain but to warn against a joint Anglo-American crusade. Also, Adams and the Monroe cabinet knew Canning had cooled to the idea of a joint declaration, and so Adams's idea was not a startling one. By that time it was either a unilateral declaration or none at all, Whitaker concluded, for Canning had veered back to a policy of rivalry with the United States rather than recognition of Latin American independence.[31]

This idea that Americans had rightly sought some cooperation with the British but had been deterred by the British themselves found considerable support from a more elaborate study of the British side published by one of Bemis's students, William Kaufmann.[32] But studies written later in the period emphasized British cooperation more

29. Samuel Flagg Bemis, *John Quincy Adams and the Foundations of American Foreign Policy* (New York, 1949), pp. 399–401.

30. Arthur P. Whitaker, *The United States and the Independence of Latin America* (Baltimore, 1941).

31. *Ibid.*, pp. 352–354, 447, 468–472, 487, 491, 493–494, 502–503.

32. William W. Kaufmann, *British Policy and the Independence of Latin America, 1804–1828* (New Haven, 1951).

and British rivalry less. George Dangerfield noted that British manufacturers had used their influence to seek better relations with the United States to encourage demands for their products.[33] Bradford Perkins, the son of the major authority on the Monroe Doctrine, Dexter Perkins, rehabilitated George Canning's policy in the last volume of his trilogy on Anglo-American relations, *Castlereagh and Adams*.[34] Perkins also gave more credit to Canning's predecessor, Castlereagh, than to any American for the improvement of Anglo-American relations.[35]

The question of who deserved the most credit for the Monroe Doctrine was still discussed, and the choice still correlated rather closely with the sentiments of the historians toward Britain. Bemis and Kaufmann, the most anti-British, gave the most credit to John Quincy Adams, who had insisted on a unilateral declaration. Arthur Whitaker and Bradford Perkins gave more credit to Monroe. But the question was no longer an emotional one, and the differences between historians had narrowed considerably. The authorship question was no longer a major vehicle to air pro- or anti-British opinions or to promote isolationism or interventionism.

The degree of expansionism inherent in the issuance of the Monroe Doctrine was somewhat more controversial, however. The major students of the doctrine, Whitaker, Bemis, Kaufmann, and Bradford Perkins, regarded it as defensive rather than expansionist. Bemis's biography of John Quincy Adams, which described the acquisition of Florida as well as other expansionist incidents in the life of Adams, made clear that Bemis would have approved of an expansionist Monroe Doctrine anyway. Bemis still regarded America's expansionism within the Western Hemisphere as glorious and necessary, condemned Jefferson's Florida policy as too weak, and praised John Quincy Adams for his acquisition of both Florida and the Spanish claim to Oregon in 1819. However much Bemis had softened toward Britain in the post-World War II era, he gave no quarter to the British in his accounts of Anglo-American rivalry in frontier territories. He justified Andrew Jackson's execution of Arbuthnot and Ambrister in Florida, and he obviously shared John Quincy Adams's emotions as he

33. George Dangerfield, *The Era of Good Feelings* (New York, 1952).

34. Bradford Perkins, *Castlereagh and Adams: England and the United States, 1812–1823* (Berkeley, 1964). The second volume was the already cited *Prologue to War*, and the first volume was *The First Rapprochement: England and the United States, 1795–1805* (Philadelphia, 1955).

35. Perkins, *Castlereagh and Adams*, pp. 200, 306–307, 340–347.

wrote that "Adams smarted under the invectives of the British . . . against American expansion through the empty Continent." Since the British had less of a stake in North America, the United States' claims seemed superior to the British in almost every instance.[36]

Bemis's praise of American expansionism occasioned less dissent in the Age of Munich than it had in the prewar era. Arthur Burr Darling, a student of Frederick Jackson Turner, contributed an influential paean to *Our Rising Empire*. He admitted that Americans would permit nothing to stand in the way of their expansion westward and that "This was hard. It was ruthless." But American expansion spread liberty, and the statesmen who supported it were the heroes of Darling's book.[37] Bernard DeVoto wrote several enormously popular histories of American expansion that shared the same spirit although his heroes were frontiersmen and settlers rather than statesmen.[38]

Historians of foreign policy did not give much consideration to Indian-white relations, but they might have found somewhat more comfort from those historians that did specialize in Indian history than they would have found in the previous era. No one was ready to defend the treatment of the Indians very strongly, and the leading summary of Indian-white relations, William Hagan's *American Indians*,[39] was relentless in describing the horrors of white conduct and the guilt white Americans bore for it. But several other historians found mitigating factors for that conduct, and a couple even defended some white policies. Alden Vaughan insisted that whatever later generations might have done, the New England Puritans had treated the Indians comparatively well. Disease had reduced the numbers of Indians in the area, so the English were actually welcomed by the Indians and did not take the land by force. Puritans had not reduced the food supply for the Indians because the Indians relied more on agriculture than on game. Puritans paid the Indians a fair price for commodities, including the land. They did not decimate the Indians in wars which, where they did occur, usually involved intertribal disputes rather than unified Indian opposition to whites.[40] Francis Prucha also defended some

36. Bemis, *John Quincy Adams and the Foundations of American Foreign Policy*, pp. 300–304, 315, 339–340, esp. p. 366.
37. Arthur Burr Darling, *Our Rising Empire, 1763–1803* (New Haven, 1940), p. 552.
38. Bernard DeVoto, *The Year of Decision: 1846* (Boston, 1943); and his *Across the Wide Missouri* (Boston, 1947).
39. William T. Hagen, *American Indians* (Chicago, 1961).
40. Alden T. Vaughan, *New England Frontier: Puritans and Indians, 1620–1675* (Boston, 1965).

aspects of U.S. policies. He even said that Jackson's policy of Indian removal was a reasonable answer to the fact that Indians were being destroyed by the effects of their proximity to white settlements. Removal was not merely a plan of ruthless dispossession.[41]

Most historians were unwilling to defend the actions of the whites as much as Vaughan or Prucha. But they were willing to see something more than greed behind these policies. This stemmed from the growing acceptance of cultural relativism and the increased sophistication of historical anthropologists in examining the entire scope of Indian life. Originally this trend had led to assigning greater guilt to the whites, for if the Indians had had a viable and valuable culture, whites could not claim that the superiority of their civilization morally justified the destruction of supposed savage cultures. But when the concepts of cultural anthropology were applied to whites as well as Indians, then white guilt for the destruction of the Indians might be mitigated. Could individual American statesmen and settlers be condemned for acting in accordance with ideas of civilization and savagism that permeated their entire culture, even though we may now be aware of the absurdity of these ideas? Roy Harvey Pearce and Robert Berkhofer brilliantly dissected the cultural assumptions of the whites and did not flinch from showing the disastrous effects they had had on the Indians. But they lightened the burden of white guilt somewhat by arguing that whites might well have been prisoners of the ideas of their own time.[42]

If historical accounts of Indian-white relations became somewhat less negative, those of the Mexican War actually became positive. Bernard DeVoto viewed Polk's policies favorably, and a polemical popular history of the Mexican War by Alfred Hoyt Bill defended them even more vehemently. Otis Singletary's summary was more academic and restrained, but it, too, saw the war as legitimized by Mexico's brutality and incompetence in its policies toward the border territories and its northern neighbor.[43]

41. Francis Paul Prucha, *American Indian Policy in the Formative Years: The Indian Trade and Intercourse Acts, 1780–1834* (Cambridge, Mass., 1962).

42. Roy Harvey Pearce, *The Savages of America: A Study of the Indian and the Idea of Civilization* (Baltimore, 1953); and Robert F. Berkhofer, Jr., *Salvation and the Savage: An Analysis of Protestant Missions and American Indian Response, 1787–1862* (Lexington, Ky., 1965).

43. DeVoto, *Year of Decision*, pp. 7–21; Alfred Hoyt Bill, *Rehearsal for Conflict: The War with Mexico, 1846–1848* (New York, 1947); and Otis A. Singletary, *The Mexican War* (Chicago, 1960).

The growing respect for Polk and the American side of the Mexican War was reflected in two polls that Arthur Schlesinger, Sr., took among American historians to determine their ranking of the best and worst presidents of the United States. In 1948, Polk was ranked tenth among the presidents and considered "near great." By 1962 he had moved up to eighth.[44] Thus, when Robert Kennedy publicly expressed regret over America's role in the Mexican War, it was not surprising that he took a pummeling from some American historians, as well as from offended Texans and assorted patriotic politicians. Allan Nevins told the *New York Times:* "The general view of historians used to be that the war was wrong; more recently they have taken the opposite view." However, Kennedy's view was the traditional view in Massachusetts, Nevins remarked backhandedly. David Donald agreed with Nevins, and the *Times* concluded that a consensus of historians found Kennedy's views to be a little old-fashioned.[45]

The consensus masked a significant division among historians who supported America's expansion and Polk's diplomacy in general. Men like Bemis, Darling, Bill, and Singletary upheld expansion both in terms of national interest and of morality. Ruthless it might have been at times, but the brutalities and incompetence of America's rivals, the relative emptiness of the continent, the spread of liberty, and the accession of strength that enabled the United States to rescue Europe from twentieth-century tyrants ultimately justified the enterprise morally. Even a strong critic of the morality of Polk and Manifest Destiny like Frederick Merk modified his attack by insisting that continentalism and imperialism never had been true expressions of the national spirit. "A better-supported thesis is that Manifest Destiny and imperialism were traps into which the nation was led in 1846 and in 1899, and from which it extricated itself as well as it could afterward."[46] A truer expression of the American spirit was its sense of mission, the protection and spread of liberty by example. The spirit of mission sought expansion only by immigration and voluntary acquisition, not conquest without regard for the wishes of others, Merk concluded.[47]

Some realist-inclined historians bridled at attempts to coat

44. Thomas A. Bailey, *Presidential Greatness: The Image and the Man from George Washington to the Present* (New York, 1966), pp. 29, 56.

45. *New York Times,* February 17, 1962, p. 1.

46. Frederick Merk, *Manifest Destiny and Mission in American History* (New York, 1963), p. 261.

47. *Ibid.,* pp. 3–23, 261–266.

American expansionism with a veneer of morality. Like Whitney Perkins, Richard Van Alstyne said this gave a pharisaical flavor to American history. It would delude the American people into a false sense of moral superiority and get in the way of a realistic assessment of foreign policy based upon power and national interest. He rejected the idea that the imperialism of 1898 had been a "great aberration," as Bemis, Merk, and others would have it.[48] He regarded the Monroe Doctrine as an expansionist statement designed to secure an empire for the United States, and he denounced Polk's policy toward Oregon and Mexico. Yet he did not condemn imperialism as a whole, only those aspects that aimed too high too quickly and risked too much. For him the drive to empire was an inherent aspect of nationalism. America was simply one part of a competitive system of national states and would have been foolish to abstain from building its empire. What was required was an acknowledgment of this natural and unavoidable selfishness and an acceptance of limits to it. Proper limits permitted compromise and avoided overly destructive wars, particularly with Great Britain.[49]

Norman Graebner's study of Oregon and the Mexican War shared much of this sentiment. Graebner was neither so critical of Polk nor so enamored of the British Empire as was Van Alstyne, but he, too, emphasized the hard, calculated motives behind American expansionism. He derided the moralistic justifications of expansion while accepting the process as natural and desirable. Graebner saw the search for Pacific ports as the key to understanding the Oregon issue and the Mexican War. Other historians had emphasized the role of the pioneers, the spirit of Manifest Destiny, or the expansionist fever generated by war on a reluctant Mexico. But Graebner argued that these factors provided neither adequate motive for the hard-headed leaders of the nation who actually made the decisions nor defined the limits the leaders set on the expansionist urge. The spirit of Manifest Destiny would have grabbed all of Oregon and all of Mexico. But Polk had a more limited, realistic goal. He wanted the major ports of the West Coast—Puget Sound, San Francisco, Monterey, and San Diego. Thus, he sought only the territory between the latitudes of 49 degrees and 32 degrees. The desire for these ports also explained the support such

48. Richard W. Van Alstyne, *The Rising American Empire* (New York, 1960), pp. vii–viii, 5–10, 204–205.

49. *Ibid.*, pp. 1–10, 98–99, 106–115, 137–144.

limited expansion received from the otherwise antiexpansionist Northeast.[50]

From the historiographical sidelines, William Appleman Williams and his fellow radicals cheered on certain aspects of the work of realists like Van Alstyne and Graebner.[51] Radicals admired the realists' frank acknowledgment that the United States was an empire and agreed with their historical narratives describing the empire's rise. But of course the radicals disagreed with the realists' acceptance of this process as an inevitable outgrowth of nationalism, of man's natural selfishness, and of strategic necessity. They argued instead that imperialism was a product of the evils of capitalism. In *The Contours of American History*, William Appleman Williams explained and traced the history of American territorial and commercial expansionism in harsh terms. He saw as particularly tragic the refusal of early liberals like Jefferson and Madison to follow their democratic and libertarian inclinations far enough to do away with private property, and he mourned their turn to frontier expansionism as a means of providing land and the economic equality they recognized as necessary to true democracy.[52] But his interpretation of early American diplomacy made even less of a dent on historiography in this era than his view of the twentieth century.

The Munich era brought little change to the historiography of Civil War diplomacy. Since neutrality was out of fashion, no one took up Frank Owsley's complaint that the North had abandoned too many neutral rights in suppressing the Southern rebellion. Instead, most historians simply repeated past attempts to show that the British government had not been unfriendly to the Union.[53] They differed only slightly in the shading of their narratives. Some praised Lincoln, William Seward, and Charles Francis Adams for their skill in checking what anti-Union sentiment there was in the British government

50. Norman Graebner, *Empire on the Pacific: A Study in American Continental Expansion* (New York, 1955), pp. v–5, 105, 126, 137–140, 151–153, 203–205, 218, 228.

51. See, e.g., Walter LaFeber's review of *The Rising American Empire* in *Studies on the Left*, 2, no. 3 (1962): 103.

52. For a full exposition of this view, see, in addition to *Contours of American History*, Williams's article, "The Age of Mercantilism: An Interpretation of the American Political Economy, 1763–1828," *William and Mary Quarterly*, 15, no. 4 (October 1958): 419–437.

53. Allan Nevins, *The War for the Union: War Becomes Revolution* (New York, 1960), pp. 242–243.

whereas others emphasized that there was little anti-Union sentiment to forestall.[54]

This sympathetic treatment of the British side of Anglo-American relations, then, was one of the more significant shifts in the historiography of early American diplomacy. So also was the more lenient attitude toward American expansion into the vacuum of power in North America. The realists' satisfaction with early American foreign policy as a model of balancing goals with power led to some debate as to which of the Founding Fathers deserved the accolades, but, all in all, America's early diplomacy was judged rather benignly. The escalation of the Vietnam War in 1965 soon disrupted this increasingly complacent historiographic scene.

54. Shading their emphasis toward British friendliness were Robert Huhn Jones, "Anglo-American Relations, 1861–1865, Reconsidered," *Mid-America*, 45 (January 1963): 36–49; Martin B. Duberman, *Charles Francis Adams, 1807–1886* (Boston, 1961); and Norman Graebner, "Northern Diplomacy and European Neutrality," in David Donald, ed., *Why the North Won the Civil War* (Baton Rouge, 1960), pp. 49–75. Shading somewhat toward the older emphasis on British upper-class hostility were J. G. Randall, the most significant scholarly biographer of Lincoln and the author of the major textbook on the Civil War and Reconstruction, and the popular historian, Jay Monaghan. See J. G. Randall, *Lincoln, the President*, 4 vols. (New York, 1945–1955); J. G. Randall and David Donald, *The Civil War and Reconstruction*, 2nd ed. (Boston, 1961); and Jay Monaghan, *Diplomat in Carpet Slippers: Abraham Lincoln Deals with Foreign Affairs* (Indianapolis, 1945).

PART SIX

The Age of Vietnam
1965-?

Escalation of the war in Vietnam shattered the parameters of debate that had dominated the post-World War II era. Disillusionment with Vietnam made radical critiques of American imperialism appear far more plausible than they had in an age when diplomatic restraint and isolation had seemed invitations to war. Vociferous nationalist interpretations of American diplomatic history dropped almost totally out of sight. The influence of hard-line realists also diminished greatly. The field was left almost entirely to the new revisionists and the "soft" realists, who, despite very serious differences, could agree that United States foreign policy had been overly aggressive in the past and should be less interventionist in the future.

The Vietnam War left its most vivid impression on the historiography of the Cold War, making accounts that were harshly critical of American policy toward the Soviets and communism far more respectable than they had been in the previous era. Changes in interpretations of earlier episodes were not so profound, but there was a general trend toward criticizing rather than justifying America's use of force in the past.

Most of these critical histories were realist rather than revisionist in outlook. This was especially the case in treatments of pre-Civil War episodes, for revisionists tended to concentrate on the modern period of American diplomacy. The new revisionist view also seemed to decline in influence somewhat as time drew America further away from the Vietnam War and confronted the nation with new challenges to its interests abroad. Still no one could afford to ignore the revisionist view any longer, and it influenced all aspects of American diplomatic history to one degree or another.

Interpretation was not the only aspect of diplomatic history that was changing in this era. Diplomatic historians were going beyond the multi-archival approach to give a new breadth and depth to their studies. Some like Akira Iriye were emphasizing the interactions of foreign cultures in addition to the more formal diplomatic relations between nations. The revisionists particularly continued to enlarge their views of the economic substructure beneath the diplomatic postures of nations. A prominent group of political scientists and historians developed a self-conscious "bureaucratic" model to describe the influence of bargaining within national bureaucracies on the development of foreign policies. The result was a continuing improvement in the quality of research and writing, but outside the subject of the Cold War there were few startling revelations from undiscovered archives. The new revisionists forced some reassessments of past events and inspired a some-what more critical tone in historical studies, but most interpretations of pre-Cold War episodes were only minor adjustments of earlier ones. No dominat-ing figures rose to fill the shoes of the giants of the past like Bemis, Beard, Dexter Perkins, and Julius Pratt. Perhaps the field had become too large and the practitioners too numerous to permit such domination. There were few topics outside the more modern period of American diplomacy that had not been covered thoroughly by several competent books, and historians had to strain to invent a topic or interpretation that was a significant improvement or change from what had already been published.

EIGHTEEN

The War in Vietnam

In 1966, Secretary of State Dean Rusk went before the Senate Foreign Relations Committee to defend the recent massive escalation of American intervention in Vietnam. Rusk carefully linked the Johnson administration's Vietnam policy to what he considered to be the realistic Cold War policies of his predecessors, referring to such successful instances of containment as the Marshall Plan, NATO, and the Korean War. Rusk described Lyndon Johnson's policy as a limited one which trod the middle path between appeasement and rollback. America was not fighting to conquer North Vietnam but merely to protect the right of the South Vietnamese to choose their own government. The United States even would accept neutralization of the area and withdrawal of all foreign troops if the freedom of the South were guaranteed. To achieve this, the Johnson administration had found it necessary to introduce large numbers of American troops into Vietnam and to expand the size and scope of American bombing raids. Nevertheless, this escalation was still a restrained and realistic action, a carefully orchestrated program seeking peace at a minimum cost to enemy as well as friend while avoiding actions which might provoke Chinese or Russian intervention. Thus, communist aggression might be contained once more.

But the war in Vietnam was containment with a difference, Rusk argued. Until recently, the communist threat had seemed a straightforward one of conventional invasion and political agitation. America's containment policy of economic aid and military alliances, backed by strategic nuclear weapons, had made such aggression appear unprofitable. The Soviet Union had seemed to accept the situation and turned toward détente. But China had remained more aggressive, calling America a "paper tiger," chiding Russia for abandoning the world revolution and urging a strategy of "wars of national liberation" to circumvent America's containment policy. Vietnam was a test case of this new communist strategy.

Rusk claimed that the revolt in the South was actually a result of aggression by North Vietnam against the vast majority of the South that wanted nothing to do with communism. The National Liberation Front was totally unrepresentative of the people of the South. No politically significant southerner had ever adhered to the NLF or its policies. Thus, the revolt undertaken by Viet Minh cadres in place in the South following the Geneva truce had fizzled in the face of the political and economic progress South Vietnam had made since 1954. North Vietnam, having triggered the revolt initially, then had to infiltrate some 63,000 trained guerrillas with numerous armaments to sustain the war. This invasion was disguised as an indigenous revolt and cloaked in the elaborate doctrine of wars of national liberation. If the United States betrayed its commitment to Vietnamese freedom, it would give the bellicose doctrine of China a victory over the more prudent policy of Russia, Rusk warned, and the outlook for world peace would be very grim.[1]

While some rumblings of dissent were being heard at the very time Rusk was testifying, his characterization of the Johnson administration's posture in Vietnam seemed to many Americans, including the authors of several historical accounts of the war, to be a logical extension of America's modern foreign policy. Wesley Fishel, Frank Trager, Chester Bain, and General Maxwell Taylor wrote of the war as a proper response to communist aggression that was in the realistic tradition.[2] Probably, if the war had ended in 1967, it would have gone down in most histories as another instance of successful, realistic, restrained containment.

1. Testimony of Dean Rusk before the Senate Foreign Relations Committee in *The Vietnam Hearings*, introduced by J. William Fulbright (New York, 1966), pp. 3–9, 227–248. See also the *State Department White Paper*, publication 7839, released in February 1965.

2. Wesley R. Fishel, ed., *Vietnam: Anatomy of a Conflict* (Itasca, Ill., 1968)— Fishel was a Michigan State University professor who served as an adviser to

But of course the war did not end in 1967. It continued for almost another decade, only to finish disastrously and ignominiously for the United States. Rusk's testimony and the contemporary historical accounts which were shaped around similar perceptions would come to be regarded as anachronistic curiosities. Except for Lyndon Johnson's own memoirs, hardly a history would appear in the 1970s that did not regard the war as a colossal blunder or worse. By the end of the war, the public mood had so altered that one poll found a majority of Americans unwilling to intervene anywhere abroad except in the case of an invasion of Canada. Historians no longer argued the correctness of the war but only about who or what was to blame for it.

Dean Rusk, Lyndon Johnson, and their historian-defenders consistently relied upon the rhetoric of restraint and realism to justify their policies. Yet some of their earliest critics were among the primary formulators of the realist ethos, including Hans Morgenthau, George Kennan, and Walter Lippmann. Kennan had taken heed of warnings against any major American involvement in Southeast Asia that had been offered as early as 1950 by John Paton Davies, one of the "old China hands" purged from the State Department during the McCarthy witch hunt. Morgenthau had visited Vietnam himself in 1955 and had castigated Diem for totalitarian policies that would drive many of Diem's noncommunist opponents into the arms of the Viet Cong. These "soft" realists would regret the fall of the South to the Viet Cong, an organization they regarded as brutal and dictatorial, but they did not believe that the area was as vital to American interests as Europe and Japan, and therefore they counseled against major military involvements in continental Asia. They were willing to settle for neutralization of Southeast Asia and the acceptance of Tito-like independent communist regimes in preference to a militaristic anticommunist crusade. With the long history of antagonism between the peoples of Vietnam and China, they had no fear that a nationalist like Ho Chi Minh would become a puppet of China. Nor did these realists think that a Viet Cong victory would have a domino effect in the rest of Southeast Asia. The nations there were too culturally and politically diverse for an event in one of them to operate so mechanically on the

---

Diem under CIA auspices. See also Frank N. Trager, *Why Vietnam?* (New York, 1966); Chester A. Bain, *Vietnam: The Roots of Conflict* (Englewood Cliffs, N.J., 1967); Maxwell D. Taylor, *Responsibility and Response* (New York, 1967); and esp. Lyndon Johnson's autobiography, *The Vantage Point: Perspectives of the Presidency, 1963–1969* (New York, 1971).

rest. Given the split between Russia and China, America's purpose should be to contain those two powers, not to oppose communist regimes that would be independent of them and contribute nothing to their strength.[3]

Had Vietnam been more important to American interests, Kennan, Lippmann, and Morgenthau still would have been doubtful that the United States could do anything to save it. They were convinced that the people of South Vietnam were thoroughly estranged from the American-backed government. These three, the consummate realists, even admitted a moral factor to the issue. A guerrilla war, "supported or at least not opposed by the indigenous population, can only be won by the indiscriminate killing of everybody in sight—by genocide." The war was impossible to win unless the United States spent its power, incurred risks, and inflicted casualties far out of balance with the interests America had at stake.[4]

But as of 1966, the realists did not extend their opposition to the war to the point of advising immediate and unconditional withdrawal. Although they regarded intervention as a mistake, they claimed it had created a new situation. Kennan thought that "a precipitate and disorderly withdrawal could represent in present circumstances a disservice to our own interests and even to world peace greater than any that might have been involved by our failure to engage ourselves there in the first place." He endorsed a strategy outlined by General James Gavin of deciding "what limited areas we can safely police and defend, and restrict[ing] ourselves largely to the maintenance of our position there."[5] Morgenthau agreed with this so-called "enclave" theory, and it became for a time the major alternative offered by the moderate opponents of Lyndon Johnson's escalation policy.[6]

The Tet offensive of 1968 and General William Westmoreland's request for substantial reinforcements undermined both the policy of Lyndon Johnson and that of the enclave theorists. The communists' offensive destroyed American confidence in the claims that search-

3. Hans J. Morgenthau, *Vietnam and the United States* (Washington, D.C., 1965); and George F. Kennan, testimony before the Senate Foreign Relations Committee in *Vietnam Hearings*, pp. 107–115. Lippmann's opinions were offered in numerous syndicated columns in the mid-1960s.

4. Morgenthau, *Vietnam and the United States*, p. 29; Kennan, in *Vietnam Hearings*, p. 110; and Ronald Steel, *Walter Lippmann and the American Century* (Boston, 1980), pp. 575–576, 579–580.

5. Kennan, in *Vietnam Hearings*, pp. 109, 112.

6. Morgenthau, *Vietnam and the United States*, p. 80.

and-destroy missions were winning the war and that enclaves could be held even if the United States were to retreat to such a policy. Sensing the turn of popular opinion, Johnson withdrew from the presidential race, halted the bombing of the North, and opened negotiations with the North Vietnamese. Johnson never admitted that his escalation of the war had been in error and denied that his turnabout constituted abandonment of his earlier policies. In his memoirs, he argued that the Tet offensive had actually been a decisive defeat for the communists, despite press reports to the contrary. He believed the communists had been so badly mauled that they had had to lessen their activities drastically while the South Vietnamese army was growing stronger. Even without further reinforcements, General Westmoreland had had enough troops in 1968 to win the war.[7] Although later analysts came to agree with Johnson that the communists had suffered badly in the Tet offensive, almost none accepted his argument that America still could have won the war without major reinforcements. Everyone else thought Johnson's policy had been either too soft or too hard.

William Westmoreland himself was the most prominent critic from the Right who thought that Johnson's policy had been too soft. Westmoreland thought it shameful that the United States had abandoned the South Vietnamese freedom-loving majority with a fraudulent cease fire that had left the North in the commanding strategic positions it had won during Tet. America could have exited from Vietnam honorably between 1963 and 1965 when the chaos of the South Vietnamese government provided a proper excuse. But once American troops had been committed, retreat should have been out of the question. The war could have been ended in a few years if the United States had struck hard at the Viet Cong in the South rather than adopting the "ill-considered policy of graduated response." Bombing the North also had been a mistake, inducing a faster flow of North Vietnamese aid southward before the South Vietnamese army was prepared for it. The war still could have been won after Tet when the communists were weakened and overextended if Johnson had permitted Westmoreland to carry out the operations he had planned over the previous two years—invasions into Laos, Cambodia, and north of the Demilitarized Zone, intensified bombing, and the mining of Haiphong harbor. With this the North "doubtlessly would have been broken."

7. Johnson, *Vantage Point*, pp. 413–418.

The general primarily blamed the press for America's failure of resolve. Reporters had convinced the American people that the South Vietnamese did not support the war, a claim contradicted by the flow of refugees southward and the persistence of the South which continued fighting even under a corrupt government. In addition, the press had convinced Americans that Tet had been a defeat for the South and the United States, when it had been the opposite. Americans had been misled by youthful and inexperienced correspondents with little knowledge of military matters or of the Vietnamese. Television had portrayed only explosions, burning buildings, and weeping casualties, not the pacification, civic action, or medical assistance offered by American troops. Westmoreland wondered "if the same uncensored comment had been coming out of occupied France during the years 1942–44 when the Allies were bombing French railroads in preparation for the invasion of Normandy, whether Allied public opinion would have supported Allied armies going ashore on D-Day."[8]

As Johnson left office, the American people were still very divided on Vietnam. Some advocated harder blows against the communists to bring victory; others argued for withdrawal as the enclave theory had lost most of its rationale. Richard Nixon cleverly played to both ends of this spectrum in his presidential campaign of 1968. Moderating his once-vehement Cold War rhetoric, he claimed to have a "secret plan" to end the war. He neglected to make clear whether this involved concessions and withdrawal or renewed efforts to force surrender. Moderates, hoping that he might mean deescalation, were cheered by his appointment of Henry Kissinger as his chief foreign policy adviser. Kissinger was a certified realist, a Harvard professor of political science who was a leading exponent of balance-of-power politics. His doctoral dissertation had extolled the stability achieved by those astute manipulators of the European balance of power at the Congress of Vienna, Metternich and Castlereagh.[9] He had been to South Vietnam in 1965 and 1966 as a consultant to the State Department and had returned with pessimistic reports of the course of escalation. In 1966, he had served as an intermediary in secret State Department efforts to open peace negotiations with the North. That

8. William C. Westmoreland, *A Soldier Reports* (Garden City, N.Y., 1976), pp. 408–410, 419–421.

9. Henry A. Kissinger, *A World Restored: Metternich, Castlereagh, and the Problems of Peace, 1812–1822* (Boston, 1957).

same year he had published an article in *Look* magazine endorsing the enclave strategy and a compromise peace.[10] Kissinger's moderation was reflected in some of the dramatic policies initiated by the Nixon administration. The Nixon Doctrine announced a reduction of America's interventionism and proclaimed that the United States would not intervene militarily in peripheral conflicts unless the threat to an ally came from a nuclear power. America might supply rhetoric, money, or materiel but not men. Thus, there would be no more Vietnams. In their policy explanations, Nixon and Kissinger publicly appealed to realist, balance-of-power justifications instead of ideology. The opening of relations with China dramatically illustrated the realist contention that communist unity no longer existed and that all strife in the Third World was not necessarily a product of a monolithic communist conspiracy. This reopening of the door to China was followed by the first Strategic Arms Limitation Agreement with the Soviet Union.

But there was another side to Kissinger's realism. His never had been the restrained and judicious realism of men like Lippmann, Kennan, and Morgenthau. Kissinger seemed harder, more rash. His academic as opposed to his more political writings were suffused with a deep pessimism. The most he seemed to hope for was that realistic, balance-of-power policies might arrest for a time the inevitable decline of Western civilization. To achieve this delay, Kissinger seemed willing to take enormous risks. For instance, in 1957 he suggested limited nuclear war as the "restrained" alternative to massive retaliation in the attempt to contain communism.[11] Although he had abandoned this alternative by the 1960s, his rather desperate outlook remained. He still believed that America was

> certain to be confronted with situations of extraordinary ambiguity, such as civil wars or domestic coups. Each successive Soviet move is designed to make our moral position that much more difficult: Indo-China was more ambiguous than Korea: the Soviet arms deal with Egypt more ambiguous than Indo-China: the Middle Eastern crisis more ambiguous than the arms deal with Egypt. There can be no doubt that we should seek to forestall such occurrences. But once they have occurred, we must find the will to act and to run risks in a situation which permits only a choice among evils.[12]

10. Marvin Kalb and Bernard Kalb, *Kissinger* (Boston, 1974), pp. 66–74.
11. Henry A. Kissinger, *Nuclear Weapons and Foreign Policy* (New York, 1957).
12. *Ibid.*, pp. 427–428.

Kissinger seemed to link every issue involving weaker nations to the competition between the super powers, dismissing as irrelevant all considerations of nationalism or necessary social change within Third World nations. He was ready to intervene almost anywhere outside the communist orbit over almost any issue because he considered the Soviet-American balance of power so delicate that any communist exploitation of strife in the Third World would undermine the basic structure of peace. Thus was justified American support for the coup in Chile and the installation of a vicious, dictatorial regime to replace the left-leaning Salvadore Allende. Thus also was justified the "tilt" toward Pakistan in its murderous war in Bangladesh since Pakistan was the conduit to China. Thus Kissinger and Nixon could give extraordinary aid to the brutal regime of the Shah of Iran, seeking to make him the military protector of the oil-rich Persian Gulf against the Soviets and Arab nationalists.[13]

Even though Nixon and Kissinger implied that the original intervention in Vietnam might have been a mistake and were ready to negotiate quite flexibly with the North Vietnamese, they insisted that since the commitment had been made, American withdrawal must be "honorable." This meant that they were unwilling to see Vietnam reunited under a communist leadership that might swing Southeast Asia into the Soviet or Chinese orbit. When the North Vietnamese and Viet Cong proved uncompromising in their demands for unification and full sovereignty, Nixon and Kissinger tried to use their improving connections with the Chinese and Russians, along with the bitter rivalry between those two allies of North Vietnam, to bring pressure on the North Vietnamese negotiating position. Determined to end the war, Nixon and Kissinger undertook savage bombing campaigns, se-

13. Kissinger may well have counseled Nixon to use somewhat more restraint in Vietnam, Chile, and Angola than Nixon ultimately used, as Kissinger often hinted privately to his former academic colleagues who were critical of these policies. But it seems clear that he did support the basic thrust of those policies. See the excerpts from Nixon's second television interview with David Frost in the *New York Times*, May 13, 1977. See also Kalb and Kalb, *Kissinger*, p. 301. For other analyses of Kissinger, see Henry A. Kissinger, *White House Years* (Boston, 1979); Tad Szulc, *The Illusion of Peace: Foreign Policy in the Nixon Years* (New York, 1978); John George Stoessinger, *Henry Kissinger: The Anguish of Power* (New York, 1976); Bruce Mazlich, *Kissinger: The European Mind in American Policy* (New York, 1976); David Landau, *Kissinger: The Uses of Power* (Boston, 1972); and Michael Roskin, "An American Metternich: Henry A. Kissinger and the Global Balance of Power," in Frank J. Merli and Theodore A. Wilson, eds., *The Makers of American Diplomacy*, 2 vols. (New York, 1974), II, 373–396.

cretly extended them into the neighboring countries of Laos and Cambodia, and then supported outright invasions of those nations. Meanwhile they hoped to disarm war critics by withdrawing American troops, ending the draft, and turning the war back over to a revitalized South Vietnamese army. Finally, after inflicting enormous damage and casualties on friends and foes alike, ruining Laos and Cambodia and endangering détente by mining Haiphong harbor just before the Moscow summit, Kissinger managed to negotiate a patchwork peace ending America's role in the war. Of course, shortly afterward, South Vietnam, Cambodia, and Laos all fell to the communist rebels.

Kissinger and Nixon, however, insisted that they had not lost the war and that their realistic policies had successfully managed to contain communism. They blamed Congress for refusing the appropriations necessary to support America's allies in Southeast Asia, and they blamed Watergate for so weakening the executive's position that the promise to renew hostilities if the communists broke their peace agreements rang hollow. They denied that the peace had been merely a "decent interval" to permit American withdrawal and prevent loss of face.[14]

Most historians, however, considered the war lost and noted particularly that Kissinger's peace had permitted North Vietnamese troops to remain in occupation of strategic areas in the South. The tremendous casualties incurred since negotiations had begun seemed to have bought no better a peace than could have been acquired at the outset of Nixon's administration. Since Kissinger had made himself the very embodiment of realism in the popular eye, this, added to the callousness of his policies toward Chile, Bangladesh, and Iran, inspired considerable challenge to the predominance of the realist outlook among intellectuals and historians. "Restrained" realists might protest with some justice that their policies should not be judged by Kissinger's more desperate outlook. Yet all of the realists had favored the containment of communism, limited wars as an alternative to massive retaliation, and a pragmatic attachment to power and interest over moral considerations in foreign policy. Many critics began to wonder whether the tragedy of Vietnam really had been an instance of an overzealous and overmilitarized containment or whether realism and containment were intrinsically flawed and inevitably brutalizing policies.

14. Kissinger, *White House Years*, p. 1470.

The moral critique of Vietnam and of the realist approach was more prominent in journalistic best sellers than in the later, more scholarly historical treatments. A good example of this was David Halberstam's *The Best and the Brightest*, a devastating journalistic dismemberment of the brilliant, hard, pragmatic, "ultrarealistic" men who had staffed Kennedy's administration, men shaped in the mold of Henry Stimson and Robert Lovett. Halberstam's heroes were the old "soft" liberals. He admired Franklin Roosevelt's World War II advocacy of anticolonialism in areas like Indo-China, a stance opposed to Winston Churchill and deprecated by realists as harmful to the war effort. He commended men like Chester Bowles and Adlai Stevenson who had questioned Vietnam intervention on moral rather than merely pragmatic grounds, and he showed how contemptuous Kennedy and his ultrarealist advisers had been toward these liberals.[15] He even praised Eisenhower and Dulles, pointing out that Eisenhower had refused to intervene militarily in Indo-China in 1954 and arguing that privately Dulles had been more flexible than Dean Acheson.[16]

Senator J. William Fulbright offered another example of the rising moral critique of realism. As a kind of mediator "between the intelligentsia and the public,"[17] Fulbright had helped to popularize the views of the restrained realists in the early 1960s. In 1964, while Fulbright was still supporting Lyndon Johnson's position on Vietnam as a moderate and realistic one, he had published *Old Myths and New Realities*, in which he had taken up Kennan's argument that it was a mistake to view the Cold War in moralistic rather than empirical terms.[18] By 1966, when he published *The Arrogance of Power*, he was still chastising liberals like Woodrow Wilson and Franklin Roosevelt in realist terms, but enough moralism had crept into his view that he could hold up Adlai Stevenson as a model of humanism against the "chauvinist" Theodore Roosevelt.[19] By 1972, his book, *The Crippled*

15. During the Cuban missile crisis, Kennedy himself had been the source of a newspaper "plant" that Stevenson, in suggesting that the United States might trade the obsolete missiles in Turkey for evacuation of Russian missiles in Cuba, had wanted another Munich.

16. David Halberstam, *The Best and the Brightest* (New York, 1972), pp. 1–33, 56, 80–81, 108, 137–145, 329–341.

17. David F. Trask, "The Congress as Classroom: J. William Fulbright and the Crisis of American Power," in Merli and Wilson, *Makers of American Diplomacy*, II, 370.

18. J. William Fulbright, *Old Myths and New Realities* (New York, 1964), pp. 4–10, 43–44, 116.

19. J. William Fulbright, *The Arrogance of Power* (New York, 1966), pp. 5, 12–13, 47–51, 72, 246–258.

Giant, placed him firmly in the liberal-moral camp. He still conceded that power politics were an improvement over an ideological, crusading policy, but he now regarded the geopolitical approach as too mechanical and amoral. His heroes had changed as well. He criticized Truman while he praised not only Franklin Roosevelt but even Henry Wallace.[20]

Another best seller that helped popularize the moral critique of realism was Frances FitzGerald's Pulitzer Prize-winning analysis of Vietnamese society during the Vietnam War, *Fire in the Lake*. FitzGerald ridiculed the American government's assertions that by backing the Saigon government it was defending freedom and democracy from communism in Asia. The "tough-minded" realists who formulated American policy had not been interested in democracy or even the Vietnamese themselves, but only in containing the expansion of the communist bloc. "But by denying the moral argument in favor of power politics and 'rational' calculations of United States interests, these analysts were, as it happened, overlooking the very heart of the matter," FitzGerald argued, "the issue on which success depended."[21]

The hearts and minds of the South Vietnamese people were precisely what must be won to win the war, but even Americans who wanted political reforms failed to realize that they were attempting what only indigenous Vietnamese could do. Here the Saigon government was as powerless as the Americans because it was thoroughly alienated from the population in the countryside. Diem and most Saigon officials still thought in terms of the old Confucian society, in which peasants obeyed the dictums of mandarins without question. But, according to FitzGerald, this society had been completely undermined by the modernizations attendant to the French and American presence in Vietnam. Plantation agriculture and mining had disrupted villages, dispossessed peasants, and destroyed the old pricing system by establishing monopolies on all new products. This placed economic power in the hands of colonial officials and those Vietnamese who had adapted to the colonial system, thus destroying the old village leadership and the respect that had existed between national leaders and the people of the countryside.

20. J. William Fulbright, *The Crippled Giant: American Foreign Policy and Its Domestic Consequences* (New York, 1972), pp. 3–4, 7–8, 11, 18–23, 28–32, 274.

21. Frances FitzGerald, *Fire in the Lake: the Vietnamese and the Americans in Vietnam* (Boston, 1972), p. 6.

Americans hoped that by reforming the army and the bureaucracy, they could establish a viable political system in the South. But the army and bureaucracy were empty shells, and there was no connection between them and life in the villages. Even those Americans who actually entered the villages to rebuild Vietnamese society were doomed to fail as their white skins and American know-how were hopelessly alien. They could not compete with the indigenous Viet Cong, who competently and sometimes ruthlessly organized the citizenry, making them intractable and hostile to both Saigon and the Americans. Thus, the political action advocated by CIA Colonel Edward Lansdale, British guerrilla expert Robert K. G. Thompson, Roger Hilsman, and other supposed political realists seemed no more realistic to FitzGerald than purely military solutions. Graham Greene's tragic portrait of a naïve Lansdale-like character in his 1955 novel, *The Quiet American*, seemed far more prescient than the heroic Lansdale surrogate created by Eugene Burdick and William J. Lederer about the same time in *The Ugly American*.[22]

Frances FitzGerald's book represented a popularization of the consensus of the few Western academic experts on Vietnam and Southeast Asia. According to FitzGerald's academic mentor, Joseph Buttinger, the author of the best history of Vietnam in the English language and a rigorous critic of American policy there, all but two authors worthy of inclusion in his bibliography on Vietnamese history were "critical of or firmly opposed to the Vietnamese war. This is not primarily the result of my preference for such authors. It is surprising (and also encouraging) that of the books published on Vietnam during the past two decades by historians, political scientists and journalists, very few were written in defense of the Vietnamese war."[23]

Equally influential in his skeptical outlook on Vietnam was the French-born journalist Bernard Fall. Fall had been reporting on Vietnam since the days of the French colonial war following World War II. Like Buttinger, Fall was no fan of the Viet Minh and the Viet Cong, but his balanced and detailed factual descriptions of North and South Vietnam undermined many of the clichés and claims U.S. government officials used to justify their policies.[24]

22. *Ibid., passim.*
23. Joseph Buttinger, *Vietnam: The Unforgettable Tragedy* (New York, 1977), p. 181. Buttinger's histories of Vietnam included *The Smaller Dragon: A Political History of Vietnam* (New York, 1958) and *Vietnam: A Dragon Embattled*, 2 vols. (New York, 1967).
24. Fall's most influential book was *The Two Vietnams: A Political and Military Analysis* (New York, 1963). He contributed many other important sketches of the

Even American government officials familiar with the Viet-namese contributed information that sometimes unexpectedly cast doubt on American policies in Vietnam. Douglas Pike, a strong sup-porter of the war, published an extensive analysis of the Viet Cong which belied government claims that the communists in the South were weak and dependent on the North.[25] Chester Cooper, a CIA analyst for Asian affairs, wrote pessimistic assessments of the war from within the government and finally in 1970 publicly summarized these analyses in his book *The Lost Crusade*.[26]

Ironically, it was probably neither the works of the moral critics nor of the Southeast Asia experts but a government study that did the most of any history to discredit the Vietnam War and undermine the realist outlook. This was the so-called Pentagon Papers compiled by the Department of Defense and leaked by Daniel Ellsberg to the press. The Pentagon Papers showed that the Tonkin Gulf attacks had taken place in waters just vacated by South Vietnamese raiders engaged, with American support, in covert raids against North Vietnam. It also showed that the Johnson administration had been formulating con-tingency plans to use just such an incident as justification for a bomb-ing campaign in the North even as Johnson was campaigning for the presidency as a moderate on Vietnam.[27]

Such revelations increased American skepticism so that the mild criticism and prescriptions of the restrained realists and liberal moral-ists seemed almost laughable to many in the face of wartime atrocities and national unrest. Radical revisionists regarded the Vietnam War as far more than a mere mistake resulting from understandable misap-prehensions about communism or overzealous applications of neces-sary realistic prescriptions for the Cold War. The radicals saw the war as the inevitable outcome of tragic evils built into the very foundation of America's political and economic capitalist system. America was fighting a calculated war in Vietnam to maintain and expand its eco-nomic system. Even if defeated there, radicals assumed that America's brutal interventionist policy would necessarily continue elsewhere.

When other historians who thought the war was the result of

---

war before he was killed in Vietnam, including *Vietnam Witness: 1953–1966* (New York, 1966), and with Marcus G. Raskin, *The Viet-nam Reader* (New York, 1965).

25. Douglas Pike, *Viet Cong: The Organization and Techniques of the National Liberation Front of South Vietnam* (Cambridge, Mass., 1966).

26. Chester L. Cooper, *The Lost Crusade: America in Vietnam* (New York, 1970).

27. Neil Sheehan et al., *The Pentagon Papers as Published by the New York Times* (New York, 1971), p. 234n.

mistaken ideas rather than economic interest pointed out that it was costing the United States far more than ever could be regained from the exploitation of Vietnam, the radicals answered in several ways. First, they said that the markets and resources of a capitalist Vietnam were essential to America's ally, Japan, rather than directly to the United States. If Japan were closed out of the Southeast Asian markets, it might be driven into a closer relationship with Mainland China to compensate for the loss.[28] Radical revisionists also argued that America's profits from control of the Vietnamese economy would be concentrated in the hands of an economic and political elite while the war's high costs would be spread over the rest of the citizenry by taxation.[29] Finally, they postulated from an economic version of the domino theory. The victory of the Viet Cong would inspire other nations to resist America's economic imperialism and threaten capitalism's necessary expansion, thus bringing about economic collapse and socialist revolution. As Gabriel Kolko, one of the most influential neo-Marxist critics of Vietnam expressed it, the economic power elite that ran the United States could not afford to withdraw from Vietnam because: "From a purely economic viewpoint, the United States cannot maintain its existing vital dominating relationship to much of the Third World unless it can keep the poor nations from moving too far toward the Left and the Cuban or Vietnamese path."[30]

There was some variation within the new revisionist camp in the degree of economic determinism that infused their analyses of the Vietnam War. Kolko was a hard-line economic determinist. But Richard Barnet, the author of the most extensive revisionist history of the war, was somewhat more eclectic in his socialism. He accepted economic interest as important to America's policy and agreed that unless American society was drastically changed, the United States would remain permanently at war. But Barnet saw the national security elite of corporate lawyers, management technicians, and military leaders that had entered government with Stimson and Lovett during World War II as the prime movers in America's policy in Vietnam. This elite had a bureaucratic momentum of its own. Thus, socialism in itself

28. When opponents of the Left branded this argument a radical contention, Noam Chomsky pointed out that it was actually an argument made publicly by people like Richard Nixon and John Foster Dulles (Chomsky, *For Reasons of State* [New York, 1973], p. 42). Chomsky was right. See Gabriel Kolko, *The Roots of American Foreign Policy* (Boston, 1969), pp. 99–100, 103–106.

29. Chomsky, *For Reasons of State*, p. 47.

30. Kolko, *Roots of American Foreign Policy*, pp. 88–91.

would not necessarily end war or imperialism although Barnet thought it would be a decided improvement over capitalism in that regard. What was needed to end American aggression was an end to the mania for growth and an acceptance of austerity. Like his fellow member of the Institute for Policy Studies, Gar Alperovitz, Barnet thought this could be achieved by a decentralized and community-controlled economy less devoted to industrial production and consumption.[31]

The variation in emphasis on economic determinism also led to differences in the accounts of Kolko and Barnet on the roots of America's Vietnam policy. Kolko and other socialists of strong economic determinist leanings like the William Appleman Williams group, saw Vietnam as only the latest of America's imperialist wars that had begun with the attempts to exterminate the Indians and followed through the Revolution, the Mexican War, up through World War II and the Cold War. Barnet accepted that view to some extent. But, like Alperovitz, he noticed more distinctions in America's policies. For instance, Barnet and Alperovitz liked American foreign policy as practiced by Franklin Roosevelt and argued that the Cold War had resulted from the harder line introduced by Harry Truman.[32]

Though such moderate revisionists as Barnet and Alperovitz were somewhat sympathetic to men like Franklin Roosevelt and Woodrow Wilson,[33] radical revisionists detested such liberals, thinking them even more aggressive and self-righteous than conservatives. They ridiculed Hubert Humphrey for his anticommunist leadership in the 1950s and his acceptance of Johnson's Vietnam policy. They quoted Adlai Stevenson's Cold War rhetoric with relish. Henry Wallace's desire to increase American trade abroad showed even him to be an imperialist. Walter LaFeber wrote an influential article emphasizing that the decision to accept French reoccupation of Indo-China after World War II was taken by Roosevelt, not Truman.[34]

31. Richard J. Barnet, *Roots of War* (New York, 1972); citations here are from the paperback version, Baltimore, 1973, pp. 5–8, 23–47, 51–56, 125–238, 206–238. The ambiguity of the Left toward economic determinism was also reflected in Noam Chomsky. He gave a very thorough economic explanation of America's role in Vietnam, then chided critics of the Left for attributing to radicals the claim that capitalism needed war to survive (Chomsky, *For Reasons of State*, pp. 64–65).

32. Barnet, *Roots of War*, pp. 17–22.

33. See Richard M. Pfeffer, ed., *No More Vietnams?* (New York, 1968), p. 93.

34. Walter LaFeber, "Roosevelt, Churchill, and Indochina: 1942–1945," *American Historical Review* 80, no. 5 (December 1975): 1277–1295.

But despite these dissimilarities in new revisionist thought, the revisionists shared an outrage at America's Vietnam policy. How could historians regard America's leaders as merely mistaken, "noble and virtuous, bewildered and victimized, but not responsible, never responsible," asked Noam Chomsky. Everyone knew that Ho Chi Minh had the support of 80 percent of the Vietnamese people. Dwight Eisenhower himself had admitted as much when offering reasons for supporting Diem's refusal to hold elections in 1956. Everyone knew that the Viet Cong was not dependent on the North and that few northerners had fought in the South until the Americans had begun sending troops. Everyone knew that neither China nor Russia had supplied much to the rebellion until America had raised the stakes of the game. The Pentagon Papers and the work of Douglas Pike, Chester Cooper, and Daniel Ellsberg made clear that the government was not deluded about what "everyone knew." Yet massive bombing attacks on the North and South continued, killing widely and indiscriminately despite Pentagon claims to the contrary while no one in the American government asked whether America should not, as opposed to could not, "pacify" Vietnam.[35] As atrocities multiplied, as government lies were exposed, as Kissinger and Nixon ordered the invasion of Cambodia and increased the bombing while calling this "deescalation" because they were removing some American troops, the new revisionist interpretation of American diplomacy gained more credence with a large number of people in the academic community. Although it never achieved dominance in American diplomatic history and began to fade once Kissinger had negotiated his patchwork truce, the revisionist view had acquired respectability, and historians found themselves compelled to deal with it in earnest.

Defensively, and in considerable confusion, the realists sought to answer the charges of liberal moralists and revisionists and to salvage what they could of their world view from the wreckage of Vietnam. Perhaps greater restraint was needed in American intervention abroad, realists admitted. But "soft" realists like Morgenthau, Kennan, and Lippmann had advocated restraint for years, especially where Asia and the less critical areas of the Third World were concerned. They also had commented on the moral costs of fighting a guerrilla war without much support from the indigenous population. Thus,

35. Chomsky, *For Reasons of State*, p. xii. For other examples of the radical critique of the Vietnamese war, see Noam Chomsky, *At War with Asia* (New York, 1970); Howard Zinn, *Vietnam: The Logic of Withdrawal* (Boston, 1967); and Carl Oglesby and Richard Schaull, *Containment and Change* (New York, 1967).

they insisted that the restrained realist view was in no way discredited by Vietnam.

Historians enamored of John Kennedy tried to show that he also might be numbered properly among these restrained realists. They insisted that Kennedy had understood the limits of America's interests and ability to affect the course of events in Vietnam. Roger Hilsman argued that just before Kennedy's assassination, the president had seemed on the verge of accepting the deescalation plans being made by a small State Department group acting under the auspices of Averell Harriman.[36] Arthur Schlesinger generally agreed that Kennedy had tried to limit America's role in Vietnam. In his history of the war, *The Bitter Heritage*, he blamed Robert McNamara and the military chiefs for the excessive commitments that did take place during the Kennedy administration. He especially chastised Dean Rusk for neglecting the secretary of state's duty to array the political against the military considerations that were so brilliantly and energetically put forward by McNamara. Thus, Kennedy had been led toward excessive intervention by the falsely rosy picture painted for him of the progress the South Vietnamese government was making in winning the war and the sympathies of its countrymen.[37] Nevertheless, Schlesinger insisted that in the end Kennedy would have kept America's role limited in Vietnam, and he blamed the major portion of the disaster on Lyndon Johnson's escalation.[38] But Schlesinger believed this error should not

---

36. Roger Hilsman, *To Move a Nation: The Politics of Foreign Policy in the Administration of John F. Kennedy* (Garden City, N.Y., 1967).

37. Arthur M. Schlesinger, Jr., *The Bitter Heritage: Vietnam and American Democracy, 1941–1966* (Boston, 1967), pp. 20–29, Schlesinger, *Thousand Days*, pp. 433–435; and Hilsman, *To Move a Nation*, pp. 523–537, 577–582.

38. The partisan nature of his defense was clear in the way he handled the history of the whole Vietnam War. He praised most Democrats while chastising Republicans. He argued that Franklin Roosevelt, whom the realists had long criticized as excessively idealistic, had actually been realistic in his seeking independence for Indo-China during World War II. However, he ignored Roosevelt's ultimate consent to French reoccupation of their empire. He emphasized Kennedy's agreement with Ridgway and Gavin in opposition to American intervention at Dien Bien Phu in 1954. But he failed to note other speeches Kennedy made at that time that were strongly pro-French and that later were very supportive of Diem. Schlesinger did not join the realists to criticize the excessive ambitions of the Truman Doctrine or the overmilitarization of American foreign policy under Truman and Acheson. He saved his criticism for Eisenhower and Dulles and argued that Kennedy had corrected their abuses by returning to a more realistic and limited policy (Schlesinger, *Bitter Heritage*, pp. 3, 7). For a critique, see Theodore Draper, *Abuse of Power* (New York, 1967), p. 50.

totally discredit containment. Johnson had misinterpreted and mis-used the honorable interventionist foreign policy that had triumphed in World War II.[39]

Schlesinger's argument that Vietnam was an aberration rather than a disproof of John Kennedy's realism found support from one other major historical work on the war published in the 1970s, Robert Gallucci's *Neither Peace nor Honor*. Gallucci agreed that Kennedy and Johnson had been led into the Vietnam quagmire by mistaken and distorted information that portrayed each step of escalation as suffi-cient to win the war. But Gallucci believed that Kennedy's open deci-sion-making process and his encouragement of debate within his administration had permitted the dissenting Harriman group in the State Department to be heard and had kept Kennedy from becoming overcommitted to South Vietnam. Thus, he might have been able politically to withdraw once the true picture of the war had become apparent to him. Johnson's refusal to tolerate such dissent made him more easily misled into escalation and the army's search-and-destroy strategy. Thus, only the minor correction of restructuring the bureau-cracy to ensure greater debate and more accurate reporting were neces-sary to secure the success of the Kennedy realist approach to foreign policy.[40]

But most other realist historians moved away from the views of Schlesinger and Gallucci. Almost no one believed that Kennedy would have withdrawn from Vietnam.[41] More importantly, most of these later historians were convinced by Leslie Gelb that Kennedy and John-son had not been misled into Vietnam but had known quite well what they were doing. Gelb had been director of the Pentagon Papers his-tory project for the Department of Defense, and from the material he had compiled, he surmised that Kennedy and Johnson escalated sim-ply because they could not afford politically to admit defeat. Gelb claimed that Kennedy and Johnson had considered virtually all views and had made all of their important decisions without illusions about light at the end of the tunnel. Political constraints had forced them to intervene gradually, always doing less than they had been told was

39. Schlesinger, in Pfeffer, *No More Vietnams?*, p. 9.

40. Robert L. Gallucci, *Neither Peace nor Honor: The Politics of American Military Policy in Vietnam* (Baltimore, 1975), pp. 1–4, 14–28, 116.

41. See Warren I. Cohen, *Dean Rusk* (Totowa, N.J., 1980), p. 192; Guenter Lewy, *America in Vietnam* (New York, 1978), p. 419. Leslie H. Gelb with Richard K. Betts, *The Irony of Vietnam: The System Worked* (Washington, D.C., 1979), pp. 92–95; and George C. Herring, *America's Longest War: The United States and Vietnam, 1950–1975* (New York, 1979), pp. 73–98.

necessary for victory and always hoping that somehow the war might be ended by compromise.[42] Wallace Thies offered some information on why these tactics had failed. In a careful inferential study of the North Vietnamese power structure, Thies speculated that a number of militant South Vietnamese led by Le Duan had won a bureaucratic battle for control of North Vietnamese policy over Premier Pham Van Dong and General Vo Nguyen Giap. Le Duan had favored all-out aid to the communists in the South while Dong and Giap had favored more moderate policies of support for the southern rebels and perhaps some compromise with the United States in hopes of protecting hard-won economic and industrial progress of the North. For Le Duan and his group, to accept a compromise peace under American military pressure and bombing would have been to admit error, to destroy their own position and political effectiveness. Thus, it would have taken far more pressure than mere American bombing to have forced North Vietnam to admit defeat, especially since the South Vietnamese government and army verged continuously on collapse.[43]

Unlike Gallucci and Schlesinger, Gelb and Thies cast serious doubts on the whole realist approach to foreign policy. The entire scheme of limited wars, fine-tuned interventions, carefully orchestrated programs of diplomatic persuasion and military coercion striving for circumscribed goals within rationally balanced power systems seemed far more impracticable than it had in the euphoria of the early 1960s. How could one mobilize opinion for such wars? Who would die willingly and heroically for such abstractions as the balance of power when principle and morality were not involved? If it were possible to mobilize opinion for such a war, how could the emotions of hatred and revenge be quelled as the deaths, mutilations, and atrocities that inevitably accompanied war multiplied? Once these emotions set in, how could the war effort be adjusted without upsetting the power balance, and how could one retreat when it became apparent that victory required an effort greater than the interests involved were worth? Most realist historians agreed with Thies that America must be

42. Gelb had published this view in a 1971 article, "Vietnam: The System Worked," *Foreign Policy*, no. 3 (Summer 1971), pp. 140–167, some eight years before his book coauthored with Betts appeared. Gallucci believed in 1975 that it was already "the new conventional wisdom" (Gallucci, *Neither Peace nor Honor*, p. 1). See also Gelb and Betts, *Irony of Vietnam*, pp. 1–2; Herring, *America's Longest War*, p. 7; and Lewy, *America in Vietnam*, pp. 418–419.

43. Wallace J. Thies, *When Governments Collide: Coercion and Diplomacy in the Vietnam Conflict, 1964–1968* (Berkeley, 1980).

more restrained in the future, avoiding interventions in marginal situations because military action simply could not be fine tuned. But such a consensus among realists was paper thin and disguised considerable disagreement, uncertainty, and confusion.

George Herring, whose book *America's Longest War* was the best short survey of the Vietnam War, concluded flatly that the containment policy was unsalvageable. He said it would be disastrous for the United States to adopt a "never again" policy and turn its back on the rest of the world, but Americans simply would have to learn to live with many international conditions and regimes they disliked. He offered no advice as to how or where intervention ever might be justified.[44]

Guenter Lewy, on the other hand, clung to the hard realist position in his book *America in Vietnam*. He was afraid that Vietnam would inspire too much rather than too little restraint in American policy. He insisted that the Vietnam War had been no more brutal than most wars and that the moral criticism of the war had gained a foothold only because American interests in the conflict had not been clearly demonstrated and the South Vietnamese government itself had been corrupt and ineffectual. Vietnam merely proved that in the future the United States should ascertain whether its national interests were substantially involved and its potential allies capable of doing their part before intervening. Interest and power had to remain the primary determinants of American intervention; whether or not the allies were democratic should not be a deciding factor.[45]

Leslie Gelb and Richard Betts offered suggestions as to how intervention could be made restrained and flexible. Since they believed that Vietnam had not been the product of misinformation, that "the system had worked," they concluded that the major barrier to restrained, realistic containment and a rational use of intervention was the political inability of the United States to withdraw once it had become committed to an intervention that proved to be ill advised. To correct this problem, they urged first that the government avoid popularizing simplistic doctrines that tended to inspire popular overcommitment to any particular action. They also thought Congress should be fortified against the presidency. It should have the power to withdraw the United States from a situation when the president had be-

---

44. Herring, *America's Longest War*, pp. 270–272.
45. Lewy, *America in Vietnam*, pp. 418–439.

come so identified with it that he was unwilling to retreat for fear of the political consequences to himself.[46]

Thus, although there was a general inclination among realists and other historians toward a greater restraint in American foreign policy as a result of the experience of Vietnam, there remained a wide range of opinion about the degree of restraint necessary, whether that restraint should be based on moral or realist principles, and whether such inhibition would require domestic reforms or even revolution. These concerns naturally led to reassessment of earlier American diplomacy. Historians approached past episodes with new questions and new attitudes, hoping not only to find the truth about the past but also seeking insights that might clarify their thinking about current foreign policy.

46. Gelb and Betts, *Irony of Vietnam*, pp. 363–365.

NINETEEN

Cold War Historiography in the Age of Vietnam

The new revisionist view of American foreign policy stirred a reassessment of many of the significant episodes of American diplomacy. But it had its most dramatic impact on the historiography of the origins of the Cold War. If containment had been a tragic and misguided policy in Vietnam, was it not possible that it had been wrong from the beginning when it was applied to the Soviet Union? Had the whole Cold War been as unnecessary as the Vietnam fiasco? Had American aggression toward the Soviet Union and other revolutionary nations been the primary cause of the nuclear terror beneath which the world had trembled all these years? The revisionists said so, and now they won numerous adherents in the historical profession and in the academic community at large.

The new revisionists were in general agreement on several basic propositions. They saw the United States rather than Russia as the primary villain in the origins of the Cold War. The United States had been by far the stronger of the two powers. Even when it withdrew most of its army from Europe, it had a far stronger navy and air force, it had a monopoly on the atomic bomb, and its economy was unharmed by the war. Certainly the United States had nothing to fear from devastated Russia, according to the new revisionists. Stalin was thoroughly conscious of his nation's weakness and made it abundantly apparent that he asked little more than friendly regimes on his borders. He did not even insist that they be communist regimes. He permitted neutralization of Finland and Austria. He tolerated non-communist governments in Hungary and Czechoslovakia until America pressured him to open them to Western economic exploitation. He even ordered the communists in areas occupied by the West to submit to right-wing governments rather than fight or disrupt them, most notably in Greece, Italy, France, and China.

Thus, according to the new revisionists, American warnings of Russian expansionism had been nothing but a smoke screen to disguise the expansionism of the United States. America was seeking to open the world's markets and resources to its own trade and investment. Given America's economic power, open economies were bound to be dominated by the United States. America's claims to be interested in democracy were suspect since, in the eyes of the revisionists, American and British actions in their own areas of occupation were fully as dictatorial and unilateral as Russia's, often involving collaboration with right-wing and even fascist elements along with violent suppression of the Left. In Eastern Europe the British and the Americans supported politicians prominent in oligarchical prewar governments that had been discredited by corruption and fascist tendencies. There was no real democratic tradition to build upon in the area, which the leaders of the West knew full well. Thus, revisionists saw the imposition of a full-fledged Russian dictatorship in Eastern Europe as Stalin's response to American aggression rather than as a preconceived Russian plan. Revisionists mitigated or deemphasized Russian conduct in the Katyn Forest massacre, the Warsaw uprising, the arrests of Polish underground leaders sympathetic to Britain, and the other actions that defenders of Western policy had seen as justification for distrust and containment of the Soviet regime.

Although the new revisionists were united on these basic issues, radicals and moderates within their consensus continued to dispute the degree of Franklin Roosevelt's responsibility for the Cold War. The publication of Gabriel Kolko's *Politics of War* in 1968 swung the pendulum of revisionist opinion rather hard in the direction of the radicals, who insisted that American foreign policy, including that of Roosevelt, had been uniformly imperialistic and aggressive throughout the nation's history. Truman had not initiated the Cold War. His policy was simply Roosevelt's "in another coating."[1] Contrary to the

---

1. Gabriel Kolko, *The Politics of War: The World and United States Foreign Policy, 1943–1945* (New York, 1968), p. 382. In a second volume written in collaboration with his wife, Kolko extended the account through 1954 (Joyce Kolko and

assertions of most other historians, Kolko argued that Roosevelt never ignored or postponed political considerations in his prosecution of the war. Roosevelt was sometimes impulsive, inept, and vacillating, Kolko conceded, but the president was never naïve or conciliatory toward the Russians. In the end, Roosevelt always decided in favor of his leading advisers. These men were thoroughly anti-Russian and determined to manipulate strategy in America's favor. This gave Roosevelt's policy a substratum of realism and consistency throughout the course of World War II.[2]

In military strategy, Roosevelt followed the advice of Marshall and Eisenhower, who Kolko found to be acutely aware of the political implications of their policies. Military arguments for an early second front in Europe were not based on a naïve attempt to win the war by avoiding the political complications Churchill was introducing with his Mediterranean strategy. American strategy was a "higher realism," a political calculation that France and Germany were more important than the Balkans. The Americans were anxious to get Allied armies into Europe to meet the Russians as far east as possible. Evidence of this higher realism was Operation RANKIN, a plan to parachute American and British troops into Germany if Germany collapsed early and provided a chance for unilateral Russian occupation. Eisenhower also had had political motives for refusing to race for Berlin. Since Yalta had already determined that Berlin would be shared, he thought it more important to take Lubeck, thus preventing Russian access to the Atlantic Coast, and to drive along the southern axis where there was opportunity to meet the Russians further east. Kolko accused the American military commanders of tawdry attempts to invite German surrenders in the West while urging German resistance in the east and insisted that the Americans had driven as far east as possible for the political effect.[3]

Kolko saw a shrewd and realistic consistency to America's economic diplomacy as well as its military strategy under Roosevelt's administration. This he ascribed particularly to Cordell Hull, whom he regarded as far more influential than had previous historians. Hull consistently sought free trade and open capitalistic societies as means to American economic dominance of the globe. Kolko saw multilateral institutions like the International Bank and the International Mone-

Gabriel Kolko, *The Limits of Power: The World and United States Foreign Policy, 1945–1954* [New York, 1972]).

2. Gabriel Kolko, *Politics of War*, pp. 8, 348–350.

3. *Ibid.*, pp. 24–30, 316–317, 373, 383–387.

tary Fund established in the Bretton Woods Agreement as embodiments of American imperialism. Taking issue with Richard Gardner's standard study of *Sterling-Dollar Diplomacy*, Kolko also accused the United States of using the leverage of Lend-Lease to acquire extortionate trade concessions from Britain as well as Russia. These economic benefits were America's primary war aims, Kolko claimed; the United States was far more interested in breaking down trade barriers than in relieving the suffering and starvation of Europe.[4]

Even if Roosevelt's political tactics shifted, his economic goals remained clear and consistent, according to Kolko. Previous historians had seen the debate over the Morgenthau plan as one between pro-Russian advisers, who wanted to eliminate the German security threat by stripping away German industries and sending them to Russia as reparations, and anti-Russian advisers, who wanted to deny Russia these reparations, thus allowing the German economy to revive and aid Western Europe's economy. Kolko regarded both plans as economically anti-Russian. They differed only in their political strategy. Russia did not want the destruction of the German economy since only a revived German economy could provide sufficient reparations for Russia's reconstruction. Morgenthau's plan would destroy this possibility. Russia would have to rely on American credits rather than reparations to rebuild its war-torn industry. According to Kolko, Morgenthau intended to use this economic leverage to force open the Russian economy and subject it to American domination.

Morgenthau's opponents, however, believed an economically restored Germany was necessary to Western Europe's recovery, so they refused to sacrifice the German economy to Morgenthau's anti-Russian strategy. They would simply divert Germany's production westward, still leaving Russia subject to the leverage of Lend-Lease and other American economic weapons. A truly pro-Russian policy, in Kolko's mind, was one that would have eliminated the German capitalist social structure that had been the basic cause of the war, restored full production in a nonthreatening German socialist system, and permitted Russia to draw reparations from that.[5]

For Kolko, Yalta was no more a sign of American cooperativeness than the Morgenthau plan. Roosevelt simply used the conference to defer most questions important to Russia, like reparations, knowing

---

4. *Ibid.*, pp. 242–279, 343; and Richard N. Gardner, *Sterling-Dollar Diplomacy: The Origins and Prospects of Our International Economic Order*, rev. ed. (New York, 1969).

5. Gabriel Kolko, *Politics of War*, pp. 314–340.

that Russia's military position was strong at that point but that America's economic leverage and control of the United Nations would place the United States in a stronger position later on. Roosevelt never had any intention of according Russia a sphere of influence or cooperating with the Soviets, Kolko insisted, and Truman simply continued his policy.[6]

Thus, the atomic bomb had played little part in starting the Cold War. America's policy had been determined by Roosevelt rather than by Truman, and this long before the bomb had become available. Contrary to Alperovitz, Kolko said that Truman had neither delayed the Potsdam Conference nor initiated the Hopkins mission primarily to give the United States a chance to demonstrate the bomb. Such a strategy would make sense only if Truman hoped to keep the Russians out of the war with Japan, only if the Americans understood the full power of the bomb, only if the Russians were unfamiliar with the bomb's development, and only if the United States ultimately was willing to use it on a recalcitrant Russia. Kolko found none of these factors prevalent. Truman still urged Russian entry into the Japanese war at Potsdam. He knew that Russian spies had revealed much of America's nuclear technology to Stalin. Neither Truman nor his advisers understood the full power of the bomb. Nor did they plan to threaten Russia overtly with its use. Like Roosevelt, Truman counted upon economic power and American domination of the United Nations to extort concessions from Stalin. The bomb only augmented these weapons. Truman did not so much decide to use the bomb as he acquiesced in the assumption prevailing throughout Roosevelt's administration that the bomb would be used as soon as it was ready. Truman used the bomb primarily to end the war quickly although he and advisers like Henry Stimson and James Byrnes welcomed any side effects it might have in pressuring the Russians. Inured to cruelty by the steadily escalating atrocities of the war, they gave little thought to the morality of the bomb. Thus, Kolko agreed in part with orthodox historians of the question like Herbert Feis.[7]

The continued adherence of Roosevelt and Truman to American global economic dominance could be seen in America's wartime relations with Great Britain as well as those with Russia, Kolko continued. Roosevelt's antiimperialist tendencies, so often praised by American liberals, were actually a thinly disguised attempt to replace European

6. *Ibid.*, pp. 145, 343–369, 398–399, 619–620.
7. *Ibid.*, pp. 398–399, 422–429, 538–561.

empires with indigenous regimes economically subject to the United States. Roosevelt had used the British need for Lend-Lease aid to bludgeon them into lowering some of the trade barriers posed by the imperial preference system. Roosevelt continued to see "underdeveloped areas primarily as a problem of raw-materials supplies, and that misery and stagnation would be the basis of such an American-led world was of no consequence in American planning for peace."[8]

Thus, America's Cold War imperialism was purposeful and calculated, not the product of mistakes or misunderstandings. America's only deviation from shrewd realism was its mistaken belief that Stalin was stirring revolution in areas occupied by the West. Stalin was betraying indigenous leftist movements and hindering necessary revolution, as was the United States. But Russia was weaker, and its imperialism was less effective. Thus, it was America's global counterrevolutionary interventionism that was the prime and "constant threat to social renovation and survival" throughout the world.[9] In a second volume, carrying the history of the Cold War to 1954, Joyce Kolko and Gabriel Kolko illustrated the extent and iniquity of the threat by describing America's many interventions against social change in places like Greece, the Middle East, East and West Europe, China, Japan, and Guatemala.[10]

Gabriel Kolko was more vehement and relentless in his Marxism than any of the other new revisionists, even the radical ones. But most revisionist histories of the Cold War written in the Vietnam era inclined toward his conclusions that economics had been more important than the atomic bomb in America's Cold War diplomacy and that there had been less contrast between the policies of Roosevelt and Truman than had been discerned by earlier moderate revisionists like D. F. Fleming and Gar Alperovitz.

Martin Sherwin's pioneering research on American atomic diplomacy helped to rebut Alperovitz's contention that Truman's use of the atomic bomb on Japan was a reversal of Roosevelt's cooperative policy. Sherwin showed more convincingly than had past historians that Roosevelt himself had been ready to use the bomb and that Roose-

8. *Ibid.*, pp. 280–313.

9. *Ibid.*, pp. 8, 620–625, esp. p. 623.

10. Kolko and Kolko, *Limits of Power*. Broad revisionist summaries of American interventionism in the Third World were Walter LaFeber's *America, Russia, and the Cold War* (New York, 1967), esp. the later editions; and Richard J. Barnet, *Intervention and Revolution: The United States in the Third World* (New York, 1968). See also Sidney Lens, *The Forging of the American Empire* (New York, 1971).

velt had also initiated the policy of withholding nuclear technology from the Russians. Sherwin argued that Roosevelt's refusal to share atomic secrets with the Soviets, rather than economic coercion, had triggered the Cold War, and he showed some sympathy for the dilemma of America's nuclear policy decision makers. Thus, Sherwin's interpretations deviated from Kolko's radical revisionism as well as from Alperovitz's. But Barton Bernstein seconded much of Sherwin's research and conclusions and incorporated them into the radical revisionist outlook. Bernstein accomplished this by describing the decision to withhold atomic information as merely an adjunct to America's Cold War policy of economic imperialism rather than as a mistaken reticence born of a natural distaste for Russia's tyranny in Eastern Europe, as Sherwin had implied it was.[11]

This revisionist emphasis on the economic dimension of the Cold War found further reinforcement in several prominent monographs analyzing specific episodes in the early Cold War period. Bruce Kuklick, a student of Kolko, argued in *American Policy and the Division of Germany* that America's economic policy toward Germany had been the basic cause of the Cold War. By insisting on multilateralism in Germany and Eastern Europe, the United States had threatened Russia's basic security. Kuklick speculated that Russia might have been more cooperative despite America's push for multilateralism if the United States had kept Germany weak and had granted the reparations and loans it had promised to Russia. But the United States had

11. Martin J. Sherwin, "The Atomic Bomb and the Origins of the Cold War: United States Atomic Energy Policy and Diplomacy, 1941–1945," *American Historical Review*, 77 (1973): 945–968; and his *A World Destroyed: The Atomic Bomb and the Grand Alliance* (New York, 1975). Bernstein's views appeared in several scattered articles and short pieces, most conveniently summarized in Barton J. Bernstein, ed., *The Atomic Bomb: The Critical Issues* (Boston, 1976); and in Barton J. Bernstein, ed., *Politics and Policies of the Truman Administration* (Chicago, 1970). An exception to this trend toward rejection of the Alperovitz thesis was Charles L. Mee's flamboyant journalistic description, *Meeting at Potsdam* (New York, 1975), which served as the basis for a prime-time television play. Mee argued that Stalin, Truman, and Churchill had all wanted a world of conflict because each thought he could advance his own nation's interest and power better in such an atmosphere rather than in one of tranquility. Pouncing on bits of information as keys to the hidden motives of each of the Allied leaders, Mee insisted that the Big Three had "rescued discord from the threatened outbreak of peace." Thus, Mee assumed that Truman's agreement to a Polish border along the western Oder constituted a cynical trading of Poland for a deal on reparations. In line with Alperovitz's thesis, Mee admitted no motive for dropping the atomic bomb on Japan but to impress Russia (Mee, *Meeting at Potsdam*, pp. xiii–xiv, 20, 33, 38, 88, 103, 110, 111, 158, 239, 261).

first tried to use its economic position to coerce Russia and then had denied the Soviets economic help while rebuilding German power and directing its economic productivity westward.[12]

While Kuklick concentrated on America's manipulation of the economic power of reparations, Thomas Paterson's *Soviet-American Confrontation* examined America's use of alternative economic weapons, Lend-Lease and loans. America had forced Stalin to turn inward and exploit his own sphere to rebuild his war-torn country. In this way, the United States had been responsible for part of the very harshness Americans feared and hated in Stalin.[13]

Yet Paterson's work also demonstrated that there still remained some significant contrasts between radical and moderate revisionists on the Cold War. Paterson might have reinforced the general inclination of the new revisionists to emphasize the economic dimensions of the Cold War and to discount any dramatic contrast between the atomic policies of Truman and Roosevelt, but he saw a greater variation in motives and conduct among the makers of American foreign policy than the radicals did. To argue that all policy derived from the nation's capitalist roots was to expand the definition of capitalism beyond usefulness, he said. Certainly America had been expansionist, but its expansionism had roots in arrogance, Christianity, racism, technology, chauvinism, and industrialism as well as in capitalism. He thought these forces might be termed more appropriately "the will to dominate" than capitalism. Paterson was the primary author of a college diplomatic history text that traced this theme back to colonial times.[14]

This characterization of American foreign policy did not necessarily make the tone of moderate revisionist histories less harsh than that of the radicals or lead to drastic differences in interpretations of specific events. There were noticeable similarities between Paterson's text and a rival text by members of the radical Wisconsin school, Lloyd Gardner, Walter LaFeber, and Thomas McCormick.[15] But the moderate

---

12. Bruce Kuklick, *American Policy and the Division of Germany: The Clash with Russia over Reparations* (Ithaca, 1972), pp. 9, 11–12, 40–41, 53, 70–73, 77–79, 82–83, 95, 104, 113, 123, 134, 142–144, 229, 231.

13. Thomas G. Paterson, *Soviet-American Confrontation: Postwar Reconstruction and the Origins of the Cold War* (Baltimore, 1973); and his "The Abortive Loan to Russia and the Origins of the Cold War, 1943–1946," *Journal of American History*, 56, no. 1 (June 1969): 70–92.

14. Paterson, *Soviet-American Confrontation*, pp. 263–264; and Thomas G. Paterson, J. Garry Clifford, and Kenneth J. Hagan, *American Foreign Policy: A History* (Lexington, Mass., 1977).

15. Lloyd C. Gardner, Walter F. LaFeber, and Thomas J. McCormick, *Creation of the American Empire: United States Diplomatic History* (Chicago, 1973).

revisionists did harbor some sympathy for the old "soft" liberals like Franklin Roosevelt, and they continued to see at least some contrast between his policies and those of his successor, Harry Truman. Paterson himself admitted that Roosevelt had begun the policy of using economic coercion on Russia by withholding negotiations on a major loan to the Soviets but argued that Roosevelt had tried to be cooperative at Yalta and that while both Roosevelt and Truman had moved in stages toward confrontation, Truman had moved farthest in that direction.[16]

Stephen Ambrose's analysis of America's World War II military strategy supported this moderate revisionist distinction between Roosevelt and Truman. Ambrose said that the strategy promoted by Eisenhower and Marshall was nonpolitical and in line with Roosevelt's desire to cooperate with the Russians. The Cold War had begun only because Roosevelt had not explained to Truman and to the American people, if he had understood it himself, that fascism, not democracy, was the sole alternative to communism in Eastern Europe. Truman had then sought to force free elections in Eastern Europe on the Russians.[17] Thomas Campbell's study of the United Nations also disputed the radical contention that Truman merely had continued Roosevelt's hostile policies. Campbell argued that Roosevelt had been seeking a cooperative internationalist policy in the United Nations as a sophisticated and not terribly reprehensible attempt to establish an orderly international setting that America's open market economy demanded. Truman, on the other hand, had used the United Nations as a masquerade for a much more belligerent attempt at coercion with economic and atomic weapons.[18] Richard Walton, in his two Cold War studies, also found at least a few praiseworthy features in the policies of "soft" liberals like Roosevelt and Henry Wallace whereas he denounced Truman and John Kennedy as unscrupulous Cold Warriors who had manufactured foreign crises to reinforce domestic support for their own hard lines.[19]

16. Paterson, *Soviet-American Confrontation*.

17. Stephen E. Ambrose, *Rise to Globalism: American Foreign Policy Since 1938* (Baltimore, 1971), pp. 48, 65, 102, 106–107, 110–111. See also his *Eisenhower and Berlin, 1945: The Decision to Halt at the Elbe* (New York, 1967).

18. Thomas M. Campbell, *Masquerade Peace: America's UN Policy, 1944–1945* (Tallahassee, Fla., 1973), pp. v–vii, 204–205.

19. Richard J. Walton, *Cold War and Counter-Revolution: The Foreign Policy of John F. Kennedy* (New York, 1972); and his *Henry Wallace, Harry Truman, and the Cold War* (New York, 1976).

The most wide-ranging and popular of the moderate revisionist accounts of the Cold War did not appear until 1977: Daniel Yergin's *Shattered Peace*.[20] In line with the moderate outlook, Yergin denied that American policy had been merely the creature of capitalism and argued that Roosevelt's policy had been a consistent one of cooperation with Russia by according Stalin his sphere without interference. Yergin had to dodge artfully to explain Roosevelt's opposition to the Churchill-Stalin spheres agreement. He also asserted confidently that Roosevelt's support for free elections in Eastern Europe had been merely for home consumption. Roosevelt had made this clear to Stalin but unfortunately not to Truman or the American people. Upon his death, the Wilsonian globalism he had kept at bay acquired influence with his successor. Roosevelt's Yalta axioms were replaced by what Yergin called the "Riga axioms."

The Riga axioms had been devised by America's early Russian experts and diplomats stationed in the capital city of Latvia prior to America's official recognition of the Soviet regime. The Riga axioms, based upon a Wilsonian view of the world, pictured Russia as a fanatical, driven, expansionist state, a view that led naturally to the idea that the Soviets would have to be contained by force. Ironically, among the perpetrators of these "Wilsonian" Riga axioms were George Kennan, Loy Henderson, "Chip" Bohlen, and William Bullitt, who considered themselves hard-nosed anti-Wilsonian realists. Some of the devotees of the Riga axioms, such as Averell Harriman, still had wanted Truman to negotiate with the Russians although Harriman advised economic pressure rather than conciliation in these negotiations. Yergin regarded this policy as less harmful than the containment policy that was actually pursued. Yergin saw Kennan's view of containment as the erection of "hostile barriers," contrasted to Roosevelt's attempts to establish "cooperative spheres." Thus, he viewed Kennan's later advocacy of disengagement as a thorough change in Kennan's outlook. Yet contrary to Kolko, Yergin regarded American leaders as sincere in their accusations of Russian expansionism and as truly offended by Russian brutality. He also had great respect for "soft" liberals Joseph Davies, Henry Morgenthau, and Henry Wallace, whom many radicals dismissed as simply another variety of Open Door expansionist. In all, his book was the most moderate in tone of the Cold War revisionists,

20. Daniel Yergin, *Shattered Peace: The Origins of the Cold War and the National Security State* (Boston, 1977).

moving rather close to the liberal moralism of David Halberstam, Frances FitzGerald, and the later works of Senator Fulbright.[21]

Kolko and the radical revisionists found their own reinforcement in several additional books. Walter LaFeber's influential survey, *America, Russia, and the Cold War*, in the tradition of the Wisconsin School, treated the Russian-American confrontation as an extension of America's historic economic expansion although LaFeber stated his thesis in a rather mild tone.[22] Diane Shaver Clemens's account of the Yalta Conference actually portrayed Roosevelt as rather reasonable in that instance, but her concluding chapter placed her firmly in the radical camp, for she wrote of Yalta as completely atypical of Roosevelt's policies before and after the conference.[23] Lloyd Gardner's *Architects of Illusion* supported this view and condemned the policies of both Roosevelt and Truman in vehement terms.[24] These books, along with the previously mentioned works of Barton Bernstein and Bruce Kuklick, provided a formidable edifice of radical historical opinion.

Although revisionists were divided in their outlooks on economic determinism and in their assessments of liberals like Franklin Roosevelt or Henry Wallace, they were united in their rejection of the idea that realists like Kennan or Lippmann had offered a reasonable alternative to the Cold War. Adding to Yergin's portrait of Kennan as a hard-line originator of the Riga axioms, Lloyd Gardner provided an acid sketch of Kennan's policies entitled "Will the Real 'Mr. X' Please Stand Up?" Gardner ridiculed Kennan's claims that any support his writings had given hard-line Cold Warriors had been the result of lapses in his language or misinterpretations by others. The apocalyptic language of his "long telegram" and "X" article had led naturally to prescriptions for global containment despite his later disclaimers, and Gardner insisted that the same could be said for Louis Halle.[25]

Ronald Steel and Barton Bernstein provided similar revisionist assessments of Walter Lippmann. They acknowledged that Lippmann had contributed useful criticisms of American globalism by urging that Russia be permitted its sphere of influence and vehemently if belatedly opposing the Vietnam War. But they bewailed Lippmann's underestimation of the relationship between economics and politics in

21. *Ibid.*, pp. 13, 309, 2–10, 43–45, 58–63, 11–12, 17–41, 67–68, 72–87, 89–90, 101–105, 134–135, 138–139, 147–151, 153–170, 181, 295–296, 314, 327, 390, 402–403.

22. LaFeber, *America, Russia, and the Cold War*.

23. Diane Shaver Clemens, *Yalta* (London, 1970), esp. pp. 268–269, 274, 279, 289.

24. Gardner, *Architects of Illusion*.

25. *Ibid.*, pp. 270–300.

American policy and criticized him for approaching American politics with no firmer ideological guidepost than pragmatism. Thus, they complained, Lippmann's criticisms, however biting, were too narrowly focused to threaten the deepest assumptions of the American public. "Where he saw innocence there was often, in fact, design; where he saw ignorance or blundering there was often purpose. In offering the counsel of realism, he failed to understand fully . . . how much his dissent was limited to means and tactics, not goals and ends," Bernstein wrote.[26]

While Bernstein, Steel, and the other revisionists attacked the Kennan-Lippmann realists and the Truman liberals, they were also rehabilitating right-wing isolationists who had been so discredited in the post-World War II era. Ronald Radosh portrayed several of these figures sympathetically in his *Prophets on the Right*,[27] and Thomas Paterson included similar analyses by new revisionist authors in his edition of *Cold War Critics*.[28]

The revisionist view was never more than a minority voice in the historical community, but the Vietnam War generated much sympathy for it among students and younger university faculty, and it could be ignored no longer by the leading diplomatic historians as it had been in the previous era. Some historians took on the revisionists directly, criticizing them in extensive reviews of their books. Orthodox historians rejected the revisionists' economic emphasis and their tendency to see every Soviet step as an understandable or even necessary response to unprovoked and aggressive actions by the United States.

26. Barton J. Bernstein, "Walter Lippmann and the Early Cold War," in Thomas G. Paterson, ed., *Cold War Critics* (Chicago, 1971), pp. 20, 22–24, 29–30, 44–45. Bernstein, a radical revisionist, was somewhat harsher in tone than Ronald Steel, a moderate revisionist with considerable affection for Lippmann, who argued that Vietnam turned Lippmann more toward radicalism at the end of his career. Steel himself had begun his career as a conventional realist, standing very close to the Lippmann view in his first major work, *Pax Americana* (New York, 1967). By 1971, however, Steel wrote in the introduction to his book, *Imperialists and Other Heroes: A Chronicle of the American Empire* (New York, 1971), that he had moved away from the liberal view that the American empire, however much to be criticized, had been motivated by benevolence and was an unintended and unwanted effect of World War II. He now doubted American motives as well as actions. Thus, his biography, *Walter Lippmann and the American Century* (Boston, 1980), criticized Lippmann from the moderate revisionist stance, see esp. pp. 486–487, 566–567. For a more complete critique of realism and its philosophical premises from the radical revisionist view, see John W. Coffey, *Political Realism in American Thought* (Lewisburg, Pa., 1977).

27. Ronald Radosh, *Prophets on the Right: Profiles of Conservative Critics of American Globalism* (New York, 1975).

28. Paterson, *Cold War Critics*.

They thought that revisionists gave too much stress to America's anti-Russian hostility in the early Cold War. Most major critics also thought that the revisionists deliberately selected sources that would emphasize economic motivation among American policy makers and would downplay their inconsistency, confusion, or good will as well as the Soviet brutality that might have justified America's caution in cooperating with Russia.[29]

Such criticisms were sufficient cause for some historians to reject the revisionist interpretation entirely and approach the Cold War just as historians had done in the immediate postwar period. For instance, two British historians, Sir John Wheeler-Bennett and Anthony Nicholls, wrote a massive history of the Cold War that blamed the conflict on Stalin's "naked ambition." They regretted Roosevelt's "appeasement" at Yalta and admired the hard-line policies of Churchill and Truman.[30]

But this book was the exception. In the wake of Vietnam, there were few historians willing to commend American foreign policy leaders for hard-line anticommunism. Almost all orthodox historians leaned toward the Kennan-Lippmann critique of America's Cold War policy and accepted the idea that the United States had been partially responsible for escalating and rigidifying the Cold War, if not for initiating it. This view became so predominant that the American statesmen of the early Cold War era and their historical defenders shifted the whole basis of their apologias. Dean Acheson, who had

29. Robert Maddox created a brouhaha by accusing revisionists of consciously distorting their histories. He did present some rather startling examples of the use of quotations out of context, and one historian was moved by Maddox's evidence to comment of another book that it would "shock even Americans who have examined the footnoting techniques of Gar Alperovitz or Charles C. Tansill" (Robert James Maddox, *The New Left and the Origins of the Cold War* [Princeton, 1973]). See also Warren I. Cohen, "New Light on the China Tangle," *Reviews in American History*, 1, no. 2 (June 1973): 295. Most critics of the Left, however, regarded the leading revisionist treatises as within the bounds of legitimate historical interpretation. For critiques of revisionist Cold War histories, see esp. Joseph Siracusa, *New Left Diplomatic Histories and Historians: The American Revisionists* (New York, 1973); Charles S. Maier, "Revisionism and the Interpretations of Cold War Origins," *Perspectives in American History*, 4 (1970): 313–350; Robert W. Tucker, *The Radical Left and American Foreign Policy* (Baltimore, 1971); Alfred E. Eckes, Jr., "Open Door Expansionism Reconsidered: The World War II Experience," *Journal of American History*, 59, no. 4 (March 1973): 909–924; and also Alfred E. Eckes, *A Search for Solvency: Bretton Woods and the International Monetary System, 1941–1971* (Austin, 1975).

30. Sir John Wheeler-Bennett and Anthony Nicholls, *The Semblance of Peace: The Political Settlement After the Second World War* (London, 1972), pp. 8, 96–97, 104, 560–561.

emphasized the strength and firmness of his stand against communism during his tenure in office, in his memoirs stressed the restraint he had shown. So did his biographers Gaddis Smith and David McLellan.[31] Michael Guhin also sought to moderate John Foster Dulles's reputation as a hard-liner, but with less success. Townsend Hoopes and Louis Gerson still portrayed the former secretary as a rigid anticommunist, with Hoopes condemning and Gerson lauding him for it.[32]

Dwight Eisenhower's reputation was the most affected by this shift of perspective, however. A wave of new publications, some of the most recent based on newly opened files at the Eisenhower Presidential Library in Abilene, Kansas, cast Eisenhower as the dominant figure in his administration's foreign policy rather than John Foster Dulles. Most also praised his restraint in such instances as the ending of the Korean War, the rejection of direct military intervention in Indo-China, and his seeking of détente with the Soviets.[33] However, most noted and some emphasized instances in which Eisenhower had not acted with such praiseworthy restraint—the CIA interventions in Iran and Guatemala, the planning of the Bay of Pigs invasion, and the establishment of the Diem government in South Vietnam.[34] But the nature of the defense of Eisenhower demonstrated the wide acceptance of the restrained realist view.

Perhaps the most influential history of the Cold War written in the restrained realist mode was John Lewis Gaddis' prize-winning book, *The United States and the Origins of the Cold War, 1941–1947*.[35] His

31. Dean Acheson, *Present at the Creation* (New York, 1969); Gaddis Smith, *Dean Acheson* (New York, 1972); and David S. McLellan, *Dean Acheson: The State Department Years* (New York, 1976).

32. Michael A. Guhin, *John Foster Dulles: A Statesman and His Times* (New York, 1972); Townsend Hoopes, *The Devil and John Foster Dulles* (Boston, 1973); and Louis L. Gerson, *John Foster Dulles* (New York, 1967).

33. Murray Kempton, "The Underestimation of Dwight D. Eisenhower," *Esquire*, September 1967, p. 108; Garry Wills, *Nixon Agonistes: The Crisis of the Self-Made Man* (Boston, 1969); Robert A. Divine, *Eisenhower and the Cold War* (Oxford, 1981); Fred I. Greenstein, "Eisenhower as an Activist President: A Look at New Evidence," *Political Science Quarterly*, 94 (1979–1980): 575–599; Peter Lyon, *Eisenhower: Portrait of the Hero* (Boston, 1974); Herbert S. Parmet, *Eisenhower and the American Crusades* (New York, 1972).

34. Blanche Wiesen Cook, *The Declassified Eisenhower: A Divided Legacy* (Garden City, N.Y., 1981); Richard H. Immerman, *The CIA in Guatemala: The Foreign Policy of Intervention* (Austin, Texas, 1982.)

35. John Lewis Gaddis, *The United States and the Origins of the Cold War, 1941–1947* (New York, 1972).

conclusions were reinforced by two historians with whom he was associated at Ohio University, Alonzo Hamby, who was the leading biographer of Harry Truman, and George Herring, who wrote an important study of America's Lend-Lease policy toward Russia.[36] Other significant works on the Cold War that took a similar Kennan-Lippmann realist view were contributed by Arthur Schlesinger, Jr., Louis Halle, Herbert Feis, Lynn Etheridge Davis, Lisle Rose, Martin Herz, and David Trask.[37]

Unlike most authors of earlier Cold War studies, these historians agreed with the revisionists that Stalin had been cautious and pragmatic rather than a fanatical ideologue of "rabid ambition" who was determined to conquer the world. They agreed that Stalin's primary goal had been security and that his ambition had been limited to securing friendly governments in Eastern Europe. They argued that America should have come to firm and solid agreements that would have accorded Stalin his sphere rather than putting off the issue and making vague and shifting demands that Stalin's suspicious nature could construe as threats to Soviet control of the area. Although these historians might disagree as to which Americans were responsible, they scorned crusading global anticommunism, McCarthyism, and excessive counterrevolutionary interventions. They particularly disliked the decision of Truman and Acheson to attack north of the 38th parallel in Korea, and, of course, they denounced American involvement in Indo-China. Not only did they agree with these aspects of Kennan's policies, but they favored Kennan's proposals for disengagement in Europe and considered Acheson's objections misguided.

However, they stopped far short of accepting the revisionist contention that the United States bore the primary responsibility for the Cold War. They did not see the flexibility and reason behind Stalin's plans for Eastern Europe that the revisionists had seen. They

36. Alonzo L. Hamby, *Beyond the New Deal: Harry S. Truman and American Liberalism* (New York, 1973); Alonzo L. Hamby, *The Imperial Years: The United States Since 1939* (New York, 1976); and George C. Herring, *Aid to Russia, 1941–1946: Strategy, Diplomacy, and the Origins of the Cold War* (New York, 1973).

37. Arthur M. Schlesinger, Jr., "Origins of the Cold War," *Foreign Affairs*, 47 (October 1967): 22–52; Louis Halle, *The Cold War as History* (London, 1967); Herbert Feis, *From Trust to Terror: The Onset of the Cold War, 1945–1950* (New York, 1970); Lynn Etheridge Davis, *The Cold War Begins: Soviet-American Conflict over Eastern Europe* (Princeton, 1974); Lisle A. Rose, *After Yalta* (New York, 1973); Lisle A. Rose, *Dubious Victory: The United States and the End of World War II* ([Kent, Ohio], 1973); Martin F. Herz, *The Beginnings of the Cold War* (Bloomington, Ind., 1966); and David F. Trask, *Victory Without Peace: American Foreign Relations in the Twentieth Century* (New York, 1968).

relied upon reports from Americans on the spot in 1945 and 1946 that the few noncommunist regimes Stalin was tolerating were actually governed from behind the scenes by communists and that Stalin's overall record there was ruthless. Revisionists might see control of Italy, Greece, and Japan by the West as comparable with Soviet rule, but orthodox historians thought there was a vast difference in the treatment accorded the inhabitants of occupied areas. Orthodox historians also insisted that the United States was neither covertly hoping for the development of governments unfriendly to the Soviets in Eastern Europe nor hoping to revive fascism there. America's leaders supported centrist parties that they considered capable of forming governments both democratic and friendly to the Soviets. Such policies were not a serious threat to Russian hegemony. These historians attributed Stalin's suspicions and reactions to quirks of character and to his guilt for earlier cooperation with Hitler rather than to anything done by the Western Allies.

Thus, most orthodox historians of the Cold War agreed that the United States had little choice but to abandon hopes of real cooperation with the Soviets and build its area of influence in Western Europe independent of Russia.[38] These historians assumed that there was a need to balance Soviet power in Europe in order to contain potential Russian expansion. But like Kennan and Lippmann, they wished that America had limited its commitments to vital strategic areas, stressed economic and political over military reconstruction, and given Russia no reason to fear that the United States would attempt to roll back Soviet influence in Eastern Europe.

Although hindsight might show that America should have left Stalin to his sphere, these historians thought it understandable that Americans and Westerners in general should be resentful of Stalin's actions in Eastern Europe and suspicious of what these actions portended for Western Europe, where strong Moscow-oriented communist parties could potentially take power. Whatever Stalin's immediate intentions—and these historians agreed that he had been remarkably

---

38. The thorough research of John Gimbel on the American occupation of Germany convinced most that the independent reconstruction of the German economy had been essential to Western recovery and that the actions of the United States there had not been part of an anti-Russian campaign so much as they had been a counter to French suspicions, although Stalin's unilateral actions in eastern Germany had done much to undermine Russia's claims on reparation from the West as well. See John Gimbel, *The American Occupation of Germany: Politics and the Military, 1945-1949* (Stanford, 1968), esp. pp. 26–31; also his *The Origins of the Marshall Plan* (Stanford, 1976).

restrained in his relations with the communist parties in the Western nations—Stalin still would not hesitate if chaos in the West gave the communist parties an opportunity to take over. In addition, even though Stalin's restraint was apparent in retrospect, he did not signal his intentions clearly at the time. His ruthlessness in action and brusqueness in negotiation could not help but raise Western suspicions.

The realists' deep hatred for Stalinist rule in Eastern Europe haunted them even as they preached that America should have understood the limits of its power and accepted the Soviet sphere. This same dilemma had driven earlier realists like Hans Morgenthau to grasp desperately for an alternative. Morgenthau had denounced Roosevelt for naïvely refusing to follow Churchill's policies. Roosevelt could have denied Russia an Eastern European sphere by bargaining with the second front, attacking the Balkans rather than Normandy, racing for Berlin, or refusing to evacuate territory east of the Yalta line, Morgenthau had said. He had advocated abandoning Eastern Europe to Stalin only as a last alternative in the unlikely event that Churchill's other policies proved impractical. But the release of additional documents and memoirs from the World War II period showed that Churchill himself had been somewhat inconsistent in his advocacy of hard-line policies, and America's military historians had already gone far to demonstrate the impracticality of his strategies. This new historical knowledge plus the growing unpopularity of the Cold War and its manifestation in Vietnam drove most orthodox historians toward the "softer" realist approach of according Stalin a firm sphere of influence. Yet it stuck in the craw of many of these realists to advocate complete abandonment of Eastern Europe to the tender mercies of Stalin. They grasped for some means of having their cake and eating it too, of giving Stalin his sphere yet avoiding the brutal consequences of this action.

Herbert Feis pointed to evidence of this dilemma in Kennan's early writings. Kennan had advocated abstention from interference in Stalin's sphere, yet the tone and context in which the advice was given implied that for Stalin to have a free hand in Eastern Europe would be reprehensible. Thus, Feis recognized some of the same inconsistency in Kennan that revisionists had seen.[39] Kennan had tried to bring his reason and emotion into harmony by arguing that Stalin would be unable to consolidate his rule in Eastern Europe without the moral and

---

39. Feis, *From Trust to Terror*, p. 37, n. 2.

financial help of the United States so that disassociation and containment would ultimately lead to a loosening of Russian tyranny there.[40] But the realists could not quite shake the thought that there might have been some alternative to outright abandonment of Eastern Europe. If it had become clear that nothing could have kept Stalin from acquiring his sphere, could Roosevelt have done something more to win Soviet concessions that would have made the sphere slightly more to the liking of the American people? If so, might this have prevented America's overreaction to Soviet rule there and helped to avoid the threats that had made Stalin's rule even harsher and more rigid?

One of those who thought so was Adam Ulam, a specialist in Russian affairs at Harvard. Ulam admitted that advocates of the Churchill strategy were "hard pressed to describe policies which could have worked." The public in the Western Allied states would not have supported a hard-line policy that risked a confrontation with Russia during the war.[41] America could have extorted from Stalin only a few minor concessions to make the Soviet sphere palatable to the West but could not have weakened or eliminated that sphere as Churchill's earlier strategy had been designed to do. Nevertheless, some minimal concessions might have been gained from Stalin. Ulam emphasized that Russia had been very weak at the end of the war, far weaker than the uninformed and clumsy American leaders had understood it to be. According to Ulam, this weakness had not brought Stalin to desire American friendship, as revisionists theorized, or to need it in order to consolidate his sphere, as Kennan had maintained. Therefore, neither open-handed cooperation nor indignant abandonment of the Soviet sphere was the proper policy for the United States. Instead, diplomatic pressure and clever, courageous negotiations might have secured some minimal liberalization of Eastern Europe.

Roosevelt and Truman could have used Lend-Lease and the inevitably short-lived atomic monopoly as bargaining counters in these negotiations. Unfortunately, contrary to revisionist assertions, they had used neither. Roosevelt had offered economic aid with no strings. He had not considered negotiating with the bomb. He had dissipated his little remaining bargaining leverage to get concessions in the United Nations, concessions which were doomed to be as meaningless

40. Kennan, *Memoirs, 1925–1950*, p. 250; see also his *American Diplomacy, 1900–1950*, pp. 66–77.
41. Adam Ulam, *The Rivals: America and Russia Since World War II* (New York, 1971), pp. 7, 96.

as the organization itself. Truman had ineptly cut off Lend-Lease, then restored it. He had not negotiated with it, with the proposed Russian loan, or with the bomb. Even when he knew of the bomb's existence at Potsdam, he had not abandoned his attempts to bring Russia into the Japanese war.[42]

Ulam argued that if Truman and Roosevelt actually had followed the economic and atomic diplomacy which revisionists accused them of following, and done so in the period between the invasion of Normandy and Japan's surrender when conditions were still fluid, they might have acquired some concessions from Stalin. Stalin might have given concrete guarantees for free elections in a neutralized Germany or similar guarantees in Poland. Perhaps there could have been more Finlands in Eastern Europe. This would have made the Soviet sphere tolerable and prevented the overreaction of the Americans that occurred later. Unfortunately, Roosevelt and Truman made unnecessary concessions because they insisted on the unconditional surrender of Japan and thus continued to need and desire Russian participation in the Pacific war. Roosevelt had turned toward Churchill's more appropriate policy at the end of his life, but Truman did not have the power and confidence of a Roosevelt, so he vacillated. His dispatch of the conciliatory Hopkins to Russia destroyed any hope of gaining concessions from Stalin through hard bargaining. When Truman finally toughened in 1946–1947, it was too late. The provisional agreements based on "previous compromises, concessions, and confusions of declarations of principles with political facts" had hardened.

Thus, by the time America had returned to the European continent with NATO, it was too late to negotiate concessions from the Russians. The Soviets had the bomb, America was in Korea, and China was communist. Also by this time Stalin was more suspicious. Until 1947 he had understood clearly that American plans had posed no real threat to him. But Stalin's misinterpretation of the Marshall Plan led him to fear that the United States actually intended to undermine his regime. Ulam still thought that the United States should negotiate a neutralization of Central Europe with the Russians, but now the terms would not be favorable enough for the American people to support them easily. Earlier, "a firm stand taken on behalf of the principles for which the war had allegedly been fought would have been not only the right but also the safe course of action."[43]

42. *Ibid.*, pp. 8, 17, 77–79, 94–95, 97–100, 102.
43. *Ibid.*, pp. 32–33, 52, 73, 66–67, 97–100, 102–103, 238.

Other realists also were tantalized by the thought that clever negotiation might have won sufficient concessions from Stalin to make his sphere more suited to Western tastes. But where Ulam saw negotiations primarily as a means of extorting concessions from a weakened Russia, most of the others emphasized concessions the West might have traded for liberalization in Eastern Europe. Martin Herz thought Roosevelt should have offered credits at Yalta in exchange for firmer guarantees in Poland. He also thought Truman should have bargained with Lend-Lease aid rather than halting it only to restore it later.[44] Lisle Rose thought that the United States should have offered atomic technology to the Soviets in exchange for a relaxation of their foreign policy. Rose argued that Stalin's aggressive moves in Turkey, Iran, Japan, and the Italian colonies well might have been his attempts to demonstrate that Russia was not about to be intimidated by the bomb.[45] Louis Halle doubted that Roosevelt could have negotiated substantial concessions from Stalin after 1942, even with the offer of financial and atomic aid. But he thought Roosevelt might have wrung something from Stalin prior to 1942 when Russia was still reeling from the German invasion.[46]

However, most orthodox historians rejected the idea that clever negotiations could have extorted or bribed substantial concessions from the Soviets. John Lewis Gaddis recalled that Congress had been dead set against sharing atomic secrets with Stalin, a point even Lisle Rose was forced to concede. Congress also had served notice that it expected Lend-Lease to be cut off immediately after the war was over, rendering moot Herz's suggestion that Truman should have bargained with it. Gaddis added that all of Roosevelt's advisers with first-hand experience in Russia, including Averell Harriman, General John Deane, William Bullitt, and George Kennan, had concluded that America should pressure the Soviets rather than be open-handed with them. Yet tactics of the sort they advocated had not worked any better than those of Roosevelt. Gaddis argued that the withholding of atomic technology and the stalling of the loan had not noticeably softened Russia's negotiating position.[47]

Stalin would not have conceded anything in such negotiations

44. Herz, *Beginnings of the Cold War*.

45. Rose, *After Yalta*, pp. 83, 121–123, 132–133, 149–150, 162. See also his *Dubious Victory*.

46. Halle, *Cold War as History*, pp. 32–49.

47. Gaddis, *United States and the Origins of the Cold War*, pp. 81–88, 254–257, 343, 356–358; and Rose, *After Yalta*, pp. 117, 175–179.

anyway, Gaddis said. Stalin was confident the United States would extend credits for its own sake to stimulate exports and avoid a postwar depression. When Roosevelt and Truman delayed the loan and reparations from the West, Stalin had extracted reparations from his own sphere rather than make concessions to secure Western credits.[48] Thus, Gaddis found America's leaders had had a very narrow range of alternatives. They could do little but abandon the Soviet sphere and build the West to contain possible Russian expansion.[49] George Herring agreed with Gaddis, and he also rejected Louis Halle's contention that better terms could have been extorted from Stalin before 1942. Herring believed that Stalin would not have kept any agreement he might have made under duress in the early stages of the war.[50]

Increasingly, the only plausible alternative to the Cold War seemed to have been abandonment of the Soviet sphere.[51] Even those who thought a better settlement might have been negotiated did not hold out much hope of winning substantial concessions from Stalin, but just enough to convince the American people of the wisdom of according the Soviets their sphere. And, as George Herring pointed out, this would have been problematical even under the best of circumstances. Openly granting a Soviet sphere went against the American grain, and to reward the Russians for minor modifications of their dominance would have been politically impossible. "The wisdom of such a course has much to commend it in retrospect, but history and experience had not prepared American leaders to act in this fashion," Herring admitted.[52]

As orthodox historians came to see fewer alternatives to according Russia its Eastern European sphere, the reputation of Franklin Roosevelt's diplomacy rose correspondingly. With the exception of the moderate revisionists, historians in the Age of Munich had generally condemned him for his naïve attempts to cooperate with the Russians. Only a few orthodox defenders pointed lamely to some of his remarks

48. Gaddis, *United States and the Origins of the Cold War*, pp. 91, 174–197, 359.
49. *Ibid.*, pp. vii, 354.
50. Herring, *Aid to Russia*, pp. 279–293.
51. E.g., Herbert Feis' new book, *From Trust to Terror*, included a repetition of his earlier wish that Roosevelt had bargained harder over Poland at Yalta, but he made clear his essential commitment to outright abandonment of Eastern Europe to the Soviets by criticizing Kennan for the ambiguity of Kennan's "long telegram" on abandonment (*ibid.*, pp. 26, 37). See also Davis, *Cold War Begins*, pp. 369–395, for a rehearsal of all the alternatives to the Roosevelt-Truman policies and the conclusion that American acquiescence with no protest whatever was the most plausible chance to avoid the Cold War.
52. Herring, *Aid to Russia*, pp. 279–293.

in the last two weeks of his life which they thought indicated he had finally caught on to the Russians. They argued that his cooperativeness at least had thrown the onus for starting the Cold War clearly on Stalin.[53] But in the wake of Vietnam, orthodox historians were less inclined to label Roosevelt unrealistic. Adam Ulam and Louis Halle continued to believe he had been inept. James MacGregor Burns' Pulitzer Prize-winning biography, *Roosevelt: The Soldier of Freedom*, portrayed Roosevelt as balancing uneasily between his idealism and realism, seeking cooperation yet delaying the cross-Channel invasion and withholding atomic information from the Soviets. Burns thought that this incongruity between Roosevelt's ends and means widened the gap between popular expectations and actual possibilities and led the Russians to suspect a plot to destroy communism.[54] But the majority of studies of Roosevelt's policies concluded that his realism had predominated over his idealism and that within the constraints imposed upon him by the conflicting demands of the Allies and domestic popular opinion, he had managed to blend cooperativeness with firmness toward the Soviets. This view was put forward most forcefully by Robert Dallek's study, *Franklin D. Roosevelt and American Foreign Policy*. It was supported by Raymond O'Connor's analysis of Roosevelt's wartime strategy, *Diplomacy for Victory: FDR and Unconditional Surrender*, Robert Divine's *Second Chance* and *Roosevelt and World War II*, along with the broader surveys of modern American diplomacy by John Gaddis and Alonzo Hamby.[55]

53. Arthur Schlesinger, George Herring, and Robert Maddox continued to hold this view on into the Age of Vietnam. Other historians like Lisle Rose, Alonzo Hamby, and John Gaddis argued that Roosevelt's contemporaneous statements to the effect that America and Russia could still cooperate reflected his true sentiments. See Schlesinger, "Origins of the Cold War," p. 24, n. 3; Herring, *Aid to Russia*, p. 290; Maddox, *New Left and the Origins of the Cold War*, passim; Rose, *After Yalta*, pp. 32–33; Hamby, *Imperial Years*, pp. 81–82; and Gaddis, *United States and the Origins of the Cold War*, pp. 172–173.
54. James MacGregor Burns, *Roosevelt: The Soldier of Freedom* (New York, 1970), pp. vii–viii, 608–609.
55. Robert A. Dallek, *Franklin D. Roosevelt and American Foreign Policy, 1932–1945* (New York, 1979); and Raymond G. O'Connor, *Diplomacy for Victory: FDR and Unconditional Surrender* (New York, 1971). O'Connor argued that Roosevelt had been fully aware of the political implications of his cross-Channel strategy. Roosevelt had wanted to attack the European mainland early, specifically in order to meet the Russians further east, and Churchill had been wrong to oppose him, O'Connor said. But O'Connor saw this as no exception to Roosevelt's cooperative policy since the Russians had wanted the same strategy. Thus, Roosevelt's policy would have pleased the Russians at the same time that

Like the moderate revisionists, the orthodox defenders of Franklin Roosevelt's diplomacy were most critical of his failure to communicate to his successor and to the American people his own understanding of the need to accord Russia its sphere in Eastern Europe. Historians writing in the Age of Munich had also noted his failure to keep Truman informed, but they had been impressed by Truman's quick grasp of affairs and his decisiveness in the subsequent crises between the United States and the Soviet Union. They had minimized signs of his vacillation, such as his use of soft-liners like Harry Hopkins and Joseph Davies for vital special missions while at the same time he was denouncing Russian policy to Molotov in the language of a mule skinner.

Early revisionists like Alperovitz had even seen such contradictions as clever delaying tactics used to disguise Truman's consistent intent to resort to atomic diplomacy. But the release of many formerly secret documents now allowed historians to see Truman's early vacillations far more clearly and trace them more elaborately. Truman's air of decisiveness, symbolized by his motto, "The buck stops here," seemed to the most prominent orthodox historians of Truman's policies, John Gaddis and Alonzo Hamby, to be a pose covering his bewilderment. Robert Dallek even argued that Roosevelt would have moved more rapidly to confront the Russians than Truman had done.[56] Patricia Ward's analysis of the diplomacy of Secretary of State James Byrnes, whom earlier revisionists had portrayed as a consistent hard-liner and virulent Cold Warrior, showed Byrnes exhibiting the same sort of confusion and improvisation as his chief.[57]

---

it would have given Roosevelt a better chance to secure a more democratic settlement in Eastern Europe. John Gaddis supported this view, pointing out that Operation RANKIN, the plan for quick U.S. and British occupation of Western Europe in case Germany unexpectedly collapsed, was intended to be carried out in cooperation with Russia. See Gaddis, *United States and the Origins of the Cold War*, pp. 75–76. For another similar analysis, see Mark A. Stoler, *The Politics of the Second Front: American Military Planning and Diplomacy in Coalition Warfare, 1941–1943* (Westport, Conn., 1977). Stoler, however, thought that the political realism of Roosevelt, along with that of Churchill and Stalin, had been too selfishly nationalistic (see *ibid.*, p. 168). See also Robert A. Divine, *Roosevelt and World War II* (Baltimore, 1969), pp. 49, 65, 70–73, 85–96; Robert A. Divine, *Second Chance: The Triumph of Internationalism in America During World War II* (New York, 1967); Hamby, *Imperial Years*, pp. 61, 81–82; and Gaddis, *United States and the Origins of the Cold War*, pp. 12–17, 31, 138–139, 172–173.

56. Dallek, *Franklin D. Roosevelt and American Foreign Policy*, pp. 533–534.
57. Patricia Dawson Ward, *The Threat of Peace: James F. Byrnes and the Council of Foreign Ministers, 1945–1946* ([Kent, Ohio], 1979).

From these detailed studies of Truman's uncertain and some-imes contradictory policies there emerged a new periodization of the Cold War that came to be generally accepted by orthodox historians. Truman's firm commitment to containment had not come immedi-ately in 1945, as the revisionists had claimed, or in 1947 with the Truman Doctrine, as earlier orthodox historians had assumed. The release of formerly secret documents, especially the printed volumes n the State Department's *Foreign Relations of the United States*, revealed that Truman had pushed Byrnes to take a harder line with the Soviets n February of 1946, following Stalin's speech and the arrival of Ken-nan's "long telegram." Historians now knew that Truman had specifi-cally approved Churchill's subsequent Iron Curtain speech, contrary to Truman's claims that he had not read the speech prior to its delivery.

Gaddis, Hamby, and other historians also argued that Truman's slide from the restrained containment undertaken in 1946 into exces-sive globalism had taken place later than previous historians had claimed. Kennan had thought it might be dated from the Truman Doctrine of 1947 which had implied a military commitment to resist communism everywhere in the world. The Truman Doctrine had been admittedly hyperbolic, Gaddis said, but all public statements tended to be so. People who complained of this underestimated the difficulty of selling the unpopular containment program to Congress. Truman and Acheson also had made follow-up statements that the doctrine did not involve a global commitment and that each case would be taken on its own merits. American restraint in China and Czechoslovakia illustrated this intention.

But the fall of China, Russia's acquisition of the atomic bomb, the Berlin blockade, and the advent of McCarthyism had made fine dis-tinctions impossible. Kennan had wanted to base American policy on the assessment of Russian intentions. But Dean Acheson and the na-tional security establishment insisted that American preparedness be based on Soviet capabilities. They had prepared a blueprint for a mas-sive military building program, National Security Council Memoran-dum 68, to permit a military response to Russian aggression anywhere in the world. Truman had hesitated to seek its implementation because of the expense involved. But the North Korean invasion of the South had opened the way, and America's military budget expanded perma-nently to gargantuan proportions. The cumulative result was in inten-sification and rigidification of the Cold War so that America could not respond properly to the increased Soviet flexibility brought about by Stalin's death. Thus, the overcommitment that the realists bewailed dated from the National Security Council Memorandum 68 and Korea, not from the Truman Doctrine of 1947.[58]

Later realists like Gaddis and Hamby did not do much to alter the overall perspective of earlier realists like George Kennan and Walter Lippmann; they simply elaborated upon it and placed it more accurately in historical context. They still saw containment as an appropriate means of maintaining the balance of power in Europe, but their inside view of the deliberations of the Truman administration brought them to emphasize the uncertainty with which Truman approached the problem and to date the establishment of a firm containment policy in 1946 rather than 1947 or 1945. They still winced at the excessive globalism, militarism, and ideological anticommunism that Truman and Acheson brought to the containment policy but dated the beginnings of these aberrations in 1949 or 1950 rather than in 1947 with the Truman Doctrine.

Thus, almost all the histories of the Cold War written in this era of Vietnam supported America's increased aversion to interventionism. The new revisionists were most adamant on this issue especially since they assumed that as long as the United States was capitalist, its interventions would inevitably run counter to progressive forces in the world. The realists were not so thoroughly opposed to intervention. They presumed that there would still be times and places where it would be justified and necessary just as it had been in World War II and to some extent in the Cold War. But their analysis of American power and interest led them to counsel far greater restraint in the future than America had shown in the past. Now too they were more willing to consider moral factors in the decision to intervene, whether as simply a realistic assessment of the conditions necessary to successful American intervention or as significant factors in and of themselves. These attitudes would influence writing on early American diplomacy just as they had influenced interpretations of Vietnam and the Cold War.

58. Gaddis, *United States and the Origins of the Cold War*, pp. 350–351, 386–402; John Gaddis, "Was the Truman Doctrine a Real Turning Point?" *Foreign Affairs*, 52, no. 2 (January 1974): 386–402; and Hamby, *Imperial Years*, pp. 109–138. See also Lewis McCarroll Purifoy, *Harry Truman's China Policy: McCarthyism and the Diplomacy of Hysteria, 1947–1951* (New York, 1976).

TWENTY

The Impact of Vietnam
on the Historiography
of Early American Diplomacy

The searing experience of Vietnam had a profound effect upon the historiography of earlier American diplomacy. As in the case of the historiography of the Cold War, nationalist bombast went totally out of fashion. So did the hard-line realism that emphasized the unavoidability of conflict and excused American movement into vacuums of power as inevitable steps to be judged only by the skill or lack of it in balancing goals with the power available. Almost all historians now recognized the prominence of expansionism in American foreign policy and regarded it more with guilt than with nationalist pride or a realist sense of tragedy and irony. Even orthodox historians came to agree that the Age of Munich had distorted the past by concentrating too heavily on political and strategic aspects of American diplomacy and ignoring the economic dimension. Many also agreed that the idealistic liberalism which they still insisted had been a sincere if misguided motivating force behind some American policy had contained elements of economic expansionism and cultural imperialism that were rightly resented by foreigners, however benevolent the intentions of the United States.

An influential minority of historians went further than this and adopted the "new revisionist" outlook on American diplomacy, insisting that expansion was not only an important element of American foreign policy but absolutely central to it and that it had been motivated primarily by economics. Three new college-level diplomatic history texts were built around this view. The earliest of these, Wayne Cole's *An Interpretive History of American Foreign Relations*, [1] tried to incorporate some of the revisionist insights into a traditional narrative that still contained large elements of the realist-idealist and interventionist-isolationist interpretive frameworks. A later text by Lloyd Gardner, Walter LaFeber, and Thomas McCormick was much more single-minded and summarized American diplomatic history from the radical revisionist viewpoint. The third of these texts, written by Thomas Paterson, J. Garry Clifford, and Kenneth Hagan, also examined American expansionism but from the moderate revisionist perspective, thus avoiding the description of expansion as an inevitable product of capitalism. [2]

The majority of historians, however, moved toward the "soft" realist position. They insisted that expansionism was only one of a number of significant elements in American foreign policy and that much of American expansion could be explained by mistaken idealism and ignorance rather than calculated and malevolent capitalist greed. Still, they admitted that this expansion often had had baneful effects, and in their analyses of specific diplomatic incidents they usually argued that a realistic course, balancing proper goals with the power available, would have been one of peaceful negotiation rather than war. They also generally argued that a realistic but nonbelligerent approach best conformed to the American ideals which most of these "soft" realists were now willing to urge as necessary to modify pure power politics. [3] In this process, the realist view lost its hard, polemical edge and, along with it, much of its power as a general organizing concept. It was difficult to predict how a historian using the realist approach would interpret any particular episode in American diplomacy except to say that he would invariably find much ignorance and blind fervor in one or another of the major American leaders involved. [4]

1. Wayne Cole, *An Interpretive History of American Foreign Relations* (Homewood, Ill., 1968).

2. Lloyd C. Gardner, Walter F. LaFeber, and Thomas J. McCormick, *Creation of the American Empire: U.S. Diplomatic History* (Chicago, 1973); and Thomas G. Paterson, J. Garry Clifford, and Kenneth J. Hagan, *American Foreign Policy: A History* (Lexington, Mass., 1977).

3. For this approach, see two other recent college texts, Daniel M. Smith, *The American Diplomatic Experience* (Boston, 1972); and Armin Rappaport, *A History of American Diplomacy* (New York, 1975).

4. See e.g., the essays collected in Merli and Wilson, *Makers of American Diplomacy* for realist critiques alternating with revisionist assessments.

This trend was well illustrated in the descriptions of the origin of American diplomatic principles offered by the nationalists, realists, and new revisionists. For instance, the fading of the nationalist view can be traced graphically in the work of Max Savelle. In 1934, Savelle had written a very influential article sketching the colonial origins of American diplomatic principles, and he had written it from a strongly nationalist point of view. He had begun with the assumption that the United States had been guided throughout its history by six rather benevolent principles—isolationism, nonintervention, freedom of the seas, the Open Door, the Monroe Doctrine, and the pacific settlement of disputes. He had searched for incidents and trends in America's colonial past that had served as precedents for these principles and had cited a few of them in this 1934 article.[5]

Thirty years later, Savelle published a far more extensive analysis of the origins of American diplomacy. But by this time neither he nor anyone else was willing to concede that the six beneficent principles he had listed in 1934 had actually guided American diplomacy consistently throughout the nation's history. So his 1967 book, *The Origins of American Diplomacy*, made only the briefest obeisance to an analysis of diplomatic "principles" and became instead a mere narrative of European and colonial diplomacy between 1492 and 1763. As the story emerged from Savelle's book, the United States had inherited a situation rather than a set of principles from its colonial past. Savelle did see expansionism as an important inheritance from America's days as part of the British Empire. The United States continued to compete with its North American neighbors for the Western lands just as it had in its colonial period. But Savelle saw defensive as well as aggressive aspects to American expansion and did not cast his narrative in a revisionist, condemnatory tone.[6]

As the nationalist view of the origins of American diplomacy faded, the realist view became more convoluted, eclectic, and uncertain than it had been in the Age of Munich. This was well illustrated by Arthur Ekirch's brave attempt to discover some consistent principles in American diplomacy and to trace their origins from the "soft" realist point of view. But, like Savelle, Ekirch found these so-called principles to be contradictory and to fluctuate from period to period and crisis to crisis. Ultimately, the only unifying theme in his book was his realist tone as he watched numerous "principles" rise, conflict

5. Max Savelle, "The Colonial Origins of American Diplomatic Principles," *Pacific Historical Review*, 3, no. 3 (1934); 334–350.
6. Max Savelle, *The Origins of American Diplomacy: The International History of Anglo-America, 1492–1763* (New York, 1967).

with contrary "principles," entirely transmogrify, and finally disappear.[7] Meanwhile, of course, the new revisionists had no trouble assessing the guiding principle of American diplomacy—expansion—and tracing its origin to the capitalist system, the heritage of British imperialism, and racism.[8]

But as nationalist and realist historians lost some of the unifying force of their explanatory frameworks, they gained in the flexibility and subtlety of their approach to particular incidents and trends in American foreign policy. They more often accented the exploitation of new historical sources and breadth of research rather than sensational new interpretations. Ernest May and Alexander DeConde wrote influential historiographical essays suggesting that historians explore cultural as well as governmental relations between nations, that they go beyond the diplomatic archives to the papers of nongovernmental personnel such as missionaries, businessmen, and tourists. Historians should discover the domestic settings within which diplomatic decisions were made.[9] In this contention they found agreement from a revisionist historiographical survey by Thomas McCormick.[10] However a slight but meaningful difference of emphasis between the approaches of May and DeConde and that of McCormick reflected the differing assumptions and methodologies of orthodox and revisionist historians.

McCormick assumed that American foreign policy was more the product of America's internal capitalist structure than a response to foreign pressures. He therefore urged historians to concentrate on the deep economic substructure underlying the froth of diplomatic decisions. When Ernest May called for attention to the domestic factors influencing American foreign policy, he was thinking less of the economic substructure than of a plurality of independent second-level

7. Arthur A. Ekirch, Jr., *Ideas, Ideals, and American Diplomacy: A History of Their Growth and Interaction* (New York, 1966).

8. See, e.g., Gardner et al., *Creation of the American Empire.*

9. Ernest R. May, "The Decline of Diplomatic History," in George Athan Billias and Gerald N. Grob, eds., *American History: Retrospect and Prospect* (New York, 1971), pp. 399–430; Ernest R. May and James D. Thomson, Jr., eds., *American-East Asian Relations: A Survey* (Cambridge, Mass., 1972); and Alexander DeConde, *American Diplomatic History in Transformation* (Washington, D.C., 1976). For an example of several essays endeavoring to follow this prescription, see Morrell Heald and Lawrence S. Kaplan, *Culture and Diplomacy: The American Experience* (Westport, Conn., 1977).

10. Thomas J. McCormick, "The State of American Diplomatic History," in Herbert J. Bass, ed., *The State of American History* (Chicago, 1970), pp. 119–141.

variables such as political parties, individual personalities, and fluctuating psychological moods. May was especially intrigued by the influence of bargaining within the bureaucracy on American diplomatic decisions, and he chaired a Harvard seminar of foreign policy experts studying this "bureaucratic" approach to diplomatic history. The members of this seminar produced several important books in the 1970s, including May's own study of the Monroe Doctrine, Graham Allison's analysis of the Cuban missile crisis, and Morton Halperin's discussion of Lyndon Johnson's decision to build an antiballistic missile system.[11]

Revisionist historians following the prescriptions of McCormick produced far fewer monographs and special studies of early American diplomacy than they did on the later period. Their views on earlier foreign policy had to be garnered from their textbooks or collections of short essays.[12] The one significant exception was Jack Ericson Eblen's study of American territorial governments, which he titled revealingly *The First and Second United States Empires: Governors and*

11. Ernest May's book on the Monroe Doctrine is discussed later on pp. 361–362. Graham T. Allison's book was *Essence of Decision: Explaining the Cuban Missile Crisis* (Boston, 1971). Morton H. Halperin's was *Bureaucratic Politics and Foreign Policy* (Washington, D.C., 1974). For further examples of this bureaucratic approach, see Morton H. Halperin and Arnold Kanter, eds., *Readings in American Foreign Policy: A Bureaucratic Perspective* (Boston, 1973). Actually this approach was a more self-conscious use of materials long a staple part of foreign policy research. It simply depended on the release of documents dealing with the lower echelons of government, supplementing previously known information about more central decision makers. Thus, historians of Anglo-American conflict during World War II, discussed at the end of the next chapter, used similar materials and approaches, as did many of the Cold War historians like Richard Barnet.

However, diplomatic historians participated little in another major trend that was affecting other historical fields, namely, methodological innovations, particularly the application of computer techniques to historical statistics. Advocates of this methodological innovation pointed to two areas in which statistical studies might be useful. First, diplomatic historians could use census, election, and congressional voting data to determine the role of popular opinion in various episodes. In this area, some historians were making headway. But in the other area, computer analysis of international systems and the likelihood of war under each system, diplomatic historians showed considerable skepticism and left the field to political scientists. For a critical analysis of this situation, see David S. Patterson, "What's Wrong (and Right) with American Diplomatic History? A Diagnosis and Prescription," Society for Historians of American Foreign Relations, *Newsletter*, 9, no. 3 (September 1978): 1–14.

12. E.g., Barton J. Bernstein, ed., *Towards a New Past: Dissenting Essays in American History* (New York, 1968); and William Appleman Williams, ed., *From Colony to Empire* (New York, 1972).

Territorial Government, 1784–1912.[13] He emphasized the autocratic features of these governments, not to mention the brutal means by which the territories had been acquired and settled in the first place. Thus, he contradicted the view of territorial government most historians had taken, in which the method the United States had used to acquire the territories had been mitigated by the beneficent policy of bringing the territories into the Union as equal states rather than holding them in perpetuity as colonies.

While Eblen's was the only overtly revisionist monograph on early American foreign policy published in this era, the influence of the revisionist view and the reaction to Vietnam did push some orthodox historians toward a more jaundiced view of the expansionism everyone recognized in the diplomacy of the nation's formative years. For instance, Alexander DeConde wrote a brief history of the Louisiana Purchase which added little new information to the story but revised the old view of the United States as passive beneficiary of Napoleon's difficulties in Europe and the West Indies. DeConde attributed the purchase far more to the aggressive expansionism of Jefferson and his administration. Jefferson had made clear to France that America intended to obtain the territory by hook or by crook. DeConde's portrait of Jefferson and the Republicans was far less attractive in this book than it had been in his earlier monographs on Franco-American relations. DeConde also used the Louisiana incident as an illustration of the continuity of America's aggressive expansionism throughout the nation's history. Clearly, his opinions had moved in response to revisionism and the atmosphere of the Vietnam era.[14]

Jefferson represented America's aggressive expansionism in still another important book published in this era, Burton Spivak's analysis of the embargo entitled *Jefferson's English Crisis.* Earlier histories of the embargo had portrayed it as an example of Jeffersonian pacifism, a pacifism praised by some idealists like Louis Sears and condemned as naïve by a whole host of realists. Spivak, however, accepted William Appleman Williams's view that Jefferson had been required to adopt such a draconian measure only because he persisted in defending America's neutral right to take up the carrying trade in French products thrown its way by the war. Instead, Jefferson should have limited the government's defense to the more proper right of the United States to carry its own products to Europe. Not only had Jefferson sought

13. Jack Ericson Eblen, *The First and Second United States Empires: Governors and Territorial Government, 1784–1912* (Pittsburgh, 1968).
14. Alexander DeConde, *This Affair of Louisiana* (New York, 1976).

these illicit war gains, but he had been ready to go to war for them. Spivak insisted that Jefferson had instituted the embargo as a prelude to war not as a substitute for it. Thus, the embargo had not been a mere continuation of the earlier Republican measures of commerical retaliation fostered by Madison during Washington's administration. It had been instead a war measure. But when American war fever died before war could be declared, Jefferson had not been able to bring himself to seek its repeal. He had simply turned away from the issue, leaving Madison to defend the embargo as a proper substitute for war and Gallatin to bear the burden of administering and enforcing it.[15]

Another area of early American diplomacy in which expansionism was pointed up and condemned by revisionist and orthodox historians alike was relations between Indians and whites. Native American activism in the 1960s focused popular attention on the plight of modern Indians and the responsibility of Anglo society for that plight. Popular works such as Dee Brown's *Bury My Heart at Wounded Knee*[16] and Vine DeLoria's *Custer Died for Your Sins*[17] denounced Anglo policy toward the Indians as outright imperialism and genocide and found considerable agreement from professional historians. Wilcomb Washburn, Francis Jennings, Reginald Horsman, and Wilbur Jacobs all wrote very comprehensive and powerful books that portrayed the effects of Anglo expansionism in all their horror and found little to mitigate the guilt for this aggression.

These historians dwelt on the falsehoods and rationalizations that whites had used historically to avoid facing the guilt and responsibility that were rightfully theirs. Anglos had known full well that the Indians were agricultural people as well as hunters; Indian agriculture had rescued the early colonists from starvation. Yet white politicians and historians had perpetuated the myth that the Indians had been merely hunters, whose inferior means of providing food had limited the population that could live on the land. Thus, they had excused the actions of white farmers who supposedly made fuller use of the land

15. Burton Spivak, *Jefferson's English Crisis: Commerce, Embargo, and the Republican Revolution* (Charlottesville, Va., 1979). Jefferson's willingness to go to war and his fading away from participation in embargo policy was reaffirmed in a fine article by Richard Mannix, "Gallatin, Jefferson, and the Embargo of 1808," *Diplomatic History*, 3, no. 2 (Spring 1979): 151–172. Reginald Stuart, however, saw Jefferson as a realistic, cautious pragmatist rather than a pacifist or liberal crusader (Reginald C. Stuart, *The Half-Way Pacifist: Thomas Jefferson's View of War* [Toronto, 1978]).

16. Dee Brown, *Bury My Heart at Wounded Knee* (New York, 1970).

17. Vine DeLoria, *Custer Died for Your Sins* (New York, 1969).

and imposed their "civilization" on the red man's "savagism." Whites had underestimated the size of the Indian population as well, which reinforced their justifications for appropriating the relatively "empty" continent. Modern historians now regarded these Anglo rationalizations as conscious distortions and had little patience with historical explanations that mitigated white guilt on the grounds that whites had been prisoners of the pervasive cultural assumptions of their time.[18] There were still a few rear-guard apologists for the Anglos, however, who used cultural assumptions as their defense. Francis Paul Prucha continued to publish prolifically. Bernard Sheehan defended this position ardently in a historiographical article on Indian-white relations although his book-length study of Jeffersonian philanthropy toward the Indians gave more stress to the baneful effects of the whites' benevolence.[19] Even historians like Sheehan who were willing to see Anglo policies and rationalizations as products of the culture and time rather than conscious genocide were offering less and less comfort to those who sought to mitigate white guilt, as demonstrated by a controversial book by Michael Rogin.

Rogin wrote a psychohistorical analysis of the assumptions of the Jacksonian era that underlay the policy of Indian removal. He concluded that they were pathological. Jackson and his generation felt enormous guilt, rage, and insecurity as the deferential, hierarchical society of the eighteenth century disintegrated and the heroism of the revolutionary Founding Fathers was replaced by the avaricious acquisitiveness of their land-grabbing progeny. The near-psychotic state of the Jacksonians required acts of heroism to prove they had not degenerated from the virtue of their forebears. War upon the Indians was the perfect answer. Jacksonians projected the illicit childhood desires they were trying to suppress in themselves onto the Indians. They saw the Indians as shiftless, sexually promiscuous, and undisciplined in their emotions, all childlike traits that members of the

18. Wilcomb E. Washburn, *The Indian in America* (New York, 1975); Wilcomb E. Washburn, *Red Man's Land/White Man's Law* (New York, 1971); Francis Jennings, *The Invasion of America: Indians, Colonialism, and the Cant of Conquest* (Chapel Hill, 1975); Reginald Horsman, *Expansion and American Indian Policy, 1783–1812* ([East Lansing, Mich.], 1967); Wilbur R. Jacobs, *Dispossessing the American Indian: Indians and Whites on the Colonial Frontier* (New York, 1972); and Wilbur R. Jacobs, "Native American History: How It Illuminates Our Past," *American Historical Review*, 80, no. 3 (June 1975): 595–609.

19. Bernard Sheehan, "Indian-White Relations in Early America: A Review Essay," *William and Mary Quarterly*, 3rd ser., 26 (April 1969): 267–286; and his *Seeds of Extinction: Jeffersonian Philanthropy and the American Indian* (Chapel Hill, 1973).

liberal competitive white society could not afford. So whites punished the Indians for these supposed sins of childhood just as they punished blacks for the adolescent sins of sexuality they also sought to reject in themselves. In the process of murdering or dispossessing the Indians, Jacksonians also could gain secure title to land, possession of which symbolized their independent manhood. Thus, those who regarded Andrew Jackson "as an acquisitive swindler—a confidence man— badly miss the point," Rogin said. "The more egregious the activity, the more he engaged in falsification of memory, denial, militant self-righteousness, and projection of his own motivations onto others." Jackson was no swindler. He was merely a murderous psychopath. That Jackson and the people he represented might be morally exempt from blame because they were insane victims of an insane liberal system might seem small comfort to those seeking mitigation for the guilt of the Anglo's ancestors.[20]

Despite the significant work being done on American Indians in this era and the general agreement that the history of white-Indian relations deserved more attention in the assessment of American history in general and American diplomacy in particular, the subject had less impact on the writing of American diplomatic history than one might have expected. Even revisionist texts and surveys that featured American expansionism passed over Indian diplomacy rather hastily.[21] And the whole idea of giving new attention to American expansionism seemed to have little effect on the authors of monographs dealing with most of the other traditional subjects of early American diplomacy. Thus, there was no great clash between revisionist and orthodox historians over the major incidents of early American foreign policy as there would be over the events of more modern policy.

Historians of the diplomacy of the Revolution, the Federalist era, the War of 1812, and the Monroe Doctrine carried on their work within the old orthodox framework. They contrasted the policies of France and England toward the new republic and assumed in the process that the United States was on the defensive in its relations with Europe rather than playing the aggressor. They still were asking

20. Michael Paul Rogin, *Fathers and Children: Andrew Jackson and the Subjugation of the American Indians* (New York, 1975), pp. 3–15, 125–138, 171–172, 190–191, 208, 212–215, 220, 246–247.
21. Arthur N. Gilbert, "The American Indian and United States Diplomatic History," *History Teacher*, 8 (February 1975): 229–241. His view is borne out in the texts of Gardner et al., *Creation of the American Empire*; and Paterson et al., *American Foreign Policy*.

whether Franklin or Jay, Jefferson or Hamilton, John Quincy Adams or James Monroe had had the more realistic program for dealing with America's powerful European adversaries. In most cases, the theses of their books were less significant than the new facts and minor correctives they turned up in their research. Sometimes these historians seemed to strain for originality, and their theses detracted from rather than added to their contribution.

One example was Cecil Currey's work on the diplomacy of the Revolution. Currey not only regarded the approaches of Jay and Adams as superior to Franklin's but accused Franklin of being a traitor, operating as a spy for the British and working against absolute independence for the United States in hopes of protecting his land speculations and other financial double-dealings. But Currey's accusations were based on guilt by association, circumstantial evidence, and tortuous reasoning. Most historians rejected his interpretation out of hand.[22]

A more trustworthy analysis of the diplomacy of the Revolution was William Stinchcombe's history of the Franco-American alliance. Stinchcombe's well-researched book was far less hostile to France and Franklin than Currey's, but he still noted considerable French skullduggery in that nation's relations with the United States and emphasized the conflicts of interest between the two allies.[23] James Hutson's work, *John Adams and the Diplomacy of the American Revolution*, acknowledged conflicts of interest between France and America and thought it fortunate that Adams and Jay had reinforced Franklin's original inclination to negotiate unilaterally. But Hutson saw John Adams's suspicions of Benjamin Franklin and France, which Cecil Currey took seriously, as near-paranoid.

Hutson, borrowing from the work of revolutionary historians like Bernard Bailyn and Gordon Wood, asserted that the paranoia of Adams was simply an exaggerated form of the suspiciousness characterizing Republican thought in that era. This distrust derived in large part from the early British reformers, the Commonwealthmen of the

22. Cecil B. Currey, *Code Number 72: Ben Franklin: Patriot or Spy?* (Englewood Cliffs, N.J., 1972). For a critical review, see Richard B. Morris in *American Historical Review*, 79, no. 2 (April 1974): 573–574. See also David Schoenbrun's unfootnoted defense of Franklin against Currey, *Triumph in Paris: The Exploits of Benjamin Franklin* (New York, 1976). The recent revelation that Currey was the true author of a book critical of the army that had supposedly been written by an anonymous high-ranking officer who had served in Vietnam cast further doubt on his accuracy with regard to Franklin.

23. William C. Stinchcombe, *The American Revolution and the French Alliance* (Syracuse, 1969).

seventeenth century, who had so influenced the ideology of the American Revolution. Hutson argued that this Republican suspiciousness had led early American diplomats to accept a very traditional and conservative outlook on diplomacy, counting on the balance of power to restrain the unbridled and nefarious pursuit of self-interest they assumed motivated all nations. Thus, Hutson contradicted Felix Gilbert's earlier influential assertions that the American revolutionaries had abandoned balance-of-power politics in favor of an idealistic reliance upon free trade to maintain peace between America and Europe. Hutson's book was provocative and his indictment of Adams's paranoid style was convincing, but his insistence that Adams's suspiciousness was shared by most American leaders, that these leaders single-mindedly pursued a balance of power, and that they gave no adherence whatever to the philosophes' praise for the peace-keeping potential of free trade, was another example of stretching a thesis too far in search of originality.[24]

Frederick Marks's *Independence on Trial* was also a valuable work, which pulled together the strands of the diplomacy of the Confederation era. But he pushed the self-evident thesis that the weakness of American diplomacy in this period had been one of the most important reasons for the writing and the ratification of the Constitution so hard that it intruded on the usefulness of the volume.[25] Similarly, Charles Ritcheson's thorough examination of British policy toward the United States in the period following the Revolution was flawed by his insistence that the British had almost always been justified in their policies whereas any American reaction had almost always been wrong-headed.[26] J. Leitch Wright provided some corrective to this Anglophilia by narrating the hostile actions of Britain's agents on the frontier, which had encouraged the Indians against the United States.[27]

24. James H. Hutson, *John Adams and the Diplomacy of the American Revolution* ([Lexington, Ky.], 1980). A good survey of the diplomacy of the Revolution was also contained in Lawrence S. Kaplan, *Colonies into Nation: American Diplomacy, 1763–1801* (New York, 1972), which noted that the origins of American diplomacy could actually be found before the Revolution in the work of the colonial agents—lobbyists sent to Parliament on behalf of the various colonial legislatures.
25. Frederick W. Marks III, *Independence on Trial: Foreign Affairs and the Making of the Constitution* (Baton Rouge, 1973).
26. Charles R. Ritcheson, *Aftermath of Revolution: British Policy Toward the United States, 1783–1795* (Dallas, 1969).
27. Of course, in doing this, Wright was operating under the increasingly unpopular assumption that the United States had the right to settle

Albert Bowman analyzed French policy toward the United States in much the same way that Ritcheson had done for the British. He provided excellent information from the French archives but exhibited an excessive favoritism toward French policies. He even went so far as to portray Talleyrand as something of a pro-American hero.[28] Alexander DeConde's study of the Quasi-War with France, which also had relied upon the French archives, had already demonstrated Bowman's main point, that after the XYZ affair had backfired, Talleyrand had tried to moderate French policy toward the United States and avoid war. But Bowman had gone too far in saying that Talleyrand was actually friendly to the United States and had sought a reasonable accommodation from the outset of the dispute over the Jay Treaty.[29]

Analyses of the American side of the diplomacy of the Federalist era seemed to be a bit more eclectic and less partisan than did analyses of the policies of America's adversaries. Specialists on the period generally found it difficult to impose a straight nationalist, realist, or revisionist view on the complexity of statements and actions of the Founding Fathers. No significant revisionist studies except Eblen's book on territorial government even made the attempt.[30] However, the influence of Vietnam and the revisionists did bring orthodox historians to acknowledge the pervasiveness of expansionism somewhat more overtly than had previous authors.

Historians assessing the period from the realist perspective also undercut the clear dichotomy between the realism credited to Hamilton and the Federalists and denied to Jefferson, Madison, and the Republicans. Lawrence Kaplan and Jerald Combs noted considerable realism on the part of Jefferson, though they thought it checked by

---

the western territories and the British had been wrong to help the Indians to resist (J. Leitch Wright, Jr., *Britain and the American Frontier, 1783–1815* [Athens, Ga., 1975]).

28. Albert Hall Bowman, *The Struggle for Neutrality: Franco-American Diplomacy During the Federalist Era* (Knoxville, Tenn., 1974), esp. pp. 228–435.

29. Alexander DeConde, *The Quasi-War: The Politics and Diplomacy of the Undeclared War with France, 1797–1801* (New York, 1966). William C. Stinchcombe convincingly refuted Bowman in a review published in the *William and Mary Quarterly*, 32, no. 1 (January 1975): 158–160. See also William C. Stinchcombe, "Talleyrand and the American Negotiations of 1797–1798," *Journal of American History*, 62, no. 3 (December 1975): 575–590.

30. Burton I. Kaufman did contribute a short article arguing rather unconvincingly that the primary thrust of Washington's farewell address was expansionism rather than nonentanglement; See his "Washington's Farewell Address: A Statement of Empire," in Burton I. Kaufman, ed., *Washington's Farewell Address: The View from the 20th Century* (Chicago, 1969), pp. 169–187.

Jefferson's obsessive partisan distrust of supposed Federalist monarchism, his idealistic attachment to pure agrarianism, his excessive fear of England, and his exaggerated notion of the beneficence of French policy toward the United States.[31] While historians were finding at least some measure of realism mixed with Jefferson's idealism, they were finding some unrealistic and romantic imperial notions mixed with Hamilton's realism.[32] This romanticism seemed especially evident during the Quasi-War with France, when Hamilton maneuvered to gain control of a substantial American army and to use it to take Spanish territory in Florida and Louisiana.[33] In the face of Hamilton's

31. Lawrence S. Kaplan, *Jefferson and France: An Essay on Politics and Political Ideas* (New Haven, 1967); and his *Colonies into Nation*. See also his "Thomas Jefferson: The Idealist as Realist," in Merli and Wilson, *Makers of American Diplomacy*, I, 53–79; and Jerald A. Combs, *The Jay Treaty: Political Battleground of the Founding Fathers* (Berkeley, 1970). Kaplan and Combs also represented two different approaches to another minor historiographical dispute. Kaplan argued that foreign policy toward Britain and France had been the major cause of the split between Hamilton and Jefferson, Republican and Federalist. Combs maintained that the foreign policy dispute reinforced and dramatized a split already apparent in the higher echelons of American politics.

32. See Combs, *Jay Treaty*.

33. All historians agreed that Hamilton had had such imperial plans, but they disagreed as to the extent of territory he had sought and the lengths to which he had been willing to go to get it. Gerald Stourzh thought that Hamilton's imperial vision had extended only east of the Mississippi (i.e., Florida and New Orleans) and had looked to sea power and Europe for the major source of American power. Thus, Stourzh said, Hamilton had always thought of himself as facing eastward when viewing a map of the United States, for he spoke of Canada as being on the left and Florida on the right of the United States. So Stourzh considered Hamilton's objections to the Louisiana Purchase as sincere ones rather than mere partisan opposition to a measure he would have been happy to have consummated if he had had the chance (Gerald Stourzh, *Alexander Hamilton and the Idea of Republican Government* [Stanford, 1970]). Stourzh found little support from other specialists in the field, who assumed Hamilton would have taken whatever he could have gotten, east or west of the Mississippi. See esp. Gilbert Lycan, *Alexander Hamilton and American Foreign Policy: A Design for Greatness* (Norman, Okla., 1970). Lycan's book was very uncritical of Hamilton, as was Helene Johnson Looze, *Alexander Hamilton and the British Orientation of American Foreign Policy, 1783–1803* (The Hague, 1969).

Historians also debated whether Hamilton actively sought war with France like many of his political allies or if he sincerely wanted peace and looked to conquest only if efforts for peace failed. Lycan thought Hamilton sincerely wanted peace, but most historians thought he wanted war, and some thought even Hamilton's support of the first peace mission to France before the XYZ affair was only a maneuver to throw blame on the French. See the previously mentioned books by Bowman, DeConde, Stourzh, and esp. Richard H. Kohn, *Eagle and Sword: The Federalists and the Creation of the Military Establishment in America, 1783–1802* (New York, 1975).

ambitions, Adams's successful maintenance of peace was now unanimously praised by historians. But, in contrast to the previous era, most accepted the idea of Stephen Kurtz that Adams made peace in the expectation that this would help rather than hurt his chances for reelection.[34]

What united all of these historians was the assumption that those Americans who had sought peace were correct and those who risked war were wrong. Thus, most praised the Jay Treaty. Those like Bowman and DeConde who denounced it did so not merely because they thought that America could have had peace and a better bargain without subservience to Britain but also because the deal the Federalists made had risked war with France. Nevertheless, all took the realist approach that some firmness and military preparation were essential to federal America.

Accounts of the diplomacy leading to the War of 1812 also emphasized the wisdom of compromise and of avoiding war. The works of Bradford Perkins and Reginald Horsman remained the standard analyses. Most historians still considered the war unwise although all but a few revisionists and Burton Spivak thought it morally justified. Historians still accepted the idea that divisions on the war were essentially partisan rather than sectional. The Republicans were at fault for not compromising to avoid war and for declaring war without adequate military preparation. However, significant new biographies, of Thomas Jefferson by Merrill Peterson, of James Madison by Ralph Ketcham, and of James Monroe by Harry Ammon, presented the Republican view with a bit more sympathy than it had been accorded in the previous era.[35]

The Monroe Doctrine would seem to have been a natural subject for a revisionist monographic treatment elaborating the role of aggres-

34. See, e.g., Clarfield, *Timothy Pickering and American Diplomacy*. Clarfield agreed with Stephen Kurtz, DeConde, Kohn, and Bowman that Adams had thought American opinion was turning against the war. Ralph Adams Brown, *The Presidency of John Adams* (Lawrence, Kans., 1975), agreed with earlier historians that Adams had known his decision for peace would hurt his popularity and destroy his political career.

35. See Marshall Smelser's volume for the New American Nation Series, *The Democratic Republic, 1801–1815* (New York, 1968). Merrill D. Peterson, *Thomas Jefferson and the New Nation* (New York, 1970); Ralph Ketcham, *James Madison* (New York, 1971); and Harry Ammon, *James Monroe: The Quest for National Identity* (New York, 1971). Victor A. Sapio, *Pennsylvania and the War of 1812* (Lexington, Ky., 1970), was quite unsympathetic to the Republicans, and his research supported the conclusions of Bradford Perkins.

sive expansionism in early American diplomacy. But such studies did not materialize. Instead, Ernest May followed his own historiographical advice and examined the domestic and bureaucratic context in which the doctrine had been formulated. He found that partisan politics rather than an economic push for foreign markets or territory was the primary determinant of the respective positions Monroe, Adams, Calhoun, Jefferson, and Madison had taken toward the British offer of a joint policy toward Latin America and the Holy Alliance. May rejected the idea that the positions of these leaders for or against the British offer could have been determined by abstract principles of diplomacy. All of them had vacillated from time to time in their attitudes toward foreign alliances. May also denied that the foreign situation had called forth their responses since he claimed that all had recognized the supposed threat of the Holy Alliance to reconquer the Spanish-American colonies as an empty one, and all had understood that Canning himself had lost interest in joint action, which rendered the question of alliance moot.

Dismissing these considerations with more certainty than perhaps was justified, May decided that only domestic considerations could have determined the positions these rivals had taken. May argued that John Quincy Adams's presidential candidacy would have been hurt by consummation of a British alliance since the British were thoroughly unpopular among the American electorate. As secretary of state, Adams would have been blamed for joining the British even if he had been an opponent of the alliance in private cabinet discussions. Thus, Jefferson and Madison, who favored Crawford over Adams for the presidency, and Calhoun, who favored himself, pushed for acceptance of the British offer knowing Adams would be blamed for it. Adams naturally resisted, and Monroe, whose primary goal was to leave the presidency with his reputation intact, gave in to Adams to avoid a fight that might tarnish his record.

The Greek Revolution also posed a partisan dilemma for Adams. If the United States recognized the independence of Greece, Edward Everett would have been the natural candidate as first American minister to the new nation. Everett was a Federalist, a very unpopular thing to be in 1823. If Adams appointed him, the electorate would be reminded of Adams's early Federalist attachments, and he would lose votes. If he did not appoint Everett, his New England constituents would be offended. Either way Adams would lose. So May concluded that Adams opposed mention of Greece in Monroe's speech not as a consistent adherent of the two-spheres approach but as a clever presidential candidate.[36]

May's argument dismissed the foreign policy factors in the decision for the Monroe Doctrine too casually. Historians with access to foreign archives and hindsight might agree that the threat from the Holy Alliance had been nil. But Harry Ammon, Monroe's biographer, pointed out that Monroe and all of his advisers except Adams seemed to take it quite seriously. Ammon's analysis of the characters of Monroe and Adams and of the domestic political relationships between the participants in the Monroe Doctrine decision led him to find May's argument unconvincing.[37]

May's book, the only significant one centered on the Monroe Doctrine in this era, may have ignored the theme of expansionism, but that theme was inevitably prominent in the historical monographs dealing with the age of Manifest Destiny, and most of them bore the imprints of disillusionment with Vietnam. Seymour Connor, Odie Faulk, and William Goetzmann resisted the trend and harkened back to Justin Smith in their analyses of the Mexican War, but they were decidedly in the minority.[38] The most critical account of the coming of the war was that of Glenn Price, who revived the charges of Richard Stenberg, that Polk had plotted to provoke Mexico into war from the beginning of his administration. Accepting in full the account of Anson Jones which had been questioned by most historians, Price assumed that Polk's agents in Texas had been ordered directly by Polk to stir up a war with Mexico that could be used as an excuse to take California. According to Price, these provocative activities indicated the true attitude of the American administration whereas any peaceful negotiations or statements deploring war were hypocritical smoke screens.[39]

The authors of the two best-researched and most complete histories of the coming of the Mexican War, Charles Grier Sellers and David

---

36. Ernest May, *The Making of the Monroe Doctrine* (Cambridge, Mass., 1975).

37. Harry Ammon, "The Monroe Doctrine: Domestic Politics or National Decision?" *Diplomatic History*, 5, no. 1 (Winter 1981): 53–70, with a response from Ernest May, *ibid.*, pp. 71–73.

38. Seymour V. Connor and Odie B. Faulk, *North America Divided: The Mexican War, 1846–1848* (New York, 1971); and William H. Goetzmann, *When the Eagle Screamed: The Romantic Horizon in American Diplomacy, 1800–1860* (New York, 1966).

39. Glenn W. Price, *Origins of the War with Mexico: The Polk-Stockton Intrigue* (Austin, 1967).

Pletcher, did not accept this plot thesis. They thought Polk would have prepared the army better, would not have made confidential predictions that war was unlikely, and especially would have avoided bringing the Oregon dispute to a crisis if he had sought to provoke a war with Mexico from the outset of his presidency. Still, the analyses of Polk's diplomacy and Manifest Destiny by Sellers and Pletcher were only slightly less condemnatory than that of Price. Polk might have wanted peace but only if Mexico and Great Britain made major concessions. Polk's policy was less consistent and more improvised than adherents of the plot thesis might grant, but it was still based on a belief that an aggressive hard line was the only way to deal successfully with contemptible Mexicans and haughty British.

Thus, Polk had been defiant, blustering, uncompromising, and patronizing throughout his diplomatic maneuvers. He had hoped to pressure Britain into offering an acceptable settlement on Oregon and to frighten and bribe Mexico into selling California. Both Sellers and Pletcher thought Polk had risked war unnecessarily with Britain over Oregon although Sellers believed that Polk's pressure tactics had been profitable for a brief period following British rejection of Polk's initial offer for a border at 49 degrees latitude. Sellers and Pletcher both agreed that Polk had not wanted war with Mexico but that he had been willing to fight rather than lose California. Both thought that the war had been unnecessary and reprehensible and that California would have come into the Union voluntarily later on. They differed only in their estimates of when Polk decided to abandon pressure tactics for war. Sellers believed that Polk had decided firmly on hostilities as soon as it was clear that Slidell would not be received, and Pletcher claimed that Polk had improvised for a few weeks longer.[40] In any case, the contention that Polk had not planned war from the beginning of his administration did little to mitigate the grasping, conniving rapaciousness of Polk and the United States as portrayed by Sellers and Pletcher. And although neither Sellers nor Pletcher had

40. Thus, Sellers thought that Polk had not made the purchase of California an ultimatum in his instructions to Slidell only because it was an instant of great tension with Britain over Oregon and that as soon as it became apparent that Slidell would not succeed, Polk had decided for war. Pletcher, on the other hand, said that Polk's later instructions to Slidell to raise the offer for California from $25 million to $40 million showed that Polk was still hoping to acquire California by means other than war at that time (Charles Sellers, *James K. Polk: Continentalist, 1843–1846* [Princeton, 1966], esp. pp. 331–338, 244–258; and David M. Pletcher, *The Diplomacy of Annexation: Texas, Oregon, and the Mexican War* [Columbia, Mo., 1973], esp. pp. 290, 591–592).

access to the Mexican archives, their accounts were so ably researched and well presented that they seemed destined to be the standard versions for some time to come.

About the only bright spot most historians saw in the era of Manifest Destiny was the Whig opposition to aggressive expansionism. Not only had the Whigs opposed the Mexican War and "54°40' or fight," but they had dampened other quarrels with the British in the Webster-Ashburton Treaty of 1842.[41] Frederick Merk reiterated this in opposition to the revisionist critics who considered aggressive expansionism the dominant passion of all Americans, and he found agreement from Pletcher and others.[42] Yet it was clear even from accounts praising the Whigs that the Whigs were not truly antiexpansionist. They simply thought the United States could peacefully absorb the relatively empty territories of the West by waiting for the indigenous population, increasingly dominated by immigrants from the United States, to request annexation as had happened in Texas.[43]

The growing interest in expansionism also somewhat touched the histories of the diplomacy of the Civil War. Its focus was Secretary of State William Seward, long recognized as a territorial expansionist but now pinpointed as the harbinger of the search for commercial hegemony and the "new imperialism" of the 1890s. Ernest Paolino, a student of Lloyd Gardner, accentuated this theme although he conceded that Seward would have been uncomfortable with the militarism and racism of the imperialists of the 1890s. Paolino also had to admit that none of the major figures of the 1890s seemed aware of Seward's prophetic visions. Thus, they were "unconscious Sewardites."[44] Given Seward's expansionism, Paolino did not think that the

41. For an excellent account, see Howard Jones, *To the Webster-Ashburton Treaty: A Study in Anglo-American Relations, 1783–1843* (Chapel Hill, 1977).

42. See Frederick Merk, *Fruits of Propaganda in the Tyler Administration* (Cambridge, Mass., 1971); Frederick Merk, *The Monroe Doctrine and American Expansionism, 1843–1849* (New York, 1966); and Pletcher, *Diplomacy of Annexation*, p. 65. See also John H. Schroeder, *Mr. Polk's War: American Opposition and Dissent, 1846–1848* (Madison, Wis., 1973).

43. Donald Spencer argued that the feverish interventionist spirit stirred by the pleas for help from Louis Kossuth and the rebels against the Austrian Empire infected Whigs as well as Democrats. Spencer said that the division between realistic restraint and emotional interventionism in the United States in the 1840s was between a realistic South and a crusading North, not between parties (Donald S. Spencer, *Louis Kossuth and Young America* [Columbia, Mo., 1977]).

44. Ernest N. Paolino, *The Foundation of the American Empire: William Henry Seward and U.S. Foreign Policy* (Ithaca, 1973), pp. 36–40, 211. The standard biogra-

secretary's proposal to Lincoln to reunite Confederacy and Union by challenging the great powers was quite such an aberration as it had seemed to historians for so many years. In this contention Paolino found considerable support, including that of the most recent and influential orthodox survey of Civil War diplomacy, D. P. Crook's *The North, the South, and the Powers, 1861–1865.*[45] Yet even for revisionists, expansionism remained a minor theme of Civil War diplomacy. All historians saw clearly that North and South were obsessed by the war itself and that European intervention in that war was the primary concern of both sides. Lynn Case and Warren Spencer contributed an extensive and virtually definitive study of France's policies toward the war but concluded that Great Britain was still the key determinant in Europe's ultimate abstention since Napoleon III had been unwilling to move without Britain leading the way.[46] Thus, Britain remained the focus for most studies of Civil War diplomacy. Historians of British policy almost all sought to revise what they thought had been an excessive emphasis on British sympathy for the North on the part of those writing in the previous era. Kenneth Bourne wrote that the trend was better characterized as a decline in enmity between Britain and the United States than as a rise in friendship.[47] D. P. Crook agreed, saying that Britain operated from cynical self-regard and moral hesitations, not lofty and generous statesmanship. "Only the rhetoric of historians who wrote during the Great Rapprochement of 1895–1930, and the wishful thinking of apostles of Atlantic unity since, have obscured that fact," he concluded.[48]

---

phy of Seward, Glyndon G. Van Deusen's *William Henry Seward* (New York, 1967), did not have this same focus on Seward's overseas ambitions, concentrating instead on his territorial expansionism.

45. D. P. Crook, *The North, the South, and the Powers, 1861–1865* (New York, 1974). Crook's emphasis on expansionism resembled that of Richard Van Alstyne rather than that of the Wisconsin school.

46. Lynn M. Case and Warren F. Spencer, *The United States and France: Civil War Diplomacy* (Philadelphia, 1970).

47. Kenneth Bourne, *Britain and the Balance of Power in North America 1815–1908* (London, 1967).

48. Crook, *The North, the South, and the Powers,* pp. v, 371. Crook condensed this book for the America in Crisis Series, and in doing so, he took some of the edge off his assertions in this regard (D. P. Crook, *Diplomacy During the American Civil War* [New York, 1975]). A similar emphasis is found in Joseph M. Hernon, Jr., "British Sympathies in the American Civil War: A Reconsideration," *Journal of Southern History,* 33 (1967): 356–367. See also Brian Jenkins, *Britain and the War for the Union,* I (Montreal, 1974); Norman B. Ferris, *Desperate Diplomacy: William H. Seward's Foreign Policy, 1861* (Knoxville, Tenn., 1976); and Adrian Cook, *The Alabama Claims: American Politics and Anglo-American Relations, 1865–1872* (Ithaca, 1975).

This portrayal of British hostility reappeared in some of the special studies of Civil War diplomacy. Frank Merli noted Britain's indifference and self-interest in its policies toward the building of ships for the Confederacy in England.[49] Mary Ellison studied the Lancashire proletariat and discovered that, contrary to legend, the cotton mill workers had not sympathized with the antislavery North.They had not helped to restrain the British cabinet from recognizing the Confederate government. In fact, British workers had sympathized with the Confederates and used what influence they had to promote a defiance of the Union blockade and restoration of the cotton trade with the South.[50] Stuart Bernath placed more of the blame for rocky Anglo-American relations with the United States because British blockade runners were captured and prosecuted without much regard for the niceties of international law.[51]

Yet overall there was an attempt to restore some sense of the delicate balance between hostility and mutual need in Anglo-American relations. This countered the excessively halcyon view that had been promulgated by historians of the World War II era who were impressed by the growth of the Anglo-American alliance in their own time. This concern for Anglo-American rivalry would be a substantial theme for historians of later American diplomacy as well. But the central factor in the historiography of later American foreign policy would still be the conflict between the orthodox and revisionist views.

49. Frank J. Merli, *Great Britain and the Confederate Navy, 1861–1865* (Bloomington, Ind., 1970).

50. Mary L. Ellison, *Support for Secession: Lancashire and the American Civil War* (Chicago, 1971).

51. Stuart L. Bernath, *Squall Across the Atlantic: American Civil War Prize Cases and Diplomacy* (Berkeley, 1970).

TWENTY ONE

The Impact of Vietnam on the Historiography of Later American Diplomacy

One of the most intense debates between revisionist and orthodox historians was over the nature and extent of American imperialism in the latter part of the nineteenth century. Orthodox historians castigated the revisionists for exaggerating the degree to which fear of industrial overproductivity and the desire for overseas markets influenced late nineteenth-century American foreign policy. After all, orthodox historians pointed out, the vast majority of American exports at this time were agricultural not industrial. William Appleman Williams responded by collecting a great number of instances in which farmers who produced these agricultural exports had agitated for foreign policies that would expand the markets for their surpluses.[1]

Orthodox historians also protested that revisionist historians were distorting American motivations when they argued that American tariff policy in the post-Civil War era had been motivated primarily by a desire for overseas expansion and economic hegemony. Paul Holbo wrote that Cleveland and the Democrats had sought lower tariffs in response to Democratic party tradition and the pressure of consumers, not the eastern industrialists' demand for foreign markets.

1. William Appleman Williams, *The Roots of the Modern American Empire: A Study of the Growth and Shaping of a Social Consciousness in a Marketplace Society* (New York, 1969).

McKinley's demand for a high tariff, on the other hand, obviously gave a higher priority to the home market than to the opening of foreign ones, Holbo continued. Answering for the revisionists, Tom Terrill recalled that McKinley had pressured for reciprocity agreements in order to compensate for the dampening effect of a high tariff on American exports. Terrill also insisted that Cleveland had remained a strong economic expansionist even while opposing territorial imperialism. This distinction was critical, Terrill maintained, for economic expansionism had persisted in American policy while territorial imperialism had faded, and it was economic expansionism that so tragically had led America to oppose revolutionary change in the twentieth century.[2]

Paul Varg and Marilyn Blatt Young showed that the China market, which supposedly had inspired American business to expand into the Far East, had been more myth than substance and that businessmen had not been truly aggressive in pursuing what economic opportunities it had to offer.[3] But Thomas McCormick countered that it was what Americans believed about the China market rather than what really existed that motivated policy and that the smallest amount of exports could be critical to the prosperity of particular businesses or even to the whole economy.[4]

Critics of the revisionists found this economic emphasis too simplistic and overdrawn and insisted that other less reprehensible factors such as benevolent missionary concerns, the fashionable cult of imperialism sweeping Europe, and the advancement of communications technology also had influenced the rise of American imperialism.[5] Yet these suggestions were offered as mere mitigations for what all seemed to agree was at least a tragic error if not a calculated and inevitable product of capitalism. Even orthodox historians accepted the economic drive for markets as more important than their colleagues in the pre-

2. Paul S. Holbo, "Economics, Emotion, and Expansion: An Emerging Foreign Policy," in H. Wayne Morgan, ed., *The Gilded Age*, rev. ed. (Syracuse, 1970); and Tom E. Terrill, *The Tariff, Politics, and American Foreign Policy, 1874–1901* (Westport, Conn., 1973).

3. Paul A. Varg, *The Making of a Myth: The United States and China, 1879–1912* ([East Lansing, Mich.], 1968); and Marilyn Blatt Young, *The Rhetoric of Empire: American China Policy, 1895–1901* (Cambridge, Mass., 1968). A previous article by Young encapsulating the thesis of her book appeared in Barton Bernstein's collection of revisionist essays, *Towards a New Past*, but she was clearly outside the revisionist consensus and more akin to the critical realists.

4. Thomas J. McCormick, *China Market: America's Quest for Informal Empire, 1893–1901* (Chicago, 1967).

5. Ernest R. May, *American Imperialism: A Speculative Essay* (New York, 1968).

vious era had been willing to allow. They also gave more attention to the inextricable mix of benevolent missionary concerns with racism and a smug sense of cultural superiority, a mix which caused such benevolence to serve both its objects and the United States rather ill in the end.[6]

The significance of economics for American foreign policy found further illustration in studies of the shaping of America's professional diplomatic corps during the Age of Imperialism. The concern for American business interests among professional diplomats emerged clearly in the studies of Richard Hume Werking and Richard Schulzinger.[7] The alliance between business interests and American foreign policy also was stressed in the revisionist studies of Wilsonian and inter-war diplomacy by such so-called "corporatist" historians as Carl Parrini, Joan Hoff Wilson, Burton Kaufman, and Michael Hogan. Orthodox historians had seen a stark contrast between Wilsonian internationalism and the isolationism of his Republican successors who had rejected the League of Nations, frustrated international trade with a high tariff, and disrupted the international economy by refusing to forgive Allied war debts. The revisionists, on the other hand, saw a basic continuity in the economic diplomacy of Wilson, Harding, Coolidge, and Hoover. All had shared a dedication to a liberal, capitalist, Open Door international economy, all had denounced socialism, and all had sacrificed democratic values to the search for order. The Republicans simply had relied more than Wilson on private corporations to enhance American interests abroad.[8]

6. The best surveys of late nineteenth-century imperialism are Milton Plesur, *America's Outward Thrust: Approaches to Foreign Affairs, 1865–1890* (De Kalb, Ill., 1971); Charles S. Campbell, Jr., *The Transformation of American Foreign Relations, 1865–1900* (New York, 1976); David Healy, *U.S. Expansionism: The Imperialist Urge in the 1890s* (Madison, Wis., 1970); and Robert L. Beisner, *From the Old Diplomacy to the New, 1865–1900* (New York, 1975), from which my own discussion of the historiography of this period has borrowed heavily. For good bibliographical and historiographical analyses see, in addition to Beisner, two articles in the *American Historical Review*: Richard N. Abrams, "United States Intervention Abroad," *American Historical Review*, 79, no. 1 (February 1974): 72–102; and James A. Field, Jr., "American Imperialism: The Worst Chapter in Almost Any Book," *American Historical Review*, 83, no. 3 (June 1978): 644–683, which includes responses by Walter LaFeber and Robert L. Beisner.

7. Richard Hume Werking, *The Master Architects: Building the United States Foreign Service, 1890–1913* (Lexington, Ky., 1977); and Richard D. Schulzinger, *The Making of the Diplomatic Mind: The Training, Outlook, and Style of the United States Foreign Officers, 1908–1931* (Middletown, Conn., 1975).

8. Carl Parrini, *Heir to Empire: United States Economic Diplomacy, 1916–1923* ([Pittsburgh], 1969); Joan Hoff Wilson, *American Business and Foreign Policy, 1920–1933* (Lexington, Ky., 1971); and Burton I. Kaufman, *Efficiency and Expansion: Foreign*

In concentrating on America's economic foreign policy, all these revisionists except Hogan emphasized the degree of Anglo-American rivalry that existed between 1900 and the 1930s, just as Gabriel Kolko had done in his study of World War II. Edward Crapol went so far as to argue that the period of the Great Rapprochement was actually an era of general and increasing rage against England.[9] Orthodox historians who emphasized the political and strategic aspects of American diplomacy, in which Anglo-American interests were more congruent, did not make so much of the differences and antagonisms between Britain and the United States. Still they acknowledged considerable contention in that relationship and were less enamored of the growing Anglo-American collaboration than had been historians writing in the Age of Munich. Bradford Perkins, who wrote the widest-ranging history of the Great Rapprochement, still stressed the growing friendship rather than the points of contention and found little to criticize in that friendship.[10] But Charles Campbell's judicious orthodox summary of the period for the New American Nation Series noted a tenuous and "hothouse" quality about the Rapprochement. He thought the United States had been overeffusive in its friendship for Britain in this period, as well as in its imitation of British imperialism. Greater moderation in the pursuit of both might have served America better.[11]

Another distinction between orthodox and revisionist historians was the degree of calculation or accident they saw in America's march to empire. This disagreement showed up most clearly in their contrasting interpretations of the Spanish-American War. Revisionists insisted that the war was a contrived step in America's search for foreign markets. Like LaFeber they attributed much to the role of business in

---

Trade Organization in the Wilson Administration, 1913–1921 (Westport, Conn., 1974); Michael J. Hogan, Informal Entente: the Private Structure of Cooperation in Anglo-American Economic Diplomacy, 1918–1928 (Columbia, Mo., 1977).

9. Edward P. Crapol, America for Americans: Economic Nationalism and Anglophobia in the Late Nineteenth Century (Westport, Conn., 1973).

10. Bradford Perkins, The Great Rapprochement: England and the United States, 1895–1914 (New York, 1968).

11. Campbell, Transformation of American Foreign Relations, p. 337; and Charles S. Campbell, "Anglo-American Relations, 1897–1901," in Paolo E. Coletta, ed., Threshold to American Internationalism: Essays on the Foreign Policies of William McKinley (New York, 1970). See also Charles S. Campbell, From Revolution to Rapprochement: The United States and Great Britain, 1783–1900 (New York, 1974). For agreement with Campbell, see Beisner, From the Old Diplomacy to the New, p. 126; see also ibid., p. 145, for Beisner's agreement with an earlier work conveying the same message—Lionel M. Gelber's The Rise of Anglo-American Friendship: A Study in World Politics, 1898–1906 (London, 1938).

pushing McKinley to declare war, and they argued that McKinley had intended to make it a war of conquest from the outset.[12] Philip Foner produced the most elaborate radical revisionist analysis of the coming of the war although it was not clear whether most revisionists were willing to accept all of the startling challenges he made to the traditional historiography of this event.

Foner argued that the Cuban rebels never had wanted U.S. intervention. They were already winning and needed nothing but American recognition of their belligerency, permitting them to obtain arms in the United States. McKinley had intervened against the will of the Cubans, seeking not to help them but to expand the American Empire. That was why McKinley's ultimatum to Spain had contained no demand for Cuban independence. McKinley intended to annex Cuba, his public statements to the contrary notwithstanding. He and Woodford had corresponded privately with enthusiasm about the prospect of annexation, and, at a minimum, McKinley was determined to prevent the rise of a radical government in Cuba. In addition, the war gave McKinley the opportunity to expand the American Empire in the Pacific. The plans to attack the Spanish fleet in Manila and the rapid occupation of the area following Dewey's victory proved this to Foner's satisfaction. McKinley had not resisted war but had merely stalled a while to prepare the military. Then he had sent the battleship *Maine* to Cuba with the intention of provoking an incident. Thus, he had embarked on an imperialist war on behalf of monopoly capitalism and its drive for markets.[13]

Foner studied the Cuban side of the Spanish-American War more thoroughly than most historians, but the evidence he produced for his assertion that the rebels had opposed American intervention was very thin, and no other significant histories of the war accepted it. Orthodox historians especially refused to believe that the conflict had begun as an American war for conquest.[14] They claimed McKinley

12. See McCormick, *China Market*, pp. 107–108; and William J. Pomeroy, *American Neo-Colonialism: Its Emergence in the Philippines and Asia* (New York, 1970), p. 32. See also the textbooks expounding the revisionist view, Gardner, LaFeber, and McCormick, *Creation of the American Empire*; and Paterson, Clifford, and Hagan, *American Foreign Policy*.

13. Philip S. Foner, *The Spanish-Cuban-American War and the Birth of American Imperialism, 1895–1902*, 2 vols. (New York, 1972), I, 168, 183–184, 216–229, 241–251, 305–310.

14. See the historiographical discussion in Gören Rysted, *Ambiguous Imperialism: American Foreign Policy and Domestic Politics at the Turn of the Century* (Stockholm, 1974), p. 18.

had been sympathetic to the rebels and had purposefully sought Cuban independence. Contrary to Foner's assertion, McKinley had told Woodford that Cuban independence was required, and Charles Campbell said the failure to make that clearer to Spain was the result of McKinley's ineptitude rather than calculation. McKinley had not rejected Spain's concessions in search of an excuse to start a war for empire. Campbell and Robert Beisner also rejected revisionist claims that McKinley had decided to occupy the Philippines even before news of Dewey's victory, thereby revealing the president's true motivations. The Philippines had come to the United States as a consequence of the war; the war had not come as a consequence of American desire for the Philippines.[15]

Thus, orthodox historians placed more responsibility upon the war itself for spurring subsequent American imperialism than did the revisionists, who saw the war as more of a way station in what was already a constant and inevitable march toward overseas expansion. Although orthodox historians like Campbell and Beisner did not consider the acquisition of colonies after the Spanish-American War to be entirely accidental or a temporary "aberration," they tended to emphasize the complexity of the situation, the variety of motives, the differing levels of intensity in those motives, and the presence of dissent in the rise of American imperialism.

Meanwhile, the revisionists insisted upon the persistence of imperialism throughout America's history and the unity of assumptions and institutions that lay behind it. Thus, a moderate revisionist, Kenneth Hagan, pointed out the continuity between gunboat interventions abroad prior to the 1890s and later imperial ventures.[16] Orthodox historian James Field, on the other hand, stressed the limited nature of American interests and intervention in the Mediterranean in the period before 1882.[17] Revisionists also tended to downplay the signifi-

15. Campbell, *Transformation of American Foreign Relations*, pp. 260–261, 268–273, 284–285; and Beisner, *From the Old Diplomacy to the New*, pp. 112–113, 118–119. See also Gerald F. Linderman, *The Mirror of War: American Society and the Spanish-American War* (Ann Arbor, 1974), pp. 9–36. Linderman also believed that the forces creating the Spanish-American War were less the first proclamation of twentieth-century capitalism than the twilight expressions of a disappearing nineteenth century. The rhetoric of the war appealed to the old localist consensus based on elemental, unambiguous moral judgment rather than the divisive, rationalist, power-oriented rhetoric of the future.

16. Kenneth J. Hagan, *American Gunboat Diplomacy and the Old Navy, 1877–1889* (Westport, Conn., 1973).

17. James A. Field, Jr., *America and the Mediterranean World, 1776–1882* (Princeton, 1969); see also his "American Imperialism."

cance and denigrate the motives of the antiimperialists who had opposed acquisition of the Philippines. They saw them as racists and free-trade imperialists, part of the continuous heritage of American imperialism. Orthodox historians cited the antiimperialists as evidence that such continuity did not exist and defended the antiimperialists' attachment to democratic principle, denying that they were advocates of an Open Door empire and pointing to the antiracists among them.[18] Orthodox historians also insisted that the antiimperialist campaign had been more than a flash in the pan. In the wake of the atrocities and sacrifices involved in the Philippine rebellion, the majority of Americans had begun to see sense in the antiimperial position, a trend encouraged by Democratic and Republican leaders who recognized in the Philippine issue a threat to the unity of both their parties.[19] As a result, the imperial spirit had evaporated quickly after the Spanish-American War, and subsequent military interventions in the Caribbean had not been launched on a wave of enthusiasm but had been reluctant and temporary enterprises undertaken only when the United States felt that chaos in the area had gone so far as to endanger American security. If American security really had been at stake in these Caribbean episodes, most orthodox historians implied that United States intervention might have been justified.[20]

But almost all of these historians now agreed that the instability in twentieth-century Latin America had not endangered U.S. security

18. Compare Pomeroy, *American Neo-Colonialism*, p. 10, with Robert L. Beisner, *Twelve Against Empire: The Anti-Imperialists, 1898–1900* (New York, 1968), and with the best of the books on the antiimperialists, Richard E. Welch, Jr., *Response to Imperialism: The United States and the Philippine-American War, 1899–1902* (Chapel Hill, 1979). E. Berkeley Tompkins, *Anti-Imperialism in the United States: The Great Debate, 1890–1920* (Philadelphia, 1970), is very uncritical and is written as though revisionist criticisms of the antiimperialists had never been made. Rubin Francis Weston, *Racism in United States Imperialism: The Influence of Racial Assumptions on American Foreign Policy, 1892–1946* (Columbia, S.C., 1972), sees racism rather than economics or territorial ambition as the primary force behind both imperialism and antiimperialism. Daniel Schirmer argues equally unconvincingly that the antiimperialists were actually radicals, allying a merchant elite, blacks, labor, and youth against imperialist bankers and manufacturers (Daniel B. Schirmer, *Republic or Empire: American Resistance to the Philippine War* [Cambridge, Mass., 1972]).

19. Rysted, *Ambiguous Imperialism*, pp. 19, 21–58, 307–311. For a contrary view, see Richard D. Challener's account of the expansionist notions of the American military following the Spanish-American War: *Admirals, Generals, and American Foreign Policy, 1898–1914* (Princeton, 1973).

20. An exception to this was Joseph S. Tulchin, *The Aftermath of War: World War I and Untied States Policy Toward Latin America* (New York, 1971). Tulchin favored absolute nonintervention.

and that American intervention simply could not produce long-term stability in any foreign nation. American interventions in the Caribbean had prevented some bloodletting and produced some reforms in politics, sanitation, and economic efficiency. But these gains were more than offset by the harm done to the standing of the United States in the eyes of Latin America. American occupiers had acquired a reputation for racism and condescension and had left the objects of intervention in a state of dependency. So even orthodox historians criticized America's military interventions and counseled far greater restraint if not total abandonment of any such policies in the future.[21]

Yet orthodox historians did not condemn America's economic hegemony in Latin America to the same extent they did the military interventions. Many recognized that economic power conferred upon the United States a disproportionate influence in Latin America, but they regarded this as virtually inevitable given the relative power of the nations involved. They were unwilling to equate this with military and political imperialism as the revisionists would. Nevertheless, the impact of Vietnam did bring most orthodox historians to oppose U.S. military intervention when it was for the protection of mere economic interests in Latin America and to support intervention only when vital

21. See William Kamman, *A Search for Stability: United States Diplomacy Toward Nicaragua, 1925–1933* (Notre Dame, 1968), who argues that in those rare instances where security might justify intervention, such intervention should be multilateral. P. Edward Haley, *Revolution and Intervention: The Diplomacy of Taft and Wilson with Mexico, 1910–1917* (Cambridge, Mass., 1970), said that Vietnam and other past interventions demonstrated that it was almost impossible to control the course of foreign revolution, however pure the intervener's motives might be, without massive force. Thus, the choice was between early massive intervention, such as Russia's in Czechoslovakia and America's 1965 foray into Santo Domingo, or the frustrating pursuit of more limited influence through diplomacy, which Haley regarded as the preferable course in almost all instances. Kenneth Grieb also advocated restraint, praising Warren Harding effusively for accepting such a policy and chastising Woodrow Wilson for intervening against Huerta in Mexico. Grieb believed that Huerta at least would have provided some stability (Kenneth J. Grieb, *The United States and Huerta* [Lincoln, Nebr., 1969]; and his *The Latin American Policy of Warren G. Harding* [Fort Worth, 1977]). More moderate but still favorable toward the restraint of the Republicans in Latin America in the interwar period was L. Ethan Ellis, *Republican Foreign Policy 1921–1933* (New Brunswick, N.J., 1968). See also Lester D. Langley, *The Cuban Policy of the United States* (New York, 1968). An exception to this trend was provided by James Hitchman and Allan Reed Millett, who argued that intervention in Cuba at the turn of the century had been justified and that the United States had withdrawn prematurely before it had made the reforms that would have given some stability to Cuba and avoided the occasion of further interventions (James H. Hitchman, *Leonard Wood and Cuban Independence, 1898–1902* [The Hague, 1971]; and Allan Reed Millett, *The Politics of Intervention: The Military Occupation of Cuba, 1906–1909* [Columbus, Ohio, 1968]).

strategic interests were at stake. Thus, the Good Neighbor policy of the 1930s and 1940s was portrayed as a model alternative to past and later American imperialism, especially in Irwin Gellman's study of Roosevelt's Latin American diplomacy.[22] American economic hegemony in Latin America received far more criticism from revisionists, who were self-consciously developing what they called "dependency theory." Holding Latin America in economic dependency they considered as bad as, if not worse than, formal political imperialism and certainly more effective. In any case, military intervention was inevitable whenever economic imperialism failed to forestall the justified nationalist and socialist revolutions that threatened American economic interests. Revisionists tended to be more critical of the conduct and results of past U.S. military interventions than orthodox historians and to see U.S. policy in Latin America as a seamless web of imperialism from the late nineteenth century to the 1970s, with alternating military occupations and withdrawals being no more than mild variations overlaying the constant of economic imperialism.[23]

The same basic conflict between revisionist and orthodox outlooks applied to American policy in Asia. The revisionists, of course, saw America's pursuit of the Open Door as a neocolonialist attempt to establish an American hegemony in Asia and dated it not from John Hay's Open Door notes but from the very outset of American trade with China shortly after the American Revolution. Although revisionists acknowledged that the Open Door policy sought economic rather than military or political dominance of Asia, they assumed as they had with Latin America that military intervention was an inevitable adjunct of economic imperialism. It was only natural that America had had to resort to force either as a means of securing stepping stones to the China market (the Philippines), to combat rival imperialisms (Japan), or to crush revolutionary nationalism that threatened American hegemony (China, Vietnam). Of course they condemned all of

22. Irwin F. Gellman, *Good Neighbor Diplomacy: United States Policies in Latin America, 1933–1945* (Baltimore, 1979).

23. See Hans Schmidt, *The United States Occupation of Haiti, 1915–1934* (New Brunswick, N.J., 1971); Jules Robert Benjamin, *The United States and Cuba: Hegemony and Dependent Development, 1880–1934* (Pittsburgh, 1977); Robert F. Smith, *The United States and Revolutionary Nationalism in Mexico, 1916–1932* (Chicago, 1972); Robert F. Smith, "American Foreign Relations, 1920–1942," in Bernstein, *Towards a New Past*; Cole Blasier, *The Hovering Giant: U.S. Responses to Revolutionary Change in Latin America* (Pittsburgh, 1976); Samuel L. Baily, *The United States and the Development of South America, 1945–1975* (New York, 1976); David Green, *The Containment of Latin America: A History of the Myths and Realities of the Good Neighbor Policy* (Chicago, 1971).

these military interventions except the war against Japanese imperialism. In that case they favored the war with Japan but condemned America's motives for it, namely, the protection of the Open Door rather than support of a progressive and independent China.[24]

Orthodox historians were also increasingly critical of America's past policies in Asia, but they endorsed the realist rather than the revisionist critique of them. They argued that the United States should have avoided the war with Japan. They despaired of the commitments to the Open Door and to China that had brought on the war, and they thought that greater accommodation of the milder forms of Japanese imperialism in China during the early twentieth century might have prevented Japan's resort to the more aggressive and brutal imperialism of the 1930s. Most of the realists followed Raymond Esthus and Charles Neu in dating America's overcommitment to the Open Door not with the capture of the Philippines nor with John Hay's Open Door notes but with the accession of William Howard Taft to the presidency in 1909.

Realists agreed that the United States had followed the Open Door policy long before Hay's enunciation of it as a policy and that Hay and Theodore Roosevelt had maintained a very limited commitment to it. Hay and Roosevelt had understood Japan's greater interests in Asia and tried to accommodate them. The only fault of Hay and Roosevelt had been their acceptance of the praise heaped upon them for the Open Door policy while they neglected to explain the limitations of American interests and power in Asia to the American people. Thus, Taft and Wilson had been able to find wide popular support for their idealistic and excessive meddling in Asia as no one considered seriously how such policies were inescapably antagonistic to Japan.

Charles Evans Hughes had stepped back to a wiser, more accommodating Japan policy at the Washington Conference on naval arms, but when he had turned his attention to other matters, the strongly pro-Chinese State Department had returned to an anti-Japanese stance. Such opposition to Japanese expansion, combined with the

24. McCormick, *China Market*; Foner, *Spanish-Cuban-American War and the Birth of American Imperialism*; Pomeroy, *American Neo-Colonialism*; and William J. Pomeroy, *An American-Made Tragedy: Neo-Colonialism and Dictatorship in the Philippines* (New York, 1974). A more moderate revisionist view is given in Jerry Israel, *Progressivism and the Open Door: America and China, 1905–1921* (Pittsburgh, 1971). For World War II, see Smith, "American Foreign Relations." An exception to revisionist approval of the war against Japan was Noam Chomsky's essay praising A. J. Muste in *American Power and the New Mandarins* (New York, 1969).

racism of America's policy toward Japanese immigration into the United States, had created an atmosphere in Japan which permitted the demands of the Japanese military for forcible expansion to gain wide support among the Japanese people. When Henry Stimson and then the Franklin Roosevelt administration had vociferously opposed Japanese expansion without possessing adequate means to enforce their opposition, the stage had been set for Pearl Harbor.[25] Pearl Harbor had led to further disasters, according to most realists.[26] The war had paved the way for the communist takeover in China and had sealed America's commitment to guide the destiny of Asia in the blood of those who had fallen in the battle against Japan; thus Vietnam.

But there was an influential minority of orthodox historians who rejected the realist argument that resistance to Japanese imperialism had been the fount of America's troubles in the Orient. Like the radicals, their sympathies were with China. Yet while they admitted the foolishness and condescension of America's meddling in Asia in pursuit of the Open Door, unlike the radicals they did not see this as threatening drastic consequences for China, Japan, or the United

25. Raymond A. Esthus, *Theodore Roosevelt and Japan* (Seattle, 1966); Raymond A. Esthus, *Theodore Roosevelt and the International Rivalries* (Waltham, Mass., 1970); Charles E. Neu, *An Uncertain Friendship: Theodore Roosevelt and Japan, 1906–1909* (Cambridge, Mass., 1967); Charles E. Neu, *The Troubled Encounter: The United States and Japan* (New York, 1975); Akira Iriye, *Pacific Estrangement: Japanese and American Expansion, 1897–1911* (Cambridge, Mass., 1972); and Akira Iriye, *Across the Pacific: An Inner History of American-East Asian Relations* (New York, 1967). Iriye's books were particularly good examples of multiarchival *and* multicultural approaches to diplomatic history. See also Robert A. Hart, *The Eccentric Tradition: American Diplomacy in the Far East* (New York, 1976); Walter V. Scholes and Marie V. Scholes, *The Foreign Policies of the Taft Administration* (Columbia, Mo., 1970); Peter W. Stanley, *A Nation in the Making: The Philippines and the United States, 1899–1921* (Cambridge, Mass., 1974); Norman A. Graebner, "Japan: Unanswered Challenge, 1931–1941," in David C. DeBoe et al., eds., *Essays on American Foreign Policy* (Austin, 1972), pp. 117–146; Waldo H. Heinrichs, Jr., *American Ambassador: Joseph C. Grew and the Development of the United States Diplomatic Tradition* (Boston, 1966); James B. Crowley, *Japan's Quest for Autonomy: National Security and Foreign Policy, 1930–1938* (Princeton, 1966); and Thomas H. Buckley, *The United States and the Washington Conference, 1921–1922* (Knoxville, Tenn., 1970). For a popular account written on the same assumptions, see John Toland, *The Rising Sun: The Decline and Fall of the Japanese Empire, 1936–1945* (New York, 1970).

26. Richard Leopold noted at a meeting of American and Japanese historians to discuss the coming of World War II in the Pacific that the American contributors to the conference "look back on the Pacific war as a mistake, one that led to many of the intractable problems confronting the United States today," while ironically the Japanese "view that conflict somewhat fatalistically, as perhaps the only instrument by which the incubus of fascism and militarism could have been exorcised" (Richard W. Leopold, "Historiographical Reflections," in Borg and Okamoto, *Pearl Harbor as History*, p. 20).

States. America's Open Door policy had been too insignificant and ineffectual to have done much harm to the Chinese or to pose much threat to the Japanese. Thus, it had neither justified Japanese imperialism nor made war with Japan likely. The United States never would have gone to war to defeat Japanese imperialism if Japan had not allied itself with Germany's far more serious threat to America's vital interests in Europe. There would simply have been an ongoing, ill-natured, but peaceful rivalry.

As Warren Cohen put it, the Open Door in Asia never had brought America's forceful intervention there. It was always the entanglement of Asian issues with a more serious threat to American interests in Europe or the Western Hemisphere that was responsible. The Philippine intervention had been a product of the quarrel with Spain over Cuba. The Japanese alliance with Germany had forced the confrontation with the United States over China in 1941. And America's fears of Russia and communism had brought intervention in Korea and Vietnam. The great mistake that had led to Vietnam had been the foolish confrontation policy toward Communist China after 1949, not the earlier Open Door policy and not the war against Japan.[27]

America's entry into World War I did not inspire much new research or interpretation in this era. The revisionist studies of Wilson's foreign policy by Carl Parrini, Joan Hoff Wilson, and Burton

---

27. Warren I. Cohen, *America's Response to China: An Interpretive History of Sino-American Relations* (New York, 1971). For a similar outlook, see Varg, *Making of a Myth*, and his *The Closing of the Door: Sino-American Relations, 1936–1946* ([East Lansing, Mich.], 1973). For an excellent historiographical survey, see May and Thomson, *American-East Asian Relations*. See also Stephen E. Pelz, *Race to Pearl Harbor: The Failure of the Second London Naval Conference and the Onset of World War II* (Cambridge, Mass., 1974); Robert J. C. Butow, *The John Doe Associates: Backdoor Diplomacy for Peace, 1941* (Stanford, 1974); and John E. Wiltz, *From Isolation to War, 1931–1941* (New York, 1968). A caustic criticism of Japanese imperialism that controversially sees Japan's atrocity-ridden march toward war as directed firmly by the Emperor himself from behind the scenes is David Bergamini, *Japan's Imperial Conspiracy* (New York, 1971). Another popular account that assumes the necessity of resisting Japan is Leonard Baker, *Roosevelt and Pearl Harbor* (New York, 1970).

As a matter of fact, most realists did not press very hard the argument that once Japan had joined the Axis, the United States could or should have avoided war in the Pacific. Such ideas, as put forward in the Munich era by Paul Schroeder and Francis C. Jones, had "found little response among other non-revisionist historians," according to John Wiltz, writing in 1968 (Wiltz, *From Isolation to War*, p. 120). Although by 1978 this view had more adherents than in 1968, the major point of most realists was that wiser American diplomacy in the period prior to the Axis Pact might have kept Japan from resorting to such desperate measures.

Kaufman concentrated on economic diplomacy and made almost no reference to the causes of American intervention into the Great War. The only revisionist account of Wilson's decision to intervene was a rather ham-handed affair by Sidney Bell that was far less sophisticated than the studies of Parrini, Wilson, and Kaufman and contributed little to the historiographical debate.[28]

For orthodox historians, Arthur Link's interpretations remained definitive. The surveys and monographs of this era reflected Link's view of Colonel Edward House, Robert Lansing, and Walter Hines Page as wrong-headed and disloyal to Wilson in their pro-Allied interventionist activities prior to the war. The argument that they had simply been more realistic than Wilson faded. This seemed to reflect increased doubts among the realists that intervention into World War I had been necessary for the security of the United States.[29] Even Link's assertion that Wilson had become involved through a "higher realism," in hopes of maintaining America's security needs and democratic ideals, did not quite eradicate from these later orthodox accounts the tinge of regret that America had joined the war.[30]

Perhaps this tone reflected some increased disillusionment with Wilson's plans for the postwar world. Two highly influential moderate revisionist accounts of Wilson at Versailles pointed to the reactionary economic and political aspects of Wilson's internationalist program.

28. Sidney Bell, *Righteous Conquest: Woodrow Wilson and the Evolution of the New Diplomacy* (Port Washington, N.Y., 1972).

29. Julius W. Pratt, *America and World Leadership, 1900–1921* (London, 1970; originally published as *Challenge and Rejection* in New York, 1967); Ross Gregory, *The Origins of American Intervention in the First World War* (New York, 1971); Ross Gregory, *Walter Hines Page: Ambassador to the Court of St. James's* ([Lexington, Ky.], 1970); and John Milton Cooper, Jr., *Walter Hines Page: The Southerner as American* (Chapel Hill, 1977). John Coogan was even more reluctant than these authors to accept the security argument for American intervention, pointing out with considerable asperity the ways in which Woodrow Wilson purposefully violated his supposed allegiance to the international law governing neutral rights and obligations on behalf of the British. See John W. Coogan, *The End of Neutrality: The United States, Britain, and Maritime Rights, 1899–1915* (Ithaca, N.Y., 1981).

30. Ross Gregory's short survey, *The Origins of American Intervention in the First World War*, stayed close to Link's interpretation in all but this aspect, with Gregory failing to mention this factor as part of Wilson's motivation. On the other hand, Patrick Devlin's extensive analysis, *Too Proud to Fight: Woodrow Wilson's Neutrality* (New York, 1975), made Wilson's desire to shape the peace almost the only motive for Wilson's decision, virtually ignoring the submarine issue. Rather unconvincingly Devlin argued that Wilson still had a political route open to noninvolvement even after Germany's announcement of unlimited submarine warfare (*ibid.*, pp. 672–678). Devlin regarded Wilson's motives as idealistic delusions rather than a higher realism (*ibid.*, pp. vii, 674–678).

Following the earlier suggestion of William Appleman Williams, Arno Mayer and N. Gordon Levin portrayed Wilson's plan for a moderate peace with Germany and the formation of a League of Nations as an attempt to combat Russian bolshevism and the radical European Left rather than an altruistic step toward forgiveness of past enemies and the spread of democracy. They saw Wilson's program as expansionist. His goal had been an Open Door world, a system that would permit American economic and cultural expansion everywhere and forestall the advance of the rival Leninist system.[31]

Mayer and Levin had considerable impact even on orthodox views of Wilson's diplomacy. The economics implicit in Wilson's programs now received more mention, and greater significance was attributed to the rivalry with bolshevism that was felt at Versailles. But orthodox historians still refused to accept either of these factors as central to Wilson's concerns. Instead, they saw Wilson's primary goal as the spread of an open democratic society. Although Wilson and his fellow Americans might have been arrogant and sanctimonious in seeking the spread of American institutions, orthodox historians were unwilling to equate this with aggressive expansionism or neocolonialism. Doubts about the wisdom of American interventionism raised by Vietnam and the revisionists did not take them this far.[32]

Still, a new respect for the motives if not the actual policies of the opponents of Wilsonian interventionism was apparent in the Age of Vietnam. Three studies of the Senate fight over the Treaty of Versailles emphasized the diversity, the relatively decent motivations, and in certain aspects the wisdom of Wilson's opponents.[33] Historians of isolationism noticed liberal as well as conservative elements that resisted the League and the march toward World War II, and they minimized

31. Arno J. Mayer, *Politics and Diplomacy of Peacemaking: Containment and Counterrevolution at Versailles, 1918–1919* (New York, 1967); and N. Gordon Levin, Jr., *Woodrow Wilson and World Politics: America's Response to War and Revolution* (New York, 1968).

32. See Samuel F. Wells, "New Perspectives on Wilsonian Diplomacy: The Secular Evangelism of American Political Economy: A Review Essay," *Perspectives in American History*, 6 (1972): 389–419; Arthur S. Link, *The Higher Realism of Woodrow Wilson and Other Essays* (Nashville, Tenn., 1971), p. 79; Keith L. Nelson, *Victors Divided: America and the Allies in Germany, 1918–1923* (Berkeley, 1975), p. ix; and Arthur Walworth, *America's Moment: 1918; American Diplomacy at the End of World War I* (New York, 1977).

33. Warren F. Kuehl, *Seeking World Order: The United States and International Organization to 1920* (Nashville, Tenn., 1969); Ralph A. Stone, *The Irreconcilables* ([Lexington, Ky.], 1970); and William C. Widenor, *Henry Cabot Lodge and the Search for an American Foreign Policy*.

the importance of ethnic elements earlier historians such as Samuel Lubell had stressed. If these historians still saw isolationism as unwise and excessively moralistic, at least they no longer regarded it as pathological.[34]

However, revived respect for the motives of the isolationists did not alter the conviction of most historians that American participation in the war against Hitler was thoroughly correct and justified. Several intensive studies of German diplomacy reinforced the findings of Hans Trefousse that Hitler had had no definite plans for the invasion of the Western Hemisphere but that if he had triumphed in Europe, the momentum of his victory and the resources made available by it would have made a future clash between the United States and the German Empire inevitable.[35]

Historians agreed that Hitler provided at least one instance in which military intervention had been correct, but they continued to debate whether Roosevelt could have brought the United States into the war earlier, as all assumed would have been desirable. James Mac-Gregor Burns, Arnold Offner, and Robert Divine all took the side of Langer and Gleason that Roosevelt had been indecisive and overly cautious in his policies toward Germany. Michael Leigh's sophisticated analysis of public opinion also concluded that Roosevelt had had more room to maneuver than his fear of congressional isolationism had led him to believe. Robert Dallek was the most persuasive advocate of the argument that Roosevelt had properly gauged the reluctance of Americans to enter the fighting and had been correct to wait for a dramatic instance of Axis aggression to bring a united America into the war. T. R. Fehrenbach, Gloria Barron, John Wiltz, and William Kinsella agreed.[36] Only one historian, Bruce Russett, dared to suggest

34. John Milton Cooper, Jr., *The Vanity of Power: American Isolationism and the First World War 1914–1917* (Westport, Conn., 1969); Manfred Jonas, *Isolationism in America, 1935–1941* (Ithaca, 1974); Cohen, *The American Revisionists: The Lessons of Intervention in World War I*; and Geoffrey S. Smith, *To Save a Nation: American Countersubversives, the New Deal, and the Coming of World War II* (New York, 1973). See also Mark Lincoln Chadwin, *The Warhawks: American Interventionists Before Pearl Harbor* (New York, 1970).

35. James V. Compton, *The Swastika and the Eagle: Hitler, the United States, and the Origins of World War II* (Boston, 1967); Saul Friedländer, *Prelude to Downfall: Hitler and the United States, 1939–1941* (New York, 1967), published earlier in Germany; and Alton Frye, *Nazi Germany and the American Hemisphere, 1933–1941* (New Haven, 1967).

36. See Burns, *Roosevelt: The Soldier of Freedom*; Arnold A. Offner, *American Appeasement: United States Foreign Policy and Germany, 1933–1938* (Cambridge, Mass., 1969); Arnold A. Offner, *The Origins of the Second World War: American Foreign Policy*

that the United States might have been better off if it had remained neutral and let Germany and Russia fight to a stalemate.[37] Meanwhile, the new revisionists continued to attack America's motives for intervention in World War II rather than the intervention itself.[38]

The only significant change in the historiography of the European aspects of World War II was the renewed emphasis on the conflicts and ill-feelings which existed between the United States and Great Britain. The opening of diplomatic and treasury documents in both Great Britain and the United States made possible the study of the undercurrents flowing beneath the carefully protected image of cooperation between the top levels of the two governments. Naval rivalry in the 1920s and 1930s was examined by Stephen Roskill and James Leutze.[39] The economic dispute involving the gold standard, American loans, the pound sterling, and the dollar stood out far more clearly in Armand Van Dormael's study of the Bretton Woods agreement than it had in Richard Gardner's earlier account of sterling-dollar diplomacy.[40] Disagreements over British imperialism were treated exhaustively in William Roger Louis's *Imperialism at Bay* and Christopher Thorne's massive multiarchival work, *Allies of a Kind*.[41] The well-known controversy over the second front also received considerable attention. Brian Loring Villa actually concluded from circumstances

---

and World Politics, 1917–1941 (New York, 1975); and Divine, *Roosevelt and World War II*. Interestingly, Divine declared in the 1979 edition of his 1965 book, *The Reluctant Belligerent*, that, under the influence of the Vietnam War, he had modified his earlier strictures against Roosevelt's slowness to intervene in World War II. See also Michael Leigh, *Mobilizing Consent: Public Opinion and American Foreign Policy, 1937–1947* (Westport, Conn., 1976); Dallek, *Franklin D. Roosevelt and American Foreign Policy*; William E. Kinsella, Jr., *Leadership in Isolation: FDR and the Origins of the Second World War* (Cambridge, Mass., 1978); T. R. Fehrenbach, *F.D.R.'s Undeclared War: 1939–1941* (New York, 1967); and Gloria J. Barron, *Leadership in Crisis: FDR and the Path to Intervention* (Port Washington, N.Y., 1973).

37. Bruce M. Russett, *No Clear and Present Danger: A Skeptical View of the United States Entry into World War II* (New York, 1972).

38. Robert Freeman Smith, "American Foreign Relations." New revisionist accounts of American intervention into World War II were as rare as their accounts of intervention into World War I.

39. Stephen Roskill, *Naval Policy Between the Wars. Vol. I The Period of Anglo-American Antagonism, 1919–1929* (New York, 1968); and James Leutze, *Bargaining for Supremacy: Anglo-American Naval Collaboration, 1937–1941* (Chapel Hill, 1977).

40. Armand Van Dormael, *Bretton Woods: Birth of a Monetary System* (London, 1978).

41. William Roger Louis, *Imperialism at Bay, 1941–1945: The United States and the Decolonization of the British Empire* (Oxford, 1978); and Christopher Thorne, *Allies of a Kind: The United States, Britain, and the War Against Japan, 1941–1945* (London, 1978).

and timing that Roosevelt had withheld a firm commitment to atomic sharing until Churchill gave his final consent to the Normandy invasion.[42] Still, none of these books went so far as Gabriel Kolko had in portraying such Anglo-American conflicts as near enmity. Instead, the picture that emerged was what one analyst called "competitive cooperation."[43] And more popular histories still clung to the emphasis on the friendship and mutual sacrifices underlying the alliance.[44]

Except in this issue of America's war against Hitler, then, historians were now more critical of twentieth-century American interventionism than they had been in the Age of Munich. Moderate and radical revisionists might disagree among themselves over the degree to which such expansion was economically motivated, but they agreed that expansionism and interventionism were the central ingredients of American foreign policy and had been generally reprehensible.

Orthodox historians were not quite so critical of American interventions and disputed the contention that expansion was the primary focus of American diplomacy. But they too had begun to doubt the advisability of many of America's interventions, and most adopted the reproving tone and outlook of the "soft" realists. They advocated a more restrained and sophisticated approach to foreign policy than the United States had taken in the past, hoping to restrict intervention to only the most crucial situations. Clearly, they supported the public mood that placed the burden of proof upon those who would demand the use of military force abroad rather than on those who would oppose it. And so it would remain until yet another traumatic crisis altered the perceptions of the American people, their leaders, and their historians.

---

42. Brian Loring Villa, "The Atomic Bomb and the Normandy Invasion," *Perspectives in American History*, 11 (1977–1978): 463–502.
43. David Reynolds, "Competitive Cooperation: Anglo-American Relations in World War Two," *Historical Journal*, 23 (March 1980): 233–245.
44. See Joseph P. Lash, *Roosevelt and Churchill, 1939–1941: The Partnership That Saved the West* (New York, 1976).

Epilogue

As the Vietnam War stumbled to its conclusion, most Americans seem to have been persuaded by the fiasco that every consideration of foreign policy—interest, power, and morality—indicated the wisdom of American withdrawal. Economic interests had never seemed much involved. The dispute between China and the Soviets and the independence demonstrated by the Vietnamese communists made America's strategic interest in a noncommunist South Vietnam seem hardly worth the expenditure of power that victory would require, if, indeed, victory was possible. Any moral content the war might have had was sapped by the authoritarianism and corruption of the South Vietnamese government, not to mention the devastating effect of the conflict on the ordinary people of Southeast Asia. The antiinterventionist atmosphere inspired by this traumatic situation affected America's outlook and policy toward the entire world.

But recent events have weakened America's abstentionist mood. Moral revulsion against intervention has been undermined by several developments. The viciousness of the successor regimes in Vietnam and Cambodia diminished American guilt over the war. The hostage issue in Iran obscured America's previous complicity in the Shah's oppressive regime, memories of which might have served as a moral brake on further intervention in the Middle East. The Soviet invasion of Afghanistan further reduced moral compunctions about an American role in the Persian Gulf. Suppression of the Solidarity union in Poland has reinforced the totalitarian image of the Soviets. Russia's extraordinary military growth has undercut the humanitarian movement to restrict military spending in the United States. President Carter's human rights campaign was too anemic, too opportunistic, and too poorly explained to give the American public a sophisticated and firm sense of the role that morality should play in foreign policy. As a result, idealism is once again being enlisted simplistically on the side of anticommunist intervention and support of pro-American regimes, however unstable and oppressive they may be. Interest as well as idealism seems to be pulling in the direction of intervention in some areas. Whereas Vietnam involved little in the way of American strategic or economic interests, the oil-rich Persian Gulf region involves both to an extraordinary extent.

Nevertheless, I believe we are still in the Age of Vietnam. None of these events have been dramatic or traumatic enough to override the "lessons" of Vietnam. The memory of that tragedy still imposes substantial constraints on the interventionist inclinations of the Reagan administration. Americans still remember the difficulties and moral dilemmas involved in fighting where large elements of the indigenous population are hostile. So, in areas of marginal significance like El Salvador, Reagan will pay a high political price if he sends more than minor amounts of arms, money, and advisors. In the Persian Gulf, where American interests are more critical, the proximity of Soviet power adds a further inhibition to a major American military intervention. And if the Russians are at all cooperative in the strategic arms negotiations, this will exert enormous pressure against Reagan's arm build-up. I suspect it would take a profound threat to America's energy supplies or an overt Soviet move against a major American ally to override the memory of Vietnam and swing the pendulum of American public opinion back to a full endorsement of large scale intervention abroad.

Until such time, most historians probably will continue to use their influence against intervention and in favor of restraint. This is all to the good, for regardless of Reagan administration policies, the objective conditions of the international scene suggest a continuing relative decline in American power and influence abroad. It may be the historians' job to explain this situation so that Americans will accept it with some serenity. Hopefully, the United States can avoid an irrational and dangerous spasm of interventionist responses to the foreign policy frustrations it will inevitably face.

By assisting in such a function, historians would be perpetuating a role they have played throughout America's diplomatic history. For while it is true that they have reflected the major swings of public opinion and even furthered them by lending them the legitimacy of the academy, they still have stood at least somewhat apart from the public consensus. In America's early years their New England perspective gave them a more restrained, Federalist view of neutrality and a more critical view of expansion than the general public seems to have had. In the first years of the 20th century their support of imperialism retained a greater sense of irony and tragedy than seems to have been present in the people at large. A greater proportion of diplomatic historians than voters seems to have kept faith with Wilsonian internationalism during the interwar years. Finally, since World War II most diplomatic historians have been to the left of the public consensus on foreign policy. Thus they have had a separate vantage point from which to offer critiques as well as explanations of past American diplomacy. In addition, regardless of their own opinions, most diplomatic historians have aired opposing points of view, recalled alternatives successful in the past, and cautioned against too dogmatic or simplistic a reading of history. This has been and should continue to be an important if modest contribution to American foreign policy.

Index

Books and articles discussed in this book will be found in this index under the author's name. Full publication information on each book and article will be found on the page number printed in italics.